Intercultural Communication for Global Business

This book brings together principles and new theories in intercultural communication in a concise and practical manner, focusing on communication as the foundation for management and global leadership.

Grounded in the Cultural Intelligence Model, this compact text examines the concepts associated with understanding culture and communication in the global business environment to help readers:

- Understand intercultural communication processes.
- Improve self-awareness and communication in intercultural settings.
- Expand skills in identifying, analyzing, and solving intercultural communication challenges at work.
- Evaluate whether one's communication has been effective.

Richly illustrated with examples, activities, real-world applications, and recent case studies that make the content come alive, *Intercultural Communication for Global Business* is an ideal companion for any business student or manager dedicated to communicating more effectively in a globalized society.

Elizabeth A. Tuleja is an Associate Professor of Management at the University of Notre Dame, USA. She teaches intercultural communication and global leadership to BBA, MBA, and executive MBA students.

"Elizabeth Tuleja has written an excellent introduction to cross-cultural behavior that has an outstanding balance. She interweaves cross-cultural anecdotes, longer cases, and a firm grasp of the major theories and approaches in the cross-cultural area to produce a highly readable, sensitive, and insightful introduction to this amazingly complicated area. I highly recommend it."

Martin J. Gannon, *University of Maryland and California State University San Marcos, USA*

"Elizabeth Tuleja brings a unique and welcome intercultural communication perspective to the field of global business. Her extensive background and mastery of the literature has resulted in an engaging book full of useful concepts, models, and real-life examples that are suitable for both newcomers to the field and experienced practitioners."

Joyce Osland, *San Jose State University, USA*

"This excellent book on intercultural communication for global business is a tool that will enhance your mindset and skill set in a way that develops cultural intelligence. It is my opinion that every business leader, politician, salesperson, negotiator, and diplomat should own a copy of this book and read it well. Just as Emotional Intelligence can be developed, so too can Cultural Intelligence be developed, and as much as we need Emotional Intelligence in our world today, we also definitely need Cultural Intelligence if we hope to lead well in this new globalized reality. This is a book you must own, and once you own, make the contents your own!"

Rob Elkington, *University of Ontario Institute of Technology, Canada, and North-West University, New Zealand*

"Tuleja provides a lucid and timely compass for navigating cultures in a rapidly globalizing, often polarizing world. Practical intercultural tools, fresh thought-provoking case studies and engaging activities offer students and professionals lit pathways for effective communications across a dizzying array of clashing cultures. Don't leave home without it!"

Joe Lurie, *University of California, Berkeley, USA*

Intercultural Communication for Global Business

How leaders communicate for success

Elizabeth A. Tuleja

Routledge
Taylor & Francis Group

NEW YORK AND LONDON

First published 2017
by Routledge
711 Third Avenue, New York, NY 10017

and by Routledge
2 Park Square, Milton Park, Abingdon, Oxon OX14 4RN

Routledge is an imprint of the Taylor & Francis Group, an informa business

Library of Congress Cataloging-in-Publication Data
A catalog record for this title has been requested

ISBN: 978-1-138-93283-8 (hbk)
ISBN: 978-1-138-93284-5 (pbk)
ISBN: 978-1-315-66864-2 (ebk)

Typeset in Bembo
by Sunrise Setting Ltd., Brixham, UK

MIX
Paper from
responsible sources
FSC
www.fsc.org
FSC® C014174

Printed and bound in the United States of America by Sheridan

To Susan, the wind beneath my wings

And to my Hong Kong friends who showed me their world

Contents

Foreword

The field of intercultural communication (IC) has advanced significantly over the past 75 years. In the 1940s through the 1950s, cultural anthropologists Clyde and Florence Kluckhohn and Fred Strodtbeck established criteria which explained societal values that illuminated social interaction styles between people of different cultures, which was useful to IC later on. In the 1950s through the 1970s, Edward T. Hall, another anthropologist, laid the groundwork for the study of IC through his work for the American Foreign Service, producing influential constructs such as high- and low-context cultures and their relative effects on communication, and space and time perceptions in cultures. For the next four decades, scholars from various fields of study such as psychology, linguistics, and training contributed to the developing discipline of IC. A few key figures are: William B. Gudykunst (theorizing about IC), Edward C. Stewart (contrast culture method, American cultural patterns), John C. (Jack) Condon (semantics, communication), Milton Bennett (linguistics, intercultural training), Young-Yun Kim (international negotiation), Stella Ting-Toomey (identity negotiation), Judith. N. Martin (communication), and of course, psychologist Geert Hofstede (cultural dimensions). Cross-cultural psychologists such as Harry Triandis, Hazel Markus, Shinobu Kitayama, and Michael Bond brought additional insights. The study of communication expanded to include scholars who researched the effect of culture on *business* communication.

In the 2000s two influential areas of study contributed to IC and business leadership: cultural intelligence (CQ), first presented by Christopher Earley, Soon Ang, and Linn Van Dyne; and the GLOBE (Global Leadership Organizational Behavior Effectiveness) ten-year study *Culture, Leadership, and Organizations,* by Robert House and others, which brought the importance of IC competence front and center in global business. The GLOBE research project was the first study of its kind, mobilizing nearly 200 social scientists from 62 countries around the world for interviews with over 17,000 employees from almost 1,000 organizations worldwide. The study sought to determine the characteristics of a global leader. As Robert House and his colleagues stated, an outstanding leader is a person in an organization or industry who is "exceptionally skilled at motivating, influencing, or enabling others or groups to contribute to the success of the organization or task" (House et al., 2004, p. 15). His colleague, Mansour Javidan, extended this definition to: "someone who is able to handle complexity, risk, and ambiguity in a fast-paced and multicultural environment successfully, because he[/she] possesses knowledge about cultural differences and mindfully reflects on behaviors, attitudes, values, and beliefs while interacting with others" (Javidan et al., 2016).

Despite the large body of research in IC and the GLOBE study in leadership, some still ignore the need for cultural knowledge and communication competence in leading global organizations. Because nation states, societies, and individuals are able to interact more easily and rapidly today than ever before, it does *not* mean that people are able to do so more effectively. Communicating successfully with people who are like you is often tricky; however, communicating successfully with people who are different from you is much harder.

Some business people assume knowledge of another culture and competence in IC are becoming irrelevant because we are moving toward a global culture. Evidence suggests that this is quite untrue. In the 21st century alone, at least half a dozen new nations have appeared, after separating from other countries, because their citizens want to retain and nurture their own cultures. Furthermore, populations who have been driven from their own land by war, climate change, and economic pressures and have migrated to new countries, bringing their own cultures with them, need IC skills, as do those who receive them. More than ever, we need to communicate with each other, seek to understand each other, and develop an unprecedented level of competence in recognizing how culture affects everything we think and do, including global leadership. That goes not only for business, but for day-to-day contacts in our lives. To connect successfully, we need knowledge, understanding, and skills.

Intercultural Communication for Global Business challenges both the business student and the business professional to become more culturally competent, what the business community now defines as *culturally intelligent*. This book is both accessible and practical, bringing together theories and concepts in applications of IC. It enables readers to put into practice—immediately—- what they read. The reader finds tools to address the inner work that is required of today's global leader, which includes first developing greater awareness of the role of cultures of people who are different, then engaging in reflection about success or failure in interactions, and finally developing skills for interacting successfully and employing them in successful communication behaviors.

This book is about how *you* can develop your own cultural competence both personally and professionally, for successful IC in global leadership.

Linda Beamer
Professor Emerita, California State University,
Los Angeles, California, USA
April 2016

References

House, R. J., Hanges, P. J., Javidan, M., Dorfman, P. W., & Gupta, V. (Eds.). (2004). *Culture, leadership, and organizations: The GLOBE study of 62 societies* (3rd edn., p.15). Thousand Oaks, CA: SAGE.

Javidan, Mansour, Teagarden, J. Mary, & Bowen, David. (2016). Global mindset secrets of superstar expats. Retrieved from www.thunderbird.edu/article/global-mindset-secrets-superstar-expats (accessed August 8, 2016).

Preface

Intercultural Communication for Global Business brings together both the foundational and the newest theories in intercultural communication in a concise and practical manner. It specifically focuses on *communication* as the foundation for all management and global leadership. As a result, this text is compact and deals with the underlying theory of intercultural communication and its practical application in the workplace. Its purpose is to give the learner, whether business students or professional, the essentials for communicating and engaging effectively in a globalized society.

Each chapter follows a systematic delivery of core concepts based upon the author's many years of teaching intercultural communication to students, managers, and executives. It begins with the fundamental question of "What is culture?" and answers the "So what?" of the important intersection of culture learning alongside business learning all the way throughout the text. It begins with examining who each of us is regarding our own individual intercultural identity, then delivers the fundamental frameworks that provide a common language for discussion, and offers multiple workplace examples across many different cultures.

Another distinguishing feature of this text is that the foundation is about discovering your own preference for communicating—and reflecting on who you are as an intercultural communicator. Much of the current business literature is calling for executives to take the time to step back and reflect on problems before acting on them. This text does just that—it encourages the reader to use several popular models from the intercultural literature to facilitate self-discovery and individualized learning.

Each chapter contains a business case study, as well as exercises for personal self-reflection and multiple resources for further reading in the teaching materials. The instructor materials provide suggested activities complete with instructions and debriefing questions, and a test bank, as well as PowerPoint slides and suggested syllabi for modular and traditional semester course planning. This text focuses specifically on communication in business, and all content (chapters, exercises, cases) surrounds the issues related to communicating effectively across cultures for global leadership. It specifically deals with the concept of cultural intelligence (CQ) by employing a user-friendly model of Knowledge–Reflection–Action (based upon David C. Thomas's rendition of CQ (Thomas and Inkson, 2009)). This text is for the learner who wants to master personal leadership development, and several key online intercultural assessment tools are suggested as ancillary materials.

The text is developed the way that the author progressively teaches throughout the term—one concept building upon another. *Intercultural Communication for Global Business* uses this developmental process to help learners grasp both theories and application. Why, you may ask, is the last chapter dedicated to leadership? Well, the entire book is about global leadership—through the lens of *communication*. The final chapter provides information—both theoretical and practical—specifically related to the development of global leadership over the past few decades.

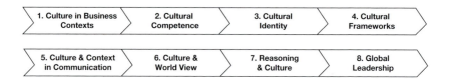

This book looks at both culture-general and culture-specific applications to business in particular and the professions in general. The culture-general approach acknowledges that it is not possible to know everything about everyone. So, the book presents some of the latest theories on cultural dimensions based upon research in anthropology, sociology, psychology, and communication. Having a general knowledge of culture provides the foundation for how a society interacts and is the first step toward moving beyond minimization of cultural differences to interaction with such differences. It also presents some culture-specific information based upon the most recent work on global leadership by looking at country clusters (GLOBE Study).

Throughout the text, there are many discussions of the challenges and pitfalls of overgeneralizing and making assumptions, and it makes a clear distinction between stereotyping and anthropological observations. In essence, this text provides a road map that helps guide its readers toward a better understanding of the complexity and challenges so that the reader can better manage cultural issues domestically and internationally.

But why the focus on communication? There are many books already on the market for international business and international management. After

20 years in the field, I strongly believe that communication is the most fundamental aspect of doing business—without it you cannot possibly expect to have productive interactions. It does not matter how adept a person is regarding her or his functional capabilities; without appropriate knowledge and behavior, it will be difficult to interact successfully with anyone. As such, *Intercultural Communication* comes from the social psychological approach and is about emotional intelligence and cultural intelligence—the ability to monitor emotions and behaviors in self and in others. *International Business* comes from a commercial approach that focuses on transactions through finance, accounting, logistics, manufacturing, and the likes. *International Management*, which includes communication, is nevertheless focused on the HR aspect of doing business—how to plan, staff, and organize personnel.

The specific focus on communication in this text is critical to helping us develop our CQ by assessing our own awareness as well as an awareness of others; without it, you may encounter many obstacles and challenges. Through definitions, examples, and illustrations, you will chart the course for your own learning and development. The text is divided into three parts: Part 1 focuses on the foundations of intercultural communication; Part 2 focuses on self-awareness and intercultural communication; and Part 3 focuses on concepts of intercultural communication.

Chapter 1, Culture in Business Contexts, lays the foundation for the text by discussing the nature of globalization and evolving demographics. It provides a rationale for culture learning—the cultural imperative of the 21st century—and attempts to define the elusive nature of culture.

Chapter 2, Cultural Competence for Leaders, examines the latest research regarding CQ and highlights several models. The Model of Cultural Intelligence is the process whereby we can develop awareness and understanding, reflect on it in a mindful way, and then practice the skills we learn in order to become competent. It is an iterative process—one that I call "cultural improvisation."

Chapter 3, Culture and Identity, asks the question—what is your individual cultural identity, which is made up of cultural, personal, and relational aspects of how you were socialized while growing up. The chapter examines such influences as ethnicity, language, gender, age, disability, social class, education, religion, and roles.

Chapter 4, Cultural Frameworks and Foundations, explains the theory behind cultural dimensions and looks at how central tendencies of a nation can be used as a starting point in order to understand difference. Dutch social psychologist and interculturalist, Geert Hofstede is famous for his initial 1970s study on workplace values that shed light into such cultural tendencies for identity, power, gender roles, dealing with uncertainty, pragmatism, and indulgence.

Chapter 5, Culture and Context in Communication, is about the socio cultural aspects of using language to communicate meaning across cultures. This chapter continues the discussion of cultural dimensions by examining Edward

T. Hall's famous work on high and low context in communication, poly-chronic and monochronic time, and spatial distance.

Chapter 6, Culture and World View, returns to the discussion of attitudes, beliefs, and values by looking at the concept of world view. This chapter asks the questions that define world view: What is reality? Who are humans? What is truth? What values are important?

Chapter 7, Culture, Cognition, and Reasoning, looks at non-Western views of intercultural communication by providing culture-specific examples to illuminate human cognition across cultures and why this matters in business. Richard Nisbett's classic study on differences between Eastern and Western thought is discussed.

Chapter 8, Culture and Leadership, examines the work of the last 15 years regarding the GLOBE Study and defines global leadership based upon new findings in cultural dimensions, leadership scales, and organization of cultures according to country clusters.

In a nutshell, this book is about developing awareness that will lead to one's curiosity for gaining more knowledge—both broad and specific—in order to reflect and put into practice what one is learning. The ultimate goal is to develop competence in dealing with cultural difference regardless of the context or the situation. Interactions with others, even those who are the most like us, are not easy. This book helps the reader identify, sort through, and put into perspective a repertoire of ways of developing CQ, which is the ability to know oneself, understand others, and then deal with the complexity associated with our globalized world.

Reference

Thomas, D. C., & Inkson, K. C. (2009). *Cultural intelligence: Living and working globally.* San Francisco, CA: Berrett-Koehler.

Part 1

Foundations of Intercultural Communication

1   Culture in Business Contexts

Commerce may be global but culture isn't . . . behind businesses there are people who have biases, expectations, and a view of life which can unexpectedly determine and form multi-million dollar decisions. Understanding that culture shapes people who shape business is vital to win.

(Pedro Pina, Google, Head of Brand Solutions, Europe)

Figure 1.1 Chinese fans—the beauty of diversity

(*Source*: Author.)

Chapter Overview

Chapter 1, Culture in Business Contexts, lays the foundation for this text by examining the questions: As leaders why should we care about the intersection of culture and business? Why are globalization and evolving demographics increasingly becoming more complex rather than simpler? What is culture? How do we identify, let alone define, something so complex and abstract? These are the key questions we will address in Chapter 1 (Figure 1.1).

Learning Objective

Understanding the nature of globalization and evolving demographics is critical for global leaders. You will examine the rationale for culture learning—the cultural imperative of the 21st century—and attempt to define the elusive nature of culture. In order to make a case for the cultural imperative, this chapter explains the historical foundations of intercultural communication by mentioning the classic works of Hall, Hofstede, Trompenaars, Kluckhohn, and others.

Key Takeaways

- Become aware of our own attitudes and assumptions about the importance of culture in leadership.
- Understand that global leadership comes from knowledge developed within the fields of anthropology, psychology, sociology, and intercultural communication.

Leadership Applications

- Technical skills are not the same as interpersonal skills.
- Leaders need to understand the impact of the "shrinking" world in that they must lead people from diverse backgrounds.

Introduction

A Cultural Faux Pas

When Bill Gates, founder of Microsoft, was in South Korea and met the President Park Geun-hye for the first time, critics were "up in arms" about his behavior. He was there to build relationships, talk about nuclear energy, and promote his new start-up, TerraPower. But why was there a media frenzy?

Gates was criticized for being too casual in his initial contact with the President. When shaking her hand he kept his left hand in his pocket. Some of the press read: "The handshake that has bruised a nation"; "Plain rude"; "Ignorance or just plain disrespect?"; "Cultural difference or bad manners?"; "A disrespectful handshake or a casual friendly handshake?" There was a notable disdain for how Gates went about establishing relationships in the East (Cho, 2013).

Why would something as harmless as leaving one hand in a pocket offend someone? This is often our reaction when we do something that contradicts someone else's expectations of proper behavior—we are incredulous that *they* don't understand *us*. Well, from a monocultural perspective, which is looking at things from one's myopic perspective, it shouldn't bother anyone! However, from a multicultural perspective (being able to see things from multiple angles with regard to cultural differences), one would have to reassess exactly *why* the action might have caused disrespect.

In Korean culture, using one hand to shake someone else's is considered too casual, something you would do with a good friend or someone younger. The other hand in the pocket symbolizes superiority and can be potentially rude when done in the wrong context or situation. South Korea is a hierarchical culture. This means that there are age-old traditions founded in Confucian practices that require one to respect the rank and order of relationships and then to maintain such an order.

Whose Rules?

Some have argued that you cannot expect a Western person to follow, say, a Confucian culture's rules nor be judged by its cultural standards. Others have reasoned that he is a "casual man . . . not bound by customs" or that he is "one of the richest men in the world and can do whatever he wants." But there is an appropriate protocol for such occasions when meeting with heads of state—regardless of how rich or down-to-earth you are. Knowing some of the proper decorum is vital in creating goodwill and developing lasting relationships—especially if you are trying to cultivate them. You have to take into account a person's status, gender, and even religion, all of which are important (Irvine, 2013).

It has often been said that "When in Rome do as the Romans do." This adage is originally attested to St. Ambrose in his liturgical advice to St. Augustine (St. Augustine had asked if he should fast on Sunday as he did in Milan—or on Saturday as was customary in Rome). St. Ambrose replied, "If you were in Rome, fast in the Roman way; if you are elsewhere, live as they do there" (WordSense, n.d.). You'll find many sayings like this in other languages. In Chinese, the translation is "Enter village, follow customs"; in Moroccan, "Do like your neighbor or move your house door"; in Polish, "When you fly among crows, you should caw like them." (Schaff, 1886).

Whether we shake hands, bow, or kiss someone on the cheek, it is important to be aware of the symbolism conveyed in the actual gesture. It is not only good etiquette, but smart business. Being aware of a counterpart's specific cultural norms demonstrates respect—and that you have spent time learning in order to develop a lasting relationship. In Japan, the subordinate is expected to bow lower than the boss. In France, you kiss a friend on each cheek, but in the Netherlands, three times. In China, you are expected to give and receive business cards with both hands while commenting on the other person's impressive credentials.

Can a cultural faux pas break a relationship or potential business deal? It depends. Can you be forgiven for a social or cultural faux pas? Of course! However, if you are to be successful as a global leader you must develop an awareness of cultural practices that carry important meaning to the people with whom you interact. You may not always get it right, but it is important to be alert and ready to adapt to the customs and practices of the people and the place you are visiting. Anything that we can do to promote respect toward a counterpart's culture or tradition is vital. So, is greeting someone correctly a social necessity? Yes, absolutely!

This book takes what is theoretical and makes it practical. It is important to know some of the foundations, because often the soft skills of doing business are overlooked in terms of the functional aspects (the skills necessary to perform accounting or financial tasks, for example). We will discuss the foundations, because this brings credibility to you as a business leader. As you will see toward the end of this chapter, the field of management is made up of a variety of disciplines—sociology, psychology and yes, communication. All of the functional skills such as knowing accounting practices, building financial models, or developing acquisition strategies do not matter much if you cannot communicate successfully. In order to lead people, you need to develop the critical skill of communication—and that is what this book is about—helping you to begin to be aware of, understand, and then put into practice communication skills developed within an intercultural framework.

Our Changing World

Our world has shrunk dramatically. With our ability to communicate 24/7 with anyone, anywhere via the Internet and smartphones; with one keystroke that brings us immediate, streaming news from all over the world; with easy access to cheaper, faster, more comfortable air travel, we have traversed the four corners of the world. Somehow we have acquired a misguided sentiment that because the world has shrunk then it will be simpler, easier, and less complicated to interact with others. However, this is far from the truth. Despite technology, treaties, or travel, our world is more complex, ambiguous, and fast-paced than ever—and it is harder to keep up with no matter how fast one's Internet connection is.

We are at a point in history where it is no longer possible to minimize cultural differences—it has been too easy to overemphasize commonalities and underestimate differences, and we have done just that. We are experiencing a new way of living. We have reached a point of no return with the cultural imperative—it is unavoidable, it demands our attention, it is an obligation, and it is a necessity if we are to survive.

So what does this have to do with business? Everything! On an organizational, team, and individual level, it means that we are now required to interact with people who are very different than us. We must learn to speak, listen, and even write with a greater sensitivity, flexibility, and openness to doing things on other people's terms, not necessarily our own.

Why is Culture Important in Business?

Globalization and Business

What is globalization? In business, it is when technology, communications, trade, tariffs, migration, and labor markets open up across borders so that free trade and capital flow unhindered by national boundaries. A more technical definition would describe globalization as: the increasing interdependence among national governments, businesses, nonprofit organizations, and individual citizens. The drivers facilitating globalization are: a) the free movement of goods, services, knowledge, and communication across national boundaries; b) the development of new technologies—think high-speed Internet and air travel; c) the lowering of tariffs and other obstacles to such movement; and d) human migration, especially from undeveloped to developed countries (Gannon, 2008).

Globalization and Society

Globalization impacts us in social and political ways as well. In the 21st century, our organizations, schools, and neighborhoods are increasingly more multicultural—we work with people of different nationalities, ethnicities, and faiths. Chances are that the person in the cubicle next to us grew up with a different language. We have round-the-clock communication—the 2014 Umbrella Revolution protests happening in Hong Kong at 7:00 pm in the evening are broadcast to us as we wake up at 7:00 am in the morning. From NYC we can hop on a plane and be in London in 8 hours, Shanghai in 14 hours, Sydney in 20 hours, Rio in 13 hours, or Dubai in 15 hours. Trade and commerce has become a global issue with the world financial crisis (the United States' subprime mortgage debacle, Spain's austerity measures, Greece's debt crisis, the Eurozone crisis and the 2016 Brexit, to name a few). Migration continues to surge as people are dispersed, seeking a better life because of economic, religious, or political reasons—whether it is immigrants from Mexico, sub-Saharan Africa, Syria, or Myanmar, we can no longer turn away.

In fact, according to the UN Global Migration Statistics, in 2013, 232 million people left their homelands in search of a better life elsewhere (compared with 175 million in 2000) (UN Department of Economic and Social Affairs: Population Division, 2013)—that is 3.2 percent of the world's population. Two-thirds of people who migrate live in Europe (72 million) and Asia (71 million). The U.S. hosts 45.8 million foreign-born people within a total population of about 330 million—that is one-seventh of the population in the third most populous country in the world. This surge of international

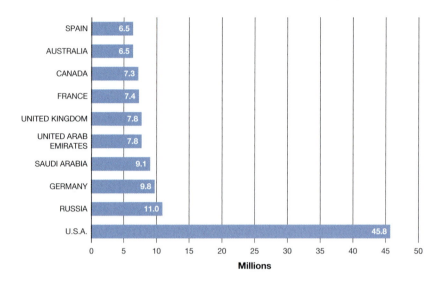

Figure 1.2 Immigrant Population in Top Ten Countries by Millions

(*Source*: United Nations Department of Economic and Social Affairs: Population Division, 2013.)

migrants came between 1990 and 2013, with about 23 million people leaving their homelands—about 1 million migrants per year (Thornhill, 2013).

And this migration is continuing to change throughout the world as history unfolds. China has plans to move 250 million rural people to cities in the next 15 years—if this is so, 70 percent of Chinese people will reside in cities—this same transition has taken centuries in Western countries (Johnson, 2013). Not to mention the mass migration of families fleeing war-torn countries, such as Syria, because of harsh governments and terrifying terrorism in the Middle East (Figure 1.2).

Globalization and Language

Immigration, increased opportunities for education, and advancement of women and minorities have created an even more multicultural society in the United States. The U.S. workforce is no longer a homogenous group of people who look, think, and behave in the same ways. The U.S. Census Bureau's *2010 Census* logs more than 330 million people living in the United States and, while over 220 million are classified as White, more than 38 million are African-American or Black, more than 50 million are Hispanic or Latino, and more than 14 million are Asian. Some 28 million more are of other races or mixed races. In the past decade, there have been large increases in the percentage of people of Asian descent, along with people of mixed and other races (U.S. Census Bureau, 2010). The fact is that more and more people do

Figure 1.3 Entering Global Village

not "fit" into any racial group. So we must be aware of this in order to gain knowledge for building competence across multiple cultures simultaneously (Figure 1.3).

The 2010 Census Bureau also reports almost 40 million foreign-born residents in the United States (U.S. Census Bureau, 2010), and *The Migration Information Source* reports that, between 2010 and 2011, the foreign-born population increased by about 400,000 people, representing a 1 percent annual increase. In the year 2011, the foreign-born population stood at about 13 percent of the total U.S. population (Migration Policy Institute, 2013), with 2 million foreign-born people settling in the United States each year. In addition, according to the Bureau of Labor Statistics 2013 report, the increase in the number of foreign-born people employed in the United States was 52 percent higher than the increase for the number of native-born people employed (U.S. Bureau of Labor Statistics, 2015). With rising investment by the United States abroad and by foreign companies in the United States, the labor force is undergoing a radical shift. For example, foreign companies with U.S. affiliates employed 5.3 million workers in 2010 (Anderson, 2012). Statistics from the Institute of International Education also show that by 2012 there were over 750,000 international students studying in the United States, up by 5.4 percent from the previous year. The overwhelming majority of them are from China (25 percent), followed by India (13 percent) and South Korea (9 percent) (Institute of International Education, 2012).

With increasing diversity comes an increase in the number of languages spoken by a country's people, so the question arises, can one language serve everyone's needs? A recent study shows that, across the business world, companies are incorporating global development programs which include the skill to speak more than one or two languages as a necessity to function successfully (Training Magazine, 2011). It has been argued by many that English will continue to be the dominant world language.

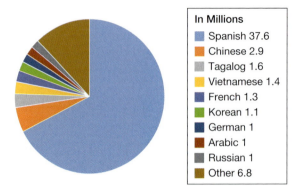

Figure 1.4 Languages Spoken in the U.S. (Other Than English). According to U.S. Census Data, 2011, Numbers Show Speakers in Millions

(*Source*: Ryan, 2013.)

However, studies contest this due to population growth in developing countries and that there will be a new linguistic order (Skapinker, 2007). By the mid-20th century only about 9 percent of the world's population spoke English as their native language, but by 2050 this will shrink to 5 percent. In fact, more people speak Mandarin Chinese than any other language (English, Spanish, Hindi/Urdu, and Arabic). English will continue to be the language of the world's commerce and investments, but it will not dominate by the number of people who speak it (Lovgren, 2004) (Figure 1.4).

The global village is more than the superficial interaction of a tourist on vacation: it is the current-day reality of savvy business professionals, community leaders, and people next door who interact each day with people from all over the world and from a variety of ethnicities and backgrounds. Globalization has come strong and it has come to stay.

As we have just discussed, we are able to cross borders with our communication, our products, our services, and our creativity through technology, travel, lower tariffs, and human migration. Therefore, if we are living in a side-by-side global marketplace, then we need global leaders who are able to identify and interact with people who have different norms, perspectives, and ideologies. Leading people is hard enough, because you deal with personality styles, backgrounds, preferences, and experiences. But by adding an extra layer of complexity that comes with leading people across borders, you will be challenged by language differences and cultural values that guarantee the potential for misunderstanding and failure. In a nutshell, we could define a global leader as someone who deals with complexity, uncertainty, and risk (Box 1.1).

Box 1.1 Starbucks' China Club

In 2006, Starbucks started a "China Club" and enrolled 300 senior officials so that they could study Mandarin language and Chinese culture. When CEO Howard Schultz was interviewed by Piers Morgan (CNN's *Piers Morgan Tonight*) in the middle of 2011, Schultz explained that Starbucks had 900 stores in Greater China and 450 on the Mainland. He said:

> I think given the opportunity and the size of what Starbucks could be in China, and the amount of Chinese Americans we have working for the company – someone came up with the idea to really start a club in which we could understand with great sensitivity and respect the Chinese culture.
>
> (CNN, 2011)

What is interesting is how little press in the United States (almost none) was given to this story.

However, in the *China Daily* and *Asia Times* there was a little more detail. *Asia Times* (June 2006) reported:

> In Starbucks' headquarters in Seattle, a group of company executives meet regularly, but not to discuss new items on the menu or what marketing campaign should be adopted. Instead, their topic of conversation is China.
>
> They are part of the "China Club," established by more than 300 senior company officials at the US coffee company. Learning to speak Mandarin recently became a new part of their routine.
>
> Starbucks chairman Howard Schultz is one of the club members. "In our Seattle office there has been such great enthusiasm and excitement for Starbucks in China. If I am not traveling, I always try to be at the meetings," Schultz said. Although China accounted for less than 10% of Starbucks' US$6.4 billion global sales in 2005, Schultz says the country will soon become the firm's largest market outside of North America. "We look at this market in terms of how quickly Starbucks has been accepted in just a few years. The market response has exceeded our expectations," Schultz said.
>
> (*Asia Times*, 2006)

What is interesting is that learning a language is not only helpful when doing business abroad, it is critical to one's survival—not just on a day-to-day basis—but for credibility's sake as well. Even just learning a small amount to show goodwill can go a long way to better cultural understanding and interaction.

A Rationale for Culture Learning

What is Culture?

In order to discuss intercultural communication, we must first define the concept of culture. Culture dictates the norms of every group. These norms, or unstated rules, are the accepted and expected ways of behaving and interacting with other people. But culture is something that we do not always see. Culture is something that we learn. Starting from infancy, we are conditioned to act, react, and learn about how people in our world do things from watching them, conversing with them, and interacting with them. In sum, culture consists of a group's communication patterns: how a group solves problems, and how a group perceives and passes on its shared values, beliefs, attitudes, and behaviors, including its perception of self, group, environment, authority, and power.

The word "culture" comes from the Latin, *cultura,* which means to grow or to cultivate. The closest meaning that the Romans might have attached to our understanding of group interaction would be *humanitas*, which was associated with human events and therefore culture. *Humanitas* is the engagement of one human being with another. Thus, knowing something about these roots can help us understand another person's world view and the most basic assumptions they hold about others who might be different (*The Free Dictionary*, n.d.).

Over the last century, key thinkers on culture, including anthropologists, sociologists, psychologists, communication specialists, and business experts, have attempted to define culture from various perspectives, frameworks, and focal points. The notion of culture is so abstract and complex that there is no end to the number of ways to define this complex human phenomenon.

Some Definitions

Anthropologist Edward T. Hall says that culture is about how we communicate, and that it is governed by hidden rules (the silent language and hidden dimension), which are reflected in both language and behavior (Hall, 1959). Interculturalist Fons Trompenaars says that culture is reflected in how a group approaches problem solving (Trompenaars & Hampden-Turner, 1998). Social psychologist Geert Hofstede argues by analogy that culture implies a kind of collective "software of the mind," learned over a lifetime of "programming" the way we do things (Hofstede, 1997). Clyde Kluckhohn and

Fred Strodtbeck, well-known anthropologists of the 1960s, construct their definition of culture around six dimensions that delineate cultural differences. Their framework focuses on value orientations that they believe all humans share in one way or another: environment, time, people, activity, responsibility, and space, which have become the basis for much of today's research on intercultural communication (Kroeber & Kluckhohn, 1952).

Current definitions of culture abound depending on different disciplines. For example, the *systems* approach includes various elements of a culture and its society, such as knowledge, beliefs, customs, and habits. Viewing cultures as *patterns* approach looks at how a society would organize the behavior of its people. There are consistent patterns of thought and action that develop over time and are transmitted from one generation to the next. And, a *group-membership* perspective of culture is about how people identify and relate to others within their in-group and sense of belonging. For the purposes of this book, culture will be defined as the values, beliefs, attitudes, and behaviors of a group of people (Baldwin et al., 2006) (see Box 1.2) (Tuleja, 2015).

To complicate matters even further as we attempt to define culture, let's look at another perspective from interculturalist Marshall Singer. He makes an interesting point regarding culture:

> [B]ecause no person is a part of all, and only, the same groups as anyone else and because each person ranks the attitudes, values, and beliefs of the groups to which he or she belongs differently, each individual must be considered to be culturally unique . . . I am not arguing that every person is a culture unto herself or himself. Culture . . . is a group-related phenomenon . . . each individual in this world is a member of a unique collection of groups. No two humans share only and exactly the same group memberships, or exactly the same ranking of the importance, to themselves, of the group membership they do share. Thus, each person must be culturally unique.
>
> (Singer, 1987, p. 3)

However we choose to define culture, it is about looking beyond our own cultural habits and biases (we will discuss this in Chapter 2) and trying to grasp the fact that everyone has different values, beliefs, attitudes, and behaviors. Culture is hard to define—it is like a puzzle—we piece it together bit by bit until we get the full picture.

The theatrical metaphor of "front-stage/back-stage" culture is helpful in explaining the elusive nature of culture (Varner, 2001). When we view a theatrical production, we are merely passive spectators observing the illusion of real events as portrayed by the actors on stage. While this can be enjoyable and entertaining, we miss out on all of the action going on behind the curtain. Perhaps we have read up on the playwright beforehand or know something of the play's theme and meaning. This understanding will surely help with the overall enjoyment of what is happening. But this is not the full view. If we

Box 1.2 The Building Blocks of Culture

Values, Beliefs, Attitudes, Behaviors

Values

The most basic of those structures are our *values*: those fundamental, unmovable tenets that make us who we are and that shape all other structures in our attitudinal system. They're a psychological assessment of those things, those concepts, and those ideas most dear to us. We acquire them at an early age from people we trust, before rational thought begins to play a role in what we know and hold to be true. The world is a particular way for us because that's what our parents, our teachers, our coaches, and our religious figures have told us. We're not in a position to challenge such beliefs—we simply accept them for what they are. Such values can (and do) change, but they do so at glacial speed.

Beliefs

Values provide the basis for our *beliefs*: those truths we hold to be self-evident because they are based on our values. If friendship, for example, is a fundamental value for us, then we believe that genuine friends will behave in certain ways and will expect certain things of us. We, in turn, can expect certain things of them and will be more than willing to go out of our way to help our friends—because we believe in them. Beliefs are what is right or wrong; true or false.

Attitudes

Attitudes, in turn, arise from and are consistent with those beliefs. It's a navigational term meaning orientation or position. Thus, an attitude gives some meaning and direction to our beliefs, serving as a guide to general thinking and our views of life over the near term. If a fundamental value of ours tells us that living a healthy lifestyle is important, then a consistent belief might be that smoking cigarettes is not a good idea. The attitude that arises from that belief would tell us, for example, that we not only shouldn't smoke, but that we should encourage others—our children, our employees, and our friends—not to smoke.

Behaviors

Behavior is the direct result of all these structures and is found at the uppermost level of our attitudinal system. It not only gives meaning and life to our more basic attitudes and beliefs, but it is the most visible portion of our system of beliefs. It may be hard to tell what a friend is thinking, but it's fairly easy to see what he or she is doing. We observe behaviors and infer the attitudes and beliefs that animate them. Behavior is often expressed in the form of an *opinion*: for the moment, at least, it's our opinion that we will vote for this person, dine at that restaurant, or purchase a particular brand. It's all subject to change, of course, and is less predictable than the underlying attitudes, beliefs, and values that support it.

Source: Tuleja, 2015, pp. 14–15

have any curiosity about theatrical workings, we might choose to go backstage after the curtain call and steal a glimpse of all of the props and mechanical devices that go unnoticed throughout the production. Or, we might have the opportunity to become stage hands ourselves and learn all of the inner workings of how the production is fabricated. In essence, we are able to understand not only *what* is happening, but *why* it is happening because of our insider's view and understanding of what is going on behind the scenes. By going backstage we have become participants. In sum, front-stage culture is *what* you see on the surface—the behaviors and practices, such as customs, food, dress, holidays, religious practices, symbols, and greetings to name a few. Back-stage culture is the "*why*" behind the "*what*" of the hidden dimensions of culture (Tuleja, 2008) (Figure 1.5).

There is a wonderful scene in the film *The Lion the Witch and the Wardrobe*, based on the book by C. S. Lewis, where Lucy meets the faun Mr. Tumnus. The meeting of this little girl and a mythical figure is quite endearing as each tries to figure out the other:

> "What are you—some kind of beardless dwarf?" asks Mr. Tumnus. Lucy holds out her hand in a gesture of friendship and he is perplexed. Sensing his hesitancy, Lucy says, "You shake it." "Oh, but why?" replies the faun. "Well, actually . . . I don't know," says Lucy.

Culture is invisible to us—we do not realize that we do things a certain way, and when asked, we really do not know the *why* behind the *what*.

Cultural Metaphors

Since we are on the topic of metaphors, let us look at another one: the iceberg metaphor. This is the most popular rendition of culture. Most of an iceberg—90 percent—is submerged below the water line, so what we see is its tip (Bruneau, n.d.). Interculturalists will describe behavior as being the tip of the iceberg. It is what we see most readily—nonverbal gestures, language, how people dress, the foods they eat, and what customs they practice. But it is what is below the water line, what we cannot see, that creates the challenge of

Figure 1.5 Front-stage/Back-stage Culture

(*Source*: Fotolia 65296493, © Diego Cervo.)

understanding someone else's culture—the attitudes, beliefs, and behaviors that support what people actually do. Understanding what is below the water line helps us to begin to decode the why behind the what (Figure 1.6).

Significance

A metaphor is a figure of speech that is representative of something else. They help us compare one thing to another—they are figurative comparisons, and like mental schema, can help us make sense out of something abstract or unfamiliar. Metaphors are abundant in human communication exchanges and we take them for granted, unaware of how much we use them. Metaphors help us make sense of common experiences and when we use them our understanding is automatic as long as we understand the connotation behind them. Every language has the possibility of containing innumerable idiomatic expressions, which lends to the creativity of how we use language (Lakoff, 1993).

Metaphors are powerful meaning-making devices and there has been a significant amount of scientific research dedicated to understanding them. We use metaphors more than we realize in our everyday life. Such metaphors are conceptual devices that aid us in transferring abstract ideas into concrete understandings. We are told that:

- Metaphors structure thinking.
- Metaphors structure knowledge.

Figure 1.6 Iceberg

(*Source*: Fotolia 103906916, © Andrew7726.)

- Metaphors are central to abstract language.
- Metaphors are grounded in physical experience (Deignan, 2005).

What We Can Learn

Here is what this means. When we encounter something new, unfamiliar, or confusing, we automatically make assumptions about our experiences by applying them to abstract concepts. In this sense, metaphors can actually shape our perception and communication. For example, we use the saying, "time is money." Time is abstract but money is concrete. We understand this intuitively and could also say, "Don't *waste* my time," "I don't *have* time," or that someone is "living on *borrowed* time" (Deignan, 2005) (Figure 1.7).

The scientific study of this theory has determined that metaphors are not simply rhetorical devices but actually conceptual tools that are linked to our thoughts, perceptions, and understanding. In other words, we use metaphors to help conceptualize our experience—and the concepts we use actually structure how we perceive and relate to everyday life. Metaphor analysis is a starting point for understanding culture's influence on who we are and how our societies function, by providing insight into understanding the elusiveness, complexity, and paradoxical nature of culture (Kövecses, 2005). For an in-

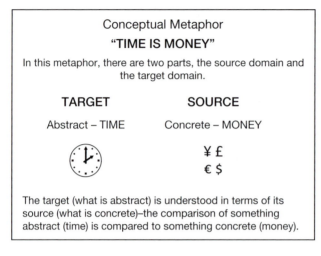

Figure 1.7 Conceptual Metaphor

depth examination of how cultural metaphors can help us understand cultural aspects of national cultures, there is a wonderful book, *Understanding global cultures: Metaphorical journeys through 32 countries*, by Martin J. Gannon (2012).

Historical Foundations of Intercultural Communication

Understanding the Field of Management's "Four Legs"

Why the study of communication and business? Well, if you think about the field of management—and this book *is* about management and leadership—it is a combination of several fields that make it what it is (anthropology, sociology, psychology, and communication). Let's break down these fields of research in the social sciences in order to see why communication in business is critical to one's ability to both function and succeed:

- Anthropology: is about the study of human nature—both past and present— and it builds on knowledge from the social, biological, and physical sciences.
- Sociology: examines social behavior that enlightens us about how people act and change within society over time.
- Psychology: involves the study of mental functions and behaviors.
- Communication: studies provide insight into the processes of human communication.

So, in business when we interact with and manage people, we are employing all four of these sciences combined. In order to be effective we need to understand human nature, social behavior, mental behavior, and how we use communication to interact with others. Think of the field of management as being the seat of a chair and the four legs (notice the metaphor used here) are these four streams of inquiry that support it—without these four legs, there would be no management!

Edward T. Hall

All of these fields of scientific inquiry had key thinkers who contributed to our understanding of the human condition: Charles Darwin and biology/ ethology (study of animal behavior and then human social organization from a biological perspective); Karl Marx and sociology/economics; Sigmund Freud and psychology; Franz Boas, Margaret Mead, and Ruth Benedict and anthropology; and Edward Sapir and Benjamin Whorf and linguistics. These key figures all had an influence on Edward T. Hall, who is credited with beginning the field of intercultural communication. Hall was an anthropologist (Ph.D. from Columbia University) who lived in the multicultural state of New Mexico and worked with the Hopi and Navajo tribes. During World War II he was in charge of an African-American squad in the Philippines and Europe.

Because of his diverse experience growing up in the Southwest and Midwestern parts of the United States as well as in Europe, his work focused on decoding what he coined as the "hidden dimensions of culture" (Hall, 1992). After World War II, he worked for the State Department and trained Foreign Service officers en route to underdeveloped countries. Hall's main teaching (based upon his research) about how different people groups view time, space, and relationships—was unheard of at that time—and quite controversial. Hall took what was theoretical (as in the discussion above) and made it practical upon writing his book *The silent language* (1959), which has led to this interdisciplinary field. Today, the Foreign Service Institute requires his readings for all recruits.

Intercultural communication is about using communication with people who are different than us. It is about how we use our collective or individual efforts; how we use power; how we interpret time and nature; how we interpret cultural identity; how our world views affect perceptions; how we persuade, negotiate, and deal with conflict. The common denominator of culture is the human condition—the variable is the mindset—or frame of reference of the individual or group of people.

Defining "Intercultural," "Cross–Cultural," and "International"

Now that we have clarified the meaning of culture and looked at the foundations of intercultural communication, it is important that we clarify some other terms. When we talk about intercultural communication, cross-cultural communication, and international communication, these terms do not mean the same things but are often used interchangeably.

Intercultural communication is the communication exchange between people who are different culturally—it examines how the specific cultural differences affect the interactions of the people engaged. For example, if you are from Switzerland and your colleague is from Singapore, the interaction would be intercultural because the communication strategies each person uses are different based upon their cultural background. The focus is on the individual as the unit of analysis.

Cross-cultural communication is not about the *interaction* of people from different cultures communicating, but the *comparison* of their differences across culture. So, if we look at our communicators from Switzerland and Singapore, and compare their communication patterns, we would be talking about a cross-cultural comparison. The study of cross-cultural communication comes from anthropology and is usually comparative in nature (Gudykunst & Mody, 2002).

International communication also involves the interaction of people from differing cultures, but it is focused on macro issues, such as governmental or political influences that affect the communication processes as people interact with each other in each respective country. For example, what is the government's influence on the process of people communicating from Switzerland and Singapore? International communication is about the power, politics, and processes of one nation influencing another. This form of communication originally comes from the study of international propaganda during World Wars I and II. The unit of analysis is therefore dependent on the country, the organization, or world systems (Gudykunst & Mody, 2002) (Box 1.3).

Many of the same principles and concepts of multiculturalism and diversity are similar to issues in intercultural communication (Beamer & Varner, 2010). However, multiculturalism deals with issues primarily regarding race, ethnicity, and gender in the fight against prejudice, bias, and discrimination that affect people who are not in a position of privilege or power. In this book, we

---

Box 1.3 Is it "Intercultural" or "Cross-cultural?"

The terms "intercultural" and "cross-cultural" are often used interchangeably. One anthropologist, William Gudykunst, has made this distinction: intercultural—involves communication between people from different cultures (examining the specific cultural characteristics of the people engaging in interaction). Cross-cultural involves comparisons of communication *across* cultures (examining the behavior of multiple cultures). The difference is between *interactions* and *comparisons* (Gudykunst & Mody, 2002, p. 34).

> **Box 1.4 Graphic Representation of our 7 Billion+ World**
>
> For graphic representations of our huge population in a shrunken world, visit this website for some astounding facts: www.7billionworld.com/.
>   You can also watch these powerful video clips:
>   www.youtube.com/watch?v=sc4HxPxNrZ0
>   www.youtube.com/watch?v=VcSX4ytEfcE
>   http://ngm.nationalgeographic.com/7-billion

will examine national cultures—the norms of large groups of people and how those values, attitudes, and beliefs shape behaviors—in order to understand the differences that exist. As we will discover in the following pages—the issues of individualism or collectivism; power and authority; or our perceptions—all affect how we view others, communicate, persuade, and negotiate. We are focusing on multiple dimensions of dealing with differences among people from many nationalities (Box 1.4).

Summary

Putting Things Into Perspective

So why does this matter? Isn't this discussion rather academic and what does it have to do with the business professional? Well, all of our learning comes from somewhere and it is important for the business person to understand the strong foundation of theories and concepts that support what happens during the communication process. As human beings we must interact with people who are different than us and, as this chapter has demonstrated, this is a challenging task!

In this chapter we have talked about culture in business contexts. We have specifically examined why culture is important in business contexts and how rapid globalization is creating a cultural imperative for more cultural competence. We looked at the history of the field of intercultural communication in order to show its importance in the business world. We also discussed what culture is and some of its many definitions so that we can begin to take what is rather abstract and make it concrete for daily experience. As we wrap up this chapter, it will certainly prove useful to provide some vivid examples of what our world looks like.

UNICEF provides us a more personal definition of globalization by looking at the global citizen: "Someone who understands interconnectedness, respects and values diversity, has the ability to challenge injustice, and takes action in personally meaningful ways." (n.d.). This definition personalizes what it means to be in such a big world. It is not just about trade, technology, and tariffs. Yes, the world is small because we are more interconnected than ever, but more importantly, globalization is about the fact that people matter.

There are currently over 7 billion people on the earth—7 billion! In 2011 the world's 7-billionth human being was born. Compare this with 1968, when there were half as many people (7BillionWorld.com, n.d.)! It is hard to wrap one's mind around this, but an excellent visual is available at www.7billion-world.com/faq.php and it is worth taking a look. If this visual was laid out flat for viewing purposes, it would be about 1 mile (1.6 km) high and 800 feet (250 m) wide!

To put this in perspective, according to National Geographic, it would take 200 years just to count out loud to 7 billion; 7 billion steps would take you around the world 133 times; shoulder to shoulder all 7 billion of us would fill the city of Los Angeles (469 square miles, 1,215 square kilometers (km^2) LA has 4 million people); 7 billion people speak more than 7,000 languages and live in 194 countries.

The shrinking world has become a cliché in recent times because the world is not shrinking; it has already shrunk! Because of the ease of travel, communication, and movement of goods, services, and people, globalization has created the need for better communication across cultures. Whether we do business across borders or within our own communities, chances are that we interact with at least someone who does not share the same language or background.

Interculturalist Marshall Singer believes that the goal for intercultural communication is not just better communication; rather successful interaction with those who are different comes through better understanding of self in relation to others. This is because conflict and misunderstanding will always be a part of the human condition and, while we can never eliminate misunderstandings because of cultural differences, misperception is less likely if we are aware of the tacit subtleties that create the potential for conflict (Singer, 1987).

Our goal for this book is to help you develop your leadership potential for more successful intercultural interactions. This book is not a quick fix with instant recipes for success; rather it is a road map that you can spread out on your table to study, to contemplate, and to choose your best route.

We will examine the basic foundations of culture learning by looking at culture-general concepts in order to apply them to culture-specific situations. Our aim is to help you cultivate an awareness of yourself, others, and to acquire and use information that will equip you to take action every time you interact with someone who approaches life from a different world view.

References

7BillionWorld.com. (n.d.). www.7billionworld.com/faq.php (accessed August 1, 2016).

Anderson, T. (2012). U.S. affiliates of foreign companies: Operations in 2010. Bureau of Economic Analysis. Retrieved from www.bea.gov/scb/pdf/2012/08%20August/0812_us_affiliate_operations.pdf (accessed August 1, 2016).

Asia Times, (2006). Starbucks soars in China. Retrieved from www.atimes.com/atimes/ China_Business/HF15Cb06.html (accessed August 1, 2016).

Baldwin, J. R., Faulkner, S. L., Hecht, M. L., & Lindsley, S. L. (Eds.). (2006). *Redefining culture: Perspectives across the disciplines.* Mahwah, NJ: Lawrence Erlbaum Associates.

Beamer, L., & Varner, I. (2010). *Intercultural communication in the global workplace.* New York, NY: McGraw-Hill.

Bruneau, S. E. (n.d.) Newfoundland Labrador, Canada, Iceberg Facts. www.new-foundlandlabrador.com/ThingsToDo/IcebergFacts (accessed August 1, 2016).

Cho, J. (2013, April 23). Koreans slap Bill Gates for "rude" handshake. *ABC News.* Retrieved from http://abcnews.go.com/blogs/headlines/2013/04/koreans-slap-bill-gates-for-rude-handshake/ (accessed August 1, 2016).

CNN. (2011). Piers Morgan Tonight: Interview with Christine O'Donnell; Interview with Howard Schultz. Retrieved from http://edition.cnn.com/TRANSCRIPTS/ 1108/17/pmt.01.html (accessed August 1, 2016).

Deignan, A. (2005). *Metaphor and corpus linguistics.* Philadelphia, PA: John Benjamins Publishing.

Gannon, M. J. (2008). *Paradoxes of culture and globalization.* Los Angeles, CA: SAGE.

Gannon, M. J. (2012). *Understanding global cultures: Metaphorical journeys through 32 nations, clusters of nations, continents, and diversity* (5th edn.). Thousand Oaks, CA: SAGE.

Gudykunst, W. B., & Mody, B. (Eds.). (2002). *Handbook of international and intercultural communication* (p. 34). Newbury Park, CA: SAGE.

Hall, E. T. (1959). *The silent language* (*Vol. 3*). New York, NY: Doubleday.

Hall, E. T. (1992). *An anthropology of everyday life.* New York, NY: Anchor Books.

Hofstede, G. (1997). *Cultures and organizations: Software of the mind.* New York, NY: McGraw-Hill.

Institute of International Education. (2012). Open doors. Retrieved from www.iie. org/Research-and-Publications/Open-Doors/Data/International-Students (accessed September 28, 2013).

Irvine, C. (2013, April 23). Bill Gates "disrespects" South Korean president with casual handshake. Retrieved from www.telegraph.co.uk/technology/bill-gates/10011847/ Bill-Gates-disrespects-South-Korean-president-with-casual-handshake.html (accessed August 1, 2016).

Johnson, I. (2013, June 15). China's great uprooting: Moving 250 million into the cities. Retrieved from www.nytimes.com/2013/06/16/world/asia/chinas-great-uprooting-moving-250-million-into-cities.html?pagewanted=all&_r=0 (accessed August 1, 2016).

Kövecses, Z. (2005). *Metaphor in culture: Universality and variation.* New York, NY: Cambridge University Press.

Kroeber, A. L., & Kluckhohn, C. (1952). Culture: A critical review of concepts and definitions. *Papers of the Peabody Museum of American Archaeology and Ethnology*, 47(1), 229–39.

Lakoff, G. (1993). The contemporary theory of metaphor. In A. Orotny (Ed.), *Metaphor and thought* (2nd edn.) New York, NY: Cambridge University Press, 202–51.

Lovgren, S. (2004). English in decline as first language, study says. *National Geographic News.* Retrieved from http://news.nationalgeographic.com/news/2004/02/0226_ 040226_language.html (accessed September 28, 2013).

Migration Policy Institute. (2013). Migration information source: US in focus. Retrieved from www.migrationinformation.org/usfocus/display.cfm?ID=931 (accessed

September 25, 2013). Corroborated with: Kandel, W. A. (2011). The U.S. foreign-born population: Trends and selected characteristics. Congressional Research Service. Retrieved from www.fas.org/sgp/crs/misc/R41592.pdf (accessed September 25, 2013).

Ryan, C. (2013). Report number: ACS-22: Language use in the United States: 2011. Retrieved from www.census.gov/library/publications/2013/acs/acs-22.html (accessed August 4, 2016).

Schaff, P. (Ed.). (1886). *Nicene and post-Nicene fathers: The confessions and letters of St. Augustine, with a sketch of his life and work* [E-book version]. Retrieved from www. ccel.org/ccel/schaff/npnf101.vii.1.LIV.html#vii.1.LIV-p10 (accessed August 1, 2016).

Singer, M. R. (1987). *Intercultural communication: A perceptual approach.* Englewood Cliffs, NJ: Prentice-Hall.

Skapinker, M. (2007, November 8). Whose language? Retrieved from www.ft.com/cms/s/0/e621ff38-8e1c-11dc-8591-0000779fd2ac.html#axzz4G7c6sSOS (accessed 2016 August 1).

The Free Dictionary. (n.d.). Culture. Retrieved from www.thefreedictionary.com/culture (accessed August 1, 2016).

Thornhill, T. (2013, September 12). More people than ever living outside their home country: Number of migrants worldwide hits 232 million. *Daily Mail.* Retrieved from www.dailymail.co.uk/news/article-2418902/More-people-living-outside-home-country-Number-migrants-worldwide-hits-232-million.html (accessed August 1, 2016).

Training Magazine. (2011). Developing successful global leaders: Tomorrow's leaders will need to be more adaptable to culture differences, geographic distance, and nonhierarchical organizational structures, according to a recent survey by *Training,* AMA, and i4cp. *Training Magazine,* May/June, 58–62. Retrieved from https://trainingmag.com/sites/default/files/trg0511-AMA-Leadership-Surv.pdf (accessed August 1, 2016).

Trompenaars, F., & Hampden-Turner, C. (1998). *Riding the waves of culture: Understanding cultural diversity in global business.* New York, NY: McGraw-Hill.

Tuleja, E. A. (2008). Aspects of intercultural awareness through an MBA study abroad program: Going backstage. *Business Communication Quarterly, 71*(3), 314–37.

Tuleja, E. A. (2015). *Intercultural communication for business.* Indianapolis, IN: Globe-Comm Publishing, 14–15.

UNICEF. (n.d.). Development aid. www.unicefusa.org/stories/pursuit-global-citizenship/7219 (accessed August 1, 2016).

United Nations Department of Economic and Social Affairs: Population Division. (2013). International migration report 2013. Retrieved from www.un.org/en/development/desa/population/publications/pdf/migration/migrationreport2013/Full_Document_final.pdf#page=7 (accessed August 1, 2016).

U.S. Bureau of Labor Statistics. (2015, May 21). Labor force characteristics of foreign-born workers summary. *Economic news release.* Retrieved from www.bls.gov/news.release/forbrn.nr0.htm (accessed September 25, 2013).

U.S. Census Bureau. (2010). Population profile of the United States: 2010 (Internet release). *2010 Census.* Retrieved from www.census.gov/2010census/data/ (accessed September 25, 2013).

Varner, I. (2001). Teaching intercultural management communication: Where are we? Where do we go? *Business Communication Quarterly, 64*(1), 99–111.

WordSense (n.d.). When in Rome, do as the Romans do. Retrieved from www.wordsense.eu/when_in_Rome,_do_as_the_Romans_do/ (accessed August 1, 2016).

Case 1

Wal-Mart in Germany

Corporate Formula Does Not Fit the German Culture[1]

Abstract

In the United States, Wal-Mart customers are greeted with a smile, escorted to the item they're looking for, and watch their purchases being bagged by an employee. These aspects of Wal-Mart's culture were a complete failure in Germany, however, when the company expanded there in 1997. Wal-Mart also failed on other counts, such as recognizing the status of unions in Germany and the importance of store location. What eventually happened to Wal-Mart in Germany, and how could it have been prevented? What did Wal-Mart learn? This case examines the cultural mishaps of America's largest discount retailer.

Introduction

Wal-Mart has become a household name in the United States, and in some parts of the world outside the United States. With low prices and a large array of products, Wal-Mart superstores have become the chosen "one-stop shop" for many consumers.

Germans, however, don't view Wal-Mart in the same way. In late 1997, Wal-Mart decided to expand into Germany by first acquiring two retailers for a total of 95 store locations. But Wal-Mart soon learned that its American model simply did not work there. On so many levels and in so many ways, it was an abject failure.

Brief Overview of Wal-Mart

Sam Walton and his brother opened the first Wal-Mart store in Rogers, Arkansas in 1962, generating more than $1 million in sales during the first year of operations. Wal-Mart expanded quickly and, by 1967, the brothers owned 24 stores with sales over $12.6 million. The company incorporated in 1969 and was listed on the New York Stock Exchange two years later. Focusing operations in small towns, in 1977, the company expanded into Michigan and Illinois and by 1980 there were 276 Wal-Mart stores across the United States (Wal-Mart Stores, 2016).

Today the company has expanded internationally and has more than 8,400 retail stores in 15 different countries and employs over 2.1 million employees across the world.

Wal-Mart opened with the intention of helping people save money on household goods and by doing so, helping to improve lives. Today the company continues to offer the lowest prices in most markets, relying on buying power with their strong supply chain. Recently, Wal-Mart focused domestic growth on the creation of supercenters, which has proved wildly successful. Additionally, the company has made significant strides toward becoming a leader in sustainability and corporate philanthropy, despite past criticism about labor practices and exploitation of suppliers.

International Development

"All around the world we save people money, so they can live better. That's good news—in any language."—Wal-Mart Stores, Inc. (Arunmaba13, 2011). In the United States, Wal-Mart customers cite low prices as the most important reason for shopping there. Its lean business model, plus the ability to reach historically high economies of scale, allow the company to dominate supplier networks.

Because of Wal-Mart's market power in the United States and its domination of supplier networks, it can continuously drive down product prices. In addition, Wal-Mart sells a full range of household products and groceries, allowing customers the increasingly ubiquitous one-stop shopping experience.

In the early 1990s Wal-Mart announced plans to take their operations global due to tough competition in the U.S. markets and the opportunities available in new markets across the world. The company realized that the United States contained only 4 percent of the world's population and that confining sales to the United States would significantly limit their ability to grow and dominate the market (ICMR, 2004).

To fulfill their global expansion goals, the company created Wal-Mart International which has grown into a $63 billion business and is the fastest-growing part of the company (Landler & Barbaro, 2006). Most of Wal-Mart's international growth comes from acquisitions, differing from their domestic strategy of building new stores. This has allowed them to penetrate new markets quickly and easily. Wal-Mart international operates in 15 markets, with a similar goal throughout—to maintain low prices by controlling cost procedures.

There are wholly owned operations in Argentina, Brazil, Canada, Puerto Rico, and the United Kingdom. In addition to its wholly owned international operations, Wal-Mart has joint ventures in China and several majority-owned subsidiaries. Wal-Mart's majority-owned subsidiary in Mexico is Walmex. In Japan, Wal-Mart owns about 53 percent of Seiyu. In Central America, Wal-Mart owns 51 percent of the Central American Retail Holding

Company (CARHCO), consisting of more than 360 supermarkets and other stores in Guatemala, El Salvador, Honduras, Nicaragua, and Costa Rica (Daniel, 2012).

Expansion into Germany

Most U.S. companies begin their international expansion in the United Kingdom due to many perceived cultural similarities to the United States. In late 1997, Wal-Mart instead opted to begin in the German market by acquiring two German retailers, Wertkauf and Interspar. Wal-Mart purchased 21 stores from Wertkauf which offered food and general merchandise to customers in the southwestern side of Germany.

This purchase was not enough to fully penetrate the German market, so Wal-Mart acquired 74 Interspar stores in 1998, which increased the total number of Wal-Mart stores in Germany to 95, making Wal-Mart the fourth largest hypermarket retailer in Germany. Wal-Mart was attempting to implement its U.S. business model, characterized by low prices, location strategy, supply-chain management, and a corporate culture that highly values hard work, conformism, and friendly customer service (Gereffi & Christian, 2009).

Following the quick purchases, Wal-Mart realized that the cultures of the newly acquired companies were extremely different from the U.S.-based Wal-Mart culture, and the stores they took on were not necessarily in the most convenient locations for customers.

In addition, Germany has stringent planning and zoning regulations, and thus Wal-Mart was unable to expand the stores' sizes to reach its economies of scale. Difficulties with local suppliers further perpetuated their logistics issues, so much so that suppliers delivering products to the distribution centers had to wait for hours to unload their cargo. This is an operational characteristic of the German distribution system that is quite different from the U.S. efficiency of lean operations.

Germany is the most price-conscious country in Europe and while Wal-Mart is known for their low prices in the United States, they were not able to generate the advantage of economies in scale necessary to be the low-price leader. Wal-Mart totaled only 95 stores, paling in comparison to their direct competitors Aldi and Lidl, both of whom have over 500 retail locations (Landler, 2006).

These factors made it impossible for Wal-Mart's U.S. business model to compete in Germany and the firm was unable to turn a profit. After years of struggling, Wal-Mart eventually halted their German operations at an estimated cost of $1 billion.

Problem and Reactions

After launching its international operations in Germany, it did not take long for Wal-Mart to see that its company culture was not catching on, nor were customers increasing their shopping at the German locations. In an attempt to boost the performance of the German locations, Wal-Mart was forced to react quickly and take action to try to adapt its culture to better suit the Germans.

One major reason that Wal-Mart's stores did not succeed greatly at first is due to cultural insensitivity. Wal-Mart did not do its research on the tradition and culture of retail shopping in Germany before entering the market, and as a result saw resistance to its stores.

Wal-Mart was forced to rescind some of its policies in order to better fit the German business model. In the United States, Wal-Mart has a greeter at the entrance to the store that is responsible for smiling and welcoming people into the store (Nussbaum, 2006). This practice was not well received by the Germans, who typically find smiles from strangers to be artificial. Some male shoppers even interpreted this smiling to be flirting (Landler & Barbaro, 2006). In order to adapt to this cultural difference, Wal-Mart was forced to remove this greeter position from its German stores.

Similarly, the cheer that Wal-Mart workers in the United States typically do each morning was not well received by the German employees. The practice had to be halted there.

In Germany, unions are particularly important, whereas Wal-Mart is used to being able to demonstrate and exercise its power rather than having to give into pressures from outside sources. One of the biggest unions in Germany, the *ver.di union*, witnessed many complaints about Wal-Mart regarding their lack of concern for the voices of the German employees. Germany has many co-determination rules which allow employees to have a voice in management decisions and to participate, whereas Wal-Mart typically ignored the German employees' input, which could have prevented many of these misunderstandings. Additionally, the *ver.di union* has complained that Wal-Mart did not keep it adequately updated on store closings. In general, Wal-Mart has not cooperated with the union to keep workers happy and motivated, producing a negative view of Wal-Mart among many Germans. Wal-Mart did not have a history of dealing with unions, and had never been forced to try to get along with unions in the way that the Germans expected it to.

In 2005, Wal-Mart released a new ethics code for its German employees. Unfortunately, the translations within the manual were far from perfect, and did not clearly translate the message that Wal-Mart was trying to send. One section advised employees to take caution with supervisor-employee relationships, which the Germans interpreted as a ban on interoffice romance.

Another section that talked about how to report unethical behavior of co-workers was interpreted as instructions on how to tattle on your fellow employees. These types of misinterpretations stem from miscommunication, and Wal-Mart did not put the proper time and effort into their translation to get its point across properly. As a result, this ethics code caused much discontent from the German employees (Ewing, 2005).

Wal-Mart found its brand name to be particularly important in the United States and used it to attract customers who knew it for its low prices and to build customer loyalty. Through its experiences in the German market, Wal-Mart came to realize that the Wal-Mart name was not as important to customers, and that this assumption had cost them greatly in terms of attracting and retaining customers (Bhan & Toscano, 2006).

In general, Wal-Mart did not do enough research on the best location for its stores. As a result, many of the supercenter stores were located on the outskirts of town, in places that people could only reach by driving. These locations were not convenient for German customers, and many found that they could get the same products for similar, if not cheaper, prices at a location that was much more convenient.

Wal-Mart initially tried to copy American tradition by having employees bag the groceries at the end of each checkout lane. This practice was not normal for German customers, and was seen as strange by many Germans who did not want a stranger touching their groceries. As a result, this practice became one more reason for Germans to choose to shop somewhere else (Landler & Barbaro, 2006). Additionally, store hours in Germany are usually shorter. Germans do not like to have to wander around a giant store looking for one thing, and did not like help finding what they need, so the help of friendly Wal-Mart employees was not popular in Germany.

One other change that Wal-Mart tried to implement was centralizing its German headquarters. Wal-Mart shut down one of the headquarters early on, forcing employees to relocate to keep their jobs. As this is a normal occurrence in the United States, many of the top German employees chose to quit rather than move. This resulted in Wal-Mart losing many talented executives because of its inability to cooperate and listen to employee needs (Landler & Barbaro, 2006).

As a result of so many of these clashes of culture, Wal-Mart did not establish a good reputation among German customers or employees. Wal-Mart found that its stores in Germany were doing nowhere near as well as its stores in the United States and other markets, mainly due to its lack of attention to cultural detail when originally implementing its plan in Germany. By the time Wal-Mart figured out its mistakes and where they could improve, it was too late to recover.

Outcome

Wal-Mart finally decided to exit the German market in mid-2006. It sold its 95 stores to the German company METRO AG, a big retailer in Germany. This sale resulted in a $1 billion pretax loss (Zimmerman, 2006). This loss does not even include the millions, and possibly billions, of dollars lost in sales each year from futile efforts to succeed in Germany.

Despite its mistakes in Germany, Wal-Mart continues to try to expand into other international markets, particularly in China. Unfortunately, Wal-Mart's missteps in Germany were costly; however, hopefully it will force them to be more culturally sensitive in future expansions.

Discussion Questions

1   Who was most affected by Wal-Mart's mistakes?
2   What sources or models can Wal-Mart use to research cultures and understand what strategies to use?
3   What considerations should Wal-Mart take into account as it tries to expand in China?
4   How could Wal-Mart have altered its international expansion strategy to account for Hofstede's dimensions and how would this have affected the end result?

Note

1 Authors: Chen-jun Yu, G., Langhamer, T., Powelson, S., Foose, B., Ripple, M., O'Neill, B., and Tuleja, E. (Ed.) (2015).

References

Arunmaba13. (2011). FDI in Indian retail market case study to Wal-Mart Mexico market. Studymode.com: Business and economy, marketing and advertising. Retrieved from www.studymode.com/essays/Fdi-In-Indian-Retail-Market-Case-661111.html (accessed August 4, 2016).

Bhan, Niti, & Toscano, Manuel. (2006). Lessons from Wal-Mart: Five common mistakes when brands cross borders. *American Institute of Graphic Arts*. Retrieved from www.aiga.org/lessons-from-wal-mart-five-common-mistakes-when-brands-cross-borders/ (accessed August 4, 2016).

Daniel, Fran. (2012). Head of Wal-Mart tells WFU audience of plans for growth over next 20 years. *Winston-Salem Journal*. Retrieved from www.journalnow.com/business/article_5ad539d5-d616-55ba-ab27-aeaf45b06074.html (accessed August 4, 2016).

Ewing, Jack. (2005). Wal-Mart: Struggling in Germany. *Bloomberg Businessweek Magazine*. Retrieved from www.bloomberg.com/news/articles/2005-04-10/wal-mart-struggling-in-germany (accessed August 1, 2016).

Gereffi, Gary, & Christian, Michelle. (2009). The impacts of Wal-Mart: The rise and consequences of the world's dominant retailer. *The Annual Review of Sociology, 35,* 573–91.

ICMR. (2004). Wal-Mart's German misadventure. Retrieved from www.icmrindia.org/casestudies/catalogue/Business%20Strategy2/Business%20Strategy%20Wal-Mart%20German%20Misadventure.htm (accessed August 4, 2016).

Landler, Mark. (2006). Wal-Mart gives up Germany—Business—International Herald Tribune. *The New York Times*. Retrieved from www.nytimes.com/2006/07/28/business/worldbusiness/28iht-walmart.2325266.html?_r=1 (accessed August 4, 2016).

Landler, Mark, & Barbaro, Michael. (2006). Wal-Mart finds that its formula doesn't fit every culture. *The New York Times*. Retrieved from www.nytimes.com/2006/08/

02/business/worldbusiness/02walmart.html?pagewanted=1&_r=2 (accessed August 4, 2016).

Nussbaum, Bruce. (2006). Did Wal-Mart smile too much in Germany? *Bloomberg Businessweek Innovation and Design*. Retrieved from www.businessweek.com/innovate/NussbaumOnDesign/archives/2006/07/why_did_walmart.html (accessed August 1, 2016).

Wal-Mart Stores. (2016). Our history: Timeline. Retrieved from http://corporate.walmart.com/our-story/heritage/history-timeline (accessed August 1, 2016).

Zimmerman, Ann. (2006). With profits elusive, Wal-Mart to exit Germany: Local hard discounters undercut retailer's prices; "Basket-splitting" problems. *The Wall Street Journal*. Retrieved from http://online.wsj.com/news/articles/SB11540723 8850420246 (accessed August 1, 2016).

Part 2

Self–Awareness in Intercultural Communication

2 Cultural Competence for Leaders

People are like puzzles—they take time and patience and curiosity to figure out.
(Author)

Figure 2.1 People/World Puzzle

(*Source*: Fotolia 21786190, © Hanna.)

Chapter Overview

Chapter 2, Cultural Competence for Leaders, examines the questions: As leaders, how can we fit together all of the puzzling culture pieces? How do we develop our cultural competence so that we can interact appropriately with people from different backgrounds? What is ethnocentrism and how do we become more culturally sensitive? What are some practical frameworks that we can use to aid us in this developmental process? These are the key questions we will address in Chapter 2 (Figure 2.1).

Learning Objective

As leaders we must understand our hidden bias and deal with the human tendency toward ethnocentrism. Social psychologists tell us that this is normal human behavior; however we must be aware of this in order to grow and develop effective intercultural communication skills.

Key Takeaways

— We all have unconscious bias that gets in the way of being non-judgmental toward cultural differences.
— Developing cultural intelligence (CQ) helps us to break away from such bias, but it is a life-long challenge that needs constant attention.

Leadership Applications

— Global leaders must work on attaining knowledge, mindfulness, and skills in order to become culturally competent.
— Global leaders can apply various models to help change behavior: the Developmental Model of Intercultural Sensitivity, the Cultural Sense-Making Model, and the Critical Incident Model.

Introduction

What's in a Name?

This would be a great question to ask on *Jeopardy*: "What is a *pe'a*?" Or, more accurately, "What is a Samoan *pe'a*?" The *pe'a* is a sacred *tatau*, which is Polynesian for "tattoo," often associated with the rite of passage for men. The sportswear giant, Nike, liked the design and incorporated it into their new product line. People from Australia and New Zealand were offended that this traditional art form was created for women's leggings—something that is only allowed for men (Ehrbar, 2013).

Nike said it meant to offend no one; rather, it was inspired by the *tataus* of Samoa, Fiji, and New Zealand. However, many Pacific islanders were offended, saying that it violated the UN Declaration on the Rights of Indigenous Peoples and that Nike should have done a better job with their due diligence.

What is your take on this? Is this political correctness or heedless ignorance of an important cultural tradition? Do companies have the right to forge ahead with innovations when launching a new product line without consultation of cultural groups that *might* be offended? How do they know who to consult? And if they consult one group, could another have potential ire toward their product?

This is not the first time that Nike has offended the public and we will discuss another case in Chapter 6. The critical issue here is that the people who run companies need to go beyond merely having excellent functional skills to develop the interpersonal and cultural skills that are critical for effective interaction.

Concerns For More Than Functional Skills

Over the past few years, the American Management Academy (AMA) has conducted annual surveys on global leadership development through the Institute for Corporate Productivity. What has been both evident and relevant to the interculturalist is now being taken seriously by the business community. Both organizations and their key leadership figures are finally beginning to realize that all of the functional and technical skills in the world cannot compare to the practical, hard reality of the soft skills (interpersonal relationships and the ability to communicate effectively) when dealing across borders.

One report by the AMA on developing successful global leaders determined:

- "Most companies continue to fail to develop global leaders, yet there appears to be a greater recognition of the link between global leadership development programs and overall business performance." (p. 5).
- "When asked to identify the single most important focus of their global leadership development programs, high-performing companies clearly focus on interpersonal influence and coalition building as their top priority." (p. 9).
- "The leading competencies that are the focus of global leadership development remain remarkably consistent over time. However, an examination of the mastery of these competencies identifies some key areas for improvement and competitive advantage." (p. 8) (AMA Enterprise, 2012).

What is apparent in this report is the *awareness* that global leadership development is critical to performance and that some effort is being made to acquire the *knowledge* necessary in order to develop interpersonal relationships; however, the mastery of *competencies* is what is lacking for the improvement of global leadership development. In this chapter we will discuss a model for intercultural competence that includes three key elements of global leadership effectiveness: knowledge, mindfulness, and behavior (Box 2.1).

Emotional Intelligence and Cultural Intelligence

This chapter examines several models for understanding intercultural competence. We will first look at the concepts of emotional intelligence (EQ) as

> ### Box 2.1 Global Firms in 2020—The Next Decade of Change for Organisations and Workers
>
> A report from the *Economist* Intelligence Unit, *Global Firms in 2020,* surveyed over 500 executives in different industries from around the world about their engagement with international business or their plans for global engagement. Seventy percent of respondents believed that their company's operational presence overseas would increase and 78 percent said that in the next three years there would be more cross-border collaboration of teams. When asked about the challenges faced while operating or competing in global markets, respondents pointed specifically to issues in cross-border communication and collaboration.
>
> Fifty percent of respondents said that communication misunderstandings have impeded their international business dealings, which have resulted in financial losses for the company and that the cause—lack of clarity in intercultural communication—is just as critical as financial gain. Another 50 percent of respondents said that the greatest threats to smooth operations are differences in cultural norms. A staggering 90 percent said that understanding cross-border communication better would improve the firm's profit, revenue, and market share and actions should be taken to educate employees regarding cross-cultural differences, yet only 47 percent said that their companies did something to help with preparedness or had an appropriate system in place for selecting people who were suited for cross-cultural dealings.
>
> Source: *Economist* Intelligence Unit: *Global Firms in 2020.* www.shrm.org/research/surveyfindings/articles/documents/economist%20research%20-%20global%20firms%20in%202020.pdf

the foundation for cultural intelligence (CQ). Then we will turn our discussion to three models that focus on developing intercultural competence. These include: the Model of Intercultural Competence (also known as the Mindfulness Model), the Developmental Model of Intercultural Sensitivity (DMIS), and the Cultural Sense-Making Model. While these concepts are abstract, they operate as crucial guiding tools when applied to practical applications.

At first glance, the notion of a global leader usually denotes someone who is able to deftly perform a merger and acquisition, or easily navigate the intricacies of global supply-chain management, or comprehend the myriad details of international accounting practices. However, it is not enough to simply possess such functional business skills in order to navigate successfully in the global business environment. Another common misconception of a global leader is that the successful leadership skills practiced in one's own culture are naturally transferable when applied to another cultural setting. We learn of many cross-border deals and negotiations that fall flat simply because due diligence has not been performed or because key players are unable to adapt readily to the challenges found in cross-cultural relations despite having performed well with their previous assignments. Research has shown that there are many differences involved in the transfer of such leadership capabilities because what may be meaningful and appropriate in one context may be insulting and improper in another, all based upon certain cultural norms for living (Hofstede, 1984).

For example, take Mark Trudeaux, a 53-year-old financial advisor and investor who had worked with European clients in Germany, Belgium, and The Netherlands. When he expanded his financial business to Asia, specifically Taiwan, he had a hard time adapting to the necessity of hospitality. After a long flight and jet lag all he wanted to do was prepare for the next day's meetings—he wanted to eat, relax with *BBC World*, and get some much needed sleep. No sooner had he showered and ordered room service than he received a message from the front desk. Ms. Huang and Mr. Tsai were waiting for him in the lobby to escort him to an elaborate banquet and evening of karaoke in his honor. It was all that Mark could do not to yell at the clerk on the other end of the line, but as soon as he hung up he cursed and threw a pillow across the room. He was exhausted, needed to prepare for his meetings, and thought it totally irresponsible not to get a good night's sleep. The last thing he wanted to do was pretend to enjoy singing songs in a smoke-filled room and down glass after glass of the strong Kaoliang spirit (distilled grain liquor).

However, after venting to himself for a few minutes, he took a deep breath, calmly put on a fresh shirt and went down to meet his gracious hosts. He knew himself well—while he would rather relax and prep for the next day, he understood that this was part of doing business in Asia and that he needed to respond graciously to this generous offer of hospitality. After all, it would be during such occasions that the real business would get done—in a tacit way—because without building strong and trustworthy relationships there would be no business. He took another deep breath, cleared his mind, and shifted his focus toward having a good time—whether this was his definition of a good time or not.

Global leaders today are required to readily adapt to change and deal with complexity across interpersonal relationships in order to flourish in an environment of ambiguity. Global leadership means that a person develops intercultural competence, which turns into cultural intelligence—CQ (Earley & Ang, 2003). Before we can talk about CQ we must first lay the foundation of EQ.

Emotional Intelligence

The concept of intercultural communication competence or CQ awareness is not new. The book *Frames of mind: The theory of multiple intelligences* (1983), by

Harvard professor Howard Gardner, introduced the idea of "multiple intel-ligences" that include both intrapersonal (understanding your own feelings and motivations) and interpersonal (understanding the intentions and motivations of others) skills. He posited that IQ (intellectual quotient) is not sufficient to explain a person's entire cognitive ability; something more was needed (Gardner, 1983). Later, Daniel Goleman, also a Harvard professor and psychologist, popularized the concept of social/EQ, which is the ability to recognize, understand, and manage emotions both in ourselves and in others. After the immediate success of his book *Emotional intelligence* (1995), the public resonated with what he had to say about "Emotional Intelligence and the Workplace" (Goleman, 1995). His idea of emotional intelligence laid the foundation for the intangible yet indispensable aspects of being a competent member of society, whether it is in the workplace or elsewhere. This com-petence, he argues, is founded in our ability to connect on an emotional and subliminal level with those around us.

In the workplace, EQ contributes 80–90 percent of the competencies that distinguish outstanding leaders from average leaders (Goleman, 1998). A person with a high EQ possesses the following attributes:

- *Self-awareness and other-awareness:* The ability to know how you are feeling and how those around you are feeling; also to know how your emotions might be affecting others. It also includes the ability to be reflective and take an honest look at oneself to monitor and keep in check one's strengths and weaknesses. While there is confidence, the EQ person does not become overconfident.
- *Self-regulation:* The ability to control your emotions and actions under pressure and think before you act. Because you are self-aware and in tune with who you are, you are able to gauge how to act and react.
- *Motivation:* The ability to be able to delay gratification for the good of the group and take a long-term approach to situations.
- *Empathy:* The insight to see what motivates others and to plan how to manage people around this. This means having empathy to understand the emotional makeup of other people and the skill in treating people according to their emotional reactions, handle conflict, work in teams, influence others, be an inspiration, help be a catalyst for change.
- *Social skills:* The ability to have the instinctive "hunch" for what to say and what not to say and how to treat people accordingly. Also, people with good social skills are strong communicators and adept at building and maintaining relationships.

Think about it. If you are managing a team of several individuals, all with different backgrounds and personalities, you need to be aware of what motivates them both on an individual level and as a group. An effective leader will listen in order to earn the individuals' confidence and respond with equanimity during a crisis. To understand others, the culturally competent leader must be aware of their own feelings, what motivates them, and what makes them "tick." For example, if you are a team leader, you would be wise to listen to your team and find out what is important to them. If the others are facing challenging circumstances, you address them while keeping your own emotions in check. You would remain calm and cool under pressure, recognizing how others around you could trigger your pressure points. You would look several steps ahead in order to foresee potential conflicts and spend the necessary time managing relationships with your team.

In the 1986 movie *Gung Ho*, directed by Ron Howard and starring Michael Keaton as Hunter Stevens, a "down and out" manufacturing town in the United States is saved by a Japanese auto company, Assan, that plans to take over their plant. Clashes of U.S. American culture and Japanese culture abound as the main character, Hunter Stevens, tries desperately to smooth over relations. Stevens is cocky at best, and his lack of self-awareness, compounded by his inadequate social skills when interacting with the Japanese, causes him to fumble around as he tries to make sense of their management style. He does, however, have a little "other-awareness"—empathy—for his fellow plant operators. By recognizing his co-workers' positions and what motivates them, he is able to rally his team around him despite the ups and downs of trying to "figure out the Japanese." Eventually he is able to self-regulate—control his emotions and actions—when working with the Japanese.

Cultural Intelligence

Like EQ, CQ has certain aspects that deal with self-awareness and other-awareness. CQ takes this even further. CQ is a person's ability to function skillfully in a cultural context different than one's own (Figure 2.2). This means that a culturally intelligent person is someone who is not only able to empathize and work well with others, but can acknowledge differing values, beliefs, attitudes, and behaviors in order to anticipate, act, and react in appropriate ways to produce the most effective results, and then to reevaluate and try acting or reacting in a different way. Described by Christopher Earley, the creator of the concept, a person with high EQ grasps what makes us human and at the same time what makes each of us different from one another. But,

> [a] person with high cultural intelligence can somehow tease out of a person's or group's behavior those features that would be true of all people and all groups, those peculiar to this person or this group, and those that are neither universal nor idiosyncratic. The vast realm that lies between those two poles is culture.
>
> (Earley & Mosakowski, 2004, p. 1)

Figure 2.2 Cultural Intelligence
(*Source*: Fotolia 72882009, © fotoscool.)

Another CQ specialist who has extended the Earley and Ang theory of CQ is Linn Van Dyne from Michigan State University. With her prolific work she breaks CQ down into four strategies: CQ Strategy, CQ Knowledge, CQ Motivation, and CQ Behavior. This framework will help us as we later talk about ethnocentrism.

- *CQ Strategy* involves your ability to make sense of intercultural experiences. We all go through a process of socialization where we acquire cultural knowledge and begin to understand it within our groups. As we begin to become aware of our cultural norms—or rules for engagement, we can begin to think critically about what is happening—we check our assumptions and think about what just happened, and we try to understand it in relation to other experiences. It occurs when people make judgments about their own thought processes and those of others. Van Dyne says, "This includes strategizing before an intercultural encounter, checking assumptions during that encounter, and then adjusting mental maps when actual experiences differ from expectations" (Dyne, 2012).
- *CQ Knowledge* is what you know about other cultures. Have you studied world history, read the newspaper, traveled, or lived in an area of the world where you had to learn something about the history, politics, religion, and social influences of its many people groups?
- *CQ Motivation* reflects your interest in not only learning about but experiencing other cultures by interacting with people from that culture. It is a person's energy and curiosity that focuses on learning as much as they can in order to function in culturally diverse situations.
- *CQ Behavior* is your ability to use both verbal and nonverbal behavior appropriately. As you build your knowledge and spend time interacting

with people from different cultures, you begin to build a repertoire of behavioral approaches. You self-monitor and choose the most appropriate behavior based upon the situation and context.

As you can see, you are already familiar with this concept of CQ because it is very similar to the EQ that you use every day to navigate the challenges of your workplace. EQ compels us to be self-aware and other-aware, and to monitor our emotions as we build relationships with people in our sphere of influence. CQ adds the extra layer of complexity, which is culture. You have to gain knowledge, try to figure out what is happening, and then be motivated to continue the learning process as you build a repertoire of behavioral approaches. Let us look at an exceptionally fluid model of CQ that focuses on the art of reflection.

Components of Cultural Intelligence

If we have all of this information at our fingertips in terms of concepts and theories, how then do we develop intercultural competence? How do we make sure that we are ready to take on the complexity of human interaction that is needed to perform business tasks across borders? Let us now look at a model of the components of CQ by David C. Thomas (Thomas & Inkson, 2009), which puts what we have just talked about regarding CQ into perspective. Thomas, an international management expert and scholar, suggests that intercultural competence can be nurtured by gaining the necessary knowledge for cultivating successful cross-cultural competencies. It is the concept of mindfulness: focused observation and critical reflection, that provides the vital link between one's knowledge and behavioral abilities when leading across cultures.

At the core of the components of cultural intelligence is the notion of mindfulness. Mindfulness is a metacognitive strategy that the culturally intelligent person must practice if they are to be successful in cross-cultural interactions. Mindfulness requires paying attention, in a reflective way, by observing the many cues in cross-cultural situations while at the same time being alert to and then monitoring personal feelings, thoughts, and actions. It means that a person is moving beyond a fixed or rigid mindset by trying to engage in cultural sense-making of situations, events, and actions that may logically fit within one's frame of reference. Cultural sense-making (which will be discussed later in this chapter) is a form of mindfulness and is a cognitive approach that helps us to organize and interpret information—a way that we can make sense of our perceived social reality (Bird & Osland, 2005).

Mindfulness originally stemmed from Eastern spiritual traditions of meditation, which prompt a person to consciously observe and change their mental habits. This form of mindfulness takes into account mental, emotional, and physical states, which help a person connect with their internal thoughts and feelings in relation to external conditions. The goal is to focus on the present moment and be aware of those mental habits (what you are thinking and how this is affecting emotional, attitudinal, or physical well-being). The outcome then is to change behavior. For example, if you are having negative thoughts and you want to rid yourself of the manifestations of those negative thoughts, you identify what might be causing the negativity and then focus on having positive thoughts. This enables you to become aware of this cycle of negativity in order to mindfully transform your thinking.

While the trend of mindfulness is not new, it is noteworthy. The construct of mindfulness has attracted significant attention in a variety of academic and professional fields. Mindfulness was introduced to the field of psychology by Judith Langer (1989) and then carried over to the field of interpersonal communication before it eventually found its way into the intercultural literature as well as the area of global leadership. In the field of education, the construct of mindfulness is often referred to as "reflective practice," and business education refers to "the reflective leader/manager" (Gosling & Mintzberg, 2003).

To this end, the opposite of being mindful is mindlessness, which is like being on autopilot. With mindlessness, there is no need to think about what you are doing because it comes naturally and is accepted and expected—you certainly do not need to question your assumptions, because you expect everything to happen the way it always has (Burgoon & Langer, 1995). This is ethnocentrism, which blinds us to the multiple reasons and possibilities behind any situation or interaction. Our goal is to strive toward a model of cultural sensitivity, which does not allow for judgment of culture, but rather a reflection of it. This reflection is essential to cultivating mechanisms to actively include diversity and intercultural relationships into our lives.

The Cultural Intelligence Model

The Cultural Intelligence Model as construed by Thomas demonstrates that having knowledge, mindfulness, and skills (also acknowledged as competencies), and using them in synergistic ways, leads to CQ. Culturally intelligent people are able to use their knowledge to understand multiple aspects of cross-cultural phenomena that come their way. They use mindful cognitive strategies that both observe and interpret any given situation and they develop a repertoire of skills which they can adapt and then demonstrate appropriate behaviors across a wide range of situations. This notion of CQ has been extended by many theorists in the field of intercultural communication (Ting-Toomey, 1999). Let us look at what this model includes (Figure 2.3).

Knowledge

Knowledge means recognizing some fundamental principles of behavior (customs, practices, rituals, greetings, language, etc.) and/or understanding something about a culture's history, politics, economy, or society. You might understand how a particular cultural group varies from your own, perhaps

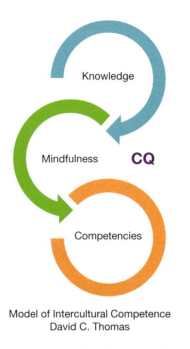

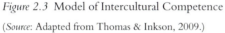

Model of Intercultural Competence
David C. Thomas

Figure 2.3 Model of Intercultural Competence

(*Source*: Adapted from Thomas & Inkson, 2009.)

regarding how people greet each other (kiss, bow, shake). You might understand that they have a different belief system than yours—perhaps they practice Shintoism or Sikhism. This is definitely favorable to lacking knowledge about a particular culture; however, simply knowing about the practices of people, society, or government is not enough. Human interaction is complex, and countless cultural intricacies and sensitivities abound, so simply having cultural knowledge—however notable this is—is not a predictor of competence. For example, even being fluent in another language is no replacement for being sensitive to people's beliefs and behaviors, although it is a step in the right direction. We have all heard of the statement—"linguistically competent, but culturally incompetent." Just because we are fluent in another language does not mean that we are adept at interacting thoughtfully and respectfully with people from another culture (Bennett, 2004).

Additionally, experiencing cultural contact—no matter the length of that contact—does not necessarily mean that a person will become culturally competent. A recent study analyzing the learning outcomes of students' academic pursuits abroad showed that it was not the amount of time spent in-country nor the act of being abroad that predicted change. Rather, it was the active and conscious effort of the students to reflect on what was happening—in real time—and then actively adjust their behaviors accordingly that made a difference. Students were able to develop this skill set through the intervention of educators who pushed them to think about what was happening and why it was happening (Vande Berg et al., 2009). This is what mindful learning about cultural differences is all about. It is about asking why and cultivating inner motivation.

Mindfulness

Mindfulness in this model indicates that what makes a difference in crossing cultures is actively paying attention to the subtle cues in cross-cultural circumstances and tuning into one's prior knowledge, thoughts, feelings, actions, and reactions to what is going on. The person practicing mindfulness is aware of their own assumptions and perceptions, and the emotions and attitudes attached to them. This person will also attempt to pay attention to the other person's actions, both tacit and explicit.

As discussed in Chapter 1, the theatrical metaphor of "front-stage/back-stage" culture is useful in thinking about mindfulness (Tuleja, 2014). Rather than having a spectator position where we take things at face value (watching what happens onstage), if we understand the working of the theater, we know what is going on simultaneously backstage. When we take things at face value, we do not get the full view. When we peek behind the curtain to see who is moving the props and signaling to actors when it is time to walk on stage, we go beyond *what* is happening to *why* it is happening.

For example, front-stage culture learning would be equivalent to talking about the importance of relationships within Chinese business by mentioning the concept of *guanxi*. *Guanxi* would simply be explained as "networking" and, in essence, the concept would be taken at surface value—its denotative meaning. However, if you wanted someone to truly understand what *guanxi* means, it would be necessary to include a discussion about *why* this is important and get into its deeper connotative meaning. How is *guanxi* experienced by the Chinese? What does it mean in terms of its web of obligation concerning its depth and duration and scope? Who starts it? How is it maintained? What are the historical underpinnings of why it is such a deep sociological factor within human relationships in China? Probing deeper into the rich traditions of the Chinese history, philosophy, and language would make the purpose of discussing *guanxi* much more meaningful.

Skills/Competence

Being skillful means that a person is able to choose appropriate behaviors (based upon developing knowledge and experience) that are suitable for a given intercultural situation. If one has developed knowledge about the culture and how it affects behaviors, then one should be able to reflect carefully on it in order to figure out its meaning. Then, the culturally competent person's aim is to figure out how to apply that knowledge by putting it into appropriate actions. Knowledge that is reflected upon deeply can result in effective behavior.

For example, the culturally intelligent person appreciates that it is not enough to simply know that formality is important in Japanese culture and that bowing is a key cultural practice. One must discern the different situations and degrees of bowing as well as aspects of the bow, such as its depth and length, the person's rank, and so forth. Also, should one bow to greet, to thank, to apologize, or even to congratulate someone? As a foreigner, you may not be expected to bow, but, if initiated, you need to understand the intricate nuances of this form of communication. It is symbolic; it is a ritual. Knowing who should bow first, how low and how long, and *why* this should be done this way in the first place involves having prior knowledge, assessing that knowledge through a cognitive process, behaving accordingly, and then reassessing what transpired based upon the nonverbal cues communicated by the other parties. Did you do it correctly? Was there subtle body language that might have signaled dissatisfaction? Could positive body language—for example, facial expressions such as a smile—mean success or could this possibly mask disapproval? Skillfulness requires constant attention and redressing the "what" and "why" of every situation.

The reason why this model of CQ is so important is that its theorist posits that the concept of *mindfulness* is the critical link between one's knowledge and one's behavioral abilities (skills, competence) when leading across cultures (Thomas et al., 2008). One must build upon one's knowledge and go beyond merely learning facts, to include analyzing one's behavior, and reflecting on it in order to build that repertoire of skillful behavior. Without this mindful, reflective practice, knowledge is empty and it will be more difficult to develop the competencies needed for intercultural interactions.

Example of the Model of Cultural Intelligence

In order to visualize what happens during this process, let us look at an example. Nancy Adler, professor of cross-cultural management at McGill University in Montreal and an expert in global leadership, tells a puzzling story in her textbook *International dimensions of organizational behavior* (Adler, 2008).

As a business person you may have strong negotiation skills back in your home country. Let us assume you operate from a Western perspective; however, the rules of the game switch when dealing with the norms of a different culture. Imagine that you are ready to close a deal with a counterpart from Qatar. You have agreed to enter into a partnership concerning a new business venture. You suggest that you meet again the following day with your lawyers so that you may finalize the details; however, your counterpart never shows up. What went wrong? Did your counterpart forget? Was he expecting a counter offer? Were you too early or was he late? The culturally intelligent person would be able to acknowledge that something was amiss and then reflect on why things had gone wrong by trying to come up with a hypothesis to test that notion. In addition, the culturally intelligent person would suspend judgment and not react negatively (see Figure 2.4).

Figure 2.4 International Men at Work

(*Source*: Fotolia 41774508, © Jasmin Merdan.)

After contemplation, you would not just focus on *what* happened, but try to determine *why* things had transpired the way they did. You might come to the realization that each of you attached different significance to the meaning of introducing lawyers at this point in the relationship. You might consider that from your Western perspective, you use lawyers to finalize agreements and the presence of your attorney signals the successful completion of the negotiation. But, you would also reason that, from a non-Western perspective, your colleague from the Arab state of Qatar on the Persian Gulf might depend on the personal relationship with you as the cementing factor and could view your suggestion of involving lawyers as a mistrust of your verbal agreement.

The culturally intelligent person revises their strategy based upon experience—it is a process of trial and error while seeking to understand the perspective of someone from a different culture. While in theory this may seem easy, perhaps by applying a formula for communication, in reality we know that it is difficult to do in practice. Let us examine this critical incident in light of the model of CQ: knowledge, mindfulness, and competence.

> *Knowledge.* If you are the person from the United States, it would work to your advantage to have some general knowledge about cultural traditions from Arab cultures. It would be even better to know something specific about the particular region in which you are interacting. Before, during, and afterwards, you would think about what you know about the situation. You would read, talk to colleagues who have done business in the area before, and ask questions. During this process you would discover that relationships are extremely important and, without investing the time to develop them, you would know that you will not be successful. You have made the time to get to know your colleagues and things are friendly and relaxed as the deal progresses, so why all of a sudden have things gone sour, when your colleague does not show up the next day?

Mindfulness. You immediately begin to reflect on what happened and why it might have happened. It is not enough to just identify what is going wrong, but careful reflection (being open to new possibilities and solutions that you have not yet thought of—all the while resisting the temptation to label and judge) may lead you to determine that you have done something wrong and perhaps offended your potential business partner. You once again think through all possible scenarios, find someone who might be able to give you insider advice, and develop a plan.

Competence. You change course and determine a way that you could re-open the conversation without insulting or alarming your potential business partner. Based upon your interactions with all involved, you proceed carefully, all the while checking and rechecking your assumptions, thoughts, biases, and actions.

This is the essence of what it means to be culturally intelligent and this is the way that we want when encountering differences in their cross-cultural immersion experiences. We want to go beyond the surface level and make deep connections to what is happening and why it might be happening. To be culturally intelligent is a continuous work in progress. It is a process that is dynamic across space and time; professionals well versed in the concept will also understand that it takes these three aspects (knowledge, mindfulness, competence) working together to yield to a successful intercultural interaction.

We have talked about what it means to be culturally intelligent and that it is truly an ongoing challenge to develop competencies. While it may indeed be a challenge, it *is* possible to achieve, and the rewards of mutual agreement and personal satisfaction are endless. Let us dig further into the finer details of these intercultural models we have considered.

Ethnocentrism and Enculturation

Social Psychology Foundation

It is human nature to think that all people are just like us. Social psychologists tell us that this is a natural part of the socialization process—there are in-groups and out-groups, and we are influenced by all sorts of people in those groups (Tajfel, 1982). Socialization is a process whereby we learn the rules and patterns of behavior (e.g., from parents, grandparents, extended families, friends, the workplace, religious places of worship, schooling, etc.). By the time we are adults, we do not even notice the cultural lenses in which we view the world. This is called ethnocentrism.

And so, we see the world through our own lenses—what we think, believe, and do seems most appropriate to us. We therefore tend to evaluate other groups according to the values and standards of our own group and inherently believe our ways of doing things are superior. Because we are self-focused and

Figure 2.5 Ethnocentric Tug of War
(*Source*: Fotolia 39829948, © Leo Blanchette.)

think *our* way of life is better than other people's ways of life, we make assumptions about others. An assumption is any belief, idea, hunch, or thought you have about a subject, idea, person, or problem. As is the often the case, our assumptions are inaccurate, which we will discuss in the next section on cultural sense-making. Ethnocentrism is a form of superiority in which you believe your way of doing things is the right and preferable way. It is a way of negatively evaluating other cultures based on your particular cultural standards. With this line of thinking we are in a perpetual tug of war (Figure 2.5).

The "I, We, They" of Ethnocentrism

Figuratively, It's Like a Tug of War

> "Others" are the ones who have culture. Not me!

> When we travel: "The 'locals' are so nice and interesting!"

> Others are the ones who pose barriers to communication. Why can't *they* understand *me*?

While it may be human nature to engage in ethnocentric thinking and behavior, becoming an effective intercultural communicator requires that we have a holistic understanding of people. Professor Hofstede says we may have "different minds" but we have "common problems" (Hofstede, 1997), and each of us faces such problems based upon our world view and life experiences. It is when we project our superiority onto others and judge their "different minds" as inferior that we block the process of understanding intercultural differences. Let us examine one way of looking at ethnocentrism.

Cross-cultural problems arise from differences in behavior, thinking, assumptions, and values between U.S. people and those from other countries and cultures with whom they associate. These cultural differences often produce misunderstandings and lead to ineffectiveness in face-to-face

> **Box 2.2**
>
> Human beings draw close to one another by their common nature, but habits and customs keep them apart.
>
> Source: Confucius

communication. A deeper understanding of the nature of cultural differences would increase the effectiveness of people in cross-cultural situations. But to reach this goal, people must first become more conscious and knowledgeable about how their own culture has conditioned their ways of thinking and planted within them the values and assumptions that govern their behavior. To be an effective intercultural communicator, it is important that we strive for *enculturation*, or the ability to look at things through other lenses. Enculturation is a social process whereby we learn the ways and manners of our culture and the "other" culture, and learn to think more broadly. When we strive for enculturation, we learn how to act and interpret other people's behavior. This helps us to become flexible and less judgmental. Interculturalist Milton Bennett invites us to think about both the visible and invisible markers of culture as we begin to understand differences (Stewart & Bennett, 1991) (Box 2.2).

Developmental Model of Intercultural Sensitivity

Bennett's framework can help us to become more conscious and knowledgeable about our ways of thinking interculturally. His developmental model walks us through five stages of the process, each representing one aspect of experiencing cultural differences (see Figure 2.6). This model is set on a continuum in which moving from left to right through the five stages of *denial, defense, minimization, acceptance, and adaptation* will bring us to a more interculturally sensitive position (Hammer, 2011; 2012). Milton Bennett has said:

> people tend to impose their own perspectives in an effort to dispel the ambiguity created by the unusual behavior of host country nationals. They are unlikely to suspend judgment about differences in behavior because they assume unconsciously that their own ways are normal, natural, and right. Those of the other culture, therefore, must be abnormal, unnatural, and wrong. This presumption of superiority of one's own culture is . . . characteristic of most peoples of the world.
> (Stewart & Bennett, 1991, p. 3)

This model is bent toward linear thinking, since Bennett stresses that, in order to achieve the ultimate goal of "integration," we must move through each

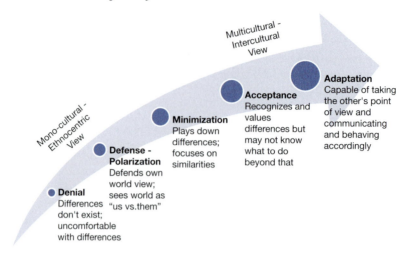

Figure 2.6 Developmental Model of IC Sensitivity

(*Source*: Hammer, 2012, p. 119.)

stage, one at a time. While a rigid model such as this has its limitations, it is nevertheless helpful to expand on the discussion of ethnocentric thinking. Therefore, while these models are not perfect, they do provide the ideal starting point when looking at the significance of CQ.

The phases are based on theoretical ideas taken from Bennett's years of teaching in intercultural training programs and are meant simply as a reference to help us analyze ethnocentricity. By identifying particular areas for self-centered thinking as related to cultural perspectives (hence, ethnocentricity), we can examine each of these stages to see where we may be affected. Bennett emphasizes action preceded by self-awareness to correct ethnocentric views and move us toward communication competence.

Stages of Intercultural Sensitivity

Phases in the Model

The first stage is *denial*. Denial means that we see no difference at all, viewing all things from our own world view or experience. It is easy, for example, to lump people into a single category, such as Asians or Americans. The former means that *all* Asians, whether Chinese, Japanese, Vietnamese, or Korean belong to the same culture. The latter usually means citizens of the United States and neglects the fact that Canadians and Mexicans are, in fact, Americans, as well.

The second stage is *defense/polarization*. This stage is characterized by excessive hostility against another culture or excessive pride in one's own. This is a stage in which we realize that there are differences but feel threatened by them, so we may insult, antagonize, or diminish others.

The third stage moves to *minimization*. This acknowledges the existence of cultural differences but claims such differences are superficial at best. While we acknowledge differences, we experience a need to maintain our feelings of cultural superiority, so we look for similarities to assuage our fears of difference. For example, if our culture celebrates birthdays in a particular way, we look for similarities in how people from another culture celebrate birthdays. It is clearly superficial, but it makes us feel better.

Moving from the third stage of minimization to the fourth, *acceptance* is the beginning of intercultural understanding. Acceptance recognizes and explores cultural differences by identifying them both by behavior, such as language, styles of verbal communication, and nonverbal communication, and by the tacit values of a given culture. These include cultural norms of interdependence and collective work products versus independent and individualistic achievement.

According to Bennett, once we move toward the acceptance stage, we can begin to adapt, which is the fifth stage of the model. *Adaptation* is the point at which we see and begin to embrace a different frame of reference (we will talk about this more in Chapter 5). Empathy is a big part of adaptation. We move from simply recognizing and respecting that others are different to empathizing with them. We try to walk in their shoes and experience (limited as this may be) things from their perspective (Bennett, 1986).

Awareness is Key

Awareness is the beginning of understanding. The more we understand, through exposure and experience, the more we will be able to develop competence, hopefully—to become more ethnorelative as the DMIS demonstrates. Ultimately, the goal is to move from a self-centered cultural orientation (monocultural) to another-centered orientation (multicultural). This model of moving from denial to adaptation is described as progressively flowing along a continuum from one spot to the next. It is important to understand that there are experiences and situations that aid and hinder this process, and these are called "trailing orientations," which pull us back into our more monocultural mindset. For more information on the DMIS and how it has been adapted into a scientific assessment tool (Intercultural Development Inventory), you can visit the Intercultural Development Inventory site at https://idiinventory.com/.

Adapting your own circumstances is essential to making the model work for you. You can even combine this model with the knowledge–mindfulness–competency model so that there is a link between the stages of cultural integration and the specific tools needed to arrive there. In the following section we will look at another model that helps us to identify our assumptions and create positive momentum toward ethnorelative thinking and behaving (Figure 2.7).

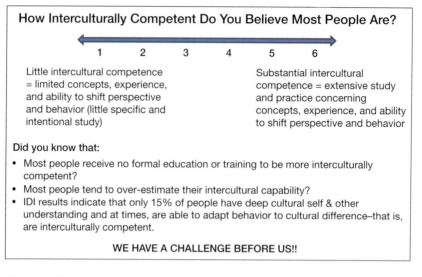

Figure 2.7 How Interculturally Competent Do You Think You Are?

(*Source*: Adapted from Hammer, 2012.)

Unconscious Bias

Think of it this way. We all have unconscious bias—we can be blinded from seeing reality as it really is. One scientific theory, the Dunning-Kruger effect, demonstrates that people have a false sense of ability and think that they are more skilled at something than they really are. Back in 1999, these two Cornell psychologists demonstrated that people did not assess their level of incompetence adequately; rather people tend to think of themselves as much more competent than others. Such lack of awareness contributes to the inability to critically analyze one's performance accurately; hence people tend to overestimate their abilities (Kruger & Dunning, 1999).

Professor Stella Ting-Toomey, best known for her work regarding identity negotiation, conceptualizes this phenomenon along four stages: unconscious incompetence; conscious incompetence; unconscious competence; conscious competence (Ting-Toomey, 1999) (Figure 2.8).

In sum, we all believe we are better at things than we really are—yet if we are willing to heighten our awareness, develop knowledge, and then reflect on our interactions with difference, then we can move away from unconscious inability to interact across cultures and move toward CQ.

Cultural Sense-Making

Mindfulness could be described in terms of another helpful model—the Cultural Sense-Making Model—which suggests another way to envision how

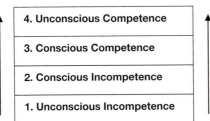

4. Unconscious Competence

3. Conscious Competence

2. Conscious Incompetence

1. Unconscious Incompetence

1. **Unawareness of our intercultural communication blunders.**
2. **Awareness of lack of intercultural competence but does nothing to change behavior.**
3. **Awareness of need to develop intercultural competence and pursues commitment to integrate.**
4. **Ability to respond naturally and appropriately based upon intercultural competence.**

Figure 2.8 Unconscious Incompetence Model

(*Source*: Adapted from Ting-Toomey, 1999, p. 52.)

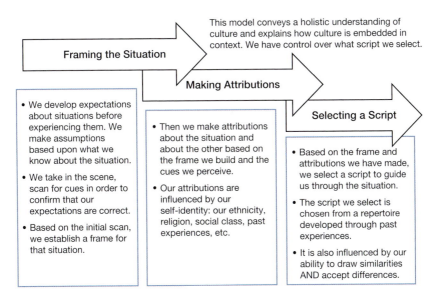

Framing the Situation

This model conveys a holistic understanding of culture and explains how culture is embedded in context. We have control over what script we select.

Making Attributions

Selecting a Script

- We develop expectations about situations before experiencing them. We make assumptions based upon what we know about the situation.
- We take in the scene, scan for cues in order to confirm that our expectations are correct.
- Based on the initial scan, we establish a frame for that situation.

- Then we make attributions about the situation and about the other based on the frame we build and the cues we perceive.
- Our attributions are influenced by our self-identity: our ethnicity, religion, social class, past experiences, etc.

- Based on the frame and attributions we have made, we select a script to guide us through the situation.
- The script we select is chosen from a repertoire developed through past experiences.
- It is also influenced by our ability to draw similarities AND accept differences.

Figure 2.9 Cultural Sense-Making Model

(*Source*: Osland & Bird, 2000, pp. 70–2.)

the culturally intelligent person can move beyond assumptions and stereotypes by actively seeking enculturation, which moves us away from ethnocentrism (Osland & Bird, 2000) (Figure 2.9).

Cultural sense-making involves reframing and changing one's script rather than restricting oneself to rigid, standard scripts. It is about changing perspective and opening up to new opportunities and ways of looking at the world. There are three steps to this process: framing, making attributions, and selecting a script.

Framing

The first step, *framing*, involves the expectations we have about a situation. Before, during, or after a situation, we think about what we know—we observe and scan for cues that might confirm our hunches. Based upon that, we create a frame for the situation.

Making Attributions

In the second step, *making attributions*, we analyze those cues and try to match them to schemas, or mental patterns that we create. These schemas are cognitive frameworks that help us to interpret unfamiliar information and experiences—and cognitive psychologists, such as Jean Piaget, have assured us that it is a natural way of learning about the world (Piaget, 2001). Making attributions is affected by our background and experiences, our beliefs, and our attitudes.

Selecting a Script

The third step is *selecting a script*, which we do based upon the frame we create and the mental patterns (schemas) that we have created, becomes our road map to navigate the unfamiliar situation. Our script is often influenced by our previous experiences and we then draw similarities or differences between what we know and what we do not know.

Example

For example, let us say you are going to a Chinese banquet where you know that there are certain foods you do not care to eat. In *framing* the situation, you set the stage, so you might think about how you have handled situations like this before. You do not want to insult your host, but you also do not want to eat something that is distasteful to you. You imagine the scene in your mind—your host offers you a delicious morsel, you refuse; the host offers it again, you refuse.

When you *make attributions* you analyze the cues of your host—he will probably smile and continue to offer you the food—at the same time, you will be trying to maintain a pleasant look on your face as well as tone while you continue to decline the food. You know that this particular culinary delight does not sit well with you, so you naturally think about how it has affected you in the past. But you also know how important formality and graciousness is within the Chinese culture—you certainly do not want to offend your host.

Finally, you will *select a script*, which might be a strategy of saying how delicious such a delicacy is and how you are honored by your host's selection of such a treat; but you also politely state that you are watching your cholesterol, so for health reasons you must unfortunately decline. This is the process of cultural sense-making. Sense-making is a way of "enculturating" a situation—where you are mindful of the situation, the ramifications if you misstep, and how you take other people's feelings into consideration. (Enculturation refers to the way a person is socialized into a certain social context.) You plan ahead to frame the situation by setting up your expectations, you then analyze the situation based upon any previous experiences or hunches regarding what you should do, and then you create a script for how you want to proceed—you script it out in your mind. This leads us to the final portion of the components of CQ, skills and competency, which are demonstrated through behavior.

Critical Incidents

Cross-cultural psychologist, Richard Brislin developed the culture general simulator model, based upon critical incidents where the observer looks at incidents for both similarities and differences among cultures (Brislin, 1986; Brislin et al., 1986). We all have anxiety, expectations, perceptions, and hidden bias when interacting with difference; cultural simulators of this sort can help us tease out what makes us uncomfortable—and even what is not accurate—thus enabling us to have a more successful interaction. We could also call them "dilemmas" as explained by cross-cultural organization experts Fons Trompenaars and Richard Hampden-Turner (Trompenaars & Hampden-Turner, 2011). They explain cultural differences in terms of dilemmas that can be reconciled by examining the cultural values and contexts of each opposing side of an issue.

Using critical incidents can be useful to tease out what actually happened in a situation and what you think happened. Critical incidents are based upon real-life scenarios and place plausible characters in an ambiguous situation where they need to identify central issues to the problem and figure out how to adjust. Readers are encouraged to put themselves in the place of the character and ask, "What happened?" and "Why?" (Brislin, et al., 1986, p. 18). Such critical incidents encourage us to practice mindful thinking in order to try to frame events from a different perspective, and most importantly, without judgment (holding back the temptation to place our own values, beliefs, and attitudes on the characters and situations). By searching for multiple meanings we can seek confirmation when possible. This is best done in pairs or small groups so that everyone can monitor each other's responses.

- After reading the critical incident, questions to ask would be: (1) What happened? Why?
- Each group member recounts what the characters said or did, focusing on the exact words and behaviors exhibited. The goal is to avoid inserting opinions and perceptions–it's hard to just state the facts!

- Other group members listen but interject when a value judgment is made.
- When value judgments or personal opinions are made (rather than simply stating the observable words or behaviors) then other questions to ask might be: What values and beliefs could have motivated the behavior? What were some of the cultural cues I might have missed or misinterpreted? How are my own values, beliefs, and attitudes affecting my perception?

See Box 2.3 for an example of a critical incident. Watch the news coverage of the famous "Korean Air Nut Rage" in the link provided. Use this critical incident to note only observable actions. What might be some alternative reasons for these actions? As a bit of background information: in 2015 the daughter of the Chairman for Korean Air became disruptive with a flight attendant when she was not served nuts in an "appropriate" manner, causing the plane to return to its gate and the defendant, Ms Cho Hyun-ah (an

---

Box 2.3 Korean Air Nut Rage

In a fit of "nut rage," Vice President of Korean Air, Cho Hyun-ah, demanded that the plane turn back to the gate because she was served nuts in the wrong way. This New York to Seoul flight should have provided her with first-class service; however, she was served nuts in a bag versus on a plate.

International media coverage shared its outrage over the nut rage, claiming, "entitlement," "emperor's daughter," and an "international disgrace" despite the fact that 40-year-old Cho Hyun-ah, an executive with the company and daughter of the company's Chairman and CEO, resigned all management posts. Her father, Cho Yang-ho, said "It's my fault; I didn't raise her right."

Amid the fervent and incessant clicking of cameras, her father, Chairman of Korean Air, gave a press conference where he bowed deeply and with eyes lowered, said, "I am truly sorry for my foolish daughter's actions that have stirred up big troubles . . . as the Chairman of Korean Air and her father, I hope for the Korean people's generous forgiveness. Please scold me. It is my fault."

The press talked about this in terms of the Korean phenomenon called "*chaebol*," which is a large conglomerate held by a family that benefits from its economic and social privileges that come from its absolute control.

Sources: www.nytimes.com/2014/12/10/world/asia/korean-air-executive-resigns-post-after-halting-flight-over-snack-service.html?_r=1; www.youtube.com/watch?v=nfzfU4tY4tc; www.youtube.com/watch?v=Y_OwkISuPNk.

executive with Korean Air), to be removed. Take note of Ms Cho's behavior as well as her father handled their apologies.

Summary

This chapter explores CQ as a core component of intercultural communication. As an extension of the idea of EQ, CQ encompasses not just an understanding of other cultures and intercultural relationships, but more importantly it advocates a grounding in mindfulness and motivating a skill set designed to respond to today's diverse cultural needs. With the aim of becoming culturally sensitive, this level of cultural competence is a gradual evolution of developing skills.

By progressing through the developmental stages of denial, defense, minimization, acceptance, and adaptation, these stages emphasize a full engagement with cultural awareness, mindfulness, and behavior. At every step of the journey, it is important to gain a wider understanding of the cultural nuances, reflect on the implications of these subtleties, and then develop the ability to respond perceptively to every situation. It is about changing perspectives, and there are a myriad ways to do so. We have discussed several helpful models in this chapter. Every model or framework has strengths and weaknesses, and can each be adapted to suit a particular context. They all, however, share in common the goals of becoming more culturally aware, mindful, and competent.

References

Adler, N. (2008). *International dimensions of organizational behavior* (5th edn.). Mason, OH: Thomson Higher Education.

AMA Enterprise. (2012). Developing successful global leaders. Retrieved from www.amanet.org/pdf/developing-successful-global-leaders.pdf (accessed on August 1, 2016).

Bennett, M. J. (1986). A developmental approach to training for intercultural sensitivity. *International Journal of Intercultural Relations*, *10*(2), 179–96.

Bennett, M. J. (2004). Becoming interculturally competent. In J. Wurzel (Ed.), *Toward multiculturalism: A reader in multicultural education* (2nd edn., pp. 62–77). Newton, MA: Intercultural Resource Corporation.

Bird, A., & Osland, J. S. (2005). Making sense of intercultural collaboration. *International Studies of Management and Organization*, *35*(4), 115–32.

Brislin, R. W. (1986). A culture general assimilator: Preparation for various types of sojourns. *International Journal of Intercultural Relations*, *10*(2), 215–34.

Brislin, R. W., Cushner, K., Cherrie, C., & Yong, M. (1986). *Intercultural interactions: A practical guide*. Volume 9. Thousand Oaks, CA: SAGE.

Burgoon, J. K., & Langer, E. J. (1995). Language, fallacies, and mindlessness–mindfulness. *Communication Yearbook*, *18*, 105–32.

Dyne, Linn Van. (2012). The four factors affecting cultural intelligence (CQ). Retrieved from www.linnvandyne.com/fourfac.html (accessed August 1, 2016).

Earley, C. P., & Ang, S. (2003). *Cultural intelligence: Individual interactions across cultures*. Stanford, CA: Stanford University Press.

Earley, C. P., & Mosakowski, E. (2004). Cultural intelligence. *Harvard Business Review*, *82*(10), 139–46.

Ehrbar, L. (2013). Pe'a tatau. www.nikeblog.com/2013/07/30/nike-pro-tattoo-tech-tights-inspired-by-fiji-samoa-new-zealand/ (accessed on August 1, 2016).

Gardner, H. (1983). *Frames of mind: The theory of multiple intelligences*. New York, NY: Basic Books.

Goleman, D. (1995). *Emotional intelligence*. New York, NY: Bantam Books.

Goleman, D. (1998). *Working with emotional intelligence*. New York, NY: Bantam Books.

Gosling, J., & Mintzberg, H. (2003). The five minds of a manager. *Harvard Business Review*, *81*(11), 1–10.

Hammer, M. R. (2011). Additional cross-cultural validity testing of the Intercultural Development Inventory. *International Journal of Intercultural Relations*, *35*(4), 474–87.

Hammer, M. (2012). The Intercultural Development Inventory: A new frontier in assessment and development of intercultural competence. In M. Vande Berg, R. M. Paige, & K. H. Lou (Eds.), *Student learning abroad* (Ch. 5, pp. 115–36). Sterling, VA: Stylus Publishing.

Hofstede, G. (1984). Cultural dimensions in management and planning. *Asia Pacific Journal of Management*, *1*(2), 81–99.

Hofstede, G. (1997). *Cultures and organizations: Software of the mind*. New York, NY: McGraw-Hill.

Kruger, J., & Dunning, D. (1999). Unskilled and unaware of it: How difficulties in recognizing one's own incompetence lead to inflated self-assessments. *Journal of Personality and Social Psychology*, *77*(6), 1121.

Langer, E. (1989). *Mindfulness*. Reading, MA: Addison Wesley.

Osland, J. S., & Bird, A. (2000). Beyond sophisticated stereotyping: Cultural sense-making in context. *The Academy of Management Executive*, *14*(1), 65–77.

Piaget, J. (2001). *Studies in reflection abstraction*. (R. L. Campbell, Trans.). East Sussex, UK: Psychology Press (original work published 1977).

Stewart, E. C., & Bennett, M. J. (1991). *American cultural patterns*. Yarmouth, ME: Intercultural Press.

Tajfel, H. (1982). The social psychology of intergroup relations. *Annual Review of Psychology*, *33*, 1–39.

Thomas, David C., & Inkson, Ker. (2009). *Cultural intelligence: Living and working globally*. San Francisco: Barrett-Koehler Publishers.

Thomas, D. C., Elron, E., Stahl, G., Ekelund, B. Z., Ravlin, E. C., Cerdin, J. L., Poelmans, S., Brislin, R., Pekerti, A., Aycan, Z., & Maznevski, M. (2008). Cultural intelligence: Domain and assessment. *International Journal of Cross Cultural Management*, *8*(2), 123–43.

Ting-Toomey, S. (1999). *Communicating across culture*. New York, NY: Guilford.

Trompenaars, F., & Hampden-Turner, C. (2011). *Riding the waves of culture: Understanding diversity in global business*. London: Nicholas Brealey Publishing.

Tuleja, E. A. (2014, May 5). The 'why' behind the 'what'—Active participants versus passive spectators in culture learning. Retrieved from http://globalbizleader.com/2014/05/ May 2014 (accessed on August 1, 2016).

Vande Berg, M., Conor-Linton, J., & Paige, M. R. (2009). The Georgetown consortium project: Interventions for student learning abroad. *Frontiers: The Interdisciplinary Journal of Study Abroad*, *18*, 1–75.

Case 2

Appropriating the Samoan Culture

Another Nike Cultural Faux Pas[1]

Abstract

In late July of 2013, Nike released a new line of tattoo-like leg tights for women, not realizing the disastrous effect it would have on the culture of Fijian, Samoan, and New Zealand people who view it as a males-only sacred rite of passage. This cultural mistake is not the first for the world's top athletic apparel and footwear company. Nike apologized and recalled all unsold tights, but how can the company make sure it does not co-opt any more cultural traditions?

Introduction

The steel elevator doors closed tightly in front of Laurissa Wilson, Chief Marketing Officer at Nike, the world's most well-known and successful sporting apparel company. Laurissa had visited the top floor before—but not on the terms she knew she would be facing today.

While driving to work earlier that morning, she received a phone call from her assistant and was quickly briefed that the Pro Tattoo Tech Tights product, launched last week, had just become an international nightmare for the company. Laurissa listened, acting as though she was shocked, but she had already anticipated the possibility of having brought to market a controversial product.

The elevator was packed and she knew she would have only a moment to reflect on what had led to this crisis. Soon, she would be on the top floor, having to justify her actions with Nike CEO, Harrison Smith.

Nike's History

Nike, Inc. is currently the number one athletic apparel and footwear company in the world. Headquartered in Portland, Oregon, it began as a small start-up run by two men in the 1960s.

Bill Bowerman, a respected track and field coach at the University of Oregon, partnered with a track star on his team, Phil Knight, to build and sell a better running shoe. Together they formed Blue Ribbon Sports in 1964. Between Bowerman testing his prototype shoes with his track team and Knight selling shoes out of his car, Nike was established.

A few years later, one of Knight's fellow Stanford graduates, Jeff Johnson, joined the pair to expedite the start-up. He developed the "swoosh" logo and marketing campaigns, thus establishing the brand of Nike that we know today. Nike revolutionized the athletic industry in the 1970s with its products. The team of three decided that they needed a brand endorser. Who better than Steve Prefontaine? (Prefontaine was a long-distance runner from the University of Oregon who competed in the 1972 Olympics.) His "fiery spirit" and remarkable career made Nike popular, taking it to a new level of growth (Nike, Inc., 2013).

That growth would continue throughout the decades. They were able to experience this resounding success through implementing successful marketing campaigns, adopting the tagline, "Just Do It," and endorsing incredible athletes such as Bo Jackson and later on Eldrick "Tiger" Woods.

In 2002, Nike took a chance at the "Secret Tournament" campaign. It was Nike's first integrated global marketing effort. It was different then their usual "big athlete, big ad, big product" campaigns, in that Nike set out to generate an experience for its consumers for the World Cup.

The use of many different advertisement channels had explosive results. Nike ads flooded all aspects of advertising: the Internet, public relations, and consumer events. In the end, it created excitement for Nike products. This marketing plan was pivotal in how Nike chose to go to market after the success of the "Secret Tournament" campaign, and contributed to the company's status as a marketing genius (Nike, Inc., 2013).

Nike continues to grow as it keeps its focus on creative marketing campaigns, international growth, and performance-enhancing innovation for athletes. Nike was also named the official sponsor of the National Football League (NFL) in early 2012.

Nike's Past Issues

Nike is not new to this type of scandal. In the last couple of years, Nike has committed numerous cultural gaffes, offending various segments of the global population. These incidents have created significant negative publicity and caused harm to Nike's reputation, since apologies become weaker the more frequently they are given.

In June of 2011, Nike released a T-shirt line with phrases such as "Dope," "Get High," and "Ride Pipe" written across the front (see Appendix 1). These expressions are traditionally associated with drug use or the act of sex. One T-shirt displayed a medicine bottle with the word "DOPE" with skateboards and snowboards spilling out of the bottle instead of drugs. The issue in this case, according to then-Boston Mayor Thomas Menino, was the promotion of drug use by a major corporation whose main target market is the younger generation (Brettman, 2011). Despite the backlash, the shirts were not pulled and Nike continued to sell them through the entirety of the campaign.

In March of 2012, Nike launched the SB Dunk Low Black and Tan sneakers. Many people are familiar with the alcoholic beverage of the same name. Traditionally, a darker beer, usually Guinness, is mixed with a lighter beer.

However, the name Black and Tan also refers to a darker period of history for the people of Ireland. Black and Tan was also the name given to a British military group that was sent to Ireland to quell the Irish rebellion against the British in the 1920s. The Black and Tan regiment was the cause of many civilian deaths. Black and Tan, or Tan, is still used in Ireland as a derogatory term for the British. It has been said that the use of Black and Tan for the sneakers is equivalent to naming them "Taliban" or "Nazi." Nike was slow to respond to criticism, but eventually a representative for Nike apologized, stating that the company meant no offense. However, the name remained and the shoe was not pulled from stock (Misener, 2012).

After the London Summer Olympics in the summer of 2012, Nike released a shirt with the words "Gold Digging" and the signature Nike check mark (see Appendix 2) to honor the 46 gold medals won by the U.S. women. In recent years, gold digging has come to refer to women who date wealthy men only for their money. The T-shirt caused additional tension because it was only available in women's sizes. While Nike never apologized, it did issue the following statement:

> Nike has consistently supported female athletes and the position they enjoy as positive role models. The T-shirt uses a phrase in an ironic way that is relevant given it was released just as the world focused on the success of female athletes.
>
> (Nazworth, 2012)

In contrast, Nike was quick to act in April 2013. Following the tragic attacks at the Boston Marathon, Nike immediately pulled its Boston Massacre T-shirt from the shelves. The design on the T-shirt referred to a four-game sweep of the Red Sox by the Yankees in 1978. The shirt is blue and white, Yankee colors, and has the words "Boston Massacre" with bloodstains on the letters (CNN Wires Staff, 2013).

The Source of the Problem

On July 30, 2013, Nike Tight of the Moment announced the release of its new Pro Tattoo Tech Tights on its blog. The company posted that the new tights were inspired by the tattoos of the Fijian, Samoan, and New Zealand people. The tights were black with white lines that created the image of tattoos, resembling the tattoos of the indigenous people of Fiji, Samoa, and New Zealand (Ehrbar, 2013).

Immediately, the public responded. Comments posted just hours after the announcement of the new tight design lamented Nike's cultural faux pas in its choice to use the tattoos of Fijian, Samoan, and New Zealand people on its apparel. On August 2, John Masina initiated a petition on Change.org asking Nike to cease production of its Pro Tattoo Tech Tights. Change.org is a petition platform providing a vehicle through which individuals can come together and campaign for change. Mr. Masina referenced the United Nations Declaration on the Rights of Indigenous Peoples in support of his claim (Masina, 2013).

What is the *Pe'a*?

The *pe'a* is a traditional tattoo that covers the body from the waist to the knees. The *tatau* process for the *pe'a* is extremely painful and is done using handmade instruments that are made of bone and wood and other natural materials. In Samoan custom, a *pe'a* is only done in the traditional way. They do not use any Western utensils or practices. The family members of the person getting the tattoo attend the ceremony to provide support during the painful process, but stand at a distance from the ceremony (Pacific Islanders in Communications, n.d.).

The *pe'a* is for males only. It is a rite of passage and a symbol of courage. It is also seen as a commitment to culture and traditions. In Polynesia, the origins of the tattoo are varied. Samoans believe that the Fijians are the originators of the *tatau*, the Fijians credit the Samoans, and the Māori of New Zealand think it comes from the underworld (DeMello, 2007).

The *pe'a* designs are done in black ink. The tattoo starts on the back and finishes on the belly button. Overall, the design is symmetrical, comprised primarily of straight lines and larger blocks. The larger blocks are traditionally found on the legs. This traditional tattoo is not something entered into lightly. It is a long, painful process. It can take several weeks to complete the *pe'a*, and the skin could take up to a year to completely heal (see Appendix 3).

In addition to abusing the symbolism behind the *pe'a*, Nike's use of the *pe'a* design on the clothing line also blatantly affronted gender norms within the Samoan culture. As previously mentioned, the *pe'a* was only given to men. Women have their own version, which is called the *malu*, and consists of a much simpler design. By using the *pe'a* on women's sheer leggings and giving the impression that a woman is wearing the *pe'a* tattoo on her body, Nike co-opted the rite of passage and commitment to cultural tradition symbolized by the practice of receiving the *pe'a*. New Zealand Parliament member Su'a William Sio, who received his *pe'a* in 1988 stated, "It's disturbing. This treasure is held dear to the Samoan community. The patterns have a spiritual meaning that come from one's family and ancestors. This just cheapens and belittles all of that. It's a total disregard of cultural protocol." (The Curatorial, 2013).

The Public's Response to Nike's Mistake

As a result of Nike using traditional, indigenous *pe'a* patterns that symbolize the commitment to the cultural tradition and values, several groups vocalized their disapproval of the clothing line and Nike's cultural insensitivity. The clothing line was offensive due to its use of indigenous cultural values and gender norms as fashion statements.

A flurry of articles and editorials emerged in countries with large Samoan populations. "To the outside world it's just a design. But to my Polynesian people, it's sacred," one individual wrote in the *Otago Daily Times* (Radford, 2013). Another commented on the Nike blog, "Every one of those curves, lines, and details has meaning. They signify our beliefs, our ancestry, our history. It is sad to have these things exploited and diluted" (Ehrbar, 2013). On Facebook and Twitter, the public demanded that Nike recall the product and pull all stock.

Only three days after the soft launch of the leggings, the petition to have the designs removed from the product line was authored on Change.org. Within four weeks of the announcement of the clothing line, roughly 1,000 individuals had supported the movement.

As stated by the Change.org petition, Nike's actions violate Article 31 of the United Nations Declaration on the Rights of Indigenous Peoples (UNDRIP), which states:

1   Indigenous peoples have the right to maintain, control, protect and develop their cultural heritage, traditional knowledge and traditional cultural expressions, as well as the manifestations of their sciences, technologies and cultures, including human and genetic resources, seeds, medicines, knowledge of the properties of fauna and flora, oral traditions, literatures, designs, sports and traditional games and visual and performing arts. They also have the right to maintain, control, protect and develop their intellectual property over such cultural heritage, traditional knowledge, and traditional cultural expressions.
2   In conjunction with indigenous peoples, States shall take effective measures to recognize and protect the exercise of these rights.

(Wiessner, 2013)

According to the UNDRIP, subtle but sustained political and societal actions have "pushed indigenous peoples and their cultures to the brink of extinction." Indigenous people have reclaimed their rights and identities as contributors to the cultural diversity on this planet, most notably, in the formation of the UNDRIP in 2007 (Wiessner, 2013).

In response to the Change.org petition, one Samoan Nike customer found "Nike's blatant disrespect and profit over [the Samoan culture] shameless and irreverent." The individual went on to write "the *tatau* is thousands of years old with a tradition of honor" and that "Nike has reduced it to $80 Spanx" (Notte, 2013) (see Appendix 4).

Nike's Response

Immediately after the launch of the new Nike Pro Tattoo Tech tights, Wilson and her team knew the corporation had committed a significant cultural error. Not only had Nike produced pants that were directly inspired by the Samoan *pe'a* pattern, but it was also using the design, which carried deep masculine significance, on women's clothing.

On August 14, 2013, only one week following the official launch of the product, Nike pulled the product from their shelves, eliminated online sales, and released the following apology:

> The Nike Tattoo Tech Tights were inspired by tattoo graphics. We apologize to anyone who views this design as insensitive to any specific culture. No offense was intended. The tights were of a limited run and no additional tights will be sold [see Appendix 4].
>
> (Notte, 2013)

Though Nike rapidly dealt with this error, those invested were left without a proper explanation or steps as to how Nike would ensure their cultural sensitivity would improve. In the case of the Pro Tech Tights, stakeholders include members of the Indigenous People of the Pacific, New Zealand, and Australian Parliament members, athletes around the world, Nike customers, suppliers, distributers, Nike, Inc., and Nike's shareholders.

Cases of Cultural Insensitivity at Nike's Competitors

Nike is not alone in making poor, culturally insensitive decisions. In late 2011, Puma launched a shoe that provoked sharp criticism from Emirati nationals (George, 2011). The limited edition shoes were released to mark the 40th U.A.E. National Day, and bore colors that closely resembled those of the U.A.E. national flag. Puma was blamed for their lack of cultural sensitivity. U.A.E. consumers found great offense in the colors of their flag represented on a product worn on an individual's feet. Upon hearing of the backlash, Puma ordered the removal of the shoes and released an apology to their customers.

In June of 2012, Adidas announced release of a line of sneakers, the JS Roundhouse Mid, a high-top lace-up with a Velcro strap across the middle with a "handcuff" that attached to the customers' ankles. A public outcry ensued immediately following the announcement of the new product. Thousands in the blogosphere took "issue with the ankle shackle, interpreting it as a historical symbol of African slavery" (*The Huffington Post*, 2012). Though Adidas initially rebuffed the comments, the athletic apparel conglomerate canceled plans to sell the shoe and apologized for any offense taken.

Next Steps

Though Nike moved quickly to respond to the public outcry, and had recalled the Pro Tech Tights, Laurissa Wilson must now assess how the egregious error was made, and ensure that Nike takes proper steps to understand their customer base while maintaining a high level of cultural sensitivity. Recognizing that the company has made several cultural mistakes in the recent past, Wilson must overhaul the process through which Nike products are developed with respect to cultural identities.

Case Questions:

1   How do the concepts of individualism and collectivism pertain to Nike and the Indigenous People of the Pacific?
2   Why were the indigenous people of Fiji, Samoa, and New Zealand offended? What identity issues pertain to the Nike Tech Tights scenario?
3   The launch of the Nike Tattoo Tech Tights offended people from various geographic regions. Explain why they experienced similar reactions.
4   Was it enough to acknowledge that the tights were "inspired by tattoo graphics," or should the company have communicated the use of the design more directly? What would Nike have accomplished by directly communicating their use of the design?
5   How can Nike improve their product-vetting process to reveal the potential for errors caused by cultural insensitivity? (List changes in how they perceive both cultures and internal process.)
6   Should a company the size of Nike be concerned with being culturally sensitive even if the negative implications do not affect their bottom line?

Appendix 1

See URL for news story and image: www.foxsports.com/other/story/nike-t-shirt-slogans-spark-controversy-062311.

Appendix 2

See URL for news story and image: www.forbes.com/sites/lancemadden/2012/08/17/i-aint-sayin-shes-a-gold-digger-but-nike-is/#10d5c80d2b5f.

Appendix 3

See URL for complete news story and image (Pacific Islanders in Communications, n.d.): www.pbs.org/skinstories/history/.

> Your necklace may break, the *fau* tree may burst, but my tattooing is indestructible. It is an everlasting gem that you will take into your grave.
>
> Verse from a traditional tattoo artist's song

The legacy of Polynesian tattoo began over 2,000 years ago and is as diverse as the people who wear them. Once widespread in Polynesian societies across the Pacific Ocean, the arrival of Western missionaries in the 19th century forced this unique art form into decline. Despite the encroachment of Christian religious beliefs that vilified tattooing as unholy, many Polynesian tattoo artists maintained their vital link to their culture's history by preserving their unique craft for generations.

In Samoa, the tradition of applying tattoo, or *tatau*, by hand has been unbroken for over 2,000 years. Tools and techniques have changed little. The skill is often passed from father to son, each tattoo artist, or *tufuga*, learning the craft over many years of serving as his father's apprentice. A young artist-in-training often spent hours, and sometimes days, tapping designs into sand or bark cloth using a special tattooing comb, or *au*. Honoring their tradition, Samoan tattoo artists made this tool from sharpened boar's teeth fastened together with a portion of the turtle shell and to a wooden handle.

> Samoan society has long been defined by rank and title, with chiefs (*ali'i*) and their assistants, known as talking chiefs (*tulafale*), descending from notable families in the proper birth order. The tattooing ceremonies for young chiefs, typically conducted at the onset of puberty, were elaborate affairs and were a key part of their ascendance to a leadership role. The permanent marks left by the tattoo artists would forever celebrate their endurance and dedication to cultural traditions. The pain was extreme and the risk of death by infection was a great concern. But to shy away from tattooing was to risk being labeled a *pala'ai* or coward and reviled by the clan. Those who could not endure the pain and abandoned their tattooing were left incomplete, wearing their mark of shame throughout their life … [continue reading at www.pbs.org/skinstories/history/]

Appendix 4

Nike yanks Samoan-inspired tattoo tights.

The footwear and apparel giant thought intricate, painful marks used for centuries as a male rite of passage would make great leggings.

Some things to consider the next time you're putting together a pair of jaunty athletic leggings, Nike: Make sure you're not co-opting an entire culture's sacred, painful tradition and, if you are, don't make it a blatant part of your marketing and promotion of the offending item.

According to TVNZ news, Nike has pulled its black-and-white women's Pro Tattoo Tech tights (pictured) after petitioners pointed out that not only was the company ripping off the Samoan Pe'a pattern that's rarely seen on folks who aren't Samoan, but it used the pattern on women's clothing when it's only applied to men.

The pants first appeared in late July and received the following shout-out on Nike's blog: "The NTM (Nike Tight of the Moment) gets all fancy pants again, this time looking to the tattoos of Fiji, Samoa and New Zealand for the latest head-turning design, the Nike Pro Tattoo Tech tights (and sports bra and bodysuit)." Even if the company didn't know that the word tattoo stems from the Samoan "tatau," it's tough to feign complete ignorance after making a statement like that.

The reaction to the stretch pants in question was particularly hostile on a Change.org petition launched on Aug. 2 to protest their sale. "I am 100% Samoan and I find Nike's blatant disrespect and profit over my culture's way of life shameless and irreverent," one comment read. "The tatau is thousands of years old with a tradition of honor and you have reduced it to $80 Spanx. Remove at once!"

[Continue reading at http://money.msn.com/now/post-nike-yanks-samoan-inspired-tattoo-tights.]

(Notte, 2013)

Note

1 This case was prepared by Lauren Newton-John, Lisa Gibboney, and Hilary Wilson under the direction of Dr. Elizabeth Tuleja.

References

Brettman, A. (2011). Nike courts controversy, publicity with drug-themed skater shirts. Retrieved from www.oregonlive.com/business/index.ssf/2011/06/nike_courts_controversy_public.html (accessed August 2, 2016).

CNN Wires Staff. (2013). Nike pulls "Boston Massacre" shirts following bombings. Retrieved from http://money.cnn.com/2013/04/23/news/companies/nike-boston-massacre-shirt/index.html (accessed August 2, 2016).

DeMello, Margo. (2007). *Encyclopedia of body adornment* Part 46 (pp. 213). Santa Barbara, CA: Greenwood.

Ehrbar, Lucas. (2013). Nike Pro Tattoo Tech tights | Inspired by Fiji, Samoa, New Zealand. Retrieved from www.nikeblog.com/2013/07/30/nike-pro-tattoo-tech-tights-inspired-by-fiji-samoa-new-zealand/ (accessed August 2, 2016).

George, J. (2011). Puma shoes with UAE flag colours taken off. Retrieved from www. emirates247.com/news/emirates/puma-shoes-with-uae-flag-colours-taken-off-2011-11-29-1.430685 (accessed August 2, 2016).

Masina, John. (2013). Cease the production of the Nike Pro Tattoo Tech tights. Retrieved from: www.change.org/en-AU/petitions/nike-cease-the-production-of-the-nike-pro-tattoo-tech-tights (accessed August 2, 2016).

Misener, J. (2012). Nike apologies for offensive "Black and Tan" sneaker. Retrieved from www.huffingtonpost.com/2012/03/14/nike-black-and-tan_n_1344197.html (accessed August 2, 2016).

Nazworth, A. (2012). Nike under fire for "Sexist" Olympic tee. Retrieved from http://investorplace.com/2012/08/nike-under-fire-for-sexist-olympic-tee/ (accessed August 2, 2016).

Nike, Inc. (2013). History and heritage. Retrieved from http://nikeinc.com/pages/history-heritage (accessed August 2, 2016).

Notte, J. (2013). Nike yanks Samoan-inspired tattoo tights. Retrieved from http://money.msn.com/now/post–nike-yanks-samoan-inspired-tattoo-tights (accessed August 2, 2016).

Pacific Islanders in Communications. (n.d.). Skin stories: The art and culture of Polynesian tattoo. Retrieved from: www.pbs.org/skinstories/history/ (accessed August 2, 2016).

Radford, Elaine. (2013). Nike Samoan Tattoo Tech tights line gets yanked after outcry. *Inquisitr.* Retrieved from www.inquisitr.com/903401/nike-samoan-tattoo-tech-tights/ (accessed August 2, 2016).

The Curatorial. (2013). Nike Pro Tattoo Tech: Tattoos, Ritual and Appropriation. Retrieved from: www.thecuratorial.com/2013/08/nike-pro-tattoo-tech-tattoos-ritual-and.html (accessed August 2, 2016).

The Huffington Post. (2012). Adidas "Shackle" sneakers cause controversy over slavery symbolism. Retrieved from www.huffingtonpost.com/2012/06/18/adidas-shackle-sneakers-controversy_n_1605661.html (accessed August 1, 2016).

Wiessner, S. (2013). United Nations Declaration on the Rights of Indigenous Peoples. Retrieved from www.un.org/esa/socdev/unpfii/documents/DRIPS_en.pdf (accessed August 2, 2016).

3 Culture and Identity

"You must be some kind of beardless dwarf," said Mr. Tumnus.
"I'm not a dwarf, I'm a girl!" replied Lucy indignantly.

(*The Lion, the Witch, and the Wardrobe*, movie of the book
by C. S. Lewis)

Figure 3.1 Lucy and Mr. Tumnus

(*Sources*: http://carlahuertacrespo.blogspot.com; http://carlahuertacrespo.daportfolio.com/gallery/842817.)

Chapter Overview

Chapter 3, Culture and Identity, examines the questions: What is your individual cultural identity? What makes up social and cultural identities and how do these affect the way we see the world? What can we learn from social influences such as ethnicity, language, gender, age, disability, social class, education, religion, and roles? Why is it important to understand concepts of race and ethnicity? These are the key questions we will address in Chapter 3 (see Figure 3.1).

Learning Objective

We must first know who we are before we can understand others. Our individual cultural identities are made up of cultural, personal, and relational aspects of how we are socialized while growing up.

Key Takeaways

— Discover your individual cultural identity.
— Consider how you negotiate your identity with others.
— Understand current ideas regarding sociocultural factors as well as race and ethnicity.

Leadership Applications

— If we are to be effective leaders, we must first understand who we are *and* what has influenced us.
— Understanding who we are will help us put into perspective our interactions with both similarities and differences as we seek to understand others.

Introduction

Cheerios and Coca-Cola Commercials

It seemed innocuous; but there was some uproar over the nature of the commercial. A little girl asks her mother if Cheerios were healthy for her daddy's heart (Demby, 2013). The next scene shows the father waking up from a nap on the couch with a mound of Cheerios stacked on top of his chest. What could be the controversy of such an endearing portrayal of a child's innocence yet deep understanding of care for her parents? The family was biracial. While this ad came and went, as did the "likes" and "dislikes" on Facebook and YouTube (there were more likes than dislikes), it still carries significant meaning for the topic of culture and identity. That same year there was another controversy regarding Coca-Cola's advertisement that aired during the 2013 Super Bowl. It was a multicultural mix of people from all walks of life singing "America the Beautiful" in various languages. Again, most of the commentary was positive, but the bad press lingered in the background (Poniewozik, 2014). In both cases, the issue of identity—one national and the other racial—were challenged (Box 3.1).

> **Box 3.1**
>
> In this book, the word "native" means "born or originating in a particular place," as in one's native country.
>
> As we continue to examine the influence of culture on leadership, we will focus our discussion in this chapter on culture and identity. We will be talking about "Who am I?" and "Who are you?" by defining these terms relating to identity. If we are to be successful in the global marketplace or with the diversity that exists in our "native" environments, then we must first seek to understand who we are, where we came from, and who/what has shaped and influenced our lives. Then we will be able to better understand others. This goes back to the basic tenet discussed regarding CQ—"know thyself" before "knowing others." The more we are self-aware, the more we are able to be mindful or reflective. The more we are able to develop competence across a wide range of situations, the better leaders we will become. This mindfulness is the key to global leadership development.

Individual Identity

Who Am I?

We have probably all been asked that requisite job interview question "So, tell me about yourself." It's both pesky and annoying but we know that eventually it will come up. What *exactly* does that question mean? Am I supposed to talk about something job related, such as how I "work and play well with others?" Or am I supposed to impress by offering something personal like a hobby that will cleverly demonstrate that I'm not boring to work with—such as the fact that I'm a competitive ballroom dancer and often try to tie in object lessons from the Latin rhythm dances such as Rumba or Samba as they apply to learning and education? I do not know about you, but often I feel like saying, "Will you throw me a bone?!" What *exactly* would you like me to talk about?

How many of us cringe at the thought of trying to guess what is on the mind of the interviewer? What is actually behind that open-ended question is merely a probe to see if the candidate knows themselves well. If they pause, then this says something about them. My guess would be that anyone would pause, because she—or he—needs to read between the lines and try to figure out whether the interviewers want some professional or personal tidbit.

So, take a shot at it: If we were just introduced as colleagues, what would you share with me in order to give an overview of who you are? "So, tell me about yourself?" If you were to describe who you are at this moment in time, what would you say about yourself? Take a moment and jot down some attributes, interests, roles, and values that make you—you. Keep these handy because we will come back to them later.

Now put this into an intercultural context—if we are asked that question about our cultural identities, how many of us would falter and be at a loss for words? What was your first reaction? To some, it may be, "I don't have any culture, I just grew up in the Midwestern United States!" The fact is, no matter who we are or where we have grown up, we *all* have an individual cultural identity. Just like above, what would you say about your culture? Where you are from? Jot down some of those ideas.

As we discussed in Chapter 1, a general definition of culture is a group-related phenomenon that includes values, beliefs, attitudes, and behaviors. Interculturalist Marshall Singer was provocative in his definition of culture as he tried to explain the perceptual approach to intercultural communication—that everyone is a member of a unique collection of groups and is therefore culturally unique. In Chapter 2 we talked about in-groups and out-groups, and how this can lead to ethnocentric thinking where we unconsciously or even consciously view ourselves as naturally superior to others. We also discussed that it is important to know yourself before you can know others—having a strong EQ enables us to do so. Now in Chapter 3 as we examine identity, we are going to look at the many aspects of life that influence who we are: ethnicity, race, language, socioeconomic status, religion, education, gender, and disability.

Social and Cultural Identities

Each of us has our own unique identity that makes us who we are. We first develop our identities through our families, from whom we learn about values, expectations for behavior, and norms for communication. Those who raise us reflect their values and beliefs through everyday interactions. As we go out into the world and make friends at school, interact with people at work, and experience life on our own, we find many other influences and experiences that shape who we are—such as with school, civic activities, and places of worship (Ting-Toomey, 1999). It is within these social contexts, according to Russian psychologist Lev Vygotsky, that we learn. Vygotsky is known for applying social learning theories to human interaction. He posits that our social environments will influence how we learn—and this obviously includes culture and its influence on how we learn the rules and standards for interaction (Vygotsky, 1978) (Box 3.2).

Enculturation and Acculturation

Since we are influenced through our numerous social environments, we gain our identity through what is called enculturation (Box 3.3). This is a life-long process within our country of origin—and especially during our formative years—that influences and shapes who we are. Those who sojourn to another culture would engage in acculturation, which is the process of learning to

Box 3.2

For an engaging exploration of "Who am I? Think again," see the following TED Talk by conceptual artist Hetain Patel: www.ted.com/talks/hetain_patel_who_am_i_think_again.html.

Box 3.3

None of us grows up in a vacuum. We all acquire and develop our identities through experiences with others in a variety of groups. We do not even realize the influence that others have on us in terms [of] meanings, values, norms, and styles of communicating.

Source: Ting-Toomey, 1999

Box 3.4

We have national identities (legal status to a nation) and our cultural identity. A nation is a group of people under the influence of an organized government within a specific territory.

Source: dictionary.com, n.d.

adapt to a new environment and set of normative standards. As renowned interculturalist Stella Ting-Toomey, a professor at California State University, Fullerton, explains, the process is incremental and cumulative, happening over time (Ting-Toomey, 1993, 2005).

For example, watch the Coca-Cola commercial celebrating U.S. American diversity regarding our immigrants from many nations (Lee, 2014). If you look at the different cultural groups represented, Sushmitha, a young woman from South East Asia who sang in Hindi, would be *enculturated* through her culture in India (if that is where she grew up) to learn the norms—or the accepted and expected ways of behaving in her country. If immigrating to the United States then, as a newcomer, she would go through the *acculturation* process of learning what is accepted and expected in the United States. Sushmitha's strength of her affiliation with her culture would be referred to as *salience*. Through both processes our identities are affected in powerful ways through the experiences we have and the people we meet (Box 3.4).

Salience in Cultural Identity

Identity is about our sense of self, or our self-image that we develop first through our families and then through the process of socialization. There are two types of identity—personal and social. Personal identity includes our unique qualities and characteristics that make us who we are. Social identity includes the many aspects of socialization that influence us, such as our cultural and ethnic membership.

Here is how one person describes her personal and social identity:[1]

> [I]t occurred to me that I am not the average American. Please hear me out before judging my ego. If I were to apply to the position of "American Identity", I might be over-qualified. My identity resume would include: Born in the U.S.A.; Caucasian; Speaks English fluently; has a law degree from an accredited U.S. law school; Makes six figures; Lives in the Suburbs; Owns a home with a garage and big yard; Owns two vehicles; Has two Caucasian children from a Caucasian husband; Is heterosexual and identifies as a female; Celebrates all major U.S. holidays; Condemns 9/11 attacks; Has no criminal record.

> In today's climate, I sound like the "upright" person that the U.S. Department of Homeland Security would not suspect of being a national security threat. . . . The same characteristics that many people believe to make me an average American, or a great one, welcome into "privileged" circles, have been reasons to exclude me from certain circles. . . . At times, I have been hailed as a stand-out by people dismissing most of the qualifications above. Ironically, the focus was on qualifications that would otherwise disqualify me from the "American Identity" position.

> My name is Samara Hakim. I speak English with an accent; my last name can be Muslim and Christian; my first name is universal. I speak several languages . . . I was born in the U.S., immigrated with my parents to Lebanon as a baby, only to return to the U.S. at the age of seventeen.

> After my return to the U.S., I have experienced life much like an immigrant would, with the questions and assumptions I have encountered. I left one home country to come back to another home country, and I have been told neither is my real home.

> I grew up Maronite in Lebanon; went to a Catholic School; was surrounded by students from various religions and countries; learned French, English, and Arabic; grew up in an affectionate home despite the turmoil of two wars. . . . My parents emphasized the value of education . . . and taught me that politics and religion do not prevent friendships unless I let them do so. To some, these facts about me would qualify me for the "Lebanese Identity" position. The same characteristics would also disqualify me in the view of many in Lebanon, and elsewhere.

> It seems that my identity becomes an issue when I am evaluated for an identity position, and when one is seeking reasons why I should not be given that position.

I have folded experiences between all the layers of my identity. I have shaped these layers and molded them with the pressures surrounding me, and that is exactly why I am not the average or typical . . . anyone. My experiences are my identity, and they have helped me get in, fit in, blend in, stand out, and stay in. My experiences are not over, and neither is my identity.

Our cultural identity is the "emotional significance that we attach our sense of belonging or affiliation with the larger culture—e.g., the larger Brazilian cultural identity or the larger Canadian cultural identity" (Ting-Toomey, 2005, p. 30).

Salience in Social Identities

There are many forms of social identities—see the illustration of the variety of social (cultural) identities as defined by social scientists William Gudy-kunst and Young-Yun Kim (Box 3.5). They argue that how we communicate plays a big role in developing and maintaining relationships within our social and cultural groups. In addition to their social/cultural categories, I would also add several other very important ones: religion, profession, and education.

We can look at our identity groups in terms of our cultural contexts and situations, such as national, family, organizational (also functional and team), or even the "host" culture if we are sojourners in another country. Within these cultural contexts lie the social influences—the forces that impact and shape us. These include: religion, family, education, profession, social class, gender, age, ethnicity, friends, region, and community (Figure 3.2).

At our core lies the foundation of who we are—our beliefs and values—which are integral to how we approach life. These are intricately tied to our sense of self and are non-negotiable. For example, our personal religious affiliation or philosophical foundation guides our everyday behaviors. While our religious and philosophical beliefs can change over time, their basic premise anchors us and provides stability. In addition to our core values and beliefs are aspects of our preferences and behaviors that are negotiable and which do not threaten our sense of self.

Here is an example of our core and negotiable values and beliefs, and how one woman explained her experience interacting with the Buddhist religion when living in Taiwan:[2]

I grew up in the Protestant faith, which has been an important part of my life and my core identity. When I lived in Hong Kong for a short time, I had many friends who were Buddhists. I was curious about their beliefs and always asked questions—it fascinated me to go to my friend's house and see her golden Buddha statue set upon an alter where she would burn

---

Box 3.5 Social Identities

- *Cultural or Ethnic Identities:* aspects of a group's cultural background—belonging to the same ethnic category (e.g., Asian American, Japanese American).
- *Language Identities:* languages often mark boundaries between our ethnic/national origins and others. Language is one major criterion for ethnic group membership.
- *Gender Identities:* the way we define our gender roles, which are the psychological traits and the social responsibilities that individuals have and feel are appropriate for them because they are male or female. Gender roles also include our sexual orientations.
- *Disability Identities:* whether we are perceived to have a noticeable disability or not. Sometimes disabilities are not noticeable.
- *Age Identities:* where we are in terms of our chronological order.
- *Social Class Identities:* where we are in terms of our position in society—not just socioeconomic, but also aspects of intelligence.
- *Role Identities:* we can define ourselves in terms of the behavioral expectations associated with a particular position in a group (e.g., multiple roles as a mother, daughter, sister, friend, employee, caregiver).

Source: Gudykunst & Kim, 1992

---

incense and pray for safety before she left the house. I wondered about the fruit she would set out every day as an offering—and then where did it go? Could you eat it? Give it away?

During the Ching Ming festival (the spring grave-sweeping festival where families will go to clean the gravesites and both honor and worship their ancestors) my friend invited me to accompany her to the site as well as a local temple. When in the temple my friend gave me incense sticks and beckoned me to follow her lead—bowing to all four directions (i.e., "corners of the world"). Out of respect for her and this tradition, I solemnly obliged and followed her actions.

At an earlier stage of my life I might have considered this to be in conflict with my core values—that is, the act of burning incense and praying to a god I did not worship would have violated my core values and beliefs. However, at this point in my life I did not look at it this way–it did not affect my core; rather it was a negotiable act done out of respect and admiration to my good friend.

In addition to group identity, individual people can become a source of identity—or role models for others. Take Carly Fiorina who was one of the

Figure 3.2 Our Core Values

(*Source*: World image by GDJ, https://openclipart.org/user-detail/GDJ [CC0], via Wikimedia Commons; Design by Author.)

first women to become CEO of a Fortune 100 company (Hewlett-Packard) as an example. She symbolized success for women and demonstrated that it was possible to break through the glass ceiling. Women wanted to emulate her— she was strong, smart, and competent as she confidently garnered the merger between HP and Compaq, no matter how contentious it was. I remember watching an interview with Neal Cavuto—he was using his typical pleasant demeanor, but relentlessly pummeled her with tough questions. She never flinched for a second. I liked this interchange so much that I used it for years when teaching media interviewing with MBA students at Wharton. Sometimes I still go back to this classic exchange.

Ms. Fiorina was totally in control and surely well rehearsed—able to rattle off statistic after statistic, keep her audience in mind, and show that she, too, could be tough at the receiving end of the hard-hitting questions. She presented herself as confident, articulate, and capable—definitely a leader. She also paid particular attention to her personal image—both on and off camera, as she was always well dressed (wearing stylish clothing that demonstrated power yet did not

Yes, I strongly believe in the concept of corporate identity.
Why do you ask?

Figure 3.3 Corporate Identity

(*Source*: www.cartoonstock.com/directory/c/corporate_identity.asp.)

compromise her femininity) and nicely coiffed. I recollect some interactions with senior female leaders at Merck & Company in Whitehouse Station, New Jersey, and noticed that all of these female executives wore the same hairstyle as Fiorina. Carly Fiorina symbolized what many women aspire to be today. Even something like how people dress or wear their hair at work can influence our identities. And to this day, as she was running for nomination to the presidency as a GOP candidate, she negotiated her identity with the American people despite her contender's attempt to poke jabs at her (Figure 3.3).

Identity Negotiation

As we interact with people and experience life, we find that we are constantly negotiating our relationships with others—this is not something about which we are aware, but it is actually a sociological phenomenon. Identity negotiation is the process that we go through when trying to figure out who we are within any given relationship. A social psychologist who studied social interaction, William Swann, came up with the phrase "identity negotiation" as a way to explain the tension that exists in all relationships as people try to deal with their expectations. This tension occurs as each person perceives the other based upon their tacit expectations of what they want out of the interaction— or the relationship. These unmentioned, often subconscious expectations create tensions because of conflicting agendas and therefore mean that each person is attempting to manage his/her own self-concept in relation to others.

We confirm our self-conceptions through our interactions with others (Swann & Read, 1981).

Canadian-born sociologist Erving Goffman also had a way for dealing with how we present ourselves in social interaction. He is known for his work on "public and private" selves in that he views everyday life as a theatrical performance where we put on a particular "face" in order to achieve our goals. For example, at work, we have our public face and show a side of us that is professional, not personal, and we change our behaviors depending on the setting and situation—as if we are on stage. As we interact with people in any given situation, we attempt to maintain our own "face" while guiding the impressions of others. Of course, when we are able to relax, we can put on our "private face" and be ourselves—like the actors walking backstage in between scenes.

During any social interaction, we regularly present ourselves (who *we* are) while simultaneously reading the presentation of others' "self" (who *they* are). Goffman came up with a book called *The presentation of self in everyday life*. He looked at human behaviors in social settings and used a theater metaphor of being "on" regarding our performance—basically how we make ourselves appear to others. He talks about similar concepts:

> When an individual enters the presence of others, they commonly seek to acquire information about him or to bring into play information about him already possessed. They will be interested in his general socio-economic status, his conception of self, his attitude toward them, his competence, his trustworthiness, etc. Although some of this information seems to be sought almost as an end in itself, there are usually quite practical reasons for acquiring it. Information about the individual helps to define the situation, enabling others to know in advance what he will expect of them and what they may expect of him. Informed in these ways, the others will know how best to act in order to call forth a desired response from him.
>
> (Goffman, 1959, p. 120)

We perform through the concept of negotiation—that each of us acquires our identity from the groups in which we interact and, based upon our development of figuring out who we are, negotiate meaning as we try to figure out who others are as well. We negotiate our daily interactions with others as we try to influence others through our identity—which is made up of our family, gender, social, and educational status (language, ethnicity, religion, political standing, etc.). "The concept [of] negotiation is defined as a transactional interaction process whereby individuals in an intercultural situation attempt to assert, define, modify, challenge, and/or support their own and other's desired self-images" (Ting-Toomey, 2005, p. 217). Depending on our personality, each of us will adjust aspects of our "presentation" according to the reactions and presentations of those around us (Box 3.6).

Box 3.6

Identity negotiation is a transactional interaction process—individuals in an intercultural situation attempt to assert, define, modify, challenge, and/ or support their own desired image (or what they believe the other person desires of them).

Source: Ting-Toomey, 2005

While we work hard (often unknowingly) to manage our perception of self as we interact with others, we also have to manage the anxiety we face when dealing with the identities of others. This is called uncertainty anxiety.

Uncertainty-Anxiety Management

It is natural that we are usually comfortable with those who are familiar to us; however, we experience anxiety when interacting with people who are unfamiliar. For example, observe any small child who hides his head bashfully and reactively moves away from a stranger who says "hello." Recently I was in the grocery store and bumped into one of my graduate students who was pushing one of those fun carts shaped like a car with his three-year-old son, Edmund, inside it. When he introduced me to Edmund, the little boy cowered and pulled away further into the little vehicle. Little Edmund was managing his uncertainty and the anxiety that went with it concerning this unfamiliar woman who had just said "hello."

Even as adults, we can experience bashfulness, and while we may not pull away physically, something goes on internally inside us. William Gudykunst's theory, uncertainty-anxiety management, refers to intergroup interaction and that we experience anxiety when interacting with people who are unfamiliar to us. We have an innate need to manage our levels of uncertainty (whether high or low), which is a cognitive ability to identify and predict the behavior of others, while at the same time managing our anxiety, which is our emotional reaction of fearing what might happen if we make a mistake. According to this theory, the person who can control both the uncertainty *and* anxiety will achieve better understanding as well as be more adaptive—the outcome being effective communication (Gudykunst & Shapiro 1996). This leads us to an understanding of how to deal with difference when interacting with someone from a different group. We all belong to a group from which we gain our identity—in fact we can belong to many groups that make up who we are. We have just explored several social identities—such as gender, religious roles, social class, age, language, or disability. One of the biggest influences in our lives can be how we identify our group membership in terms of race and ethnicity.

Group Membership

What are race and ethnicity? Trying to trace the etymology for the word "race" is an elusive process. It is supposed that the French got it from the Italians (*razza*, which means "species" or "kind"), who introduced it into the English language in the mid-1500s. The word "ethnicity" is a little easier to identify because it comes from the Greek "*ethnikos*" (meaning "of a nation") or "*ethnos*," which also means "race" (O'Connor & Kellerman, 2009).

Ethnicity

Ethnicity relates to sociological factors that can include a shared language, nationality, religion, cultural traditions, and group history. For example, the Kurds from the mountainous Kurdistan region that expands into parts of Iran, Iraq, Turkey, and Syria are non-Arab people who identify themselves as their own group—although they are a group without a recognized nation. They are generally Muslims and speak the Kurdish language as well as Arabic, Persian, and Turkish languages, depending where they live. However, a small number of Kurdish people can also be Christians or Jews or Yazidis (those who combine aspects of Islam, Judaism, and Christianity). Depending on geography and religion, Kurdish people will identify themselves within different group memberships.

Ethnicity is defined in terms of shared ancestry. It can be actual or presumed. Often people will associate with a particular group based upon family stories passed down from generation to generation—there is a nostalgic or emotional interest in being associated with a particular group—and, whether actual or imagined, the person will self-identify and believe to be part of that group. Their salience, or emotional connection to the need to belong, creates bonds to a particular group membership (Diffen LLC, n.d.).

One example of this phenomenon is quite interesting: Kyle Merker does a TV commercial spot for Ancestry.com. He opines (see Figure 3.4):

> "Growing up we were German. We danced in a German dance group. I wore lederhosen." He goes on to say that he tried to track down his family tree but couldn't find a single German relative. So he had his DNA tested. "The big surprise is we're not German at all—but Scottish and Irish. So I traded in my lederhosen for a kilt."
>
> (AncestryDNA, 2016)

Race

In the United States, originally, using the term "race" meant placing people into groups based upon physical characteristics such as bone structure, eye color, skin color, and hair—and these characteristics were supposedly the result of distinctive genetic differences. The first U.S. Census is as old as the

Figure 3.4 German Lederhosen

(*Source*: Fotolia 80960006, © Magann.)

presidency of the United States—being conducted in 1790, a year after George Washington was inaugurated. According to Census.gov, there were five categories: two for white males ("over 16" was used to determine young men for military duty, as well as to gauge industrialization); one for white females; one for other free people; and one for slaves. At that time in history, this is what the population focused on in the newly formed republic. Actually, this is the first known national counting of people in any country (Cortés, 2013). Today, the U.S. Census is a way of categorizing people—supposedly for Federal funding. The census claims that the categories it uses are not meant to define race through genetic classifications; rather its rationale is to reflect the current social definitions as demarcated by the people within the country (U.S. Census Bureau: FAQs, n.d.) (see Box 3.8).

The idea of race has changed because of the determination that the concept of race is not scientific (the definition of race is currently disputed in biology and anthropology circles as not having biological merit); rather it is political and social (*Harvard Magazine*, 2008). As humans, we are part of the human species "homo sapiens" and, while people may look different because of facial features, skin, eyes, and hair color, there is much variation in the categories we assign to people. Social mores and attitudes as well as political agendas determine how people are perceived and treated—race is a social construct (Box 3.7).

In the PBS Series *Race: The Power of an Illusion*, the authors introduce the topic of race and then summarize with "Ten Things Everyone Should

Box 3.7 What the Experts Say about Race

What is the difference between race and ethnicity?

> While race and ethnicity share an ideology of common ancestry, they differ in several ways. First of all, race is primarily unitary. You can only have one race, while you can claim multiple ethnic affiliations. You can identify ethnically as Irish and Polish, but you have to be essentially either black or white. The fundamental difference is that race is socially imposed and hierarchical. There is an inequality built into the system. Furthermore, you have no control over your race; it is how you're perceived by others. For example, I have a friend who was born in Korea to Korean parents, but as an infant, she was adopted by an Italian family in Italy. Ethnically, she feels Italian: she eats Italian food, she speaks Italian, she knows Italian history and culture. She knows nothing about Korean history and culture. But when she comes to the United States, she's treated racially as Asian.

Source: Conley, 2003

Box 3.8

In ancient times, people did not associate race with the physical, but with religion, status, social class, and language. Race is a relatively modern idea.

Know About Race." They say, "Our eyes tell us that people look different. No one has trouble distinguishing a Czech from a Chinese. But what do those differences mean? How does race affect people today?" This series makes the following comments about the category of race (Fredrickson, 2013):

1   Race is modern social construction of identity: In ancient times, people were not classified according to their physical attributes; rather religion, status, and language.
2   Race is not genetic: There is no such thing as a gene that differentiates members of a "race" from another. Therefore race is not biological.
3   There are no subspecies of humans: Humans have not evolved into subspecies; rather, humans are the most similar of all species.
4   Skin color doesn't define race: Humans inherit traits independently from another—so skin color isn't connected to the genes that create blood type, hair, or shape of eyes—or intelligence or any other abilities.

5   Variation comes within and not between people of different "races." Only a small amount of variation exists in human beings. If you pick two random people from the same people group, for example, a Czech person, they can be just as genetically different than a Czech and a Chinese person (Box 3.9).

The U.S. Census on Race and Ethnicity

U.S. Census information on racial categories contains six categories: American Indian or Alaskan Native, Asian, Black/African-American, Hispanic or Latino, Native Hawaiian or other Pacific Islander, White. These categories date back to the 1970s and it is said that the creation of such categories was supposed to help against discrimination. The rationale for collecting data on race is to assist Federal programs in determining policy decisions especially related to civil rights, such as equal employment opportunities, and to assess health and environmental risks (U.S. Census Bureau: FAQs, n.d.).

But how can people be defined in the same way? In the table below, notice the many inconsistencies with the categories. The U.S. Government agrees that its definitions are not perfect, but insists that it needs these racial classifications in order to combat inequality in terms of education (data show that schools are even more segregated than in the 1960s); wealth gaps (there is a huge disparity between African-Americans and Whites); health issues (the highest rate of diabetes is found in Native Americans); crime (incidents of hate crimes against Arab and South Asian Americans has increased since September 11, 2001); and poverty—one in four Latinos live at the poverty level (DeNavas-Walt & Proctor, 2015). In talking about the U.S. Census and race, Former Supreme Court Justice Harry Blackmun said, "Race is a double-edged sword, but we must overcome centuries of inequality before

---

Box 3.9 Race: The Power of an Illusion (PBS)

In the United States, race and freedom evolved together. The United States was founded on the radical new principle that "all men are created equal," but the early economy was based largely on slavery. How could this anomaly be rationalized? The new idea of race helped explain why some people could be denied the rights and freedoms that others took for granted. . . . Race is a powerful social idea that gives people different access to opportunities and resources. Our government and social institutions have created advantages that disproportionately channel wealth, power, and resources to white people. This affects everyone, whether we are aware of it or not.

Source: Fredrickson, 2013

Table 3.1 U.S. Census and Race Categories

American Indian or Alaskan Native	Origins from North, Central, South America with tribal affiliation
Asian	East and South East Asia: China, Japan, Korea, India, Pakistan, Malaysia, Philippines, Thailand, Vietnam, Cambodia
Black or African-American	Origins from black racial groups of Africa
Hispanic or Latino	Cuba, Mexico, Puerto Rico, South America, Central America, Spain
Hawaiian or Pacific Islander	Origins from Hawaii, Guam, Samoa, other Pacific Islands
White	Origins from Europe, Middle East, North Africa

(*Source*: U.S. Census Bureau, 2013.)

we can unmake it. . . . In order to get beyond racism, we must first take account of race. There is no other way." (Cheng, 2013).

   The 2010 Census did not work, because it included two separate questions about race and ethnicity. First, people were asked if they were Latino, Hispanic, or Spanish. The second question asked people to identify one or more options (out of 15) about their racial categories. This forced a large percentage of respondents to check the vague and unhelpful "some other race" category (Table 3.1 and Figure 3.5) (Krogstad & Cohn, 2014).

Latino/a and Hispanic Cultures

The Census questions are unclear, complicated, and often do not make sense to any of us who have to answer them. A study by the Pew Research Center explains that, according to policy, the term "Hispanic" is not considered a race but an ethnicity. This study showed that two-thirds of Americans who checked "Hispanic" on the 2010 Census considered their background as part of their race. This demonstrates that current U.S. racial categories are not relevant to today's view of race and ethnic identity as socially constructed (Gonzales-Barrera & Lopez, 2015).

   In fact, if you ask ten people what the term "Hispanic" or "Latino" means you'll probably get a variety of different answers. The definition varies depending on who you talk to. In Texas and New Mexico, people might refer to themselves as Hispanic (usually a U.S.-born Mexican). In New York City or Miami, depending on who you talk to, it might be Latino. Or Hispanic. The denotative, or dictionary meaning, is that Hispanic is about language and Latino about geography. For example, if you are from Brazil you would be Latino (male) or Latina (female), because your mother language is Portuguese and not Spanish. If you are from Spain (Iberian Peninsula) then you would be Hispanic and not Latino (Figure 3.6) (Fernandez, 2013).

   Because of this critical issue, in 2020 the U.S. Census Bureau plans to change its social categorizations to reflect the multi-"racial" makeup of U.S.

Instructions from 2010 U.S. Census:

Note: Please answer BOTH Question 8 about Hispanic origin and Question 9 about race. For this census, Hispanic origins are not races.

Question 8: Is Person 1 of Hispanic, Latino, or Spanish origin?
☐ No, not of Hispanic, Latino, or Spanish origin
☐ Yes, Mexican, Mexican Am., Chicano
☐ Yes, Puerto Rican
☐ Yes, Cuban
☐ Yes, another Hispanic, Latino, or Spanish origin-Print origin, for example, Argentinean, Colombian, Dominican, Nicaraguan, Salvadoran, Spaniard, and so on.

Question 9: What is Person 1's race?
☐ White
☐ Black, African Am., or Negro
☐ American Indian or Alaska Native – Print name of enrolled or principal tribe.

☐☐☐☐☐☐☐☐☐ ☐ ☐☐☐☐☐☐☐☐☐

☐ Asian   ☐ Japanese   ☐ Native Hawaiian
☐ Chinese   ☐ Korean   ☐ Guamanian or Chamorro
☐ Filipino   ☐ Vietnamese   ☐ Samoan
☐ Other Asian-Print race, or   ☐ Other Pacific Islander-Print race, for
for example, Hmong, Laotian,   example, Fijian, Tongan, and so on
Thai, Pakistani, Cambodian, etc.

☐ Some other race-print race

☐☐☐☐☐☐☐☐☐ ☐ ☐☐☐☐☐☐☐☐☐

Figure 3.5 Instructions from 2010 U.S. Census

-Hispanic refers to people of Spanish-speaking origin *(language)*
-Latino refers to people of Latin American origin *(geographic)*

Figure 3.6 Differences between Latino/Latina and Hispanic

Pew Research Study: Experimental Question Combining Race and Hispanic Ethnicity for 2020

Question 8: What is Person 1's race or origin? Mark X in one or more boxes AND write in the specific race(s) or origin(s).

☐ White-Print origin(s), for example, German, Irish, Lebanese, Egyptian, and so on.

☐ Black, African Am., or negro-Print origin(s), for example, African American, Haitian, Nigerian, and so on.

☐ Hispanic, Latino, or Spanish origin-Print origin(s) for example, Mexican, Mexican Am., Puerto Ricam, Cuban, Argentinian, Colombian, Dominican, Nicaraguan, Salvadoran, Spaniard, and so on.

☐ American Indian or Alaska Native-Print name of enrolled or principal tribe(s), for example, Navajo, Mayan, and so on.

☐ Asian-Print origin(s) for example, Asian Indian, Chinese, Filipino, Japanese, Korean, Vietnamese, Hmong, Laotian, Thai, Pakistani, Cambodian, and so on.

☐ Native Hawaiian or Other Pacific Islander-Print origin(s) for example, Native Hawaiian, Guamanian or Chamorro, Samoan, Fijian, Gongan, and so on.

☐ Some other race or origin-Print race(s) or origin(s).

☐☐☐☐☐☐☐☐☐☐☐☐☐☐☐☐☐☐☐☐☐

Figure 3.7 Pew Research Study: U.S. Census Experimental Question Combining Race and Ethnicity

(*Source*: Krogstad & Cohn, 2014.)

citizens. The next Census will include a combined race and ethnicity question where respondents can check boxes and then fill in an accompanying space about their specific origins. So, in order to accommodate the multiracial makeup within the United States, the U.S. Census has created new forms to allow people to check more than one box (see Figure 3.7). However, not everyone has the same definition of what these categories mean. For example, Hispanic and Latino refer to the following: Cuban, Mexican, Puerto Rican, South American, Central American, and Spanish (this definition depends on who you talk to. Some people interchange Hispanic and Latino; others strongly oppose this).

National Differences in Identity

But nations differ in how they, as a society, approach classifications. In the United States people are usually classified by their ancestry, so technically the Moroccan American citizen would be considered African-American.

However, in Brazil, people are classified by what they look like, using a large number of categories (Wiki South America, 2016). Today race and ethnicity often overlap, as shown in Figure 3.8, "Main *Ethnic* Groups In Brazil." Brazil has many more racial categories than the United States. Brazil classifies people based upon main ethnic groups (Indian, White, Black, Asian) and mixed race (Pardo), which includes Mulatto, Cafuzo, Caboclo, Juçara, and Ainocô. Governments throughout the world are challenged regarding how to keep track of the diversity within their nations.

The point is that our individual interaction within our many groups shapes both us and our groups—one affects the other. As we have seen in the revamping of U.S. Census questions, it is not sufficient to check one box—or even two—our backgrounds are too complex to be defined by simplistic (and outdated) categories. No matter our nationality, one thing for sure is that our main group membership is made up of many different aspects of our social identities, with race and ethnicity being major aspects from where we may or may not get our identity salience.

In many cultures people are known by their group membership through their name. For example, Chinese surnames come first to represent the association with the family. So if you are greeting a female named Hua Huang you would say, "Huang ni hao" or "Ms. Huang hello." It is also common to greet someone by asking what their surname is: "Ni gui xing?" or "What is your family name?" The reply would be "Wo xing Huang" ("My surname is Huang") or "Wo jiao Huang Hua" ("I am called Huang Hua").

Names in Spanish-speaking countries can be complicated because there are two surnames—the first is the father's and the second is the mother's. The father's name is considered the surname (family name) which is passed on

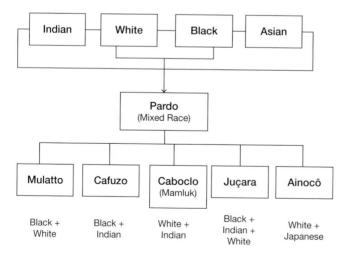

Figure 3.8 Main Ethnic Groups in Brazil

(*Source*: Wiki South America, 2016.)

to children. So if the father's name is Jose Cardona Delgado and the mother's name is Marisol Sandoval Peres and they have a child named Marcos, his name would be Marcos Cardona Sandoval. This process of naming brings together generations of families whose names are never forgotten.

Identity can even come in a number. People identify with many things—even area codes. A National Public Radio (NPR) segment talked about how New York's Public Service Commission has created another area code for Manhattan. But New Yorkers were upset, saying that when they were forced to change to a new area code "it felt like we were being banished to a separate island." People become emotionally attached to their area code. The number 917 may not mean much to someone else, but it carries a sense of belonging to the person who has lived in that "area" for many years and then is told they need to change those three digits in their phone number. One person even said, "Having my 917 area code is tangible proof that I got here first, that I've been here." Another person, who opened a restaurant in Manhattan, insisted they receive the familiar 212 area code, because "the 646 just didn't speak to our NYC roots and the brand image needed for the restaurant" (Babin, 2015).

As we wrap up our discussion regarding group membership—and specifically race and ethnicity—it's important to understand two things. First, each of us does have a unique identity, which is based upon our family, our upbringing, and the many social influences on our lives, as well as our distinctive personalities. Second, in any given country—or nation group—there are many cultures and subcultures. While we could talk about Chinese culture in general, there are 56 different ethnic groups that comprise the makeup of China—each has its own culture (Central Intelligence Agency, n.d.). While the Han Chinese make up the overwhelming majority at 92 percent, the other 8 percent of ethnic minorities in this population of 1.4 billion people provide both important and varied traditions and customs. For example, on any given day at the Forbidden City in Beijing, Chinese people travel from all over the country to this historic site and many wear their traditional clothing or headwear to demonstrate their pride and group membership. It is quite an experience!

So we can't say that all Chinese people are the same. China is a multinational nation. Besides ethnicities, China can also be broken into 23 provinces (e.g., Yunnan, Hubei, Liaoning), 4 municipalities (Beijing, Tianjin, Shanghai, Chongqing), 5 autonomous regions (Guangxi, Inner Mongolia, Tibet, Ningxia, Xinjiang), and 2 special administrative regions (Hong Kong and Macau). North, south, east, west, each region or even city will display different characteristics (Travel China Guide, n.d.).

How can you possibly define an entire people group? If you use the term "Asian American," does that apply to being Korean? Japanese? Indonesian? Thai? According to Geert Hofstede's work (which we will talk about in Chapter 4), we can generalize large groups of people based upon the central tendencies of the cultural dimensions that apply to those groups. Asian cultures, in general, tend to be based upon a collective rather than individual unit. So we could say, "People from Asian cultures tend to. . . ." However, we cannot overgeneralize to *all* members of the many cultures and subcultures, let alone individuals, within any group (nation, country, etc.).

In the past, anthropologists had traditionally focused on the cultural variety of subgroups *within* a given society. Today, anthropologists examine the subgroups and their cultures in order to understand the larger society. In other words, it is the *groups* that comprise a society and not the society that comprises the groups. Perhaps a vivid example is needed.

Individual Cultural Identity

Remember in Chapter 1 we talked about Marshall Singer's stimulating perspective on culture—that we are culturally unique? It is worth repeating here:

> Each individual in this world is a member of a unique collection of groups. No two humans share only and exactly the same group memberships, or exactly the same ranking of the importance, to themselves, of the group membership they do share. Thus, each person must be culturally unique.
>
> (Singer, 1987, p. 3)

Let us look at a creative way for understanding cultural identity. Take a few moments to ponder Singer's analogy of culture via a cake metaphor. What do you think about his idea below and how do you make sense of this in light of your own understanding of culture?

> A chocolate cake is different than a fruit cake, yet they are both cake. They have more in common with each other than either does to a chocolate candy bar. But that doesn't distract from the fact that the chocolate in the cake and the chocolate in the candy bar are much more similar to each other than they are to any of the other ingredients of either the cake or candy bar.
>
> (Singer, 1987, p. 2)

This analogy shows us that we need look past our initial perceptions and experience things on a deeper level. At first glance, one might think we have more in common with someone who outwardly looks like us (the chocolate cake to the chocolate candy bar), but, upon closer inspection, we turn out to have more in common with those who do not look just like us (the chocolate cake to the fruitcake). You choose the dimension—regardless of the form of the confectioner's delight (or our culture) we usually have a few "ingredients" that make us very similar to that person. We can be much more similar to individuals outside of our culture because we have one part of us, whether it be an interest, belief, etc., that makes us so close. When discussing this in class,

I recall the story of a male student of mine (from the United States) who was working at the same summer internship with a female student (from India). He commented that they were different genders, came from different geographical parts of the world, had different backgrounds and beliefs, and looked different. However, because of their hard work and push to get the coveted job offer at the end of the summer, they became good friends over some common interests and life situations. While they were from different "categories," they shared a similar "ingredient" that made them become friends.

On the contrary, here is a situation that did not go well—a friend of mine asked for advice in the hope that he could gently bring up an issue of concern to his boss. He worked in a small insurance company that prided itself on hiring people from a variety of backgrounds. As the general manager, he was in charge of handling the day-to-day issues that came up with both the company and the employees. He had a good rapport with his direct reports and they respected and admired him. So when this incident happened, they asked him to let the boss know that, while he meant well, he was way off. You see, the boss wanted to get to know his employees better and to help them feel included, so he arranged for a *Cinco de Mayo* celebration. Good music, good food, good fun. Right? Well . . . actually . . . no! What he did not realize was that, while his staff was Hispanic, they were from different countries including Puerto Rico, Guatemala, and the Dominican Republic. While from his perspective the boss was trying to be considerate, he actually was minimizing the fact that there were differences among these groups—and, he wasn't aware that *Cinco de Mayo*—a national holiday—is celebrated by people from Mexico!

Summary

At the beginning of this chapter you were asked to reflect on "Who am I?" Now that you have read through this chapter with multiple explanations, write down all of the things that identify you—roles, relationships, occupations, status, etc. What are the ones that are most important to you? Which identity in particular has shaped your individual identity? Which has shaped your group-membership identity? What are the values and beliefs held by this primary group? What are your values and beliefs? Do these differ from your primary group? Now that you have an idea about who you are, what might this say to you as a global leader? Being able to articulate something about our individual nature is extremely helpful in placing ourselves where we are at in the world. The more we know about ourselves, the more equipped we are to learn about others.

There are many forms of identity and we have talked about them—personal, family, and social. We have talked about primary and situational identities—some can be changed; others cannot. We have talked about the fact that we are influenced by our culture, starting the moment we take our first breath until the moment we take our last. Our self-image is shaped by those with whom we interact during our formative years and beyond; we tend to be comfortable with those who are like us and less comfortable with those who are not like us. Because we tend to be comfortable with the familiar, we find it hard to interact across cultural borders.

Why is this important for business leaders? Knowing about who we are, how we are socialized regarding our identities and how we *negotiate* the meaning of our identities of others will help us on our quest for developing self-awareness, understanding, mindfulness, and competence.

Social psychologist Kurt Lewin has said, "Generally, in every situation, the person seems to know what group he belongs to and to what group he does not belong. He knows more or less clearly where he stands, and this position largely determines his behavior." (Tuleja, 2015, p. 124). Such differences in the way people identify with self and the environment, as we have discussed in this chapter, clearly affect how we interact in the workplace. As global leaders, we must work even harder to understand these particular hidden dimensions of culture in order to be more effective at work and at home, when we are overseas, or in conversation with those whose cultural traditions are much different from our own. Remember, *culture is not value-neutral.* You need not embrace or praise the practices of another culture, but you certainly must try to understand them.

Notes

1 Excerpts from "I am not the average American," by Samara Hakim (www.linkedin. com/in/samarahakim; www.facebook.com/TheCultureFactor/). E-mail corres- pondence, October 1, 2015.
2 Libby Lang. E-mail correspondence, March 31, 2015.

References

AncestryDNA. (2016). Lederhosen [Television commercial]. *Headline News.* Retrieved from www.ispot.tv/ad/7c4Y/ancestrydna-lederhosen (accessed July 15, 2016).

Babin, J. (2015, December 3). New area code gets a "meh" from some New Yorkers. *Marketplace.* Retrieved from www.marketplace.org/2015/12/03/life/new-area- code-gets-meh-some-new-yorkers (accessed July 15, 2016).

Central Intelligence Agency. (n.d.). China—The world factbook. Retrieved from www.cia.gov/library/publications/the-world-factbook/geos/ch.html (accessed July 15, 2016).

Cheng, J. (2013). Go deeper: Sorting people. *RACE—the power of an illusion* [PBS documentary]. Retrieved from www.pbs.org/race/000_About/002_02-godeeper. htm (accessed July 15, 2016).

Conley, D. (2003). Ask the experts: What our experts say. *Race—the power of an illusion* [PBS documentary]. Retrieved from www.pbs.org/race/000_About/002_04- experts-03-02.htm (accessed July 15, 2016).

Cortés, C. E. (Ed.). (2013). *Multicultural America: A multimedia encyclopedia* (Vol. 1, pp. 88–90). Los Angeles, CA: SAGE.

Demby, G. (2013, January 31). That cute Cheerios ad with the interracial family is back. *NPR.* Retrieved from www.npr.org/sections/codeswitch/2014/01/30/268930004/ that-cute-cheerios-ad-with-the-interracial-family-is-back (accessed July 15, 2016).

DeNavas-Walt, C., & Proctor, Bernadette D. (2015). *Income and poverty in the United States: 2014* (U.S. Census Bureau Current Population Reports, 60–252). Washington, DC: U.S. Government Printing Office.

dictionary.com (n.d.). Nation. Retrieved from www.dictionary.com/browse/nation (accessed August 1, 2016).

Diffen LLC. (n.d.). Ethnicity vs. race. Retrieved from www.diffen.com/difference/Ethnicity_vs_Race (accessed July 15, 2016).

Fernandez, S. (2013, August 7). Hispanic vs. Latino: What's the difference? *Hispanic Houston.* Retrieved from http://hispanichouston.com/hispanic-vs-latino-whats-the-difference/ (accessed August 1, 2016).

Fredrickson, George M. (2013). *Race—the power of an illusion* [PBS documentary]. Background readings. Retrieved from www.pbs.org/race/000_About/002_04-background-01-x.htm (accessed August 1, 2016).

Goffman, E. (1959). *The presentation of self in everyday life.* Garden City, NY: Double-day–Anchor.

Gonzales-Barrera, A., & Lopez, M. H. (2015, June 15). Is being Hispanic a matter of race, ethnicity or both? Pew Research Center. Retrieved from www.pewresearch.org/fact-tank/2015/06/15/is-being-hispanic-a-matter-of-race-ethnicity-or-both/ (accessed August 1, 2016).

Gudykunst, W. B., & Kim, Y. Y. (1992). *Communicating with strangers: An approach to intercultural communication* (2nd edn.). New York, NY: McGraw-Hill.

Gudykunst, W. B., & Shapiro, R. B. (1996). Communication in everyday interpersonal and intergroup encounters. *International Journal of Intercultural Relations, 20*(1), 19–45.

Harvard Magazine. (2008, May to June). Race in a genetic world. *John Harvard's Journal.* Retrieved from http://harvardmagazine.com/2008/05/race-in-a-genetic-world-html# (accessed July 15, 2016).

Krogstad, Jens M., & Cohn, D'Vera. (2014, March 14). U.S. Census looking at big changes in how it asks about race and ethnicity. Pew Research Center. Retrieved from www.pewresearch.org/fact-tank/2014/03/14/u-s-census-looking-at-big-changes-in-how-it-asks-about-race-and-ethnicity/ (accessed August 1, 2016).

Lee, J. (2014, February 5). Coca-Cola Super Bowl ad: Bilingual girls explain meaning. *USA Today.* Retrieved from www.usatoday.com/story/news/nation-now/2014/02/05/coca-cola-super-bowl-ad-america/5224595/ (accessed August 1, 2016).

O'Connor, P. T., & Kellerman, S. (2009, June 1). Why is the human race called a race? Grammarphobia. Retrieved from www.grammarphobia.com/blog/2009/06/why-is-the-human-race-called-a-race.html (accessed August 2, 2016).

Poniewozik, James. (2014, February 2). Coca-Cola's "It's beautiful" Super Bowl ad brings out some ugly Americans. Retrieved from http://time.com/3773/coca-colas-its-beautiful-super-bowl-ad-brings-out-some-ugly-americans/ (accessed August 1, 2016).

Singer, M. R. (1987). *Intercultural communication: A perceptual approach* (p. 2). Englewood Cliffs, NJ: Prentice-Hall.

Swann, W. B., & Read, S. J. (1981). Self-verification processes: How we sustain our self-conceptions. *Journal of Experimental Social Psychology, 17*(4), 351–72.

Ting-Toomey, S. (1993). Communication resourcefulness: An identity-negotiation perspective. In R. Wiseman, & J. Koester (Eds.), *Intercultural communication competence* (pp. 72–111). Newbury Park, CA: SAGE.

Ting-Toomey, S. (1999). *Communicating across cultures.* New York, NY: Guilford Press.

Ting-Toomey, S. (2005). Identity negotiation theory: Crossing cultural boundaries. In W. B. Gudykunst (Ed.), *Theorizing about intercultural communication* (p. 217). Newbury Park, CA: SAGE.

Travel China Guide (n.d.). Map of China provinces & cities. Retrieved from www. travelchinaguide.com/map/china_map.htm (accessed August 2, 2016).

Tuleja, E. A. (2015). *Intercultural communication for business* (p. 124). Indianapolis, IN: GlobeComm Publishing.

U.S. Census Bureau: FAQs (n.d.). How are census data used? Retrieved from https:// ask.census.gov/faq.php?id=5000&faqId=979 (accessed August 2, 2016).

U.S. Census Bureau. (2013). Race: About. Retrieved from www.census.gov/topics/ population/race/about.html (accessed August 1, 2016).

Vygotsky, L. S. (1978). *Mind in society: The development of higher psychological processes.* Cambridge, MA: Harvard University Press.

Wiki South America. (2016). Culture of Brazil. Retrieved from https://southamerica258. wikispaces.com/Brazil+Culture (accessed August 1, 2016).

Case 3

Cheerios Commercial

Thirty Seconds that Caused 30 Days of Controversy[1]

Abstract

General Mills' Cheerios commercial in 2013 depicted a biracial family that subtly reinforced negative stereotypes of the African-American population. Through this commercial, ethnocentrism, racial salience, and minimization of differences were portrayed. General Mills can learn to be culturally intelligent by developing knowledge of the African-American culture, being mindful of the differences between the African-American culture and the larger American culture, and implementing cross-cultural skills.

Introduction

On May 27, 2013, Cheerios premiered a new commercial on national television. At a kitchen table, an adorably curious little girl asks her mother if Cheerios are really as good for the heart as her father told her. Her mother responds that Cheerios have whole-grain oats that positively contribute to heart health. The little girl smiles and runs out of the kitchen. Then, later that same afternoon, the daughter's father is seen taking a nap on the couch. As he wakes up, Cheerios fall to the carpet. The daughter had placed a handful of Cheerios on her father's heart. The commercial ends with the word "LOVE" displayed on the screen.

The following day, the commercial appeared on Cheerios' YouTube page. Within days of airing, comments filled the Cheerios YouTube page expressing outrage about the actors and content of the commercial. The mother was Caucasian. The father was African-American and the daughter was biracial. Instantly, Cheerios found itself at the center of a controversy, with newsrooms, bloggers, the actors themselves, and the Internet community weighing in at overwhelming numbers (Goyette, 2013b). The comments were divided between strong support and firm opposition. The disapproval of the commercial did not come from Caucasians only; members of the African-American community were also displeased.

The controversy is difficult to understand because of the variety of interpretations of the commercial. Cheerios thought it created an ordinary scene with a family interested in heart health, but racial undertones played a key role in the commercial's reception with audiences. The racial nuances shown through the interactions of the family highlighted the complex history between Caucasians and African-Americans. This case discussed how Cheerios' lack of cultural sensitivity and historical knowledge could be interpreted as inattentive to the African-American community. The case will do so by first discussing the company profile, changing demographics in the United States, cultural history of the African-American population, and racial stereotypes in advertisements. It then reviews the commercial and subsequent controversy, concluding with a brief evaluation.

Company Profile

General Mills

General Mills Inc. was founded by Illinois Congressman Robert Smith in 1856. It is headquartered in Golden Valley, Minnesota. The corporation is primarily concerned with food products. General Mills sells products in over 100 countries, with offices or manufacturing facilities in more than 30 countries. Global net sales for General Mills were $17.8 billion in fiscal year 2013 (General Mills, n.d.).

General Mills' sales are categorized into three primary business segments: (1) U.S. Retail, (2) International, and (3) Convenience Stores & Foodservice. U.S. Retail is divided into seven business segments, the largest of which being Big G Cereal, which includes all of General Mills' most iconic cereal brands. One of those brands is Cheerios. Big G Cereal accounts for 22 percent of U.S. Retail's net sales in the fiscal year of 2013.

Cheerios

Cheerios is a brand of breakfast cereal manufactured by General Mills and was introduced on May 1, 1941 as "CheeriOats" (Banken, 2013). The name was changed to Cheerios in 1945 (Cheerios, n.d.). Cheerios targets women and consumers in their forties and is a family brand—the women that the company targets are making the purchasing decisions for the household (Howard, 2003). Cheerios has expanded to include 13 variants of the oat-bran cereal. Almost half a million cases of cereal are produced and shipped across the United States every week (Banken, 2013).

Changing U.S. Demographics and Target Markets

The changing demographics in the United States since the advent of Cheerios in the 1940s is one that greatly affects the amount of product sold and indicates which consumers are more likely to buy certain products over others, especially when it comes to how those products are advertised (Nielsen, 2012).

In 2012, the number of African-Americans neared 43 million, which represents about 13.7 percent of the U.S. population. "Since 2000, the total U.S. population only increased by 11.3 percent, while the [African-American] population increased by 17.9 percent, a rate that is 1.6 times greater than overall growth." (Nielsen, 2012). Generally, African-Americans make shopping trips more often, but this greater frequency of shopping is coupled with less spending during each trip and making smaller purchases based on short-term needs and not on deal availability. Brand-name products are, in total, 82 percent of African-American households' purchases, while only 31 percent of their purchases are private labels (Milwaukee Black Business, 2015). Of African-American consumers, 81 percent find that products are more relevant to them that are advertised on African-American media. Seventy-eight percent of African-Americans would prefer to see a higher number of African-American models/actors appearing in advertisements. A little over than half say that, if the advertising positively portrayed African-Americans, they would be inclined to purchase a product. Overall, African-Americans are more likely to exercise their buying power when they are reflected in advertisements (Nielsen, 2012).

Generally, Caucasian consumers are less confident about global brands. "That is, they do not find them to be any more exciting than other brands, and they do not believe their product quality is necessarily higher." (Dimofte et al., 2010, p. 84). Nevertheless, Caucasian consumers do agree that global brands possess higher social status. Although the attitudes and perceptions of Caucasians tend to be less optimistic than those of consumers that are minorities, they still match non-Caucasian spending for global brands. This exemplifies a paradox within the Caucasian consumer community (Dimofte et al., 2010).

The African-American Population

In order to understand the controversy that was stirred up following the Cheerios commercial and how the advert was ultimately inattentive to the African-American community, it is important to offer a brief cultural history of African-Americans, interracial marriage, and current marriage trends.

A Brief Cultural History

African-Americans are descendants of slaves. Slavery was a system that entrenched the superiority of Whites over Blacks. This superiority was based on skin color and other superficial physical characteristics. As such, slavery was a dehumanizing practice that still has lasting effects. After slavery ended, African-Americans found themselves unable to return to their countries of origin as a result of slavery codes and the "uprootedness forced on them by slaveholders" (Ting-Toomey & Chung, 2005, p. 92). With no other options, they were forced to adapt to the dominant culture—a culture that emphasized their inferior status.

Caught between two cultures, African-Americans embrace aspects of both. From the American culture, African-Americans value individualism. For example, African-Americans place the needs of their own nuclear family before the needs of the wider community. From the African culture, people would include a network of important people in addition to their families—extended families of aunts, uncles, cousins, and long-time friends. However, African-Americans value collectivism as well. It is quite common for African-American grandparents to live in the same home as their grandchildren. Both individualism and collectivism are cultural values that make up a person's identity dimension (Tuleja, 2009).

Presently, the relationship between African-Americans and Caucasians has improved but the hierarchy that existed during slavery is still present. African-Americans are still assigned an ethnicity on the basis of their skin tone. "Ethnicity is basically an inheritance wherein members perceive each other as emotionally bounded by a common set of traditions, worldviews, history, heritage, and descent on a psychological and historical level." (Gudykunst, 2005, p. 216). This imputed ethnicity on African-Americans has influenced their social relationships, particularly marriage.

A Brief History of Interracial Marriage

Race relations between Caucasians and African-Americans are difficult to understand because of our complex history. After slavery was abolished, Jim Crow laws continued the discrimination against African-Americans. One of the many restrictions under these laws was that African-Americans and Caucasians could not marry. It was not until the 1960s that interracial marriages were legally recognized and protected. In 1967, the U.S. Supreme Court in the groundbreaking *Loving v. Virginia* decision prohibited anti-miscegenation laws, laws that restricted African-Americans from marrying Caucasians. Now, interracial marriages account for 8.4 percent of U.S. marriages today, or 1 out of 12 marriages (The Associated Press, 2012). Currently, more African-American men marry outside of their race than African-American women. In 2008, 22 percent of African-American men married outside of their race. Comparatively, only 9 percent of African-American women are in interracial marriages, "making them the least likely of any race or gender to marry outside their race and the least likely to get married at all" (Davis & Noll, 2010).

Current Marriage Trends

Despite the change in the law and the rise in interracial marriages, interracial marriages are still only slowly gaining social acceptance. The assumptions of deep racial differences further compound the problem because "people believe mixed race to be an anomaly rather than a norm" (Maillard, 2013). Likely, modern advertisements have not reflected the changing racial makeup of marriages in the United States due to this common misconception.

In the African-American community, the disproportionate number of men marrying outside their race has generated a backlash by African-American women. Some African-American women resent Caucasian women, seeing them as "staking claim to a 'good black man'" when already "there is not enough of them" (Goyette, 2013a). On the same note, the dwindling numbers of eligible African-American men has drastically decreased the number of married African-American women, since African-American women are the least likely to marry outside their race.

Racial Stereotypes in Advertisements

When it comes to advertising, commercials have reinforced gender and ethnic stereotypes rather than attempted to accurately reflect African-American culture. Until the 1960s, commercials overwhelmingly employed only Caucasian actors. After this, advertisers began creating commercials depicting more racial diversity, "but nearly always in an understated, somewhat subtle manner" (O'Barr, 2010). The 1980s television sitcom, the Cosby Show, is an example of television embracing a broader view of an African-American family but there are countless more negative depictions that outweigh this view.

African-American actors have had to navigate an industry dominated by Caucasians who have narrowly defined their roles. Since African-Americans are usually portrayed one-dimensionally, television stereotypes can "reinforce widely held notions about black sexual prowess, criminality, and laziness" (Wilkerson, 1993). African-American men are usually portrayed as the side-kick to a Caucasian friend, the comedic relief, the athlete, the highly sexualized womanizer, the absent father, or, perhaps the most damaging, the drug-dealing criminal and gangster (Smith & Darron, 2013). Even when African-American men are shown in a positive light, it is usually under the "theme of protecting whiteness and its virtuous subthemes of justice and freedom" (Smith & Darron, 2013). With the control of the industry still in the hands of Caucasian executives, it is difficult to show the spectrum of the African-American experience. Despite the increase in African-Americans shown on television, subtle racial stereotypes still persist.

On the other hand, Caucasian women are often portrayed as submissive and demure. They are also shown as having a higher socioeconomic status than their minority counterparts. Caucasian women are shown to be highly engaging parents, taking an active interest and role in their children's lives.

The Controversy

A Timeline and Key Facts

Taking the above discussion regarding demographics, culture, and stereotypes in advertising, we can now turn to the controversy ignited by the Cheerios commercial. Below is a timeline of key events between May 27, 2013 and July 14, 2013.

May 27, 2013: Cheerios aired a commercial with a Caucasian mother, an African-American father, and a mixed-race daughter. In the commercial, the mother responded to the daughter's question that indeed Cheerios are good for the heart as her father had told her previously. In the next scene, the father wakes up from a nap in the middle of the afternoon with a pile of Cheerios over his heart.

May 28, 2013: The Cheerios YouTube channel uploaded the commercial produced by the advertising company Saatchi & Saatchi. The video received over 4.1 million views. The comments were so racially charged that Cheerios decided to disable the comments section on the video.

In the days after the video was uploaded to YouTube, the video received a range of reactions from support to racist statements about the interracial family. The controversy received news coverage in the *Huffington Post*, *The New York Times*, and *Slate*.

June 2013: Executive Vice-President of Marketing for Cheerios Camille Gibson issued the following response to the controversial advertisement: "Consumers have responded positively to our new Cheerios ad. There are many kinds of families, and Cheerios celebrates them all. Ultimately we were trying to portray an American family, and there are lots of multicultural families in America today." (Stump, 2013).

July 14, 2013: Many parodies of the video appeared on YouTube. The-FineBros YouTube Channel uploaded a video featuring reactions from children to the controversial video. The video received over 3.82 million views and over 40,000 comments (Berman, 2013).

Summary

Television is ubiquitous. In 30 seconds, commercials capture our attention and advertisers hope to influence our buying behaviors. The subtle racial undertones in the way the family was portrayed struck a chord with viewers. Viewers had strong initial reactions that sparked a deeper national conversation about interracial couples and biracial children on television. In a precarious position, the widely negative responses put the impetus on Cheerios to evaluate the message of the commercial and respond accordingly.

The Controversy

Reevaluating Cheerios' Decision

Cheerios is an iconic brand. In order to maintain African-American consumers, Cheerios needs to portray African-Americans positively. To do so, Cheerios must increase awareness of African-American history and reflect that awareness in advertisements. It appears that Cheerios created a commercial without understanding the cultural dynamics of portraying an interracial couple. The difficulty with this case is that on the outside it appeared that Cheerios was being progressive and culturally sensitive by depicting an interracial marriage. However, Cheerios was actually subtlety perpetuating negative stereotypes by the way they portrayed this young girl's African-American father. This in turn angered many consumers who voiced their opinions in the YouTube comments section of the commercial.

After disabling the YouTube comment section and reflecting on the controversy, Cheerios' Executive Vice-President of Marketing Ms. Camille Gibson had to issue a response. Ms. Gibson had to synthesize the competing perspectives from viewers and construct a statement that reflected Cheerios' support or apologies for the misstep. Before Ms. Gibson made her statement, what were some of the considerations she factored in when meeting with Cheerios executives? In attempts to make a statement that reflects cultural sensitivity, Ms. Gibson should have taken into account the following questions:

Discussion Questions

1   What was your initial reaction after seeing the commercial and how Cheerios portrayed the new American family?
2   What were some of the issues with Cheerios' response to consumer reaction given that Cheerios disabled the YouTube comment section, but continued to air the commercial?
3   How does the complicated history between African-Americans and Caucasians in the United States impact the family portrayed in the commercial?
4   Was there an alternative to Cheerios' decision to dismantle the comments section of its YouTube page after racist comments appeared?
5   How does the interaction between the actors in the commercial relate to gender and ethnic stereotypes?
6   In the future, what can Cheerios do to increase cultural intelligence and reflect this knowledge in their advertisements?
7   People were upset with the portrayal of the father's role in the commercial. Why?

Note

1 Authors: Carmen Wu, Lauren Lymen, Alex De La Flor, and Elizabeth Tuleja (Ed.).

References

Banken, Coco. (2013, August 5). 5 Things you didn't know about Cheerios. Taste of General Mills, 2013. Retrieved from www.blog.generalmills.com/2013/08/5-things-you-didnt-know-about-cheerios/ (accessed October 10, 2013).

Berman, Jillian. (2013, June 5). Cheerios exec on ad featuring mixed race couple: We were reflecting an American family. *The Huffington Post*. Retrieved from www. huffingtonpost.com/2013/06/05/cheerios-ad-mixed-race-couple_n_3390520. html (accessed October 10, 2013).

Cheerios. (n.d.). What's the story behind Cheerios? Retrieved from www.cheerios. com/Articles/Whats-the-story-behind-Cheerios (accessed August 1, 2016).

Davis, Linsey and Noll, Eric. (2010, June 4). Interracial marriage more common than ever, but Blacks still lag. *ABC News*. Retrieved from http://abcnews.go.com/WN/Media/black-women-marry-interracial-marriage-common/story?id=10830719 (accessed October 9, 2013).

Dimofte, C. V., Johansson, J. K., & Bagozzi, R. P. (2010). Global brands in the United States: How consumer ethnicity mediates the global brand effect. *Journal of International Marketing*, *18*(3), 81–106.

General Mills. (n.d.). Company Overview. Retrieved from www.generalmills.com/en/Company/Overview (accessed August 1, 2016).

Goyette, B. (2013a, May 15). Cheerios commercial featuring mixed race family gets racist backlash. *The Huffington Post*. Retrieved from www.huffingtonpost.com/2013/05/31/cheerios-commercial-racist-backlash_n_3363507.html (accessed August 1, 2013).

Goyette, Braden. (2013b, May 31). Cheerios commercial featuring mixed race family gets racist backlash (Video). *The Huffington Post*. Retrieved from www. huffingtonpost.com/2013/05/31/cheerios-commercial-racist-backlash_n_3363507. html (accessed October 10, 2013).

Gudykunst, W. B. (2005). *Theorizing about intercultural communication*. Thousand Oaks, CA: SAGE.

Howard, T. (2003, May 12). Cheerios ads turn trucks into sweethearts. Retrieved from http://usatoday30.usatoday.com/money/advertising/adtrack/2003-05-11-cheerios_x.htm (accessed October 10, 2013).

Maillard, Kevin Noble. (2013, June 27). The myth of rarity. *The New York Times*. Retrieved from www.nytimes.com/roomfordebate/2013/06/13/is-interracial-marriage-still-scandalous/interracial-couples-are-still-seen-as-rare (accessed October 10, 2013).

Milwaukee Black Business. (2015, March 3). The power of the Black consumer: Why African-American spending is still growing in 2015. Retrieved from www. mkeblackbusiness.com/the-power-of-the-black-consumer-why-african-american-spending-is-still-growing-in-2015/ (accessed October 10, 2013).

Nielsen. (2012, September 21). *African-Americans still vital and growing in the U.S.* Report. Retrieved from www.nielsen.com/us/en/insights/news/2012/report-african-americans-still-vital-and-growing-in-the-us.html (accessed October 10, 2013).

O'Barr, W. M. (2010). The rise and fall of the TV commercial. *Advertising & Society Review*, *11*(2). Advertising Educational Foundation. Retrieved from Project MUSE database: http://muse.jhu.edu/journals/advertising_and_society_review/v011/11. 2.o-barr.html (accessed October 9, 2013).

Smith, P. D., Darron, T. (2013, March 14). Images of Black males in popular media. *The Huffington Post*. Retrieved from www.huffingtonpost.com/darron-t-smith-phd/black-men-media_b_2844990.html (accessed October 9, 2013).

Stump, Scott. (2013, June 3). Cheerios ad with mixed-race family draws racist responses. *Today News*. Retrieved from www.today.com/news/cheerios-ad-mixed-race-family-draws-racist-responses-6C10169988 (accessed October 10, 2013).

The Associated Press. (2012, February 16). *Interracial marriages in the U.S. hit all-time high 4.8 million. NY Daily News.* Retrieved from www.nydailynews.com/life-style/interracial-marriages-u-s-hit-all-time-high-4-8-million-article-1.1023643 (accessed August 3, 2016).

Ting-Toomey, Stella, & Chung, Leeva C. (2005). *Keys to understanding cultural and ethnic identities. Understanding intercultural communication* (pp. 85–102). Los Angeles, CA: Roxbury.

Tuleja, Elizabeth. (2009). *Intercultural communication for business* (pp. 1–22). Mason, OH: South-Western.

Wilkerson, Isabel. (1993, August 15). Television; Black life on TV: Realism or stereotypes? *The New York Times.* Retrieved from www.nytimes.com/1993/08/15/arts/television-black-life-on-tv-realism-or-stereotypes.html?pagewanted=all (accessed October 9, 2013).

Part 3

Concepts of Intercultural Communication

4 Cultural Frameworks and Foundations

The nature of management skills is such that they are culturally specific: a management technique or philosophy that is appropriate in one national culture is not necessarily appropriate in another.

(Hofstede, 1984, p. 81)

Figure 4.1 Moroccan Slippers, Tangiers, Morocco

(*Source*: Author.)

Chapter Overview

Chapter 4, Cultural Frameworks and Foundations, examines the questions: How do you measure culture? What is the science behind it? Is not generalizing an entire culture sophisticated stereotyping? These are the key questions we will address in Chapter 4 (Figure 4.1).

Learning Objective

All leaders need the proof that what they espouse is credible. This chapter investigates the theory behind cultural dimensions and looks at how central tendencies of a nation can be used as a starting point in order to understand difference. Dutch social psychologist and interculturalist Geert Hofstede is famous for his initial 1970s study on workplace values that shed light into such cultural tendencies as identity, power, gender roles, dealing with uncertainty, pragmatism, and indulgence.

Key Takeaways

— Cultures can be measure based upon group tendencies.
— The field of intercultural communication has robust scientific evidence to support its claims.
— Values are part of human existence, and are consistent and stable over time.

Leadership Applications

— Leaders who know that the principles they follow are backed by strong validity and reliability can engage difference with confidence.
— It is important to see differences in order to understand how to react in different situations.

Introduction

In this chapter we will examine specific frameworks of culture known as "cultural dimensions" by discussing their origins, current debates, and future extrapolations. Cultural dimensions are a means of systematically breaking down cultures into similarities and differences in order to appreciate the natural variations that exist between groups of people that form societies—we can interchange "nation," "nation state," and "country" to signify a society. Based on these contrasting views of how people live in society, this chapter will examine the work of Dutch psychologist Geert Hofstede, whose prolific research has contributed valuable insight into cultural patterns across societies. While Hofstede is not the only social scientist who has studied culture, his groundbreaking work has made its mark on the systematic empirical study of intercultural issues, so we will begin with his work. In later chapters we will discuss other noteworthy researchers.

As we discussed in Chapter 1, culture is a complex concept and has been defined in innumerable ways, depending on the academic or professional context in need of a definition. What would you think if someone defined the concept of culture with a computer metaphor: culture is like the collective programming of the mind. What is your reaction to this statement? Does it intrigue you? Bother you? Or is it a nonissue? These are the ideas we will discuss in this chapter.

Why We Need Cultural Dimensions

When Proctor and Gamble (P&G) attempted to enter the Italian market with the green Swiffer mop, they learned some pretty impressive information about Italian women and their cleaning habits—they have some of the cleanest homes in Europe. On average, it is estimated that Italian women spend 21 hours on cleaning per week as compared to 4 hours by U.S. American women. The weekly routine includes washing kitchen and bathroom floors at least four times a week, along with regular ironing of clothes, even under-garments, and sheets (Ball, 2006). This means they buy lots of cleaning products. With this information, P&G did not do any due diligence by performing focus groups to collect data. They thought they could just sweep it under the rug. Italian women would love the Swiffer Wet Mop because it would cut down on the amount of time spent cleaning. However, the product failed miserably, because the P&G brand management team failed to understand the reasons *why* Italian women preferred to clean their way.

Convenience and saving time are not important to Italian women—strong detergents and fastidiousness are. Women needed to be convinced that a spray coming out of a plastic mop would be as strong as putting "elbow grease" into scrubbing floors by hand with a sturdy bucket at their side. While the value of "quick and easy" products is appreciated by U.S. American women, Italian women perceived this as cheating. They preferred to do things the old-fashioned way. Labor-saving devices such as washing machines and dish-washers did not gain popularity in Italy as they did in other countries until the 1960s, because after World War II Italy remained one of the poorer countries (Ball, 2006). Even today, young women in the workplace prefer—and take great pride—in meticulous attention to the cleanliness of their homes. At the time of this product flop (2006), it was estimated that only 30 percent of households had a dishwasher because women were convinced that these machines could not clean as well as they could (Ball, 2006).

We can draw important cultural lessons from this failure by examining *what* happened in relation to *why*. This is where the use of cultural dimensions—showing differences and similarities of cultures is useful. If we compare the United States with Italy, U.S. Americans tend to be *fixed* in nature since they generally prefer to follow schedules and strictly manage their time. Getting things done quickly and efficiently are valued as good, whereas taking too much time to complete a task (such as hand scrubbing a kitchen floor four times a week) is a poor use of time management—after all, you could spend your time better on something else. On the other hand, Italians prefer a *fluid* orientation, which means a looser management of their time—rather than do, they prefer to be. Things get done and, when they are done, the amount of time spent and the thoroughness dedicated to a task is considered worthwhile. Had P&G spent some time in due diligence trying to understand the *why* behind the *what* of cultural values, they could have saved time, money, and lost productivity. *This* is why we need to understand cultural dimensions, which are based upon human values.

Understanding Human Values

Every society has values and value systems. A value is an enduring belief that one way of existence (thinking, believing, doing) is better than another. A value system is the composite of principles and rules that people in a society learn in order to help choose how to interact and navigate through life. This is how the early 20th-century psychologist Milton Rokeach described the value concept (Rokeach, 1973). Values are made up of cognitive, affective, and behavioral aspects and help guide humans in preferring one behavior over another. We make choices—one thing over another—so there is a constant comparing of opposites. We learn these values at an early age, implicitly taught by those who raise us and influence our early development, which have a tremendous impact on us. "Values can serve as standards that guide our choices, beliefs, attitudes, and actions" (De Mooij, 2014, p. 54). In the hierarchy of values and attitudes, values are the stable, enduring guides related to social attitudes and beliefs (Inglehart, 1990); attitudes are oriented toward situational contexts. Within our value systems we have value orientations which can be rank-ordered on a continuum. For example, democracy, freedom, fairness, achievement, cooperation, and caring are values, and the degree to which we place these on a continuum—from high to low—demonstrates one's orientation. And such values are shaped by one's culture, which has a tremendous impact on both collective and individual values, attitudes, beliefs, and behaviors.

Cultural Dimensions 101

Geert Hofstede, a prominent researcher and brilliant statistician, described culture as the collective programming of our mind. He explained that norms, the accepted and expected ways of living, are formed from within the collective group interactions of people and subsequently influence us in ways that we are not even aware. In his 1980 book, *Culture's consequences* (Hofstede, 1980), Hofstede advanced the idea that "cultural dimensions" are aspects of culture that can be measured against other cultures. He used continua to contrast differences in order to demonstrate how a particular culture could be more or less of any particular dimension—for example, some cultures like the United States generally tend to be more individualist in their social makeup.

Individualist and collectivist are social dimensions (not political) that mean the degree to which people will integrate into their primary groups (family and extended family). In individualist societies, people will have a looser connection usually only with immediate family, as well as the expectation for independence from the family once one becomes an adult. In collectivist societies, people will be tightly connected to their extended family from birth through death.

In the late 1960s and into the early 1970s, Hofstede performed what was the most comprehensive study at that time, regarding how culture influences values in the workplace. Hofstede's concept of analyzing survey data at the national (country) level that quantified distinct cultural differences started with his landmark analysis of workplace values in subsidiaries at IBM across the world. He himself describes his foray into this type of research as almost an accident, when he all-of-a-sudden found himself in the possession of an enormous amount of data that had been collected from 100,000 surveys from over 50 countries. As he began to analyze the data, he found that responses to the surveys demonstrated that there were definite national trends, with the majority of the population being at one end or the other along bi-polar continua. This resulted in the discovery of correlation of information at the country level, which was very different than when analyzed at the individual level. It is from there that he fashioned his theory of identifying cultural differences among nations based on a scale from 0 (low) to 100 (high). He describes his findings:

> So it seemed that employees of this multinational enterprise . . . could serve for identifying differences in *national* value systems. The reason is that from one country to another they represented almost perfectly matched samples: they were similar in all respects except nationality, which made the effect of national differences in their answers stand out unusually clearly.
>
> (Hofstede, 2011, p. 6)

Within these distinct patterns of both similarities and differences among societies, definite trends emerged by grouping certain phenomena together. This was all based upon statistical relationships. Originally, there were four distinct dimensions: power distance, uncertainty avoidance, individualism/collectivism, and masculinity/femininity, with a fifth dimension of long-term/short-term orientation to time added by Canadian psychologist Michael Harris Bond. Professor Bond was living and researching in Hong Kong, and had produced a separate study on the Confucian Values Survey (Bond, 1988; Hofstede & Bond, 1988). Today there is a sixth dimension, indulgence/restraint (Hofstede & Hofstede, 2010; Minkov, 2011).

Mental Models

Before we talk about the six dimensions, let us examine why Hofstede uses the computer metaphor of programming the mind. Figure 4.2 shows the different

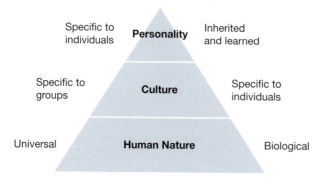

Figure 4.2 Three Levels of Mental Programming

(*Source*: Hofstede & Hofstede, 2010, p. 6.)

levels of mental programming. At the deepest level (the base of the pyramid) is human nature. Because of human nature, there are many behaviors and understandings that all people share even though they come from different cultures. Next is the middle level of culture which is based on common experiences that we share with a particular group of fellow human beings. Cultural values, attitudes, and assumptions about proper behavior give us something in common with a definable group of others, but not with all of them—this could be a national culture or a work culture. At the top, or the shallowest level, is personality. Our personality is based upon genetic makeup and personal experiences that make each of us unique. Because of personality, each of us has many behaviors and understandings that are quite different from those of others, even though they come from the same culture.

This model reminds us that culture, while a key influence in all aspects of our lives, may not always account for every difference. Sometimes the confusion or frustration that we experience could be simply a personality trait. For now, we will distinguish among cultural dimensions by using the continua that demonstrate opposing poles of attitude and behavior.

Let us explore Hofstede's premise and how that relates to intercultural communication and global leadership. All people have a tendency toward certain cultural orientations that are subconsciously held and which affect them in their day-to-day interactions. Hofstede defines these orientations as dimensions, which are "an aspect of a culture that can be measured relative to other cultures" (Hofstede & Hofstede, 2010, p. 26). More than four decades later as studies have been expanded there are now six universal categories, or cultural dimensions, which affect how we interact with others who are different from us. These include: expressions of individualism and collectivism; use of power and authority; attitudes toward uncertainty and change; customary roles of masculinity and femininity; perception of short-term and long-term time; and preferences for indulgence and restraint.

Hofstede's Six Culture Dimensions

Power Distance

Power distance relates to how we measure inequality in our society—who are the more powerful members with the authority to make decisions and rules? As a result, people will accept and expect power that is unequal and act accordingly without need for added justification of why (see Table 4.1). Hofstede comments that, while power and inequality are present in all societies, some are more unequal than others and, as a result of being in a low-power position "inequality is endorsed by the followers as much as by the leaders" (Hofstede, 2011, p. 9). This means that a society—or an organization—will function properly only when it is socially stratified: everyone has a place with different rights and responsibilities to be fulfilled for the good of the society (Box 4.1).

Table 4.1 Hofstede's Power Distance

Power distance	*High power distance*	*Low power distance*
- *Work* - *Boss* - *Employee* - *Education* - *Family* - *Religion*	• Hierarchy and centralization in business and government • Respect is expected toward authorities • The boss is a benevolent autocrat • Employees told what to do • Governments based on control of votes/change is by force • Education is teacher centered • Parents expect obedience • Elderly are revered and respected • Religions have hierarchy of religious leaders	• Flattening of hierarchy with those in higher positions • Employees are almost equal with bosses • The boss is a democratic leader • Employees can express ideas • Governments based on majority of votes/change is peaceful • Education is student centered • Children expect equality • Elderly are neither revered or respected • Religions have equality of believers
How to Interact	• Recognize leader's authority • Decision-making is based upon position power • You may need to wait for the person at the top to authorize or make a decision before you can act	• People more inclined to work in teams • Decision-making is based upon the boss's leadership skills • Everyone expects to be involved in the decision-making process

(*Source*: Adapted from Hofstede, 1980, pp. 37, 43.)

Box 4.1 "In Hierarchical Tradition"

In hierarchical and traditional societies, these inequalities have existed for centuries and are understood (if not tolerated) by the broad majority of people, usually out of economic and political necessity. The people must accept and obey a political system that controls them, their government, and their economy in a top-down fashion, making power of all sorts less accessible to them.

Source: Wibbeke & McArthur, 2008

Saudi Women Vote

For example, the Saudi government is an absolute monarch, meaning that there is no elected legislature, and this leaves little room for citizens to participate in politics. However, people *can* run for municipal councils, which are popular-elected bodies where council members oversee local projects and approve their budgets. Yet they do not have fiscal authority on how the money is spent (Stancati & al Omran, 2015). This type of control conditions people to accept this centralized authority and, while they may not agree with the rules, they nevertheless must accept it as a way of life. Recognition of power and its status differentials among individuals is expected, rewarded, and reinforced. The Hofstede research plots the Saudi Arabian culture as having a strong power distance (90/100), which determines the importance placed on power structure and how individuals recognize and accept the power/status differences.

An interesting event happened on December 12, 2015. Saudi women were allowed to vote for the first time and even run for local municipal elections. Yet while they were allowed to run for office there were additional restrictions placed on their campaign—because there is strict gender segregation the female candidates were not allowed to interact directly with male voters—instead they had to rely on male proxies, speak behind screens, and use social media (Stancati & al Omran, 2015). While this practice also relates to gender differences (which we will discuss later), combined with power distance there is a strong effect on women's rights in the kingdom. In Saudi Arabia, the following are cultural norms (what is accepted and expected practice) in that women need the approval of a male guardian (father, husband, brother) in order to:

- Marry (or divorce).
- Enroll in a university.
- Obtain a passport or travel abroad.
- Visit a male doctor (must have male relative present) unless an emergency.
- Obtain a driver's license.

To make sense of this culture, it can be compared across other cultures according to the Hofstede model. For example, the United States (40/100) exhibits more egalitarian tendencies, which means that people expect to minimize power structures in favor of emphasizing the equality and status among individuals. This lower power distance means that people see themselves more as equals. There is no question over a woman's autonomy to vote, travel, marry, or divorce.

Applied to business, a low-power distance organization would be what Peter Senge calls the learning organization (Box 4.2). This organization is comprised of a group of people who are free to unleash their creative capabilities and contribute to its betterment. In essence, the freedom to create and learn from one another allows information to flow freely and flattens the hierarchy. When layers of hierarchy are flattened, it takes less time for senior-level leaders to receive information, process, and respond to it. It can also reduce overhead costs to improve profitability. Additionally, low power distance means that subordinates rely on their boss's leadership skills in decision-making, whereas high-power distance subordinates rely on position power.

When I lived in Hong Kong, I remember the frustration of going to the Personnel Department at the university where I was on the faculty in the business school. When I came to ask a basic question, if the director was not there, or busy in a meeting, the assistant could not provide information for me because she was not allowed to take the initiative to do so. I would have to come back at a time when the person in charge could help me. It was my responsibility to make sure I had an official appointment to get my question answered.

Another interesting custom that took much getting used to was purchasing an item in a large department store. Unlike in most Western countries, there were no cash registers by department. You had to make your request to the salesperson in the department where you were shopping, and they would write up a receipt for you to take to the central register in the middle of the store. You would pay there, be given a receipt and then you would go back to the department that was holding your item, give them the receipt, and wait for the clerk to go back to the storeroom where they had put your merchandise for safekeeping. Finally, you received your item after they checked, rechecked,

---

Box 4.2

Learning organizations [are] organizations where people continually expand their capacity to create the results they truly desire, where new and expansive patterns of thinking are nurtured, where collective aspiration is set free, and where people are continually learning to see the whole together.

Source: Senge, 1990

He who is able to conquer others is powerful; he who is able to conquer himself is more powerful—Lao-tzu

Ancient China was ruled by emperors through dynastic control within China. Their power was ascribed and the emperor was considered god-like and exhibited autocratic control. Chinese opera is often used to tell stories of the ancient dynasties and dramatizes the intrigue of the conquests of powerful rulers. Chinese opera (京剧 *Jīngjù*), established during the Tang Dynasty (618–97), is one of the oldest art forms. It combines literature and art with music played on traditional instruments (erhu, gong, and lute), to tell stories of love and loyalty, war and power.

Figure 4.3 Chinese Opera-Power, Beijing

(*Sources*: Photo, Author; AncientMilitary.com, n.d.; Yanchen, 2009.)

took your receipt, and produced another receipt with an official "chop" (stamp) for proof of purchase.

Centralized power is quite different than localized power. For example, London Business School professors Robert Goffee and Gareth Jones believe that leaders are born by flattening the hierarchy between them and their direct reports. Rather than establish social distance, they propose executives know their employees so that they can know what is going on. Accordingly they believe that distance is necessary only for strategic planning and that balance between operational closeness and long-term strategic planning takes effort. When achieved, this flatter hierarchy helps senior executives achieve a flexibility to communicate with their employees and adapt accordingly. In turn, eliminating multiple layers of management creates trust that paves the way for speedier decision-making and the ability to react to crises more quickly (Goffee & Jones, 2006) (Figure 4.3).

Individualism and Collectivism

Individualism and collectivism deal with how we tend to interact with others in individual or collective ways—Do we think in terms of "me" or "we?" Do we have strong ties with our clan, family, or in-group where there is cohesion, loyalty, and respect for members of the group? Or are those ties looser and less defined by expectations that we act for the good of the group

Table 4.2 Hofstede's Individualism—Collectivism

Individualism–collectivism	Individualism	Collectivism
Work Boss Employee Education Family Religion	• Task completion takes priority over relationship • Workers are responsible for their productivity • Boss will praise you for taking charge • Say what you think • You are in charge and should take care of yourself—independence is expected • Education is about learning how to learn • In the classroom, individual opinions are expected • Move out on your own • Do what is best for your self-actualization	• Relationship takes priority over task • Groups are responsible for their productivity • Boss will praise the group for working together • Maintain harmony • You belong to your in-group and are protected in exchange for loyalty and respect • Education is about learning how to do • In the classroom the group generates opinions • Live with family • Do what is best to maintain cohesion and respect for family
How to Interact	• Recognize individual accomplishments • Ask the group's leader for a response • Encourage expression of own ideas • Expect change to happen immediately	• Recognize group's accomplishments • If needing a response, let the group decide and then one person reports back for the group • Respect those who are older and wiser • Introduce change slowly because of long-standing traditions

(*Source*: Adapted from Hofstede, 1980, pp. 67, 73.)

and therefore can act in our own interest first, which means less responsibility for other's well-being and less interpersonal connection beyond family and close friends (see Table 4.2, Figure 4.4 and Box 4.3).

Familismo

An example of collectivism is *familismo,* a core cultural value of Hispanic or Latino people where there is a strong connection and identification to both nuclear and extended families that include aunts, uncles, and cousins, and close family friends. Duty to family, which includes the extended family, requires loyalty and constant interaction. It is best exemplified in the relationship of the compadres, or godparents, who pledge to share a parenting role of the child who is baptized. While this co-parenting role forms a bond between child and

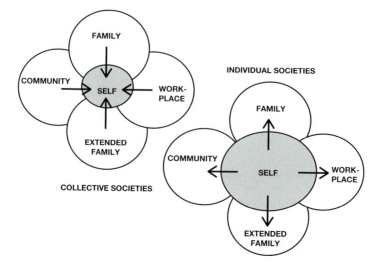

Figure 4.4 Individualism–Collectivism

Box 4.3 "Our Cultures of Origin"

Our cultures of origin—Mexican, Puerto Rican, Salvadoran, Cuban, Colombian, or other Spanish-speaking countries—are rooted in family, in connecting, helping each other become the best we can be, putting our children first, and supporting each other through good times and bad.

Source: López, 1999

---

godparent, it also solidifies the relationship between the parents and god-parents. This practice creates a life-long bond (Sanchez, 2015). Family is everything in this collectivist culture and living close by translates into caring for each other and socializing on a daily basis. Along with this comes the respect and adherence to the traditional roles of the Hispanic–Latino family—a deep sense of family responsibility, close adherence to traditional gender roles, with the father as the respected authority of the family, and sons being allowed to gain independence sooner than daughters (although this is relaxing), and respectful treatment of older adults.

Educational Systems

In terms of education, individualism and collectivism are demonstrated differently. In the United States, there are some U.S. student behaviors that international students may find surprising or that would be considered disrespectful in their country. For example, students may sit in class with their feet on the chair or desk in front of them and may even eat or drink in class.

Students freely interrupt lectures to ask questions or even to raise objections to what is being said. In general, these behaviors do not necessarily denote disrespect unless done in a belligerent or aggressive manner. In fact, one way in which a U.S. student shows respect for their teacher is by being an active participant in class. While every professor has different expectations and limits for their students, they generally expect students to actively participate in class—sometimes the teacher will ask the questions and expect a reply; other times students will join in and make their own query or comment.

This is quite different than in many other places in the world where students know the power distance and requirements for formality in the classroom and therefore give respect to their teachers. Students are expected to deport themselves through active listening and note-taking from the lecture, which is more didactic than transactional. When I taught in Hong Kong I had to learn to adjust my teaching expectations and styles for my students. My typical practice of calling on students (in my mind, inviting them into the learning process) to allow them to demonstrate mastery over the topic, just did not work. I constantly had silent stares that made me wonder if they had prepared for class or I was a bad teacher. With this method I just could not expect to get a response back from individuals. But I observed that, while students would not speak up in class, they were constantly whispering to each other. Were they bored or were they helping each other perhaps with an English vocabulary word? So, rather than single out a student, I put them in small groups with discussion questions. It was their responsibility to select one student to report back for the group. It worked well. The students saw themselves first and foremost as part of the group so to speak out individually would be sharing their point of view versus the group's view. Asian cultures accept and reinforce conformist practices—it is better to conform to the group's expectations than to stand out on your own.

Ubuntu

Another form of collectivism is the African concept of *Ubuntu*. The essence of *Ubuntu* is that humans cannot exist without each other. Translated from the Bantu languages in southern Africa it means, "I exist because you exist." This concept is not limited to South African countries but is practiced throughout Africa, in Tanzania and Uganda, "*Obuntu*" and, in Zimbabwe, "*Unhu.*" It is a way of life that promotes generosity, hospitality, kindness, and self-sacrifice—all ways to build empathy in relationships. Put simply, "A person is a person through other persons," or "I am because of who you are" (Chibba, 2013). Archbishop Desmond Tutu popularized this tribal concept during his anti-apartheid campaign in the 1980s. He explained:

> One of the sayings in our country is Ubuntu—the essence of being human. Ubuntu speaks particularly about the fact that you can't exist as a human being in isolation. It speaks about our interconnectedness. You can't be human all by yourself, and when you have this quality—Ubuntu—you are

known for your generosity. We think of ourselves far too frequently as just individuals, separated from one another, whereas you are connected and what you do affects the whole World. When you do well, it spreads out; it is for the whole of humanity. . . . A person with Ubuntu is open and available to others, affirming of others, does not feel threatened that others are able and good, based from a proper self-assurance that comes from knowing that they belongs in a greater whole and is diminished when others are humiliated or diminished, when others are tortured or oppressed.

(Rich, 2012)

Rice Farming

Another example of collectivism is the practice of rice farming in Asian and South East Asian countries. A recent study in the journal *Science* revealed the differences between rice cultures that seed interdependence and wheat cultures that sow independence (Talhelm et al., 2014). Rice farming is more complex, requiring the cooperation of an entire village because of the complex irrigation system that must be managed and maintained in order to drain water into the paddies. There is constant building, dredging, and draining involved. In turn, this contributes to developing collectivistic tendencies that are passed down from one generation to another. Wheat cultures tend to be more individualistic because there is less dependence on others for water—when it rains, it rains (Kuo, 2014). So if you are a rice farmer and your house is at the bottom of the hill then you had better have good relations with the person who is at the top of the hill and controls the water flow! Or if you live at a higher level and need to borrow a domestic animal from a neighbor below you, if good relationships are maintained then there should be reciprocity. This concept will be elaborated upon in Chapter 7.

Doing and Being Mindsets

In the workplace, an individualistic practice would mean placing task before relationships in terms of wanting to get down to business—we call this doing versus being. Rather than entering into a phone call or business meeting by asking about health or family, you would launch into the issue at hand right away. A colleague who just moved to Qatar found himself in this position. He worked for a software company and was hired to oversee the systems management of a newly formed company. As he was in charge of averting crises by constantly "putting out fires," he was in the habit of calling an employee and immediately asking them to help with an issue. Or, he would walk down the hall and pop his head into someone's office and say, "Hello—it's happened again, I need you to run interference." He eventually realized that he had to ease into the conversation even if it meant exchanging a brief pleasantry. What is interesting is that he was originally from Jordan so he knew about the customs of Middle Eastern countries, but, having lived in the United States for a number of years, he had grown accustomed to efficiency (see Table 4.3).

Table 4.3 Characteristics of Individualism and Collectivism

Individualism	*Collectivism*
Family/Relationships	**Family/Relationships**
• Nuclear family • Set out on own; earn your own living • Speak one's mind (tell honest truth) • Independence	• Extended family • Loyalty to group; earnings to help • Consider effect of honesty on others • Interdependence
Communication	**Communication**
• Meanings are in words • Silence is abnormal • Direct confrontation accepted • Express personal opinions • Freedom to say no	• Meanings are in actions • Silence is normal • Direct confrontation considered rude • Personal opinions do not exist • Must say, "We will think about it"
Work	**Work**
• Act according to self-interest • Task over relationship • Guilt (one's own conscience) • Think in terms of "I" • Self-respect (individual)	• Act according to group's interest • Relationship over task • Shame (group conscience) • Think in terms of "we" • Face (point of view of society)

Uncertainty Avoidance

The next cultural dimension is uncertainty avoidance. Uncertainty is part of life as we simply cannot know the future—we all live with it. But some cultures deal with uncertainty differently than others—should we try to control the future, or should we just "go with the flow" and see what happens? This is also known as control and constraint.

Uncertainty avoidance is about how a society tolerates ambiguity or the degree to which people feel anxiety when they find themselves in unfamiliar or uncertain situations. It is "the extent to which the members of a culture feel threatened by ambiguous or unknown situations and have created beliefs and institutions that try to avoid these" (Hofstede, 2011, p. 6). Normally the highest degree of uncertainty avoidance is found in collective societies because of the need to act interdependently as well as the fact that such societies also have a higher power distance. Hofstede describes it as the extent that a culture programs its members to feel either uncomfortable or comfortable in unstructured situations. Unstructured situations are novel, unknown, surprising, and different than usual. Such cultures try to "minimize the possibility of such situations by strict behavioral codes, laws and rules" (The Hofstede Centre, n.d.a) and do not tolerate deviant opinions from what is expected from those in power. It is important to note that uncertainty avoidance is not about risk—in every culture you find people taking risks whether it be in the stock market, entrepreneurial ventures, or deciding to sell a business. It is about minimizing what might happen when one deviates from the accepted and expected norm (Table 4.4).

Table 4.4 Hofstede's Uncertainty Avoidance

Uncertainty avoidance	Strong (high) avoidance	Weak (low) avoidance
- Work - Boss - Employee - Education - Family - Religion	• Uncertainty is a threat and must be fought • Is suspicious of differences: what is "different is dangerous" • There is a need for clarity and structure • There is an emotional connection to rules even if one doesn't follow them • In education, teachers are still respected if they say they do not know	• Uncertainty is essential in life and it must be accepted and even embraced • Values difference: what is "different is curious" • There is familiarity with disorder and ambiguity • There is blatant reaction to rules • In education, the teacher is the sage with all of the answers
How to Interact	• Be clear with expectations and timelines • Provide clear details • Check back and offer assistance before the deadline	• Be careful of needlessly imposing rules or restrictions • Be willing to ask questions for added input

(*Source*: Adapted from Hofstede & Hofstede, 2010, pp. 125, 134.)

Greek Debt Crisis

We can look at Greece for an example of uncertainty avoidance. Greece was hit hard after the 2008 financial crisis. To make matters worse, in 2009 they announced that they had been understating their deficit figures (Alderman et al., 2015). On the verge of setting off a new international financial crisis, they took a bailout from the European Commission in 2010 and then again in 2012. Of course, with the bailout came austerity measures such as higher taxes, lower pensions, and decreased government funding for social services. However, even though the country was managing to stay afloat by starting to pay off its creditors, Greece was imploding, with its economy shrinking by 25 percent and unemployment rising by 25 percent. In 2015 Greece wanted to renegotiate their bailout loans and months of negotiating ensued, with the newly elected prime minister walking away and calling for a referendum—60 percent of the citizens said no to more austerity measures. The country defaulted on its International Monetary Fund (IMF) payments and was reprimanded for not following the rules (Hartmann, 2015).

We have learned some lessons from Greece—while the government struggles with corruption, it is not so much the spending but insufficient revenue that has caused their problems (Johnston, 2015). Greece has an extremely high level of tax evasion from both the self-employed and upper-middle-class professionals, which has added to its financial collapse. One estimate is that Greece loses up to €20 billion in tax evasion per year (Smith, 2015). In addition to white-collar tax evasion, there is the shadow-market tax evasion, with estimated billions never reported through the underground economy (Transparency International, 2013). Why is this so astounding?

Law professor at the University of Athens, Aristides Hatzis, connects it to the lack of trust ingrained in the Greek psyche dating all the way back to the Ottoman Empire's occupation. Centuries ago, you were patriotic if you eluded taxes, which were considered theft, so citizens fought back. Today people distrust the government as corrupt, inefficient, and unreliable, allowing for many forms of political corruption, including lack of transparency, poor law enforcement, and government impunity. "Normally taxes are considered the price you have to pay for a just state, but this is not accepted by the Greek mentality" (Karnitschnig & Stamouli, 2015, p. 17). Tax evasion is a social norm and a way to fight back against the corrupt government.

Greece has the highest possible score for uncertainty avoidance: 100, which makes for an anxious and stressful approach toward life. Hofstede explains it this way through Greek mythology—it is like the Sword of Damocles hanging over the society (Bird, 2015). In business, a high-uncertainty-avoidance culture (averse to change) means that employees would rather stay with one organization for life, there are many rules and regulations within a centralized system, employees are used to formality, decisions cannot be made individually but rather through consensus, and one needs the approval of a senior official before any decisions or plans can be implemented. On the flip side a low-uncertainty-avoidance culture (embraces change) is open to innovation, more willingness to take risks, can make decisions unilaterally and have more flexibility and creativity in implementing ideas, work atmosphere is informal and relaxed, and rules are flexible.

Harvard business professor George Serafeim explains the uncertainty avoidance of Greece this way:

> all parties agree that the Greek economy will have to become more competitive. Many politicians and commentators mention two critical factors in accomplishing this: increasing innovative capacity and reducing bureaucracy. Both are important, but they are far more difficult to achieve than many understand because they are, to a significant extent, influenced by culture.
>
> (Serafeim, 2015)

Greece needs to embrace ambiguity and come to grips with unstructured situations, volatility, rules, and change (Box 4.4).

According to Prof. Serafeim, there is a correlation between uncertainty avoidance (Hofstede's Index), bureaucracy (World Bank ranking), and innovation (European Innovation Index). Greece scores the highest on both uncertainty avoidance (100) and bureaucracy (61) and lower on innovation (38).

> ## Box 4.4 Harvard Business Professor George Serafeim
>
> Bureaucracy, laws, and rules exert particular influence in Greece because they help make life more structured and less uncertain. In Greece, acquiring construction permits, registering property, and enforcing contracts in courts require vast amounts of paperwork and time. . . . Because of the aversion to risk they are unlikely to invent new products, processes, or business models. This helps to explain why Greece has one of the lowest license and patent revenues from abroad as a percentage of its GDP, as well as one of the lowest contributions from high-tech product exports to its trade balance.
>
> Source: Serafeim, 2015

In its company are Slovenia and Italy. Countries that have low-uncertainty-avoidance and low bureaucracy have high innovation, such as Sweden, Denmark, and the United Kingdom. This enables high levels of scientific research, venture-capital financing, and healthy partnerships between public and private entities. Because of a less bureaucratic government, people spend less time with red tape and more time developing their businesses, which benefits everyone.

Masculinity and Femininity

Masculinity and femininity, like some of the other terminology used by Hofstede (see Table 4.5), seems to be a rather odd way to name the phenomenon of traditional socioemotional roles, but these are based upon the Latinized words for manlike and womanlike (a man can be called feminine and a woman masculine). A "masculine" culture refers to a society that leans toward competition, achievement, and success, which are typically considered masculine roles within traditional society; whereas a "feminine" culture values cooperation and caring. This means that in masculine cultures the emotional gender roles are distinct—they focus on what one should feel having been born as a boy or a girl—boys should be assertive, tough and grow up to be focused on material success; girls are encouraged to focus on the quality of life. So men should deal with facts and women with feelings. In a feminine culture there is more role separation—where men can be can be modest, tender, and focused on the quality of life, and both men and women can deal with facts and figures. Also, religion in masculine societies focuses on God as the father; in feminine societies religion focuses on fellow human beings (10 minutes with, 2014).

How do these role divisions within societies play out in business? In feminine societies you are expected to balance family and work—this is the norm. In masculine societies work takes precedence over family activities. One's work is an acceptable excuse to work long hours or cancel a vacation

Table 4.5 Hofstede's Masculinity–Femininity Dimensions

Masculinity–femininity	Masculine	Feminine
- *Work* - *Boss* - *Employee* - *Education* - *Family* - *Religion*	• Maximum differences in social/emotional roles • Work comes first; family second • Men should be assertive and ambitious; women may be assertive and ambitious • Men deal with facts • Boys never cry and fight back; girls can cry but not fight	• Minimum differences in social/emotional roles • Family comes first; work comes second • Both men and women should be caring • Women deal with feelings • Both boys and girls can cry but never fight
How to Interact	• People probably expect male/female roles to be different • People may have different expectations from male/females in their social roles	• Make sure job descriptions and expectations are nondiscriminatory • Be careful to treat men and women the same • Be careful of sexist language

(*Source*: Adapted from Hofstede, 1997, pp. 96, 103.)

because of important deadlines. This would be less likely in a feminine society—family should not be neglected (Box 4.5).

Nordic Cultures

In countries like Sweden, Norway, and Finland, there is low masculinity, which means that traditional roles are equally distributed between men and women. For example, the *Economist* reports that Sweden has such a strong parental leave policy that 90 percent of fathers use it, because they receive similar benefits as the mother. Back in the 1970s Sweden became the first country in the world to use a gender-neutral paid parental allowance as well as leave, which means that parents can split their time to care for the newborn, all the while receiving 90 percent of their salary for up to 180 days (Storø & Jansen, 2007).

In Norway, the past 30 years have seen men taking a dominant role in childrearing, with a jump in paternity leave skyrocketing from 4 percent to 85 percent. A professor of social work at a university in Oslo said:

> The participation of Norwegian men in child rearing and child care has changed dramatically. This change can be characterized as a movement away from the traditionally distant father, whose main task in the family was to financially support his wife and children, to becoming a father who is actively engaged in the daily lives of his children.
>
> (European Union, n.d.)

Box 4.5 Norwegian Men and Raising Children

Over the past 20 years, the participation of Norwegian men in child rearing and child care has changed dramatically. This change can be characterized as a movement away from the traditionally distant father, whose main task in the family was to financially support his wife and children, to becoming a father who is actively engaged in the daily lives of his children. The young Norwegian man of today is increasingly interested in his children. This entails playing a greater role in their daily care. Since 1993 in Norway, the father has had the right to take a paid six-week leave of absence from work, when his child is born. In the following years, the number of men who have done so has increased from 4 percent to 85 percent. Apparently, Norwegian men have discovered the positive sides of fathering and spending time with their children. Taking part in the child's everyday life is done with pride and joy.

Source: Storø & Jansen, 2007

Because of generous government subsidies, it is easier now for parents to take time off from work without any detrimental effects on their career trajectory—it is expected and employers welcome it. This behavior has become a norm within society.

And, Finland also has strong family and social support for working parents. Leave is broken into three parts, almost as long as one year: maternity leave 18 weeks; parental leave 2 weeks; paternity leave 9 weeks. In addition, all working parents are entitled, by the government, to shorter working hours from the end of the parental leave until the end of the child's second year of school (S. H. for *The Economist*, 2014).

Another way that masculinity and femininity have been described is goal orientation (winning and decisiveness are important in society) and process orientation (process and consensus are important to society) (Smit, 2012). Femininity in Nordic countries can be explained as modesty, equality, and sympathy for the "underdog," as compared to the masculine traits of standing out, competing, and admiring winners. Aligned with femininity is the Law of Jante, which translated roughly means "do not think you are more special than others" (Box 4.6). There are many principles, five of which are:

- You are not to think you are anything special.
- You are not to think you are as good as us.
- You are not to think you are smarter than us.
- You are not to convince yourself that you are better than us.
- You are not to think you know more than us.

You are not to emphasize your success over that of the group—this is antithetical to "bigging up" (British slang) for the outrageous boasting and puffing up of candidates on the famous *Apprentice* show. In the United States, when asked, "What do you do?" people are quite eager to reveal their self-importance; however in Scandinavian and Norwegian countries what you say might break the rule of Jante. For example, a simple five-word sentence, "I run my own business" could be interpreted as, "Do you think you're so good that you don't have to be a regular worker?" (Rohrer, 2013).

Japanese Valentines—a Cross-Cultural Comparison

While this phenomenon of femininity is typical of Nordic countries, which has a definite effect on the workplace, there are other customs that make an interesting impact on social norms. According to Hofstede's research, Japan has one of the highest masculinity rankings in the world. However, when it comes to adopting the Western holiday of Valentine's day, the roles are reversed.

The conception of "Valentine's Day" began as early as ancient Roman fertility rituals and morphed into various practices throughout the Middle Ages to the Renaissance and now into modern times. The 17th-century custom of sending a card eventually found its way to the United States in the 18th century (History.com Staff, 2009).

Today it is estimated that in the United States alone about 1 billion cards are sent each year on Valentine's Day, approximately 35 million boxes of candy are consumed, and roughly 220 million roses are grown for the occasion. Jewelry is

---

Box 4.6 The Law of Jante

Some see the mindset embodied in the Law of Jante as a barrier to entrepreneurial and national economic success, while others see it as a tool that has hedged Scandinavians against failure, preventing them from taking the same economic risks that led much of the Western world to the brink of financial apocalypse beginning in 2008. There was no housing bubble in Sweden, in part because it would seem antithetical for anyone to take on more debt than necessary for essential living, where the chief consideration when contemplating a housing upgrade would be not "How much will the bank lend me?" but "Is an extra bedroom really necessary?" (Of course, Sweden had its own major financial crisis in the early 1990s. But the country got out of it by making the banks pay mightily for their overindulgence and for any bailout money they received from the government. In the end, the Swedish taxpayer lost nothing and the economy rebounded quickly.)

Source: Harress, 2013

entirely another dimension to this holiday! All in all, it has also been estimated that anywhere from $14 to $20 billion are spent annually by U.S. Americans in their pursuit of love. Traditionally, it has been the man's responsibility to express his affection and appreciation for the woman, but, as we know, it really depends on the individuals involved (History.com Staff, 2009).

In Japan, however, Valentine's Day is the day for women to pursue men with gifts of chocolates and, since the 1950s, has become a booming business, with estimates as high as $5 billion in sales for all things Valentine (Hadfield, 2014). It has been said that, since Japan is not traditionally an expressive culture in terms of showing affection or emotion, there needed to be an outlet for women to be able to express their love. (Of course, some will argue that this is a marketing strategy for chocolate companies!) Today we can debate how times have changed, but it is nevertheless an interesting cultural and historical perspective to ponder. So, for women in Japan, it is more complicated than for women in the United States since there are different levels of gift-giving and the *types* of chocolate given. And, depending on what is given, it sends a specific message to the recipient.

Chocolates that are given to a special man are called "*honmei choco,*" which means he is a "prospective winner" and the object of her love interests. Chocolates that are given to co-workers and other nonromantic male friends are the obligation chocolates called "*giri choco.*" As times change, so do the customs and now it is customary for women to exchange gifts with female friends, so this is called "*tomo choco*"—or—"friend chocolates." And, as all traditions advance over time, men are starting to give women chocolates on Valentine's Day, called "*gyaku choco,*" which means "reverse chocolate." But, it is more common for men to reciprocate a month later, on March 14, which is called White Day. Men are expected to reciprocate (with more expensive chocolates), as it is customary within Japanese culture to return favors—a serious social obligation that should never be ignored (Figure 4.5).

Figure 4.5 Japanese Valentine

(*Source*: Fotolia 5713536, © Maria Bell.)

The concept of *"giri"* is an age-old social practice of mutual obligation among the Japanese—you enter into a web of friendship and obligation that continues for a life-time of sharing and reciprocating favors. It is similar to the mutual trust/obligation of the Chinese concept of *"guanxi."*

So, when it comes to masculine or feminine roles during Valentine's Day in Japan, the roles reverse, with women pursuing men during the Day of Love.

Long-Term/Short-Term Orientation

Long-term/short-term orientation refers to how a society values traditions and values—whether holding onto values that are steeped in a society's history and tradition dating back centuries and millennia, or whether they are more recently created. This dimension was not originally part of the first set of four, but was added later in 1988 when Hofstede realized the strong correlation of Michael Harris Bond's Chinese Value Survey (Hofstede & Bond, 1988) dimension, which was initially called "Confucian Work Dynamism." Long-term values included perseverance, thrift, relationship status, and shame. Short-term values were associated with quick decision-making and self-autonomy.

Bond's premise was that countries in East Asia had common cultural roots that date back in history—and he named this "Confucian Dynamism" because many of the teachings of Confucius speak of the nature of relationships and status, perseverance, shame, etc.—as Hofstede explains (see Table 4.6):

> The positively rated values of this dimension were already present in the teachings of Confucius from around 500 BC. There was much more in Confucius' teachings so Long-Term Orientation is not Confucianism *per se,* but it is still present in countries with a Confucian heritage.
>
> (Hofstede, 2011, p. 5)

All societies will maintain their connection to the past while living in the present and planning for the future. But how a society prioritizes these aspects of living and relating to "what has been lived" will be different. For example, a long-term-oriented society will place great emphasis on traditions and "times gone by," and subsequently venerate the heroes, stories, and even myths with such reverence; whereas a short-term-oriented society still remembers the past, but with less intensity and less adherence to the past's influence on the present.

Siddhartha River of Life

One of the best examples to help us understand long-term orientation is the Buddhist belief system. Buddhism is based on the teachings of Siddhartha Gautama, which began in the 5th century BCE in northeastern India. Perhaps we remember the classic book that many of us read in high school, *Siddhartha,* about the young man's quest to find life without suffering and to reach an enlightened, perfect state of Nirvana. In Siddhartha's journey, he kept

Table 4.6 Hofstede's Long-Term/Short-Term Dimensions

Long-term and short-term	Long-term	Short-term
Work Boss Employee Education Family Religion	• The past is important history is to be revered • Traditions are to be honored • Thrift and perseverance are important • Students think success and failure are the result of luck • High valued is placed on education	• The future is important new experiences will come • Traditions should be adapted • Serving others is important • Students think success and failure are earned through effort • High value is placed on self-actualization
How to Interact		
	• Respect rules and traditions • Reward loyalty • Do not lose face	• Find your own destiny and make changes • Reward adventure • Be respectful of others but first respect yourself

(*Source*: Adapted from Hofstede, 1997, p. 173.)

encountering the river, which symbolized the cyclical nature of life. Buddhists believe in this cycle of life——birth, life, death, and rebirth—which goes on throughout eternity, and that the cycle can be broken only if they reach enlightenment. In the story, the ferryman helps Siddhartha understand that the river represents the transcendence of time and that life, with its past, present, and future, are one and the same (Hesse, 2009).

In Sanskrit, the name Siddhartha सिद्ध (*siddha*), means one who has accomplished his goal. In Eastern philosophy, goals (and life in general) are viewed as cyclical and not linear as the Western world sees life (Campbell, n.d.). India scores 51 on this dimension which shows a preference for a more pragmatic approach to life. The belief in "karma" or "what you do now decides your destiny" is important in Indian philosophy and also promotes a pragmatic approach to life whereby people accept many truths that depend on the seeker.

In the workplace, long-term orientation means more flexibility in changing plans rather than adhering to punctuality, because reality is constantly changing and it is up to each person to discover their fate (The Hofstede Centre, n.d.b). Long-term orientation means that managers must rely on long-term relationships for building their business, whereas short-term orientation means that business people rely heavily on technology for interactions.

While meeting styles depend upon the type of organization, you generally have the Western style—e.g., high-tech industries that follow schedules and meeting agendas, or the more traditional companies that can appear to be informal, with people coming and going or answering a text in the middle of a meeting. With traditional companies, it will take one longer to establish the business relationship and the cycle of business could very well be conducted along the lines of nonbusiness-related meetings and events. It is necessary to engage in the small talk and show that you understand the importance of building trust and credibility for long-term interaction.

Indulgence and Restraint

"Indulgence and restraint" refers to the new dimension that has grown out of this ongoing research, namely by Bulgarian linguist Michael Minkov and his study of the World Values Survey (Hofstede & Hofstede, 2010). "Indulgence" refers to societal standards for immediate gratification of basic human needs in order to enjoy life; "restraint" stands for a society that believes one should control and regulate gratification—and does so through strict social norms.

The indulgence and restraint orientations deal with how children are socialized into society and the extent to how they are taught to control both desires and impulses—weak control is indulgence; strong control is restraint. If we return to India as an example, we will note that it scores 26 out of 100 on this dimension, which means it has strong restraint. This society places emphasis on hard work to obtain what one needs to live versus emphasis on leisure time and the delayed gratification of what one wants. Social norms play a big part in the perceptions regarding people who overdo their indulgence in life (Table 4.7).

Baby Boomers/Millennials

Probably one of the best examples of indulgence and restraint can be found in generational differences between Millennials and Baby Boomers. Baby Boomers grew up in the post-World War II generation. Times were tough but taking a turn for the better. Children born during the new millennium were the first generation to have their own personal computers and mobile phones. According to a Pew Research study on social and demographic trends (Pew Research Center, 2010), Millennials are confident, self-expressive, and want to be treated as special. It has been said that many have been raised by helicopter parents who take care of everything from managed play dates to defending their child's right to earn an A in math, to liaising with a coach to get their child on the team. This creates an over-dependency on parents yet an independency on getting what they want. Of course, not everyone has these tendencies; but such an outlook on life certainly conflicts with the previous generations that did not expect the same things out of life.

Young people today have a singular focus on what they deserve because of their special circumstances—a rather particularistic viewpoint that will be discussed more in Chapter 6. For example, in talking with a friend (Baby Boomer) who is a physician, I learned that newly minted doctors are being

Table 4.7 Hofstede's Indulgence–Restraint Dimensions

Indulgence–restraint	Indulgence	Restraint
Work Boss Employee Education Family Religion	• Work hard and play harder • Anything is possible • You are in control of your destiny • Freedom of speech is important • Many people describe themselves as happy as a life goal • Save but also spend for today	• Work hard and work even harder • Pessimism and cynicism • What happens to me is fate • Freedom of speech would be nice • Fewer people describe themselves as happy • Save for the future; spend only what is necessary for today
How to Interact	• Realize that others might be insulted or cautious about your comments on life, lifestyle, etc. • Others might not take you seriously	• Realize that others may not always show emotions • Remember that what is fun may be defined and/or perceived differently

(*Source*: Adapted from Hofstede, 2011, p. 16.)

more discriminate about what their work hours will be—based upon the opinion that they have worked extra hard to obtain their degree because of the exorbitant loans needed to complete their education. Rather than understand the norms for hierarchy—more experienced doctors choose their own schedules whereas new doctors are assigned their schedules—many from today's generations expect that they will get what they want from the start. There is often an expectation that not only should one search for the perfect dream job but that one deserves it.

Another friend of mine told me about an astounding example of indulgence at its best. His daughter was playing violin in a youth symphony orchestra and, the day of the concert, one of the members of a particular quartet did not show up. No phone call, no text message, nothing. My friend's daughter volunteered to sight-read for the missing violinist, which she did to the relief of the other three musicians. At the end of the day of performances, the tradition was to give everyone a small trophy. One of the coordinators of the group wanted to make sure that the absentee musician did not miss out on her trophy (Figure 4.6)!

In the workplace, this can be a challenge for managers in midlife who are used to working hard in order to achieve status, respect, and reward. In a cultural clash between generations, the older generation asks, "*What* needs to be done?" while the younger generation asks, "But *why?*"

Now that we have discussed the six dimensions of culture, it is important that we talk about the controversial nature of this research that classifies cultures.

Figure 4.6 Trophy: Earned or Indulgent?

(*Source*: Fotolia 50586796, © Dmitry Erashov.)

Challenges to Cultural Dimension Theory

Debating Theories

It is important to understand the scientific debate about this type of research because it relates to our ongoing discussion throughout the book regarding generalizations and sophisticated stereotypes. Any serious discussion of leadership must be credible, so while this book focuses on the practical aspects of leading in a diverse world, all of the information is based upon established and tested theories. Controversy of this study abounds, with the critics both criticizing the methodology and claiming that it is not possible to rank an entire nation on only one side of the continuum or the other, thus making it infeasible that any culture could be both individualistic and collectivistic depending on situation and context.

Hofstede's ideas were new and creative but controversial since a paradigm shift was occurring in social science at that time. It was a new way of thinking that rocked tradition and, because of this, Hofstede is probably one of the most respected yet criticized social scientists of the 21st century—at least he is one of the most quoted! When any paradigm shift occurs, those who stand out with new ideas are harshly criticized (Kuhn, 1996), as was Hofstede.

Despite the challenges of unrelenting criticism, this paradigm-shifting research is sound, respected, and constantly updated (Hofstede & Hofstede, 2010). And, a multitude of researchers have both replicated and varied the Hofstede studies and come up with largely similar and expanded results— external validation is a good thing! We will discuss one such study, the GLOBE Study (Global Leadership Organizational Behavior Effectiveness) (House et al., 2004) in Chapter 8. The main point to remember is that culture is not something that can be objectified. It is complex; it is multilayered; and the Hofstede's dimensions help us make sense out of such complexity through relative comparisons.

Cultural Generalizations

This begs the question: Are generalizations considered labels or stereotypes? Milton Bennett, a prominent U.S. scholar in the field of intercultural education, who is based in Milan, Italy, says:

> Good cultural generalizations are based on systematic cross-cultural research. They refer to predominant tendencies among groups of people, so they are not labels for individuals. A given individual may exhibit the predominant group tendency a lot, a little, or not at all. So cultural generalizations must be applied to individuals as tentative hypotheses, always open to verification.
>
> (Bennett, 2001)

As a strong proponent of the cultural generalization method, Bennett explains: "For global managers, using cultural generalizations is the best way to combine cross-cultural knowledge with openness to individual differences. This combination of knowledge and openness translates into the strongest climate of respect for diversity, and thus, to competitive advantage" (Bennett, 2001). Generalizations are helpful as long as we realize that the results of any study may or may not be applicable to specific individuals or events. We will discuss this more in Chapter 6 when we talk about stereotypes and world views.

For now, let us assume that generalizations are good ways to help us create schema—or mental models for understanding differences compared to our perspective. Analyzing the differences and similarities relative to our vantage point is what the Hofstede dimension research is all about. To demonstrate, Hofstede uses a vivid analogy—if you were to pick up a map of the world—often it is the practice of the company that publishes the map to put their continent in the middle—that becomes the vantage point for all observation. As a matter of fact, if you have studied the Chinese language or its history, you would know that the word for China (*zhongguo*) means "middle kingdom" [*zhōng*—中 middle or center; 国 *guó*—country]. Ancient Chinese during the Zhou Dynasty (1046–256 BCE) believed that China was at the center of human civilization. This would make sense because it was the longest-reigning dynasty (Time Maps, n.d.). It is probably correct in assuming that each culture group believes that it is the center of the universe!

Paradoxes of Culture

The careful reader will realize that the Hofstede rankings are to be used merely as a guide for initially understanding culture. The emphasis is on the collective phenomenon with attention to the aggregate results of any given people. For example, we can say that China tends to be a collectivistic society but current social changes (such as the one-child policy and the broadening of the middle class) are affecting this core dimension as young people become more individualistic. It is therefore necessary to gather more information and use the findings merely as a starting place. Also, while the results of the Hofstede dimensions are categorized by country, we know that with any given national country there are many cultural groups—such as ethnicity (China has over 56 ethnic minorities) or language (Canada has a majority of English-speaking inhabitants and a minority of French speakers in Quebec) (Statistics Canada, 2015). Actually, only 10 percent of the 200+ national cultures can be considered monocultural (Gannon, 2008) (Box 4.7).

What began as a study about workplace values revealed glimpses into standard tendencies of cultural differences across national borders. Hofstede's work is accessible because he was able to take culture's complexity and explain it in measurable terms. As leaders it is critical to understand that all cultures have contradictions and inconsistencies—these are called paradoxes. Martin J. Gannon—renowned scholar on cultural metaphor—describes paradox as a statement that seems to be untrue but is in fact true. It is the simultaneous existence of two contradictory or inconsistent elements that represents the essence of paradox (Gannon, 2008). Paradoxes are complicated since we can agree or disagree with them based upon our individual experiences. Just because you prove a paradox exists does not eliminate it:

> Paradoxical values coexist in any culture; they give rise to, exist within, reinforce, and complement each other to shape the holistic, dynamic, and dialectical nature of culture. Seen from the Yin Yang perspective, all cultures share the same potential in value orientations, but at the same time they are also different from each other because each culture is a unique dynamic portfolio of self-selected globally available value orientations as a consequence of that culture's all-dimensional learning over time.
>
> (Fang, 2012, p. 25)

This is because each of us looks at reality in different ways—all based upon our frames of reference. An example might be from the architectural term, "less is

---

Box 4.7

"Culture is more often a source of conflict than of synergy. Cultural differences are a nuisance at best and often a disaster."

Source: *The Economist*, 2008

Box 4.8 What is a Paradox of Culture?

A paradox is something that seems false, but in fact is true—it is when you have conflicting, contradicting, or inconsistent information that confounds your ability to create mental representations—or categorize—what you are experiencing. If we accept both elements as possessing truth (called the "dialectal") then we can try to figure out the reasons for contradicting stimuli.

Source: Gannon, 2008

---

more," where in this school of thought the more elaborate the structure, the less attractive it is. Paradoxical values exist within any society because of the unique attributes of people who make up the culture. So, it is not possible to say, "All Irish are. . ." All Germans are . . . " All Indonesians are. . . . " Rather, we can say, "Generally, Irish people value. . . ." Or "Generally, Germans might think that. . . ." Or Indonesians tend to believe. . . . " (Box 4.8).

Nomunication

For example, Japanese act in a highly formal way (uncertainty-avoiding behavior) when dealing with others in a business setting; however, in the context of drinks after work they will be informal and direct. You may work side by side someone for 10–12 hours a day, but drinking with colleagues after work can almost be a requirement. Add to that karaoke singing and people who are raised since childhood to be restrained and show good face will come alive with emotion and enthusiasm. After-hours drinking is actually when tense issues at work are allowed to be aired. It is called "nomunication." In Japanese, *nomu* means to drink and combined with the English word, communication, it explains how people can "loosen their tie" or "let down their hair." With a tradition of drink until you fall down, if you have a problem with someone, you can bring it up, apologize, perhaps laugh, and forget about it. What goes on in the party stays at the party and the problem is never mentioned again. To do so would lose face (Box 4.9).

Value Trumping

On two levels this can be a paradox. Japanese cultures are highly relational— does not this practice contradict the value of maintaining relationships? To bring up a problem during working hours would make people unhappy, create disharmony for the day, and cause someone to lose face (you never criticize or openly disagree with someone). However, after hours, the value of harmony is trumped by the value of honesty. This value trumping takes place within certain contexts where certain values take precedence (Osland & Bird, 2000).

Box 4.9 The History of Karaoke

Karaoke is a relatively recent practice that began in the early 1970s by a struggling musician, Daisuke Inoue. He played in small snack bars, typical hangouts in Kobe City, Japan, and one day a businessman he knew asked him to record a few songs to accompany his poor voice when he had to entertain business clients. Inoue obliged his friend who became so popular with his clients that he asked for more recordings. Eventually Inoue asked a friend who was good at electronics to make a device (called the Juke 8) and karaoke was born. Through word of mouth the concept caught on and because Inoue did not patent his device he never made a fortune. The name also came about by chance and actually means empty orchestra (*karappo okesutura*) which was shortened to karaoke. The word karaoke has been adopted into Japanese dictionaries as well as the *Oxford*.

Karaoke is a paradox in the high context, high power distance culture of Japan. The Asian phenomenon of karaoke allows businessmen to loosen their ties and let it all hang out during an evening of drinking and socializing. In generally face-saving cultures such as Japan and South Korea, great care is taken on hiding one's true feelings since it is more important to respect the harmony needed for group interaction. In a karaoke situation where the rules are to drink and let loose it is acceptable to be raucous and even tease your boss; the next day it is back to business as usual. This serves as an example of value trumping while the values of respect and proprietary behavior (the figure) take precedent in most situations, it can be moved aside in certain contexts (the ground), in essence being trumped by a secondary set of values such as informality and directness.

Source: Madrigal, 2013

Also, Japanese are highly task focused during the day and private matters are not discussed. Showing that you can open up after hours can go a long way to building trust in relationships, even if it means dealing with disorder during a drunken night out. The next day you'll be back to business.

Or what about the Buddhist monk in Thailand who takes an oath of poverty, giving up all worldly possessions to pursue enlightenment? Perhaps it might seem contradictory to see a monk walking down the streets of Chiang Mai with an iPod in his hand, or bartering for jade in the jade market with a flashy Rolex on his wrist (see Figure 4.7). Certain contexts mean that certain values take precedence. Value trumping is based on the Gestalt principle of figure/ground. At times one value is dominant (figure), while at others, the same value blends into the background (ground). When looking at something our eyes focus on it in relation to its surroundings. You could even say that the words you are reading on this page are only visible because of the white background supporting them (Soegaard, n.d.) (Box 4.10).

Figure 4.7 Monk in Bangkok, Thailand

(*Source*: Fotolia 19176406, © Ana.)

Box 4.10 Can a Culture Be Simultaneously Low Context and High Context?

Since Edward T. Hall arranges cultures on a continuum going from low-context to high-context communication, he seems to suggest that a low-context culture cannot be high context. However, his descriptions of cultures argue against this proposition. For example, he describes the high-context way that the Japanese communicate with one another but the low-context way that they communicate with Westerners . . . . The karaoke bar is a Japanese innovation and it is popular in other Asian nations presumably because it allows for the expression of low-context behavior and serves as an emotional outlet for such rules-focused and high-context cultures. Even when businesspeople from a high-context culture entertain their counterparts from a low-context culture in a karaoke bar, they tend to move away from high-context behavior toward low-context behavior. We can, then, accept Hall's basic formulations about low-context and high-context communications and cultures, but with caveats. While it is possible to describe the dominant profile of a culture as either low context or high context, we must realize that cultures can be both low context and high context but in different situations and contexts.

Source: Gannon, 2008

Summary

Culture is complex and in order to understand it we need ways to identify similarities and differences. The Cultural Dimension method enables us to compare and contrast elements of cultures based upon careful research of human values surveys that are generalized across cultures. We are then able to make comparisons that help us identify what we know and put it into perspective regarding what we do not know. As long as we do not overgeneralize by saying that all people act or believe a certain way, we can say with confidence that science shows people in any given society have certain norms and values that reinforce their behavior. And, every society is made up of unique individuals who will deviate from the norm; however, central tendencies toward certain norms and values can be measured and are stable over time.

This chapter has demonstrated sound theory of intercultural communication with robust scientific evidence to support its claims. We have learned that cultures can be measured based upon group tendencies, such as individualism and collectivism; power; uncertainty; gender; and orientation to time. Such dimensions are based upon values, which are an integral part of human existence. Leaders who know that these cultural principles are backed by strong validity and reliability can confidently interact with others while continuing to learn about cultural differences.

References

10 minutes with. (2014, November 18). 10 minutes with . . . Geert Hofstede on masculinity versus femininity 10112014. Retrieved from www.youtube.com/watch?v=Pyr-XKQG2CM (accessed June 19, 2015).

Alderman, Liz, Kanter, James, Yardley, Jim, Ewing, Jack, Kitsantonis, Niki, Daley, Suzanne, Russell, Karl, Higgins, Andrew, & Eavis, Peter. (2015, November 9). Explaining Greece's debt crisis. *The New York Times.* Retrieved from www.nytimes.com/interactive/2015/business/international/greece-debt-crisis-euro.html?_r=0 (accessed August 1, 2016).

AncientMilitary.com. (n.d.). The government of Ancient China. Retrieved from www.ancientmilitary.com/ancient-china-government.htm (accessed June 19, 2015).

Ball, Deborah. (2006, April 25). Women in Italy like to clean but shun the quick and easy: Convenience doesn't sell when bathrooms average four scrubbings a week. *The Wall Street Journal.* Retrieved from www.wsj.com/articles/SB114593112611534922 (accessed August 1, 2016).

Bennett, M. J. (2001). *Intercultural competence for global leadership.* Retrieved from www.idrinstitute.org/allegati/IDRI_t_Pubblicazioni/4/FILE_Documento.pdf (accessed June 20, 2015).

Bird, M. (2015, February 25). This is the real reason Greece has a massive tax-evasion problem. *Business Insider.* Retrieved from www.businessinsider.com/this-is-the-real-reason-greece-has-a-massive-tax-evasion-problem-2015-2?r=UK&IR=T (accessed August 1, 2016).

Bond, M. H. (1988). Finding universal dimensions of individual variation in multicultural studies of values: The Rokeach and Chinese value surveys. *Journal of Personality and Social Psychology, 55*(6), 1009.

Campbell, Mike. (n.d.). Siddhartha. Retrieved from www.behindthename.com/name/siddhartha (accessed August 1, 2016).

Chibba, S. (2013, September 19). Ubuntu is about relationships. *Media Club South Africa.* Retrieved from www.mediaclubsouthafrica.com/land-and-people/3479-ubuntu-is-about-relationships#ixzz3yAaGyQBI (accessed June 19, 2015).

De Mooij, M. (2014). *Global marketing: Understanding cultural paradoxes* (4th edn.). Thousand Oaks, CA: SAGE.

European Union. (n.d.). Finland: Universal services and financial benefits to promote the well-being of all children and families. Retrieved from http://europa.eu/epic/countries/finland/index_en.htm (accessed August 1, 2016).

Fang, T. (2012). Yin Yang: A new perspective on culture. *Management and Organization Review, 8*(1), 25–50.

Gannon, M. J. (2008). *Paradoxes of culture and globalization.* Thousand Oaks, CA: SAGE.

Goffee, R., & Jones, G. (2006). *Why should anyone be led by you?: What it takes to be an authentic leader.* Cambridge, MA: Harvard Business School Press.

Hadfield, J. (2014, February 13). Japan gets in the mood for love this Valentine's Day. *The Japan Times.* Retrieved from www.japantimes.co.jp/culture/2014/02/13/general/japan-gets-in-the-mood-for-love-this-valentines-day/#.VviYbpMrLVq (accessed August 1, 2016).

Harress, C. (2013, August 23). The law of Jante: How a Swedish cultural principle drives Ikea, Ericsson and Volvo, and beat the financial crisis. *International Business Times.* Retrieved from www.ibtimes.com/law-jante-how-swedish-cultural-principle-drives-ikea-ericsson-volvo-beat-financial-1397589 (accessed June 19, 2015).

Hartmann, M. (2015, July 6). The absolute moron's guide to the Greek debt crisis. *New York News & Politics.* Retrieved from http://nymag.com/daily/intelligencer/2015/07/greek-debt-crisis-the-absolute-morons-guide.html# (accessed August 2, 2016).

Hesse, H. (2009). *Siddhartha/The Dhammapada.* New York, NY: New Directions.

History.com Staff. (2009). History of Valentine's Day. A+E Networks. Retrieved from www.history.com/topics/valentines-day/history-of-valentines-day (accessed June 19, 2015).

Hofstede, G. (1980). *Culture's consequences.* Beverly Hills, CA: SAGE.

Hofstede, G. (1984). Cultural dimensions in management and planning. *Asia Pacific Journal of Management, 1*(2), 81–9.

Hofstede, G. (1997). *Cultures and organizations: Software of the mind: Intercultural cooperation and its importance for survival.* New York, NY: McGraw-Hill.

Hofstede, G. (2011). Dimensionalizing cultures: The Hofstede model in context. *Online Readings in Psychology and Culture, 2*(1), 6, 9, 16.

Hofstede, G., & Bond, M. H. (1988). The Confucius connection: From cultural roots to economic growth. *Organizational Dynamics, 16*(4), 5–21.

Hofstede, G., & Hofstede, G. J. (2010). *Cultures and organizations: Software of the mind* (3rd edn.). New York, NY: McGraw-Hill.

House, R. J., Hanges, P. J., Javidan, M., Dorfman, P. W., & Gupta, V. (Eds.). (2004). *Culture, leadership, and organizations: The GLOBE study of 62 societies* (3rd edn.). Thousand Oaks, CA: SAGE Publications.

Inglehart, R. (1990). *Culture shift in advanced industrial society.* Princeton, NJ: Princeton University Press.

Johnston, M. (2015, November 4). Tax evasion plagues Greece. *Investopedia.* Retrieved from www.investopedia.com/articles/investing/090815/tax-evasion-plagues-greece.asp (accessed August 2, 2016).

Karnitschnig, M., & Stamouli, N. (2015, February 25). Greece struggles to get citizens to pay their taxes. *The Wall Street Journal*. Retrieved from www.wsj.com/articles/greece-struggles-to-get-citizens-to-pay-their-taxes-1424867495 (accessed August 2, 2016).

Kuhn, T. S. (1996). *The structure of scientific revolutions* (3rd edn.). Chicago, IL: University of Chicago Press.

Kuo, L. (2014, May 14). Does growing rice make you less individualistic? *The Atlantic*. Retrieved from www.theatlantic.com/international/archive/2014/05/does-growing-rice-make-you-less-individualistic/370857/ (accessed June 20, 2015).

López, R. A. (1999). Las Comadres as a social support system. *Affilia*, *14*(1), 24–41.

Madrigal, A. C. (2013, December 18). Someone had to invent karaoke—this guy did. *The Atlantic*. Retrieved from www.theatlantic.com/technology/archive/2013/12/someone-had-to-invent-karaoke-this-guy-did/282491/ (accessed June 19, 2015).

Minkov, M. (2011). *Cultural differences in a globalizing world*. Bingley, UK: Emerald Group Publishing.

Osland, J. S., & Bird, A. (2000). Beyond sophisticated stereotyping: Cultural sense-making in context. *The Academy of Management Executive*, *14*(1), 65–77.

Pew Research Center. (2010, February 24). Executive Summary. Millennials: Confident, connected, open to change. Retrieved from www.pewsocialtrends.org/2010/02/24/millennials-confident-connected-open-to-change/ (accessed June 19, 2015).

Rich, J. (2012, August 22). Embracing the spirit of Ubuntu. *HuffPost Healthy Living*. Retrieved from www.huffingtonpost.com/dr-judith-rich/ubuntu_b_1803189.html (accessed June 19, 2015).

Rohrer, F. (2013 May 7). The apprentice: A lesson from Sweden. *BBC News*. Retrieved from www.bbc.com/news/magazine-22398633 (accessed June 20, 2015).

Rokeach, M. (1973). *The nature of human values*. New York, NY: Free Press.

Sanchez, E. (2015, July 17). Latinos live familismo. *HuffPost Latino Voices*. Retrieved from www.huffingtonpost.com/american-heart-association/latinos-live-familismo_b_7818240.html (accessed June 19, 2015).

Senge, P. (1990). *The fifth discipline: The art and practice of the learning organization*. New York, NY: Doubleday.

Serafeim, G. (2015, March 13). If Greece embraces uncertainty, innovation will follow. *Harvard Business Review*. Retrieved from https://hbr.org/2015/03/if-greece-embraces-uncertainty-innovation-will-follow (accessed August 2, 2016).

S. H. for *The Economist*. (2014, July 22). Why Swedish men take so much paternity leave. *The Economist*. Retrieved from www.economist.com/blogs/economist-explains/2014/07/economist-explains-15 (accessed June 20, 2015).

Smit, C. (2012, July 9). Masculinity and femininity. *Culture Matters*. Retrieved from http://culturematters.com/masculinity-and-femininity-culture-matters/ (accessed August 2, 2016).

Smith, H. (2015, May 2). Use your credit card to fight tax evasion, Greek tourism chief urges visitors. *The Guardian*. Retrieved from www.theguardian.com/world/2015/may/02/greece-tourists-credit-cards-tax-evasion (accessed August 1, 2016).

Soegaard, M. (n.d.). Gestalt principles of form perception. Interaction Design Foundation. Retrieved from www.interaction-design.org/literature/book/the-glossary-of-human-computer-interaction/gestalt-principles-of-form-perception (accessed August 2, 2016).

Stancati, M., & al Omran, A. (2015, December 14). Social media lifts Saudi women in vote. *The Wall Street Journal*. Retrieved from www.wsj.com/articles/social-media-lifts-saudi-women-in-vote-1450132404 (accessed August 1, 2016).

Statistics Canada. (2015). Immigration and ethnocultural diversity in Canada. Retrieved from www12.statcan.gc.ca/nhs-enm/2011/as-sa/99-010-x/99-010-x2011001-eng.cfm (accessed August 2, 2016).

Storø, J., & Jansen, A. (2007). The Norwegian man as father. Child Research Net. Retrieved from www.childresearch.net/papers/parenting/2007_05.html (accessed August 2, 2016).

Talhelm, T., Zhang, X., Oishi, S., Shimin, C., Duan, D., Lan, X., & Kitayama, S. (2014). Large-scale psychological differences within China explained by rice versus wheat agriculture. *Science*, *344*(6184), 603–8.

The Economist. (2008, November 8). Geert Hofstede. www.economist.com/node/12669307 (accessed August 1, 2016).

The Hofstede Centre. (n.d.a.). India. Retrieved from http://geert-hofstede.com/india.html (accessed August 3, 2016).

The Hofstede Centre. (n.d.b.). Canada. Retrieved from http://geert-hofstede.com/canada.html (accessed August 3, 2016).

Time Maps. (n.d.). Overview of the history and civilization of ancient China. Retrieved from www.timemaps.com/civilization/Ancient-China (accessed June 20, 2015).

Transparency International. (2013). National Integrity System Assessment—Greece. Retrieved from https://issuu.com/transparencyinternational/docs/greece_nis_en?e=2496456/1424394 (accessed August 1, 2016).

Wibbeke, E. S., & McArthur, S. (2008). *Global business leadership* (2nd edn.). New York, NY: Routledge.

Yanchen, Z. (Ed.) (2009). Symbolism of Chinese opera masks. Retrieved from www.cctv.com/english/special/operamaster/20090619/108284.shtml (accessed June 20, 2015).

Case 4

Best Buy

Is China Ready for the Big Box?[1]

Abstract

With a population of 1.4 billion people (The World Bank, n.d.) and a growing
economy, China presents an attractive market for retailers looking to expand.
Best Buy is no exception, and in 2003 it opened operations in China. By 2011,
Best Buy was operating nine of its "Big Box" stores throughout China.
However, the strategy that resulted in great success throughout the United
States was not effective in China and, in February 2011, Best Buy closed all of its
stores in the country. The closures of Best Buy's stores in China were the direct
result of the company's lack of awareness of the cultural and infrastructural
complexities present abroad. As Best Buy seeks to reenter China through the
already established Five Star Appliance stores, it can aim for success by first taking
into account the Chinese market, culture, and consumer habits.

Introduction

Best Buy entered the Chinese market in 2003 and by 2011 had nine stores
throughout China; yet had to shut down all of them suddenly. The closures of
Best Buy stores in China were the direct result of the company's lack of
awareness of the cultural and infrastructural complexities present abroad. As
Best Buy seeks to re-enter China through the already established Five Star
Appliance stores, it can aim for success by first taking into account the Chinese
market, culture and consumer habits.

Best Buy Background

In 1966, Dick Schulze and a partner founded Sound of Music, a Minnesota-
based home and car audio store. Due to the growth of the audio market,
in 1971, Schulze decided to expand the number of stores across the state. As the
number of stores increased, Best Buy's product line expanded to include home
appliances and audio-visual equipment (Funding Universe, n.d.).

The company changed its name to "Best Buy" after Schulze's largest store
was destroyed by a tornado. In order to sell the inventory that survived,

Schulze dedicated his entire marketing budget to promoting a parking-lot sale. The success of the sale became the footprint of Best Buy's current business model: providing a wide variety of products at the lowest prices. Best Buy's signature business model became the source of the company's tremendous growth. Between 1984 and 1987, it expanded from 8 stores to 40, and sales jumped from $29 million to $440 million (Funding Universe, n.d.).

In 1989, Schulze revolutionized the retail industry by introducing the Concept II warehouse-like store format to Best Buy's business model. Concept II allowed Schulze to reduce the number of employees while increasing the quality of customer experience. Customers could now see, feel, and touch a variety of products that they wished to buy. In addition, customers received Best Buy's signature customer service, which has since become a key factor in the company's growth. Concept II stores were such a hit that, in 1994, Schulze introduced Concept III stores, which were even larger (Funding Universe, n.d.).

Today Best Buy has grown to over 3,000 stores worldwide using their Concept III "Big Box" stores. The company now sells products ranging from consumer electronics, computing and mobile phone products, entertainment products, appliances, and other related services, generating revenues of $50 billion per year. The company's operations have expanded beyond its retail stores to include call centers and online retail operations under a variety of brand names, including Best Buy, Best Buy Mobile, The Carphone Warehouse, Five Star, Future Shop, Geek Squad, Magnolia Audio Video, Pacific Sales, and The Phone House (MorningStar, 2012). (See Appendix 1 for highlights of Best Buy's history.)

China

Before discussing how Best Buy attempted to expand its operations to China, it is necessary to review Chinese history, culture, and economy to gain a better understanding of the challenges Best Buy would eventually face. China is the most populous country and the second largest economy in the world. China has had a long history of dynastic rule, starting with the Shang (Yin) dynasty in the 17th century BCE and ending with the Qing dynasty in 1912, at which time the Republic of China was established and the Nationalist Party came to power. However, the country remained politically fragmented, and it was only in 1949 that the Communist Party gained control of Mainland China (Central Intelligence Agency, n.d.).

Since 1949, China's population has grown rapidly from 563 million people to 1.4 billion today. While the population grew rapidly, economic growth was slow. The country was faced with severe famines and general unrest (Chirot, 1996). However, Deng Xiaoping assumed power of the country after Mao's death in 1976 and made significant economic and social reforms. Deng Xiaoping liberalized the economy to encourage market-driven economic reform and initiated the "one-child" policy to curb the rapidly growing population. Since these reforms, the living standards in China have increased dramatically, and China has become a major player in the global economy.

China's GDP has more than quadrupled since 1980, and consumption has also grown at a rapid pace. A recent study by the Economic Intelligence Unit indicated that China's retail spending has increased at an annualized rate of 12 percent (Wang, 2010). While Chinese spending has increased, the spending patterns are unique to their culture. A McKinsey study indicates: "Chinese consumers regard the interests of their families more than their Western counterparts and use word of mouth to research products" (McKinsey & Company, 2010). Moreover, they place more emphasis on value rather than product brands. Chinese consumers like bargaining and frequent local neighborhood stores, as cities are highly congested and driving can take too long.

Chinese culture is also heavily influenced by the concept of *guanxi*, which loosely translates to connections or relationships and is based on the traditional values of loyalty and accountability. Having good *guanxi* can determine the fate of a business. Properly addressing *guanxi* can help businesses gain a better understanding of local markets, attract the best talent, and secure strong business associates. In addition, it can prevent holdups or potential barriers concerning a company's business in China. The Cultural Orientations Indicator (an online tool for determining cultural preferences for communication and behavior) for China supports these findings, as it shows that people in China are both collectivistic, placing a high value on family, and particularistic, treating similar decisions differently based on the circumstances. (See Appendix 2, Table 4A2.1.) In terms of consumption patterns, these indicators might suggest that consumers favor certain markets/stores over others even though they have similar features and prices.

While Chinese consumers place a heavy emphasis on value, the market for luxury goods in China has also grown at a rapid pace. High-income families are more brand conscious and have increased their spending on clothes, shoes, and other fashion items (McKinsey & Company, 2010). While their purchasing of certain items has increased, their spending on other items has decreased. Chinese consumers are prudent and do not spend beyond their means. This prudence is easily visible through China's personal savings rates, which were nearly 37 percent in 2009. Given these dynamics and the level of growth in China, Best Buy's potential in China was seemingly limitless. According to McKinsey, the Chinese consumer electronics market has been growing at a compound rate of 12 percent a year and was expected to reach about 1 trillion Yuan ($125 billion) by 2010 (von Morgenstern et al., 2006). (See Appendix 3.) It is this growing market and influencing culture that Best Buy attempted to enter and to expand its business.

Best Buy in China

In 2003, Best Buy opened up operations in China by establishing a sourcing office in Shanghai. To facilitate its expansion, in May 2006, Best Buy purchased a 75 percent stake in Jiangsu Five Star Appliance Co. in an effort to more easily move into the Chinese market. Five Star Appliance was founded in 1998 as a wholesale electronics business in China, with their first retail stores opening in 2001. Five Star is currently the third-largest appliance and consumer electronics retailer in China, with over 131 stores across eight of China's provinces. They primarily operate in air-conditioning, video and audio products, and digital communication (Best Buy, 2012). In 2007, Best Buy opened its first store in China, an 8,000-square-meter store in Shanghai, with the intention of bringing a brand new, customized shopping experience to Chinese customers. Best Buy hoped to first saturate its presence within one of China's largest cities and optimize its existing supply chain before expanding across China. By 2009, Best Buy had opened 9 stores throughout China, with multiple locations in Shanghai and Beijing in addition to 170 stores under the Five Star Appliance brand. China looked to be a market with endless potential for Best Buy to grow its revenues and profits. However, Best Buy's entrance into the Chinese market presented numerous unforeseen hurdles that have led to the company's inability to gain a market share in China.

As Best Buy entered China, the company failed to recognize the unique composition of China's retail landscape. Best Buy entered China using the same approach as in the United States, where it competes with a few Brick and Mortar companies such as Sears. In China, there are numerous outlets for consumers to purchase their electronic products. This fragmented market consists of both large national players, such as Carrefour and Suning, and thousands of family owned "mom and pop" electronic stores, where bargaining over price is the preferred way of doing business.

The level of traffic in China's metropolitan cities contributes to the popularity of these smaller, local stores. China has one of the greatest car adoption rates in the world, and when coupled with an older infrastructure, China can be one of the most traffic-congested areas of the world. Due to this amount of traffic, Chinese consumers tend to prefer shopping closer to home rather than traveling across the city to a Best Buy. This differs greatly from Best Buy in the United States, where the level of traffic affects few Best Buy locations. Best Buy apparently failed to recognize the impact of traffic on consumer shopping habits in China.

Traffic congestion was not the only hurdle Best Buy faced, for the physical size and layout of Best Buy's Concept III stores posed further problems as it entered the Chinese market. Given the population density in Shanghai, premier retail space, especially at the level needed for a signature Concept III store, is very costly, resulting in a high fixed-cost investment for Best Buy. Further problems with these large stores arose from the number of product lines offered in each store. According to Shaun Rein, Managing Director of China Market Research Project and a contributor to *CNBC*:

> Best Buy ultimately opened a giant flagship store in downtown Shanghai. The store was selling far too many product lines in a location where

consumers literally needed to walk up several stories to reach the entrance. Seeing the mistake, local competitors like Suning and Gome opened small stores right next to Best Buy on the ground level with convenient access and sold only high demand, high margin products.

(Rein, 2012) (See Appendix 4)

Not only did Best Buy pay substantially for its real estate, but the company also lost sales to its smaller, neighboring competitors.

In addition, Best Buy's business model differed greatly from other retailers entering China. According to Vivian Ni, Best Buy's major Chinese competitors lease separate parts of their stores to retailers of distinct brands, earning profits from the so-called "entrance-fee" and by taking a portion of every retailer's sales profit. Best Buy, on the other hand, purchases all of its products directly from suppliers and prices them independently. This results in Best Buy keeping large quantities of inventory in stock, a major challenge for Best Buy in China considering the difficulties of managing its supply chain given China's complex infrastructure (Ni, 2011).

Not leasing floor space also affected Best Buy's relationship with its suppliers. According to Fried and Chinnareddy (2012), Best Buy's relationship with its suppliers became strained due to this different business model in China. The suppliers viewed Best Buy as "erecting a 'wall' between suppliers and the customer, rather than a 'bridge' thereby creating both *guanxi* and face problems for Best Buy." Under the concept of *guanxi*, it is important to include those parties within your personal network when taking action because all parties must feel that their intentions and goals are being considered. Best Buy's failure to include its suppliers conflicted with the Chinese way of doing business (Fried & Chinnareddy, 2012).

Another obstacle in China for Best Buy was centered on the company's core values. In America, the Best Buy brand is synonymous with customer service, value, and quality. However, in China these values do not resonate the same way within the Chinese electronics consumer. In China, when consumers make a purchase, they value a fair price over the fixed costs associated with products at Best Buy. Potential customers were going into Best Buy stores in Shanghai, browsing the items, but then going out and bargaining for the products at the smaller stores. Best Buy was unable to compete on price when consumers could bargain their way to paying the lowest prices elsewhere.

The idea of bargaining to achieve a desired price contributes to a major misconception regarding companies that attempt and fail to enter the Chinese market. The misconception is that companies entering China fail because the Chinese are "cheap" and do not provide significant margins for foreign companies to survive. This could not be further from the truth. In China, consumers are actually willing to pay more for premium products. According to McKinsey, the Chinese are willing to pay for better value and quality, and are spending more time researching and are exploring product nuances.

The Chinese are highly brand cautious and demand high-end products at the right price. McKinsey also highlights that "45 percent of Chinese believe that higher prices correspond to better quality, compared with just 16 percent in the United States and 8 percent in Japan" (Atsmon & Magni, 2012). While Best Buy did carry many of these big-ticket items, selling them was not one of the company's core capabilities.

Many consumers commented that the Chinese name of Best Buy—*Baisimai*—was a bad one for marketing. *Baisimai* literally means, "to buy after thinking 100 times." This suggested to the Chinese consumer that they must "beware" before making a purchasing decision at Best Buy. However, because the Chinese are collective in nature, they much prefer to go by their peers' recommendations when making a buying decision. In other words, they do not want to have to "think 100 times" about something—they'd like to trust their friend who says an item is a great product (see Appendixes 5 and 6). The store's name may have led to lost sales opportunities for Best Buy due to the distrust it suggested to the Chinese consumers.

Best Buy's failure to consider these cultural and infrastructural complexities was eventually too difficult for the company to overcome. On February 22, 2011, Best Buy announced that it would close all nine of its Chinese stores; six in Shanghai, one in Beijing, one in Suzhou, and one in Hangzhou. Following the announcement, a couple of stores remained open to handle after-sales issues. Outside these stores, there were long lines of dissatisfied customers waiting for the doors to open and their issues to be dealt with (China.org.cn, 2011).

Food Bazaar

An International Success Story

Given the hurdles noted above of a U.S. company attempting to enter China, it could be easy to assume that success is difficult to achieve when companies make the move to expand abroad. For example, similar to China, India is a country characterized by cultural diversity and rapid economic growth. Foreign companies have been trying to enter India's retail sector and capitalize on the large spending of middle-income consumers. Several companies, including the United Kingdom's Marks and Spencer and the United States' Wal-Mart, have entered the Indian economy but have failed to establish a strong presence. On many occasions, the failure to succeed has been because these companies failed to understand the cultural complexities and tastes of Indians. For example, when Marks and Spencer launched in India, it only sold polo shirts for men in five different colors. However, Indians like bright colors and were not very interested in purchasing the "dull"-colored shirts that were available. Marks and Spencer (Orange, 2010) has since learned and now offers polo shirts in 16 different colors in India, compared with only five in the United Kingdom (PwC, n.d.).

While many companies have failed to attract Indian consumers from their traditional markets to more modern ones, there are some that have succeeded. In a slightly different sense, national cultures can have many subcultures and a new idea or model can be akin to breaking into a foreign market. Taking a Western idea and trying to be innovative in your own country can be as difficult as marketing to a foreign society. For example, one of the most prominent of these successful companies has been India's own Food Bazaar. Food Bazaar was started by Mr. Kishor Biyani, who wanted to emulate India's traditional marketplace in an economically efficient, modern wholesale environment. Indians traditionally shopped for food items in small local markets. They are accustomed to shopping in crowded spaces where they can bargain for, as well as touch and feel, the vegetables they buy.

When Food Bazaar was initially launched, it was a typical Western grocery store with clean aisles that were organized meticulously. This ambience attracted a select audience, but isolated the mass audience that Food Bazaar was hoping to attract. Even though prices were competitive, and sometimes even lower than local shops, Food Bazaar did not do as well as it had expected. However, Food Bazaar learned quickly and adapted to its customer's needs. It maintained the Western concept of convenience but combined it with Indian values (Pantaloon Retail, n.d.).

Food Bazaar changed the look and feel of its stores to reflect a local market. The company made the aisles narrower, creating the impression of a crowded market. There were large open buckets with vegetables/food items where consumers could touch and choose the items they wanted to buy. Moreover, in an effort to replicate the satisfaction of bargaining, Food Bazaar had certain days when items would be cheaper. Additionally, its focus is on opening newer and smaller-sized stores in city neighborhoods or as a part of its other stores rather than following the model adopted by other big-box stores. This was because Indians are used to shopping for food in their neighborhood.

Given these changes, Food Bazaar gained popularity and became one of the largest food retailers in the country. As of now, they have over 214 stores in 90 cities in India. Food Bazaar is a success story of a company adapting to a country's culture. This one example highlights that success is possible through the examination of consumers' culture and reflection as to how to best reach those consumers. Food Bazaar's success is one that also suggests the potential that Best Buy can reach as they seek to reenter the Chinese market.

Best Buy's Second Chance?

In July 2012, Best Buy decided to make another attempt at entering the Chinese market. This time, they would do so with only their Best Buy Mobile brand. Best Buy would enter through 14 Five Star Appliance retail stores in Nanjing. By doing this, Best Buy would attempt to take advantage of Five Star's experience and success operating in this market, with the intention of building the brand enough to someday have independent Best Buy Mobile retail stores in China (ChinaTechNews, 2012).

With the lessons from their recent failure fresh in their minds, Best Buy is once again attempting to expand into China. It is yet to be seen whether or not Best Buy will be able to leverage Five Star Appliance's capabilities to make this second attempt a successful one.

Discussion Questions

1   What are the cultural differences that may have led to the Best Buy's failure in China?
2   Given what you have learned in this case, what information or study would you have done before entering the Chinese retail market?
3   What should Best Buy consider if they want to enter another Asian market?
4   Do you think they would face similar challenges as in China; or could they be different? Why/why not?
5   How should Best Buy deal with the implications of the Chinese translation of their name?

Appendix 1

Timeline of Best Buy's History

See the following website: www.bestbuy.ca/en-CA/Pressroom/Press-RoomInfo.aspx.

Appendix 2

Table 4A2.1 Cultural Orientations Indicator Comparison Between China and United States

China	U.S.A.
Sense of self	
Constraint	Control
Private	Private
Hierarchy	Equality
Collectivistic	Individualistic
Competitive	Competitive
Order	Flexibility

Table 4A2.1 (continued)

China	U.S.A.

Interaction style

China	U.S.A.
Fluid	Fixed
Being	Doing
Indirect	Direct
Instrumental	Instrumental
Formal	Informal
Particularistic	Universalistic

Thinking style

Multi-focus	Single focus
Past	Future
High context	Low context
Inductive	Inductive
Systemic	Linear

(*Source*: www.berlitz.com/Corporate-Solutions/Global-Leadership-Training/GLT-Web-based-Solutions/COI-Assessment/191/.)

Appendix 3

See the following websites for more information on Chinese consumer spending:

> www.goldmansachs.com/our-thinking/macroeconomic-insights/growth-of-china/chinese-consumer/
> www.mckinsey.com/industries/retail/our-insights/mapping-chinas-middle-class
> www.mckinsey.com/business-functions/strategy-and-corporate-finance/our-insights/why-chinas-consumers-will-continue-to-surprise-the-world.

Appendix 4

See the following website for an image of the Best Buy store in Shanghai: www.flickr.com/photos/kreep/369762272.

Appendix 5

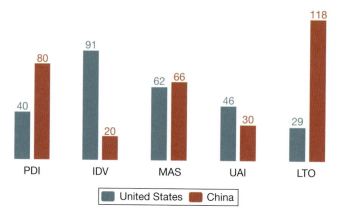

Figure 4A5.1 Hofstede Dimension Comparison, United States versus China

(*Source*: https://geert-hofstede.com/united-states.html.)

Appendix 6

Cultural Orientations Indicator

Continua and Definitions

The Cultural Orientations Indicator (COI) is an online cross-cultural assessment tool that has three dimensions that provide a way for us to understand and discuss with others how we prefer to interact, process information, and view ourselves in their work environment (Schmitz, 2012).

Note

1 Authors: Ashuman Beri, Steve Robinson, Mary Jo Sorrentino, Angelo Vargas, and Elizabeth A. Tuleja (Ed.)

References

Atsmon, Yuval, & Magni, Max. (2012). Meet the Chinese consumer of 2020. Retrieved from www.mckinsey.com/insights/asia-pacific/meet_the_chinese_consumer_-of_2020 (accessed March, 2012).

Best Buy. (2012). Extending the reach Best Buy vendor portal. Retrieved from www.extendingthereach.com/wps/portal/!ut/p/c0/04_SB8K8xLLM9MSSzPy8xBz9C-P0os3gLAwMDZydDRwMgw8LA08DJ08zJw9LY3d9cvyDbUREAPwtU5w!!/ (accessed September 10, 2012).

Central Intelligence Agency. (n.d.). *The world factbook: East & Southeast Asia*. Retrieved from www.cia.gov/library/publications/the-world-factbook/geos/ch.html (accessed September 17, 2012).

China.org.cn. (2011, February 26). Best Buys' 3pm opening leaves hundreds waiting. *Shanghai Daily*. Retrieved from www.china.org.cn/business/2011-02/26/content_22009402.htm (accessed September 23, 2012).

ChinaTechNews. (2012). Best Buy attempts new strategy for China via mobile channel. Retrieved from www.chinatechnews.com/2012/07/01/16447-best-buy-attempts-new-strategy-for-china-via-mobile-channel (accessed September 22, 2012).

Chirot, Danil. (1996). *Modern tyrants: The power and prevalence of evil in our age* (p. 8). Princeton, NJ: Princeton University Press.

Fried, Andreas, & Chinnareddy, Aditya. (2012). *3 Key trends in China*. Retrieved from www.hsp.com/blog/2012/7/3-key-trends-china (accessed September 20, 2012).

Funding Universe. (n.d.). Best Buy Co., Inc. history. Retrieved from www.fundinguniverse.com/company-histories/best-buy-co-inc-history/ (accessed August 1, 2016).

McKinsey & Company. (2010). *2010 annual Chinese consumer study*. Retrieved from http://csi.mckinsey.com/Knowledge_by_region/Asia/China/2010_annual_Chinese_consumer_study.aspx (accessed September 19, 2012).

MorningStar. (2012, March 3). XNYS: BBY Best Buy. Form 10-K. Retrieved from http://quote.morningstar.com/stock-filing/Annual-Report/2012/3/3/t.aspx?t=XNYS:BBY&ft=10-K&d=d8a03cd525497f4c3735de3612d09b02 (accessed September 15, 2012).

Ni, Vivian. (2011). Best Buy's withdrawal: American morals fail to transcend Chinese consumer market. Retrieved from www.china-briefing.com/news/2011/03/02/best-buys-withdrawal-american-morals-fail-to-transcend-chinese-consumer-market.html (accessed September 15, 2012).

Orange, Richard. (2010). M&S eyes up India a second time. Retrieved from www.thenational.ae/business/m-s-eyes-up-india-a-second-time (accessed September 16, 2012).

Pantaloon Retail. (n.d.). Food bazaar. Retrieved from www.pantaloonretail.in/businesses/food-bazaar.html (accessed September 18, 2012).

PwC. (n.d.). Winning in India's retail sector. Retrieved from www.pwc.com/in/en/assets/pdfs/rc-publications/WinningSector.pdf (accessed September 17, 2012).

Rein, Shaun. (2012). *Rein: Why global brands fail in China*. Retrieved from www.cnbc.com/id/46009614/Rein_Why_Global_Brands_Fail_in_China (accessed September 22, 2012).

Schmitz, J. (2012). Understanding the cultural orientations approach: An overview of the development and updates to the COA. Retrieved from www.culturalorientations.com/SiteData/docs/ArticleUnd/616d3a22b5d5d472/Article%20-%20Understanding%20the%20Cultural%20Orientations%20Approach.12.06.2012.pdf (accessed September 20, 2016).

The World Bank. (n.d.). China. Retrieved from http://data.worldbank.org/country/china (accessed September 27, 2012).

Wang, Helen H. (2010). China's booming consumer market. Retrieved from www.forbes.com/sites/china/2010/08/27/chinas-booming-consumer-market/ (accessed September 15, 2012).

von Morgenstern, Ingo Beyer, & Shu, Chris. (2006). Winning the battle for the Chinese consumer electronics market. Retrieved from www.mckinseyquarterly.com/Winning_the_battle_for_the_Chinese_consumer_electronics_market_1855 (accessed September 16, 2012).

5 Culture and Context in Communication

One of the most effective ways to learn about oneself is by taking seriously the cultures of others. It forces you to pay attention to those details of life which differentiate them from you.

(Edward T. Hall, *The silent language*, 1959, p. 54)

Figure 5.1 Man Running in Desert

(*Sources*: Fotolia 76780059, © corbis_micro; Fotolia 90303201, © Antonioguillem; Fotolia 51995494, © Maridav.)

Chapter Overview

Chapter 5, Culture and Context in Communication, examines the questions: What exactly *is* communication and how can business people be on the same wavelength when interacting with someone who is very different? What does context have to do with effective intercultural encounters? What do time and space have to do with communication context? And, what role does language play when leaders try to navigate the often choppy waters of cross-cultural interactions? These are the questions we will address in Chapter 5.

Learning Objective

Chapter 5, Culture and Context, is about the connection between culture and language and its effect on how we communicate and interact in business. This chapter continues the discussion of cultural dimensions by examining Edward T. Hall's famous work on high and low context in communication, polychronic and monochronic time, and spatial distance.

Key Takeaways

- Culture and language are interconnected and affect how we communicate.
- Some messages are explicit and others are implicit and it is up to us to read between the lines.
- Successful communication occurs when people are on the same frame of reference.

Leadership Applications

- To be a CQ leader, it is necessary to grasp the nuances of both spoken and nonspoken communication.
- As business professionals we should care about the intersection of culture and communication so that we are ready to do business.

Introduction

It is All About Frame of Reference

The story goes like this—a young man got his break in the world of advertising for a beverage company and was given an assignment in the Middle East. His campaign flopped. Seeing how dejected he was, his best friend asked him, "Why weren't you successful with the soft drink ad campaign?" He replied—"I was confident that I could make a clever sales pitch in the rural areas even though I can't speak Arabic. So I designed the campaign without any script—there would be three pictures within the ad. The first showed a man lying in the desert sand, dying of thirst. Then, the man drinks our beverage. After being revived he jumps up and runs on his way, totally refreshed." "Brilliant," cried his friend. "Not really," sighed the young man. "I didn't realize that in Arabic you read from right to left." In reality, situations like this happen in the business world *all* of the time (see Figure 5.1). We think we know what to do and how to say things, but often we realize that we have missed the point!

Global leaders must have control of their language choices and realize that what they say or express through nonverbal communication can have a tremendous impact on those from different cultural groups. In the following section are some real business blunders that will put a smile on your face. All of them involved miscommunication. All of them could have been avoided by a culturally competent leader.

Frame of Reference

Miscommunication in International Business Blunders

Let us look at some real examples of how businesses have miscommunicated about their products (Ricks, 2006). Unfortunately, we usually only hear about the incidents that have had negative consequences. But, that is how we learn. Then we will talk about how leaders can ensure that such blunders do not happen to them.

When Gerber introduced its line of baby foods into the African market, they wanted to keep things simple—both financially and with their advertising campaign. So, they did the same thing as always by using the identical packaging as in the United States—little glass jars with the picture of the baby on the label. Regrettably, they had not done their due diligence to learn what is customary regarding advertising in African culture. Only later did the Swiss company learn that, since most people in Africa do not read English, companies normally put a picture on the *outside* of what the container has on the *inside*. Gerber did not sell much baby food in Africa as a result.

What about the former Swiss company, Schweppes (now Cadbury-Schweppes)? Schweppes wanted to market their tonic water in Italy. This company tried to do its due diligence and hired a translator. But, instead of translating "tonic water" into "*aqua tonica*," the translator made a mistake and translated it into "*aqua di toletta*," "toilet water." Schweppes also did not make any money that year.

What about an enterprising American T-shirt maker in Miami who printed shirts for the Spanish-speaking market to promote the Pope's visit in 1987? Instead of "I saw the Pope" (*el Papa*), the shirts read "I saw the potato" (*la papa*) (see Figure 5.2). Not good for business or diplomatic relations! Not to mention the upset it caused with the religious community. An error such as not knowing the masculine (*el*) and feminine (*la*) pronouns in Spanish made the meaning entirely different. The "Popetato" became a collector's item.

Pepsi used its slogan "Come Alive with the Pepsi Generation" for advertising in Taiwan. They translated this into Chinese too literally and it came out as "Pepsi brings your ancestors back from the grave." This is a big cultural faux pas, because in Chinese tradition there is worship of ancestors, celebrated on a day called Tomb Sweeping Day (清明节, *Qīngmíng jié*). It is a one-day holiday that has been celebrated in China for centuries. This festival is a time to commemorate and pay respect to a person's ancestors, with families

Figure 5.2 "I saw the potato"

Figure 5.3 Chinese Characters for Coca Cola

visiting the gravesite, often from a great distance, in order to reunite with those who have passed on. Family members carefully remove weeds from the gravesite, sweep and clean up around the tombstone, as well as make repairs and burn incense and paper money.

Here is another one. Coca Cola's "Coke Adds Life" slogan translated into Chinese came out as "Bite the wax tadpole." The people at Coca Cola then researched over 40,000 characters to find the phonetic equivalent that had a much better effect: "*ke*" (happy) "*kou*" (mouth) "*ke le*" (happiness) which means, "Coke brings happiness to the mouth" (Figure 5.3).

Triangle of Meaning

Ogden and Richards' Model

So we have looked at miscommunication; let us look at how we can become better communicators. We'll start with the process of communication—how we actually communicate—remember, awareness is key and the more we understand how the communication process works, the better we can avoid such business blunders.

In English "to communicate" comes from the Latin verb *communicare*, which means "to make common to many" or "to share." As we try to share our ideas to others in ways that are common or familiar, we often can miss the mark. You see, any meaning we try to convey is subjective and depends on the person who attaches meaning to it. For example, if two people are communicating and are not thinking on the same wavelength, while the message is being shared, the meaning is not. If your partner says to you, "I know we've talked about getting a dog for a long time, let's go adopt one," You become excited because you recently watched a movie that had a loveable bulldog named Winston, and immediately fell in love with the saggy–baggy, floppy–wrinkly, good-natured breed. That weekend, you set out for the pound and when you get there your partner gets excited at seeing a German Shepherd. Your heart sinks because in your frame of reference, you wanted a ridiculously endearing English Bulldog, not a sleek and cunning German Shepherd (Figure 5.4).

Irish playwright George Bernard Shaw once said, "The problem with communication . . . is the illusion that it has been accomplished." This is a perfect example of the "Triangle of Meaning," which is about how symbols are associated with the things they represent (Ogden & Richards, 1927). It is actually a simple model that takes an abstract concept and makes it concrete. A *symbol* is anything to which people assign meaning, such as words, diagrams, colors, etc. The *referent* is the concept or idea that a symbol will evoke in the mind of an interpreter. A communicator is referred to as an *interpreter*. As interpreters we hope to select symbols that others will understand in the same way we do. We can miss connecting with someone over the *translation* of the meaning (or semantics), as in the example of translating English concepts to Chinese. We can miss being on the same wavelength through *things*, such as in

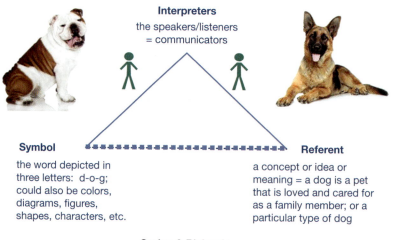

Interpreters
the speakers/listeners
= communicators

Symbol
the word depicted in
three letters: d-o-g;
could also be colors,
diagrams, figures,
shapes, characters, etc.

Referent
a concept or idea or
meaning = a dog is a pet
that is loved and cared for
as a family member; or a
particular type of dog

Ogden & Richards

Figure 5.4 Triangle of Meaning

(*Sources*: Tuleja, 2015, p. 45; Fotolia 59460433, © jagodka; Fotolia 61245378, © otsphoto.)

the dog example. We can miss being on the same wavelength through *words* (or symbols) that are used to communicate products, as we saw in some of the examples at the beginning of this chapter. I love the cartoon by Gary Larson where the goggle-eyed space creatures have landed and are meeting the earth people with dictionary in hand. The one alien says to the other as it grabs the dictionary, "Take me to your stove? . . . You idiot! Give me that book!" We know how difficult it is to try and find the right word when we are trying to communicate in another language. The words carry meaning only in the minds of the interpreters, and if we are not both on the same wavelength, then we have not communicated successfully.

Lost in Translation

Translating Meaning

When I lived in Hong Kong, I was doing a research project with the Marriott Corporation to look at the communication practices of its employees (Tuleja et al., 2011). In preparing a survey for managers in Hong Kong and China, my team and I had to consider collective group accomplishments rather than individual. When we examined an original question in English, "How good are you at . . . ?" we had to consider the cultural context. While this question would seem appropriate in Western culture, it could have a different meaning within the Chinese collective context. It might be construed as "bragging" since Chinese people often do not want to create disharmony by bringing bad favor and a loss of "face" to their boss or organization. The Chinese translation had to be more appropriately construed (and then translated) as, "I am *capable* of getting others" . . . (我很能讓其他人对我作出正面的回应: *Wǒ hěn néng ràng qí tā rén duì wò zuò chū zhèng miàn de huí yìng*). Saying, "I am good at . . . , " is difficult for a Chinese person to admit, especially an older person. Saying you are good at something is not humble; but saying, "I can do something" is acceptable.

Translating Ideas

We can also miss being on the same wavelength about our *ideas*. One of my all-time favorite cartoons is Dilbert on a first date. He says to his date, "I know it's only our first date, but what do you think of me?" She says to him, "You remind me of Elvis." In Dilbert's mind he is thinking "Sexy!" but his date is thinking "Dead!" Surely his love life was not where he wanted it to be (Box 5.1).

Translating Things

Another example can be found in the different names used for things. It is easy to assume that just because one speaks the same language, they use the same

> **Box 5.1**
>
> If you would like to show your intellectual proficiency at work, you can refer to this concept of "frame of reference" from the linguistic field of semiotics, which is the study of signs and symbols, and communicative behavior (both spoken and nonverbal).

language. For instance, British English and North American English have more differences than merely spelling. It is easy to misinterpret what someone says based upon how they define the term. In the United Kingdom, people wear trousers rather than pants; the U.S. "elevator" is, in British English, a "lift," a cookie is a "biscuit," the trunk of a car is a "boot," a truck is more often called a "lorry," and a stove is a "cooker."

Translating Symbols

We can also miscommunicate by using the wrong *symbol*. Symbols are arbitrary by themselves, but they carry meaning and are recognizable when we assign meaning to them. That is why we have communication problems when we interpret symbols—and words—differently, or if we do not recognize them (Figure 5.5).

Even punctuation—symbolism itself—can affect business dealings if the meaning is not clear to both communicators. Here is a situation where problems occurred with the misplacement of a comma, which had a disastrous impact on the bottom line for Lockheed Martin in 1999—this catastrophic accounting mistake was called the "70 Million Dollar Comma." As reported in the Associated Press in London on June 19, 1999, "Bad punctuation left Lockheed Martin with a $70 million bill after a misplaced comma gifted a customer with overgenerous contract terms" (CNN Money, 1999). This international contract with the U.S. aerospace company misplaced the comma by one decimal point within the very equation that adjusted the sales price with inflation changes. The European style reverses the comma and decimal point; many times the punctuation that will be used to set off thousands is nonexistent. This punctuation causes confusion with the meaning of the numbers. So, in the United States it would read 70,000,000.00; in Europe, 70.000.000. The customer didn't budge, expecting Lockheed to stick to their original deal. The customer was never identified to the public! It leaves us wondering what the person who made the egregious error is doing today.

Why is it that we only hear of the failures and mishaps in international business? Well, we learn from them and they do make the news! I do want to include a successful example, but I first have to give you one more unsuccessful one to see how the company turned things around.

Symbols for money–these four are probably the most familiar.

£ $
¥ €

- But what about this one? It's a Russian Ruble. ₽

- Or this one? It represents the Turkish Lira. ₺

- Or what about this? It's the Greek Drachma. 𝒟ρ

- Or the Rupee, found not only in India, but Pakistan, Sri Lanka, Mauritius, Nepal, and the Seychelles. ₨

Figure 5.5 International Monetary Symbols

McDonald's Comeback

Can you remember when you were a kid and first went to a McDonald's fast-food chain? I can! Think about what the building looked like. Did it have the notable red and white brick tiles, the golden arches, and was it a drive-up building? Or was it a more modern one, where you could go in and sit down? Nostalgia sweeps in like high tide as I remember the thrill of being a little kid in the back of my parents' tan Plymouth station wagon, waiting—with anticipation—to have a treat of that little hamburger, the salty fries, and the delicious root beer. I would sit in the back of the station wagon with my brothers and we would eat our treats.

Now picture an image of Ronald McDonald—the tall figure, all yellow and red, standing stiffly, although happy, outside the restaurant. McDonald's smiling icon, Ronald McDonald, is recognizable to many people around the world. Not all of us may like clowns (!), but there is something so simple about Ronald McDonald and his silly smile that makes him inviting.

Let us discuss the unsuccessful example. McDonald's has many versions if its famous figure—one of them is a relaxed version of Ronald sitting on a bench. His arm is nonchalantly draped on the back of the bench with one leg casually crossed over the other. His smile is wide and his body language is inviting—it "says," "Come join me and we'll chat over a strawberry milk-shake." Well, this is what it might say to *some* people—but to others it could be extremely insulting. When this version of the Ronald McDonald figure was placed in front of the restaurant on the island of Malta there was an immediate outrage in the community and people boycotted the fast-food chain (Verluyten, 2010).

What happened? What went wrong? How could anyone be offended by this yellow and red clown with a goofy smile who was just sitting on a bench?

Think about where Malta is—it the island just off the tip of the boot of Italy, in the Mediterranean Sea. Very close, across the Mediterranean, is Tunisia in northern Africa—a Muslim country. Naturally, there are many Tunisian tourists as well as immigrants who live in Malta. In Muslim cultures, showing the bottom of your foot is considered an egregious error—it is rude and insulting. The bottom of the foot is considered dirty—both with practical and deeply religious connotations. This mistake demonstrated the insensitivity of the U.S. McDonald's Corporation in that the executives were not aware of this important cultural issue—it not only insulted the people, but also showed an ethnocentric—or self-focused attitude of the U.S. American people toward the Muslim population—and created negative feelings (actually perpetuating the stereotype of the "ignorant American").

This was a major communication blunder—if we look at it from the Triangle of Meaning perspective, at the bottom left corner of the triangle is the *symbol*. As we recall, the symbol could be a word, concept, diagram, color, emblem, sign, character, and so on [this particular symbol is the figure of Ronald McDonald sitting on the bench with the bottom of his foot showing]. At the right bottom corner of the triangle is the referent—the idea, feeling, impression, or meaning that people attach to the symbol (in this particular instance the impression was negative—showing the bottom of one's feet is offensive for both cultural and religious reasons). At the top are the *interpreters*— the communicators. While a U.S. American executive might have in her or his mind the positive meaning of a "laid-back" happy clown that will welcome guests to the establishment, and children will be happy to have their pictures taken with it, to a Muslim customer, this clown sitting there with his foot in the air would be such an offense that many people would recoil with displeasure and shock, wondering how insensitive a multinational company could be to insult their customs and religion. The interpreters would not be able to connect the dotted line at the base of the triangle and therefore not have the same referent for the symbol—they would both be on different frames of reference.

Learning From Mistakes

But, we can all learn from our mistakes, as did McDonald's. They turned around their approach in Thailand. The executive team learned their lesson from the island of Malta and spent time on the much-needed research into cultural customs and came up with a more successful figure when they opened their restaurant chain in Thailand. Thailand's culture has a history of formal politeness and respect, so, when you meet someone, you place your hands together (thumbs touching and fingers pointing upward) and say, "*Sa-wat-dee*." It means "blessing," "good fortune."

It only seems natural that the figure of Ronald McDonald should do the same—so when McDonald's entered the Thai market, they created the Ronald McDonald figure standing tall with his hands in the prayer position. This statue was well received. If we look at it in terms of the Triangle of Meaning, the symbol is the figure of Ronald McDonald with his hands in a prayer position. The referent is the meaning that people attach to the symbol (in this case, the connotation was positive).

The interpreters—the communicators—were both on the same frame of reference—both parties had the same idea about the symbol, so they had successful communication. The meaning of the hands folded in prayer (*sa-wat-dee*—blessing/good fortune) is a positive force that welcomes people into the restaurant. The McDonald's executives learned from their mistakes and were able to now show respect for the Thai people and their culture. They were able to connect the dots between the symbol *and* the referent.

The importance of the Triangle of Meaning is that we must strive to be on the same frame of reference. When we act as interpreters, we hope to select symbols that others will understand in precisely (or approximately) the same way we do. Remember what we said in the beginning of our discussion about the Latin verb for "communication?" If two people are communicating and are not thinking on the same wavelength, while the message is being shared, the meaning is *not*.

Major missteps in multinational companies caused by well-meaning but ineffective business leaders can be incredulous and costly. But missteps are common when leaders do not take the time to do their due diligence.

Context and Communication

Edward T. Hall

What is your response to the following quote by anthropologist Edward T. Hall, who is author of the seminal work on intercultural communication called, *The silent language*: "One of the most effective ways to learn about oneself is by taking seriously the cultures of others. It forces you to pay attention to those details of life which differentiate them from you." (Hall, 1959, p. 54). You probably would agree. This quote fits what we have been talking about in terms of the connection of emotional intelligence and cultural intelligence. We first learn about ourselves and then we learn about others. Hall defines culture as how we communicate, and states that it is governed by hidden rules (the silent language and hidden dimension)—these are reflected in both language and behavior. As global leaders it is essential to be ready for these tacit aspects of culture and communication that present themselves in daily interactions.

Hall is credited with founding the scholarly field of intercultural communication based on his work with the Hopi and Navajo Indians of the Southwestern United States, as well as his work with the Japanese as a Foreign Service Specialist. From both his research and his foreign-service work, he developed a continuum along which he charted the communication patterns of different cultures. Communication follows a definite pattern, it is learned, and it can be analyzed just as we do with culture (Hall, 1959). This is the notion of high- and low-context cultures. In *high-context* cultures, meaning is derived from the subtle, tacit actions and reactions of the communicators and not necessarily the words they use. Communication will also be less direct. Relationships are especially important, so the manner in which something is said, and the attention paid to the audience for those remarks are carefully observed. For example, silence can mean that a person is thinking, is showing deference, or is simply taking the time to respond while observing the reactions of the receiver. A speaker from a high-context culture will understand the importance of that silence and will infer that implicit meanings often speak louder than words.

Low-Context Communication

A *low-context* culture relies more on the explicit or actual words that are spoken. Emphasis is placed on being direct, and receivers are meant to respond to the verbal code in more literal ways. The task is more important than the relationship, so low-context speakers will use clear language, and a lot of it, to get the point across. Low-context speakers are uncomfortable with silence and quickly will try to fill it with more words. Such speakers may interpret silence as a lack of understanding and will, therefore, feel as if they have to explain in more detail. Figure 5.6 depicts the names of a number of nations plotted along a diagonal continuum. You will notice that the Eastern (Asian) cultures are positioned toward the high-context pole. Mediterranean cultures are positioned in the middle, while Western cultures (U.S., Canada, and Western Europe) fall closer to the low-context pole (Leeds-Hurwitz, 1990).

High-Context Communication

In a high-context culture meaning is derived by what is *not* said, with people grasping the subtext within the context of what is being discussed. Here is an example that can help us visualize what high context means. The ancient Chinese symbol for listening includes not only listening with the ears but with the heart and eyes as well (U.S. Department of State, n.d.) (see Figure 5.7). We listen with our ears to hear the word, the tone, and the pitch; we listen with our mind to understand to analyze and to broaden our perspective; we also listen with our eyes to see the facial expression, to read the body language; and we listen to our heart to feel the emotions, to empathize, and to respond. This ancient Chinese character is made up of six radicals (components of the character that add semantic meaning and also phonetic sound). On the left we have "ear" and below it is "king," which means we should listen to the king and never interrupt. On the top right is "ten" and "eye," which, put together, means to focus on the king with ten eyes. The radical for "one" means to not only focus, but do so with undivided attention. Finally, the bottom-right radical means "heart." So one listens to the king with ears, eyes, and heart—giving full respect and devotion.

Also, the semantics (meaning) of certain phrases can mean different things in different languages. For example, in Japan, if you ask "Where are you going?" it is more of a social question—politeness, where you do not expect an answer. In the United States to ask "Where are you going?" would be an information question. However, in the United States one would say, "Hi, how are you?"

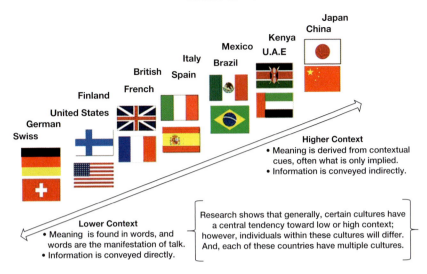

Figure 5.6 High- and Low-Context Cultures

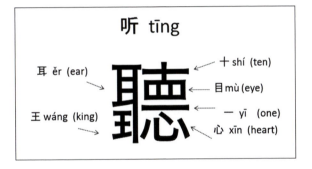

Figure 5.7 Chinese Character for Listening

while passing an acquaintance on the street. The status quo is to keep walking—you are generally not interested in hearing how that person is. But in Mexico or the Middle East, one would expect to stop and talk about one's day or family. In China, a common way to greet people is to ask if they have eaten or not with the greeting, "*Ní chī le ma?*" While the syntax of these sentences imply an answer—"I'm fine" or, "Yes, I have eaten" the semantics—or meaning—of the sentence is based upon context. This expression is also considered a social question versus an information question. If you know that this is a convention of language, then you'll know how to respond. If not, you'll be wondering why people always ask you if you have eaten when they meet you!

Finnish people tend to be high context when listening without interruption. Foreigners tend to stereotype Finns as taciturn, wondering whether they are even listening. But this is cultural tradition to show respect to the speaker by listening intently. India also has a high-context practice that shows respect. Have you ever wondered when you watch a Bollywood movie why characters are always using the suffix, "*jee/ji*" at the end of an elder's name? This is a form of honorific that shows respect. Another aspect of high context is that preserving harmony and strengthening relationships is more important than exchanging information. Japan has a high-context concept of *tatemae*, which means "someone who is direct and objective," and *honne* is the "unspoken meaning." In Japan if a guest has overstayed their welcome, the host could never make them lose face by saying it is time to go. Instead, the host will ask if the guest would like to eat a breakfast dish called *bubuzuke*. This signals to the guest that they have overstayed their welcome and it is time to leave (Nishimura et al., 2008)!

Direct and Indirect Communication

Related to high- and low-context communication is the concept of direct and indirect communication. Cultural groups have general tendencies toward one or the other with—of course—many variations in between. We constantly have to remember this caveat. All generalizations are a starting-off place for us to bring awareness into our interactions. Even how we organize presentations are influenced by culture. Direct communication is straightforward, with explicit expectations communicated to employees. In multinational companies, there would be a need for overcommunication of key messages, project plans, and so on, to make sure that people were all on the same frame of reference regarding timelines, project details, and work expectations, with conflict being handled immediately. An indirect form of communication would be more implicit and often an intermediary would be used to deal with conflict, with the emphasis on "saving face" (Table 5.1).

For example, in Madagascar there is a four-point organizational pattern that follows the indirect form of public address (Jaffe, 1995):

Table 5.1 Direct and Indirect Communication

Direct	Indirect
Offers frank opinion	Refrains from stating personal opinions
Uncomfortable with silence	Silence is a time to reflect before responding too hastily
Comfortable challenging or contradicting other's ideas	It is more important to preserve harmony and save face
Uses "I" words—"In my opinion," "I think"	Uses "We" words and qualifiers—"In our humble opinion," "We might agree"
Be succinct—get to the point	Say only what is needed

(*Source*: Hall, 1990, p. 49.)

1   First, the speaker would humbly apologize for interrupting everyone's daily routine to make their statement. This demonstrates someone's humility in being given the honor to speak.

2   Then, the speaker would thank all those in authority—there is a formula to this—first God; the president and government officials; village headman (chief) and elders; and then family and people in attendance. It is a very collective way of acknowledging everyone from top to bottom.

3   The speaker moves on to use stories and illustrations to make his or her point—often with the use of proverbs and adages to demonstrate wisdom from the past.

4   Finally the speaker closes by not only thanking the listeners, but by blessing them as well.

Whereas, in the United States, if you are advising someone on how to make a public address, you would probably stick with the old adage—"Tell us what you're going to tell us; tell us; then tell us what you told us." This is a three-point organizational strategy that starts with the main idea (deductive approach); then gives detailed support with examples; then wraps up by restating the main point in a circular conclusion.

Does this mean that all people doing business in Madagascar are going to use the four-point indirect form of public speaking? Of course not; however, knowing something about the speaking strategies of people from a culture with whom you are doing business can help you stay calm and regroup when your meeting inevitably does not go in the direction or take the form you had anticipated.

Designer Yang Liu created a brilliant infographic series called *Ost trifft West* (East versus West) that contrasts Eastern and Western communication patterns, values, and behaviors (see Figure 5.8). Its simplicity is profound as she demonstrates the fundamental differences between the East and the West, inspired by her experience having grown up in China and living in Germany. In this example she depicts direct versus indirect communication.

Handling Conflict

Another way of looking at directness and indirectness is how we handle conflict. I like the definition used by the Cultural Orientations Indicator, which is an online cross-cultural assessment tool that measures one's cultural preferences regarding interaction styles, thinking styles, and identity (TMC, n.d.). Indirect communication would indicate handling conflict and giving feedback discreetly, with an emphasis on saving face, whereas direct communication would do so in a straightforward and explicit manner.

As an indirect communicator you believe that conflicts out in the open are not beneficial to a cohesive workplace so you work around the conflict—some would call this being passive. You might use metaphors to express

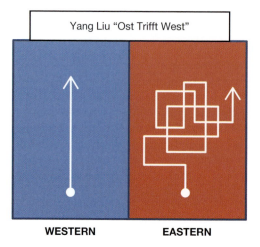

Figure 5.8 Yang Liu "Ost Trifft West"

(*Source*: Adapted from Yang Liu "Ost Trifft West," n.d.)

disagreement and if that does not work, find a third party to mediate. Having things out in the open makes you nervous and uncomfortable, especially the display of emotions.

You believe that open conflicts are not beneficial to the parties involved. You may prefer passive resistance or the use of subtle or metaphoric expressions of disagreement, critical feedback, or dissenting views, as well as the use of formal or informal mediators (arbitrators, colleagues, friends, etc.) to address, manage, and resolve contentious issues. Situations that require you to bring contentious issues into the open are uncomfortable for you. Openly displayed tensions can disturb you deeply.

Direct communication would be the opposite—you would handle the controversy by talking about it. For example, let us say you have to give one of your employees her annual review. She is competent, skilled, and has been an integral part of the team—a star performer. However, her communication style is abrupt, acerbic, and negative, which intimidates her team members, who have complained to you. All efforts of indirect expressions of discomfort by team members have not registered and no change has come about. So as you plan your approach you decide to be direct with your communication from the perspective of helping her understand the need to improve personal accountability with team members rather than emphasizing how to improve her performance (Figure 5.9).

Saying "No"

Not everyone says "no" in the same manner. Not everyone uses the expression of "thank you" and "please" in the same way. For example, in India, you

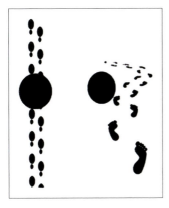

Figure 5.9 Handling Conflict Directly or Indirectly

would only say "thank you" if you knew someone well—that person would be in your inner circle—otherwise there is no social expectation that one would go out of their way to express thanks for a service. When saying "no," people from India can have a difficult time because they do not want to create conflict that will erode the harmonious relationship. Steve Mezak, CEO of Accelerance, a global software outsourcing company, and author of the book *Software Without Borders*, has written a humorous yet accurate account of how people using different language can have vastly different interpretations. He says, "So here's a short guide to help my fellow culturally challenged Americans on how to know when an Indian programmer (manager, team lead, etc.) means 'no'" (Box 5.2).

Monochronic and Polychronic Time

Monochronic

Another important finding of Hall is that some cultures are traditionally monochronic. In such a culture, time is thought of as being linear. People are expected to do one thing at a time, and they have little patience for lateness or interruptions. There is an emphasis on freedom and opportunity that come to people who work hard. Employees know implicitly that they must agree to specific deadlines and in order to meet those deadlines it is necessary to explicitly deal with what it means to be "complete." People who relate to monochronic time understand it in terms of isolated events—time is not continuous—it is discrete and divided up into fixed components such as minutes, hours, days, and weeks. These components are meant to be organized, accounted for, and scheduled. Detailed planning with spreadsheets and lists to keep track of procedures, tasks, and deadlines is essential. Daily routines are expected to be kept and respected. If there is a meeting, show up

Box 5.2 The 7 Ways an Indian Programmer Says "No" by Steve Mezak

No response = NO

When you are busy dominating a conversation about your software development you may notice your Indian programming team is not saying much in response. Be careful! It's not awe. They are probably disagreeing with your ridiculous approach or unrealistic release date.

Changing the subject = NO

Technical managers can be easily distracted by interesting programming questions. But don't forget to circle around to get the answers you need to important questions. For example:

STEVE: Will the software be finished by Thursday?

SANJEEV: I wanted to ask you about the Foobar module ...

STEVE: (*excited about the new functionality Foobar brings to the software app*): Yeah, we are really looking forward to that feature!

SANJEEV: Yes, it is very cool. Will it be made available for all users?

STEVE: Oh yes, especially managers. Remember when a manager clicks the Foobar button the screen displays the monthly Foobar report in the upper right corner . . . . .

(No, the software will not be finished by Thursday.)

Postponing an answer = NO

When you ask, "Will the software be finished by Thursday?" listen for responses like "I'll get back to you on that ..." or "I'll have to ask the team ..." that may seem reasonable but probably mean no. After all if the answer was truly yes then an Indian would say it. There is some chance "the team" will provide the reassurance to say yes later, but for now consider the answer is no, the software will not be finished by Thursday.

Repeating the question = NO

Especially repeating the question multiple times:

STEVE: Will the software be finished by Thursday?

SANJEEV: This Thursday?

STEVE: Yes, we want the support team to try it out on Friday so you have until the end of the day on Thursday.

SANJEEV: Thursday afternoon?

(The software will not be finished by Thursday.)

Turning the question = NO

If the response is another question back to you like, "Do you think we can get everything done by Thursday?" or "Is Thursday still a good day for you?" (Then plan for a delay.)

Hesitation in answering = NO

If the answer is really yes then an Indian programmer will blurt it out quickly. But if there is any hesitation, unusual facial expressions or body language then it means the actual answer is a pain-causing "no" that gets expressed as a noncommittal response.

A conditional yes = NO

I was stranded in the Mumbai airport on a rainy night last year when my flight was canceled. I learned that a Cathy Pacific flight was scheduled to leave at 3am heading in my intended direction (but was probably already full up). I asked the agent anyway, a kind-hearted middle-aged Indian man, "Can you get me on the Cathy Pacific flight to Singapore?"

"That would be difficult" he said.

In New York, my response might have been, "Okay, let's do it!" But on that rainy night in Mumbai I recognized his true meaning and knew instantly that the answer was no. I was put up in a Marriott hotel for the night and left on a flight the next evening.

As a general shortcut in communication with your Indian programming team, remember that the absence of "yes" in a conversation really means "no" and you should adjust your plans accordingly. Bugs, unclear requirements & technical challenges in software development are unavoidable no matter what country you are in. The trick is to identify these problems quickly and address them.

Mezak, 2012 (used with permission).

and do not be late. If your boss has asked you to focus on a specific project, then you are expected to work until it is finished before moving on to another task. To bounce back and forth between tasks is seen as wasting time, but is also uncomfortable to the person who tends to be single-focused (monochronic) in nature. Work is present-focused and people want quick results—this contrasts with the fluid focus of polychronic cultures (Table 5.2).

In the United States, we have many sayings for time:

- Time is money (see Figure 5.10).
- Don't waste time.
- Don't throw your time away.
- Lost time is never found again.
- Don't steal time.

Polychronic

In polychronic cultures, time is cyclical and there is a relaxed sense to when someone must be someplace "on time." Punctuality takes on a different

Table 5.2 Monochronic/Polychronic Time

Monochronic time	Polychronic time
Short-term focus and commitment	Long-term focus and commitment
One thing at a time	Many things at a time
Be punctual	Be flexible
Committed to task at hand	Committed to relationships
Single-focused	Multi-focused
Deadlines should be followed strictly	Deadlines are merely guidelines
Low-context communicators who need explicit information	High-context communicators who can read between the lines
Privacy is respected	Public connection is respected

(*Source*: Hall & Hall, 1987, pp. 16–17.)

Figure 5.10 Time is Money

(*Source*: Fotolia 80839183, © Stepan Popov.)

meaning, and it would be more appropriate to show up later than the time discussed. People who are polychronic have a different relationship to time—for them it is continuous and even cyclical, one event flowing into another, like a continuous river. At work they prefer unstructured time and find it easy to multitask to get things done. They meet deadlines, but they do it in a way that makes sense to them—in their way—in their own time. I had a boss years ago who had lived and worked in East Africa for many years. He never wore a watch. He knew it was time to teach his class when he heard the sounds of people moving in the hall. His internal clock enabled him to listen to the cues of movement and sound (Hall, 1990).

Also, in polychronic cultures it is acceptable to interrupt someone during a meeting by answering the phone or allowing an assistant to stop you full sentence to relay an important message. I remember a number of years ago having dinner in Beijing with a Google executive and one of my students (the executive was one of her mentors). My student was excited to be able to invite me, her professor, to have dinner with him and experience "high-flying" life in Beijing. However, over a meal of duck tongue, I remember basically only making a few customary greetings while the executive spent the entire dinner on his phone. My student and I had an enjoyable time discussing the cuisine in his absence.

It is important not to associate polychronic cultures and their people as lazy—it is just a different way of getting things done. Time is relaxed rather than rigid. Tony Cohen's book *On Mexican Time* delightfully explains his observations on Mexican life when he moved to San Miguel de Allende (State Symbols USA, n.d.). Time moved more spherically there, which allowed him to catch his breath and move to an adagio versus allegro rhythm. In Mexico, if you want someone to show up on time, you say, "*en punto,*" which means "on the hour" or "on the dot." If you arrange to meet friends at 9:00 pm and you want people to be on time, you must say, "*Nos vemos a las nueve en punto*" otherwise 9:00pm can flow into 9:30 or even 10:00pm. If someone tells you that they will do something in "just a minute," and they say, "*un momentito,*" you could be waiting 20 minutes or even an hour to get it done.

Lapses in frames of reference occur all too often when one counterpart is thinking that something will get done by the end of the week and the other is thinking that it will get done when it gets done. Both have two different perspectives of what means "get it done" and, if they do not make their meaning common between them, there will be definite frustration, and per-haps missed deadlines.

I used to live in Albuquerque, New Mexico, the Land of Enchantment. I love the symbolism on the State flag—the symbol of the red sun on a bright yellow background. The sun is an ancient Zia symbol which is represented by a circle with four points radiating from it, all with four bars on each point. These represent the four points of the compass (north, south east, west), the four seasons of the year (spring, summer, fall, winter), the four times of each day (morning, noon, evening, night), and the four seasons of life (childhood, youth, middle years, old age). There are four sacred obligations that go with these aspects of life: develop a strong body, a clear mind, a pure spirit, and care of others. This symbol is a reminder of the polychronic attitude toward the time of life—it is cyclical with everything being in its proper place—direc-tions, times of day, four physical-environment seasons, as well as the devel-opmental seasons of a person's life—even the reminder of the importance of creating synergies for good living (State Symbols USA, n.d.).

A while back, I saw a T-shirt with the sun symbol with a caption below it, "*Carpe Mañana,*" which means seize tomorrow (see Figure 5.11). It is a play on words from the Latin aphorism *Carpe diem*, which means "seize the day" and comes from the Roman poem *Odes* (23 BCE), by Horace. This is a great example of polychronic time (James, 2008).

Here is another example of polychronic time, which is more cyclical in nature than monochronic time. In Greek mythology, the Sphinx sat outside of Thebes and asked this riddle of all travelers who passed by. If the traveler

Figure 5.11 Carpe Mañana—Seize Tomorrow!

failed to solve the riddle, then the Sphinx killed them. If the traveler answered the riddle correctly, then the Sphinx would destroy herself. The riddle: What goes on four legs in the morning, on two legs at noon, and on three legs in the evening? Oedipus solved the riddle, and the Sphinx destroyed herself. The solution: A human, who crawls on all fours as a baby, walks on two legs as an adult, and walks with a cane in old age. Of course morning, noon, and night are metaphors for the times in a person's life (University Press Inc., n.d.).

Space

One other area of importance is the study of how humans use space, called "proxemics"(Hall, 1966). Hall developed a theory that, apart from human sensory devices, our perception of space is patterned by culture. The way we use and organize space is internalized on an unconscious level and informed by our cultural influences (Hofstede would call this the programming of our minds). Hall created the notion of personal space—the proverbial bubble that surrounds each of us, which is 4 feet/1.22 meters. Intimate space is the closest space that surrounds us—this is only intended for close friends and intimate relationships—the intimate distance is 1.5 feet /0.46 meters. Social space occurs in—obviously—social interactions with people we know or even strangers—there is a safe distance of about 12 feet/3.66 meters. Public space is the area of space that provides a distance of some 25 feet/7.62 meters where we can be impersonal or even anonymous. Have you ever noticed being uncomfortable in a situation where you might have backed away from someone who was standing too close in "your space?" Perhaps you remember the *Seinfeld* sitcom episode of the "Close Talker" (Itsbeginningtolook, 2009). Anyone who has had this experience understands when someone invades their space (Figure 5.12).

When I lived in Hong Kong I was amazed at how people used space. With over 7 million people crammed into the New Territory and Hong Kong Island, an area slightly smaller than New York City, it was a challenge to navigate one's space, especially in the MTR underground subway. Whether walking or standing, if any space whatsoever in front, behind, or to the side

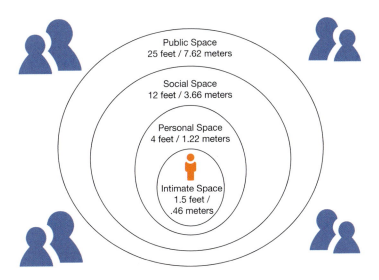

Figure 5.12 Public and Private Space

(*Source*: Hall, 1966, pp. 117–25.)

opened up it would be filled immediately. People were constantly in my space and it was a way of life that I needed to get used to—or spend my days in rush hour needlessly frustrated. I learned to never open a door for people, or gesture to someone to enter an elevator first: I would never get in! Westerners are accustomed to standing in an elevator in such a way that maximum space is maintained between people. When in Hong Kong, you learn quickly that just when you think the elevator is full, several more can be squished in. Again, just when you think the door will close, several more people will push their way in! Space has different meanings to people and their perceptions of what is acceptable and what is not.

The Cultural Anthropology of Traffic Patterns

Watch examples of traffic patterns in Malmo, Sweden, then Mumbai, India, and finally, Ho Chi Min City, Vietnam (see Box 5.3). What do you notice? What are the patterns and who has the right of way? In private cultures, value is placed on distance with clearly marked boundaries and order. In more public cultures, value is placed on proximity and overlapping, permeable boundaries. Notice how the traffic flows around objects—the bigger vehicles giving way to the smaller—and so on. It might not appear like this at first, but look again and see the rhythm and flow of people and scooters, cars and buses.

The scene from *Midnight Cowboy* is a relevant example of personal space. In this scene, Dustin Hoffman defends his personal space. But is it not paradoxical

> ## Box 5.3 The Cultural Anthropology of Traffic
>
> From time to time, URL links to videos go down. If this happens, try Googling the subject and/or obtain the movie to watch. All movies mentioned in this text are worth watching and analyzing for cultural concepts:
>
> - Malmo, Sweden: www.youtube.com/watch?v=_ThTGG69w84
> - Mumbai, India: www.youtube.com/watch?v=2fRyqP0aHtQ&feature=related
> - Ho Chi Min City, Vietnam: www.youtube.com/watch?v=4phFYiMGCIY
> - *Midnight Cowboy*: www.youtube.com/watch?v=c412hqucHKw
> - *Outsourced* Train Scene: www.youtube.com/watch?v=up-tsl855hw

that on a crowded city street—whether New York, Hong Kong, or London—people basically live their lives in the public yet perhaps want to establish their own personal space? As previously mentioned, in Hong Kong, people do not mind closeness—they actually subconsciously close the gap when walking on the MTR subway. If you pause, you may get run over; if there is a spot of space, someone will fill it—even if it means they are in your face or end up tripping you by accident. This reminds us that cultures are complex and contradictory. Another telling example is from the film *Outsourced*. Watch the clip and notice the utilitarian use of relative space on the train.

People are comfortable with different space between them when greeting. The French kiss on both cheeks. The Dutch give three kisses. The Japanese bow and the depth depends on the rank of each person. In Venezuela people give a huge hug—an *abrazzo*. In China people rarely hug. For Arabs, the space that is comfortable for ordinary social conversation is approximately the same as that which Westerners reserve for intimate conversation. Therefore, Arab culture does not have the same concept of public and private space that Western cultures do. Westerners, in a sense, carry a little bubble of private space around with them.

Summary

Communication is more than exchanging words. Communicating across cultures is all about the context. As leaders we need to know some aspects of how language works, as we learned through the Triangle of Meaning. If we are not on the same frame of reference, then miscommunication occurs because each person has different expectations for what the words or symbols or gestures mean. We can also apply the concepts of high and low, direct and indirect communication, and target culture-specific aspects of people with whom we interact. How we use time as well as how comfortable we are when people get into our space are important considerations for any business professional. As we have learned in this chapter, if we do not understand the subtleties of a language and culture, then we can fall prey to the costly business blunders talked about in this chapter. Being a culturally competent leader means that we discover the hidden dimensions of language in our everyday interactions.

References

CNN Money. (1999, June 18). Lockheed's $70M comma. Retrieved from http://money.cnn.com/1999/06/18/worldbiz/lockheed/ (July 28, 2016).

Hall, E. T. (1959). *The silent language.* Garden City, NY: Doubleday.

Hall, E. T. (1966). *The hidden dimension.* Garden City, NY: Doubleday.

Hall, E. T. (1990). *Understanding cultural differences: German, French, and Americans.* Yarmouth, ME: International Press.

Hall, E. T., Hall, M. R. (1987). *Understanding cultural differences: Germans, French, and Americans.* Yarmouth, ME: Intercultural Press.

Itsbeginningtolook. (2009, December 4). Social awareness—close talker.wmv. Retrieved from www.youtube.com/watch?v=NGVSIkEi3mM (July 28, 2016).

Jaffe, C. (1995). *Public speaking: A cultural perspective.* Belmont, CA: Wadsworth.

James, P. (2008) Seize the day and savour it: Horace's carpe diem. Retrieved from www.open.edu/openlearn/history-the-arts/history/classical-studies/seize-the-day-and-savour-it-horaces-carpe-diem (July 28, 2016).

Leeds-Hurwitz, W. (1990). Notes in the history of intercultural communication: The Foreign Service Institute and the mandate for intercultural training. *Quarterly Journal of Speech, 76*(3), 262–81.

Mezak, S. (2012, April 11). The 7 ways an Indian programmer says "no." *Accelerance.* Retrieved from www.accelerance.com/blog/the-7-ways-an-indian-programmer-says-no (July 28, 2016).

Nishimura, S., Nevgi, A., & Tella, S. (2008). Communication style and cultural features in high/low context communication cultures: A case study of Finland, Japan and India. In A. Kallioniemi (Ed.), *Renovating and developing subject didactics. Part 2.* Proceedings of a subject-didactic symposium in Helsinki, February 2, 2008 (783–96). University of Helsinki. Department of Applied Sciences of Education. Research Report 299.

Ogden, C. K., & Richards, I. A. (1927). *Meaning of meaning.* New York, NY: Harcourt Brace.

Ricks, D. A. (2006). *Blunders in international business.* Malden, MA: Blackwell Publishing.

State Symbols USA. (n.d.) Flag of New Mexico. Retrieved from www.statesymbolsusa.org/symbol-official-item/new-mexico/state-flag/flag-new-mexico (July 28, 2016).

Training Management Corporation (TMC). (n.d.). Meet the cultural navigator. Retrieved from www.culturalnavigator.com/CN7/login.aspx (July 28, 2016).

Tuleja, E. A. (2015). *Intercultural communication for business.* Indianapolis, IN: Globe-Comm Publishing.

Tuleja, E. A., Beamer, L., Shum, C., & Chan, Elisa K. Y. (2011). Designing and developing questionnaires for translation across cultures. *IEEE Transactions on Professional Communication, 54*(4), 392–405.

University Press Inc. (n.d.). Greek myths: Oedipus. Ancient Greece. Retrieved from www.ancientgreece.com/s/GreekMyths/Oedipus/ (July 28, 2016).

U.S. Department of State. (n.d.). Active listening. Retrieved from www.state.gov/m/
a/os/65759.htm (accessed August 1, 2016).

Verluyten, S. P. (2010). *Intercultural skills for international business and international relations.*
Leuven: Acco.

Yang Liu Designs. (n.d.). Projects, Ost trifft West. Retrieved from www.yangliudesign.
com (accessed September 20, 2016).

Case 5

Target Corporation

The "Urine Sandal"[1]

Abstract

"*Orina*" means "urine" in Spanish. But it also means "peace" in Russian—ostensibly the only meaning the Target Corporation had when it used the word to name its new foot sandal in February of 2013. It did not take Latino news outlets very long to protest the *orina* name, resulting in great embarrassment for the second-largest retailer in the United States. What should be Target's response, and how can the retail giant recover respect from the Latino community? What steps can Target take to assure this does not happen again?

Introduction

Jessica Deede sat at her desk, staring blankly at the papers in front of her. Her phone rang unremittingly, as reporters pestered her for Target's official comment on the events of the last three weeks. Within this short time span, Target had managed to mistakenly name two products in an offensive manner. A plus-sized dress was named "Grey Manatee," only to be followed by a sandal the next week named "orina," which translated to "urine" in Spanish. It fell to Jessica Deede—the spokesperson for Target—to determine how best to communicate the issues with consumers and the media.

Background

The Beginnings

After a successful career in banking and real estate, George Dayton moved from New York to Minneapolis to explore business opportunities. In 1902, Dayton created the Dayton Dry Goods Company, which would grow to be one of the largest retailers in the world (Target Brands, n.d.a).

By 1960, The Dayton Company had grown into the leading department store in the Midwest (Target Brands, n.d.a). After brainstorming ways to reach larger audiences of shoppers, a discount retailing operation was launched. Industry experts considered this mass-market approach very risky; it did not seem wise for the company to shift focus from traditional department-store retailing. Despite the risks, company leadership recognized an opportunity to create a new type of mass-market discount retailer that provided high-quality products to value-oriented consumers.

The management aimed to create "a store you can be proud to shop in, a store you can have confidence in, a store that is fun to shop and exciting to visit" (Target Brands, n.d.a); thus the discount retailer was named Target. In 1962, St. Louis Park, Crystal, and Duluth, Minnesota, hosted the grand openings of the Target flagship model (Target Brands, n.d.a).

By 1975, Target had grown to be the greatest revenue generator of the Dayton conglomerate (Target Brands, n.d.a). Over the next 15 years, Target aggressively expanded its presence from the Midwest to all of 47 states. To better reflect their core operations and strategy, The Dayton Company elected to change its name to The Target Corporation in 2000 (Target Brands, n.d.a).

On its 50th Anniversary in 2012, Target reported sales of nearly $70 billion (Target Corporation, TGT: New York, 2012), solidifying its position as the second-largest discount retailer in the United States. From its humble beginnings, Target has definitely grown into a premier vendor of trendy, high-quality, and reasonably priced goods.

Organizational Structure

In addition to its main retail subsidiary, the Target Corporation is broken down into several subsidiaries (Target Corporation, TGT: New York, 2012):

- Financial and Retail Services—Issues and oversees Target credit cards, as well as gift-card operations.
- Target Sourcing Services—Logistics service that globally sources and locates merchandise around the world in order to create a fluid and dynamic supply chain.
- Target Commercial Interiors—Designs services and furniture for professional offices.
- Target Brands—Oversees and operates Target's private labels and products.
- Target.com—Operates a variety of online e-commerce initiatives, including the flagship target.com.

Products and Image

Target has achieved such great success by creating significant competitive advantages in product differentiation. Over the years, management has successfully achieved the goal of providing "everyday essentials and fashionable, differentiated merchandise at discounted prices" (Target Corporation, TGT: New York, 2012). This objective has created a clear and sustainable alternative to Wal-Mart's (Target's primary competitor) price leadership in the discount retailing industry.

Featuring exclusive products from a number of stylish boutiques, Target augmented its discounter reputation with a trendy one. Target owns a number of private labels, which it operates as a part of its core business (Phillips, 2012). Also, Target has engaged in a number of high-profile design partnerships across merchandise lines, ranging from apparel to kitchenware. Target worked with designers Mossimo and Isaac Mizrahi in apparel to create new lines that complement its own labels (Barwise & Meehan, 2004). Each of the brands, private and partnership, has a specific product-positioning that appeals to Target's overall broad customer base.

Target's design partnerships have enabled them to adopt a theme: "cheap for chic." Consumers have accepted and responded favorably to the retailer's ability to provide stylishly designed products at affordable prices.

Consumer Profiles

Traditional Target Markets

Although Target has developed a competitive advantage through its "choice for cheap" strategy, they have never been able to compete with major rival Wal-Mart from a price perspective. Thus, their target market has always been a bit different. They strategically aim to cater to a different consumer base.

The median age of a shopper in 2012 was 40, with a median household income of approximately $64,000. Approximately 43 percent had children at home and about 57 percent had completed college (Target Brands, n.d.b). These figures speak to Target's target: while they function as a discount retailer, they aim to target middle-class consumers who prefer trendy apparel and goods at reasonable prices.

Changing U.S. Consumer Demographics

With the aging of the Baby Boomer population, the average age in the United States is increasing. However, the Hispanic and Latino populations remain relatively young; this demographic group is poised to experience the largest growth of any group by 2050 (Llopis, 2013). In fact, Hispanic/Latino populations accounted for nearly half of the U.S. population increase between 2000 and 2011 (Llopis, 2013). And, by 2019, minority children will be in the majority (U.S. Census Bureau, 2011).

With this growth in population, the Hispanic/Latino demographic is expected to be a primary driver of workforce supply-and-demand. Businesses will need to adjust their advertising and product offerings to cater to the preferences of this new target audience. This will require a significant amount of shifting, as Hispanic/Latino consumption preferences differ from that of traditional Caucasian target audiences.

Hispanic and Latino Consumption Patterns

The median age of the Hispanic and Latino market segment is 28 years old, with a median household income of $65,233 (DeNavas-Walt & Proctor, 2015). Despite the similarity of these numbers to those of Target's traditional customers, consumption patterns still differ widely.

For example, Hispanics/Latinos spend 68 percent more time viewing videos on the Internet, and 20 percent more time watching videos on mobile devices than non-Hispanics/Latinos (The Nielsen Company, 2012). The marketing and advertising implications are obvious; businesses will need to expand to online and mobile video platforms in order to reach this target audience. How will this impact the product portfolio these companies invest in, and what kinds of marketing and advertising strategies will they have to adapt to?

Also, Hispanics/Latinos demonstrate distinct product consumption patterns and have differing behavioral purchasing habits than the overall population. The demographic makes fewer shopping trips per household and spends more money per trip (The Nielsen Company, 2012); essentially, Hispanics/Latinos are bulk buyers. Given the collectivist and *familioso* nature of Hispanic/Latino families, this behavior makes sense. Rather than having individuals buy what they alone desire and need, families will often go out together and engage in bulk shopping.

This provides opportunities, but also downsides for businesses. While more spending on shopping trips implies larger revenue streams, infrequent trips imply that a loss of loyalty could be deadly. Businesses will need to differentiate themselves and advertise effectively to keep Hispanics/Latinos engaged as customers.

A Failure of Intercultural Communication

The Urine Sandal

In April of 2013, Target made a branding mistake that offended the wider population. In an apparently harmless act, Target chose to name a sandal "orina."

"*Orina*" is a word that means "peace" or "peaceful" in Russian, which is the image that Target was attempting to convey to its customers. However, the meaning in Spanish is drastically different; the direct translation of "*orina*" means "urine" (Sheets, 2013).

Naturally, the brand name offended many Spanish speakers. But more than the offensive name, consumers seemed to be outraged by Target's lack of oversight and review in brand naming. A popular consumer blog titled "Consumerist" wrote the following:

> It's not so much that urine is offensive — hey, we all gotta pee — but it does display an apparent lack of attention to detail on the part of a

national retailer. Does no one speak Spanish at Target HQ or have access to this thing we call Google?

(Quirk, 2013)

Other blogs and online sites followed in this example, and Target caught on to the news quickly. Within a day, the "orina" branded products had been removed from Target.com. Unfortunately, the media storm did not end with the removal of the products and the blog posts; the following day, major news outlets began to report on Target's mishap. When Jessica Deede, a spokesperson for Target, was asked to comment by *The Huffington Post*, she responded by noting that in "realizing this name could be misinterpreted, we [Target] are taking steps to remove the name from the sandal" (*The Huffington Post*, 2013).

While this may have been enough to calm the storm under normal circumstances, consumers and bloggers soon realized that this name calamity was not the only instance of Target's poor branding.

Dresses for the Manatees

Just a week earlier, Target had apologized for electing to label a plus-sized women's dress as "Manatee Gray" (Rupar, 2013). (A manatee is a large sea cow that can weigh up to 1,300 pounds.) Although Target did not mean to be crass, this act was still seen as one of insensitivity. In fact, Target had branded the dress as such due to the color scheme; in the past, Target had branded petite clothing, towels, and rain boots as manatee gray (Weber, 2013).

As was evident in the "orina" situation, Target had unknowingly communicated the wrong message to consumers. Through the abundant negative blog posts and unfavorable media coverage, it was clear that consumers were beginning to feel that Target was not putting much thought or effort into the formulation of communication with consumers.

Summary

Clearly, Target suffered by virtue of its own mistakes, and its reputation took a hit. Branding is key to the success and profitability of such discount retailers, and such errors come with tremendous costs. Although their intentions were good, Target's failure in planning and consideration seemed to lead to a failure in communication.

Given the collectivist nature and bulk-buying consumer behavior of Hispanics/Latinos, significant action needs to be taken to remedy this situation quickly and effectively. A failure to do so may lead to a decline in revenues and failure to capitalize on the fastest-growing demographic in the country.

How can Target ensure that branding mishaps do not happen again? How can they begin to heal their reputation and move away from being "sloppy" branders? What steps need to be taken to mend relationships with consumers and ensure that the high-quality standards are renewed? These are the critical issues that Target's management faces.

Discussion Questions

1 Taking into consideration the Triangle of Meaning (simply put, that there is a strong relationship between words, actual concept, and listener), what was the root cause of this mislabeling?
2 What actions can be undertaken by management to ensure that this type of branding mishap does not happen again?
3 What are the optimal ways for Target to communicate with customers and the media in order to mend relationships and heal its reputation?

Note

1 Authors: Patel, K., Kenney, K., Martinez, A., and Tuleja, E. (Ed.).

References

Barwise, Patrick, & Meehan, Seain. (2004, August 16). Bullseye: Target's cheap chic strategy. Harvard Business School. Retrieved from http://hbswk.hbs.edu/archive/4319.html (accessed May 1, 2013).

DeNavas-Walt, C., & Proctor, B. D. (2015, September). Income and Poverty in the United States: 2014, Current Population Reports. Retrieved from www.census.gov/content/dam/Census/library/publications/2015/demo/p60-252.pdf (accessed August 6, 2016).

Llopis, Glenn. (2013, January 9). Advertisers must pay attention to Hispanic consumers as rising trendsetters in 2013. *Forbes*. Retrieved from www.forbes.com/sites/glennllopis/2013/01/09/advertisers-must-pay-attention-to-hispanic-consumers-as-rising-trendsetters-in-2013/ (accessed May 1, 2013).

Phillips, Cheryl. (2012, May 5). The shops at Target launch: Five trendy boutiques start shopping frenzy. *Examiner*. Retrieved from www.examiner.com/article/the-shops-at-target-launch-five-trendy-boutiques-start-shopping-frenzy (accessed May 1, 2013).

Quirk, Mary Beth. (2013, April 9). Target probably didn't check Spanish dictionary for "urine" before selling "orina" sandals. *Consumerist*. Retrieved from http://consumerist.com/2013/04/09/target-probably-didnt-check-spanish-dictionary-for-urine-before-selling-orina-sandals/ (accessed May 1, 2013).

Rupar, Aaron. (April 12, 2013). Target renames "orina" sandal after learning word means urine in Spanish. Citypages Blogs. Retrieved from http://blogs.citypages.com/blotter/2013/04/target_renames_orina_sandal_after_learning_word_means_urine_in_spanish_image.php (accessed May 1, 2013).

Sheets, Connor Adams. (2013, April 12). "Orina" sandal scandal: Behind Target's odd name choices. *International Business Times*. Retrieved from www.ibtimes.com/orina-sandal-scandal-behind-targets-odd-name-choice-1189743 (accessed May 1, 2013).

Target Brands. (n.d.a). Target through the years. Retrieved from https://corporate.target.com/about/history/Target-through-the-years (accessed May 1, 2013).

Target Brands. (n.d.b). Corporate fact sheet. Target quick facts. http://pressroom. target.com/corporate.

Target Corporation (TGT: New York). (2012). Target 2012 10-K. Retrieved from http://investing.businessweek.com/research/stocks/financials/secfilings.asp?ticker= TGT (accessed May 1, 2013).

The Huffington Post. (2013, April 9). Target to rename "orina" shoe after learning it means "urine" in Spanish. Retrieved from www.huffingtonpost.com/2013/04/09/ target-orina-shoe-urine-spanish-translation_n_3046787.html (accessed May 1, 2013).

The Nielsen Company. (2012, April 17). Young, mobile, and growing: The state of U.S. Hispanic consumers. Retrieved from www.nielsen.com/us/en/newswire/ 2012/young-mobile-and-growing-the-state-of-us-hispanic-consumers.html (accessed May 1, 2013).

U.S. Census Bureau. (2011). Population by sex, age, and Hispanic origin type. Retrieved from www.census.gov/population/hispanic/data/2012.html (accessed August 6, 2016).

Weber, Peter. (2013, April 5). How Target fixed its "manatee gray" plus-size debacle. Yahoo! News. Retrieved from http://news.yahoo.com/target-fixed-manatee-gray-plus-size-debacle-094700278.html (accessed May 1, 2013).

6 Culture and World View

Faith is to believe what you do not see;
the reward of this faith is to see what you believe.

(Saint Augustine)

Figure 6.1 World Religion Symbols. Can you identify these? See end of chapter for
answers

(*Source*: Kok, n.d.)

Chapter Overview

The key questions covered in Chapter 6 will be: What is a world
view and how does this affect our outlook on life and therefore how
we approach business problems? What is the role of perception in
our intercultural interactions? What is the difference between a

stereotype and a generalization? We progress in this order by building one aspect upon the other: we all have a world view(s); we all have perceptions about other people's world view(s); we can form stereotypes or create prototypes based upon our perceptions and experiences (Figure 6.1).

Learning Objective

Chapter 6, Culture and World View, returns to the discussion of attitudes, beliefs, and values by looking at the concept of world view. We will do this by looking at more theories related to intercultural communication, such as the work by two anthropologists, Kluckhohn and Strodtbeck, who studied the Navajo and Hopi Indians in the Southwestern United States. They developed a framework called the Value Orientations Model that addressed questions about human nature, people and nature, and sense of time, activity, and social relations. You will begin to see the overlap of the theorists mentioned throughout this book and that there are common themes in the research that help support our practical application of these concepts in our everyday leadership challenges.

Key Takeaways

—   World views can be invisible forces that impact our lives and professions.
—   Understand how culture influences the way individuals view the world.

Leadership Applications

—   You will be challenged to consider how to adapt your leadership/ communication style to interact more effectively with someone with whom you work. You will be able to consider: upon what world views might that person be operating?
—   Awareness and knowledge are not enough. Examine one of your own cultural perspectives and try to view it from someone else's. What might be *their* perspective for why you think, believe, or behave in a certain way?

Introduction

Nike Air Bakin' Goes Up in Flames

Every multinational company has its challenges. Back in 1997 Nike created a design to go on the back of one of its basketball shoes—the Air Bakin'—which were fiery flames on the back of the shoe that said, "Air." However, members of the Muslim community were insulted because the logo looked more like the Arabic script for "Allah." Since these shoes were being sold in the Middle East, Nike had to recall 38,000 pairs worldwide. Nike had no intent to insult, so it redesigned the logo, but altered it only slightly—unfortunately it was almost identical to the original. The Council on American–Islamic Relations (CAIR) got involved and Nike had to issue an apology and ended up building three playgrounds in three Islamic neighborhoods. This particular sports shoe had been dubbed, the "Air Allah" and had news titles claiming, "The Air Bakin' does not speak Arabic" (Jury, 1997).

Depending on your world view, this could put a smile on your face or make you gasp. Or maybe it would make you wonder what all the fuss was about—like Roy Agostino, the spokesperson for Nike. As a leader he had to learn the hard way that one cannot underestimate what seemed like an insignificant symbol used when creating, making, or marketing a product (see Figure 6.2). In a situation like this it is easy for both sides to be upset with the other—Nike wondered why this mattered in the big scheme of things— the logo simply had a few wavy lines meant to symbolize fire. That anyone would be offended—even when they made the effort (at great cost) to redesign the image—was incomprehensible. But from another perspective, the Muslim community was troubled that this *did not* matter to Nike. It was inconceivable that anyone could blatantly insult God in such a manner. This basketball shoe basically insulted the very essence of being Muslim. There was a clash of world views.

In the Islam religion, Muslims believe that the sole purpose of their exist- ence on earth is to submit to and worship Allah. So, they incorporate religion into every part of their day with discipline and utmost respect. One way to show reverence to God is through cleanliness, hence why Muslims take off their shoes and wash themselves before entering a mosque to pray. To have

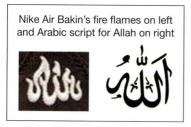

Figure 6.2 Nike Air Bakin's Fire–Arabic Script

a symbol that resembled the name of God on the bottom of a shoe was blasphemous since the foot is unclean. As we discussed in Chapter 5, symbols are powerful because they hold important meaning to the person who makes sense of that meaning. In Islamic tradition one cannot create images of Allah or his prophet Muhammad, let alone relegate the script that signifies God to the back of a shoe. The symbol on the shoe signified disrespect and was utterly unthinkable.

As global business leaders it is not possible to be privy to every belief system, custom, norm, or even vocabulary. However, the savvy global business leader is going to be proactive because of both their awareness *and* desire to understand how to communicate with those who are not like them. And, when they do misstep—which happens to all of us—as a culturally intelligent communicator they will do what they can to make sure that communication channels are open in order to solve the misunderstanding. The following section explains why world view matters.

World View

Definition

World views attempt to answer four basic questions about humans and the universe: What is reality? Who are humans? What is truth? What values are important? The term "world view" comes from the German word, "*weltanschauung*," which is "*welt*" (world) + "*anschauung*" (perception, or view). Emmanuel Kant is credited with first using the term to describe a person's observations or perceptions about the world (Dicks, 2012, p. 22). A world view is basically a person's beliefs about life and the universe—one's core assumptions of what is.

In his fascinating book *An African Worldview: The Muslim Amacinga Yawo of Southern Malaŵi*, Ian Dicks says this about world view:

> Worldview is at the most fundamental level of culture. It is the core, so to speak, and affects people's beliefs and practices. If one could peel back the layers of a culture, starting with surface behavior, practices and customs, the deepest layer would be a people's worldview. In order to gain an understanding of a people's worldview, one must trace the source of the underlying assumptions. This source is the stories, especially those stories that people hear from childhood to adulthood, and especially so during liminal [e.g., rite of passage] periods in their lives. These "stories" need to be examined, as far as possible, together with the rituals to which they belong and against the life setting and context of the people.
>
> (Dicks, 2012, p. 12)

No matter who we are or where we live, whether we get our information through modern technology or more modest means, we have the innate need to figure out the world within our own experience. World view is found within the stories, traditions, and memories our family and friends pass on to us. These stories about existence and survival help us to make sense out of the world. It is how we figure it all out.

Value Orientations

Kluckhohn and Strodtbeck Orientations

Since so much of the field of intercultural communication comes from anthropology, let us look at how two anthropologists, Clyde Kluckhohn and Frederick Strodtbeck, tried to make sense of human world view via their work in the Southwestern United States in the 1940s and 1950s through the Harvard Values Project (Hills, 2002). They set out to investigate the core values of different cultures with the hypothesis that all cultures have a limited set of common human problems that need solutions. Kluckhohn and Strodtbeck concluded that there were five human concerns that all societies are based upon: human nature; people and nature; time sense; activity; and social relations. They hypothesized that intercultural understanding could be improved by exploring any culture's five concerns (Kluckhohn & Strodtbeck, 1961) (Table 6.1).

Their work originally included Zuni and Navajo pueblos, a Mexican American village, and Mormon and Texan communities (Gallagher, 2000), providing groundbreaking research at the time. Of course their theory has been tested with other cultural groups since, for example by Rokeach (1979), Schwartz (1992), and of course Hofstede (2001). While they used the term "values," it is more accurate to use the term "orientation" because Kluckhohn and Strodtbeck sought to study the foundational assumptions upon which a culture will build its value system (Gallagher, 2001). As we have seen in Chapter 4, regarding Hofstede's cultural dimensions, having frameworks such as these can help to identify hidden differences (Kluckhohn and Strodtbeck, 1961). They developed a range of responses for each of the value orientations. For example, if we look at "human nature," which asks the question, "What is the basic nature of people?" we get a range. For example, in Christian tradition, the response would be that human beings are born with an evil nature; in Judaism, people would have both good and bad; and in Islam, people are born good but become corrupted by the world.

Examples of Value Orientations

Let us look at an example of how this framework plays out in the workplace. If you work in healthcare you need to ensure that your staff understand the medical needs of ethnic communities which are influenced by the socio-emotional needs as well. People who come from ethnic or cultural backgrounds hold different outlooks on what constitutes medical practice; for

Table 6.1 Kluckhohn and Strodtbeck's Value Orientations Model

Orientation	Range		
Human Nature: What is the basic nature of people?	Evil: People are born "bad" with selfish tendencies and must become good	Mixed: People have a bit of good and bad in them	Good: People are born good and become corrupted by the world
People and Nature: What is the basic nature of humans?	Subordination to Nature: Humans yield to nature and its external forces	Live in Harmony with Nature: People flow with nature and must learn to be in harmony with it	Mastery Over Nature: People try to control nature; nature is there for us to use
Time Sense: How do people think about time?	Past: People learn from history & traditions to guide their life	Present: People live in the moment; today is what is important	Future: People look ahead to plan goals –sacrificing now ensures security
Activity: What is the preferred approach to activity?	Being: People take time to pause and live in the moment	Becoming: People are in-process of becoming	Doing: People are action oriented; rewards come through achievement
Social Relations: How do humans form their social organization?	Hierarchical: Decisions made by those with the right authority. Protection from benevolent boss/leader	Collective: Decisions made by group consensus	Individual: Decisions made by personal autonomy

(*Source*: Adapted from Ting-Toomey, 1999, p. 60.)

example, there has been much documentation in recent years about the Hmong people's response to Western medical practices. The Hmong come from southern China, Laos, Thailand, and northern Vietnam (Bankston, n.d.). They believe that illness is spiritual in origin, called "*Quag Dab Peg*," and happens when the soul separates from the body. Traditional treatment would include a shaman ritual (Fox, 2012). Ultimate decisions about medical care must be made by the elder of the family—usually the oldest male in the family.

In Pacific Islander groups, the extended family can have a strong bearing on the care of a family member, who should not be left alone. Oftentimes, the entire family will come to comfort their relative and provide basic care. The wisdom and insights from the older members of the family are important when hearing the doctor's diagnosis, so they must give their opinions. Thus, respecting those who are older and wiser honors the interests of the family over the individual. This has also been documented regarding Latino and African families as well. Attitudes toward mental health can be varied, such as in India and Pakistan, where such an illness can affect the family's place in society. In Vietnam, there is an emphasis on achieving a balance of hot and cold poles within the body which should not be disturbed (EuroMedical Link, n.d.). So, some people would approach Western medical practices as contradicting their need for balance with nature. If we look at the "People and Nature" orientation, where the main question is, "What is the basic nature of humans?" there would be a range, from humans yielding to nature (if you get sick, it is fate and you must accept it) to living in harmony with nature (finding remedies from nature) to mastery over nature (controlling an illness through a man-made drug) (Box 6.1).

In this book we keep talking about a person's values, beliefs, and attitudes. We all start from a specific point of view. Based upon this view or, as we are discussing in this chapter, a world view, we make assumptions of what life is all about and how we are going to act. In order to underscore this point, let us look at some of the major world views, as explained through some dominant religious beliefs.

Overview of World Religions and Belief Systems

How many religions or belief systems exist in the world today? I've seen indications of anywhere between 4,000 and 6,000. A 2010 Pew Research Center study examined the size of major religious and nonreligious groups in the world based upon global population and came up with the following:

- Christians, 2.2 billion (32 percent).
- Muslims, 1.6 billion (23 percent).
- Nonreligious affiliations, 1.1 billion (16 percent).
- Hindus, 1 billion (15 percent).
- Buddhists, 500 million (7 percent).
- Folk/traditional religions, 400 million (6 percent), including: African traditional religions, Chinese folk religions, Native American religions, Australian aboriginal religions.
- Other religions, 58 million (1 percent), including: Bahá'í, Jainism, Sikhism, Shintoism, Daoism, Zoroastrianism.
- Jews, 14 million (0.2 percent) (Pew Research Center, 2012).

While we are able to count the number of major and minor religions (by population), it is difficult to put a definite label on each, because within each religion (or belief system—a religion is a belief in a god or group of gods—a supernatural being) are myriad forms of practice. For example, in Christianity, one could compare the Roman Catholic, Protestant, and Eastern Orthodox traditions. Broken down further, each tradition has different denominations which are subgroups that have their own traditions and identities, but still ascribe to the major tenets of the faith. Within these subgroups there are sub-subgroups that could be divided along the lines of conservative or liberal theology, and so on.

Box 6.1 World View—A Clash of Perspective

A colleague of mine was travelling in Morocco and was an avid photographer who enjoyed candid portrayals of people in their everyday lives. She loved to capture the essence of human movement and interaction with objects and asked my advice on how she should handle her picture-taking ethically. I suggested that she always ask for permission—even if she had to use gestures—and to be respectful. When she returned she told me of the varied responses—one upset her greatly. She was in a marketplace and was off to the side trying to be inconspicuous while taking pictures of some women buying rice. The colorful sacks that displayed different varieties of rice, beans, and nuts were so artistic as the late afternoon sun filtered through the awnings above. She snapped a couple of shots of the women reaching for the merchandise as the merchant filled their bags. The merchant caught her out of the corner of his eye and rushed over with a scowl, shaking his hands for her to go away. She complied and moved away and decided to focus on the bags and bundles of various foodstuffs—inanimate objects should be within limits, she thought. Again, the merchant saw her, rushed over and tried to grab her camera, yelling at her. She was overwhelmed and stood frozen as a colleague rushed over to help her. A push-pull situation developed.

She felt terrible and we reviewed the various angles of why the shopkeeper might have been angry. As we tried to be mindful of the situation—frame it, make attributions, select a script—it became evident that the nature of *her* perspective on what can be photographed—whether it is animate or inanimate—can have different meanings to different people. My colleague assumed that taking pictures of bags of rice or vegetables stacked on a table would be acceptable. However, some who might be tired of tourists invading their everyday lives might find that as an intrusion on their privacy. Regardless of the object, lack of respect for one's property, even in the public square, was unacceptable; hence, the man's hierarchical and collective social order was upset (see the Value Orientations Model (Table 6.1)) and it was necessary to protect and preserve the safety and privacy of these women.

For the sake of discussion, the following provides a very brief and general overview of some of the major belief systems of the world.

Hinduism

Hinduism is based mostly in India and is a belief system that is made up of many gods. Some Hindu followers will call it a religion; others will call it a belief system. The holy texts of Hinduism, called the Vedas, or Books of Knowledge, were first written in Sanskrit about 1200 BCE to 100 CE. These books focus on the supreme reality of the universe. There are many different Hindu practices with a flexible belief system and no central religious authority. Also, there is no single Deity; rather millions of gods and goddesses can be worshipped—from a statue to a tree. Therefore, religion and culture are interchangeable concepts. Moral values include nonviolence, compassion, purity, self-control, and generosity.

The major tenets are:

- The reincarnation of the soul—there are many rebirths until one's karmas have been resolved and the soul is liberated.
- The belief that the universe is undergoing an endless cycle of recreation.
- The belief in many divine beings from the supernatural.
- The belief in the divinity of the four Vedas (a collection of inspired songs) (BBC, n.d.a).

In Hinduism there are infinite gods and goddesses that become embodied via idols, or a guru, or in a temple, or in things. Hinduism is a henotheistic religion, which means you can believe in one god yet acknowledge that there are others as well, which is the practice of bhakti. Another example of henotheism is from Greek mythology—Zeus, who was the highest-ranking god of all the other Olympian gods. Such faiths are among the most tolerant (New World Encyclopedia, 2014).

One's present position in life is a result of actions in a previous life and this explains why there is suffering and evil. Hinduism seeks eternal relief from karma's law—to reach Nirvana means you have broken the cycle of birth–life–death. "Karma" means "action" in Sanskrit and has been compared to Newton's law of cause and effect that states, "every action must have a reaction" (Brahma Kumaris: World Spiritual Organization, n.d.). There is good karma and bad karma, and what we do initiates forces in our life—what happens is for a reason—and, whether good or bad, these forces are meant to teach versus punish. Submission to life's forces and how we react leads us to Nirvana (Box 6.2).

Box 6.2 Karma

Every action generates a force of energy that returns to us in like kind … what we sow is what we reap. And when we choose actions that bring happiness and success to others, the fruit of our karma is happiness and success.

Source: www.chopra.com/the-law-of-karma-or-cause-and-effect

Buddhism

Buddhism originated in India in 520 BCE through Siddhartha Gautama, an Indian prince who went on a quest to find inner enlightenment. It is practiced in India, South East Asia, China, Japan, South Korea, and Nepal. Buddhists meditate for self-discipline as a way to purify one's self from all worldly yearnings. To Buddhists there is no god or creator. To believe is to be one with reality.

The major tenets are:

- Suffering exists (Dukkha). There are many causes of universal suffering.
- There is a cause for suffering (Samudaya). We all seek things that do not bring us fulfillment.
- To transcend life is to be reincarnated (Nirvana). People are reborn in a different context.
- There is an end to suffering (Nirodha). To be free we must find Nirvana, which is the final state of being liberated from the cycle of death and rebirth.
- To end suffering, one must follow the Eightfold Path (Magga). This consists of discernment/wisdom, virtue/morality, and concentration/meditation (Robinson, 2009).

Judaism

Judaism was founded in approximately 2000 BCE and is one of the first monotheistic religions. The biblical figure Abraham is considered the father of Judaism because he made a covenant with God and therefore was promised the Holy Land. The religious texts include the Torah (Hebrew Bible), which was originally written in Hebrew. The Torah grounds Judaic tradition in religious, ethical, and social laws, while the Talmud (means "study" in Hebrew) is a collection of ancient rabbinic teachings.

There are three divisions of Judaism. The Orthodox division is a traditional practice with a strong emphasis on following the law as set forth by the Torah, and families follow strict dietary codes by keeping the household kosher (pure) as a symbol of piety and obedience. Only men can become rabbis. The Conservative division blends traditional forms of worship and diet with contemporary practices, and women can become rabbis. The Reform division blends contemporary and liberal approaches to Judaism—the Talmud is not authoritative, and women can become rabbis. Judaism has diverse views today, but there is a constant thread running through, "a sacred narrative expressing their relationship with God as a holy people" (Patheos Religion Library, n.d.)

The major tenets are:

- God is eternal and created the universe and humans (in his image).
- God is a spirit.

- God knows the thoughts and deeds of humans—humans have two natures, one good and one evil—neither is inherent, but people become what they do.
- There is a heaven which is for the righteous and a hell for the malevolent. Jews are God's chosen people awaiting the coming of the Messiah (WorldviewU, n.d.).

Christianity

Christianity originated in the 1st century CE, after the death of Jesus in 33 CE, and follows his life, teachings, and death/resurrection. It is a monotheistic (Trinitarian) religion, believing in only one God, who is made up of three parts (Holy Trinity: God the Father, Son (Jesus Christ), Holy Spirit). "Trinity" means "tri" (three) and "unity" (one) and is an abstract concept that transcends our three-dimensional world. It has been described as multiplying $1 \times 1 \times 1 = 1$, as well as adding $1 + 1 + 1 = 3$. All three are one yet all three are unique. Another analogy is water in all three forms of liquid, vapor, and ice.

The major tenets are:

- God is omniscient and creator of all things.
- God is a just God, expecting followers to adhere to the moral standards of the Ten Commandments; yet, God is also loving and relational.
- People can approach God through prayer, fasting, and tithing, but more importantly through faith.
- Humans are fallen (because of original sin) and need a savior, Jesus, to intervene between humans and God, who forgives anyone who seeks forgiveness.
- Christians believe that Jesus was the promised one—Messiah—predicted in the Old Testament. He lived as a human (God incarnate), was crucified, and rose from the dead (BBC, 2009a).

Islam

Islam is a monotheistic religion and Muslims are its followers. They worship Allah (Arabic for "God"), who revealed himself in 622 CE through the last prophet, Muhammad. The Qur'an is God's word given to Muhammad through a vision that he was the last of a number of prophets God sent to teach his law, including, Abraham, Moses, and Jesus. Jesus is revered as a special prophet and Muslims believe in the virgin birth; however, they do not believe that Jesus was God. Muslims believe that God is powerful but unknowable and strive to intertwine faith with practice. There are several things necessary for both faith and practice.

The five pillars of faith are:

- Profession of faith (Shahada)—"There is no God but Allah and Muhammad is his prophet."

> ## Box 6.3 What is: Islam, Muslim, Arab, an Arabic Speaker?
>
> – Islam is a religion.
> – A Muslim is a person who follows the religion of Islam.
> – Arabs are a people whose place of ethnic origin is the Arabian Peninsula.
> – Arabs speak the Arabic language but can choose any faith.
> – Muslims can have any native language; however, the Qur'an is written in Arabic.
> – Indonesia has the largest population of Muslims in the world.

- Daily prayers (Salat)—Muslims pray up to five times a day (whether in a mosque or on their own in a private place, they must face Mecca—the holy city).
- Give alms (Zakat)—Muslims are expected to help those in need, giving generously of time, service, and finances.
- Fasting during Ramadan (Sawm)—during the ninth month of the Islamic calendar, Muslims are expected to fast from dawn to dusk.
- Pilgrimage to Mecca (Hajj)—If possible, Muslims are expected to make a pilgrimage to Mecca (Muhammad's birthplace and where he had his first revelation) during their lifetime to walk around the Kaaba. The Kaaba is a square building and is the most sacred shrine believed to have been the place constructed by Abraham (Ibrahim) and his son, Ismail (BBC, 2009b) (Box 6.3).

Other Religions and Belief Systems

Of course, there are many, many other belief systems. The following is a brief layout of them. The important point is that all of us have a view of the world based upon our values and beliefs, and these world views shape and guide and influence who we are and what we do. Understanding that belief systems are foundational to one's core can help us better understand the cultural differences that we will encounter in our work and in our communities (BBC, n.d.b).

- *Agnosticism:* A belief that maybe God exists, but concludes that this is hard to prove. There is neither faith nor disbelief in God or gods.
- *Ancestor worship:* The belief that one must revere ancestors' spirits because they have the power to influence the lives of the living. Therefore it is necessary to keep relations good with those who have gone before.
- *Atheism:* A belief system—not a religion— based upon the disbelief in the existence of God or the need to explain the existence of the universe. Atheism comes from "a" (without) and "theism" (belief in God or gods). There are many reasons for nonbelief in a supreme being, such as

insufficient evidence to support it. Atheists follow moral codes for what is good or bad, but this excludes any religious foundation.

- *Bahá'í:* "Bahá'í" means "glory of God" in Arabic. This religion was founded by an Iranian, the Báb (meaning "the gate"), who claimed that another prophet would follow those who had come before—Abraham, Moses, Jesus Christ, and Muhammad. The faith is progressive by accepting all religions as having truth and that the most important aspect of life is to seek unity.
- *Confucianism:* A philosophy that follows a collection of ethical and moral teachings. Founded in the 6th to 5th century BCE by K'ung-fu-tzu, whose teachings created a system of social and political ethics meant to guide people toward proper behavior in everyday life. Confucian philosophy valued hierarchy, group orientation, and tradition, and emphasized that it was important to hold to filial piety, kinship, and loyalty as an indication of the important obligations within the established order of relationships.
- *Daoism:* Founded by Lao-zi (or Lao-tzu), this is an ancient Chinese philosophy, emphasizing the opposites of Yin and Yang as complimentary forces. "Dao" means "the Way." This philosophy complimented Confucius's teachings of social harmony in that people should seek harmony with nature through mystical experience of inward focus.
- *Jainism:* An ancient religion originating in India that teaches spiritual liberation of the soul. This is achieved by belief that the way to liberation and bliss is to live a life of harmlessness and renunciation. All living beings (including plants and animals) have souls and it is critical to treat all with respect and gentleness. All followers practice the three jewels: right belief, right knowledge, and right conduct.
- *Mormonism:* Founded in the 19th century by Joseph Smith and later promoted by Brigham Young in Salt Lake City, Utah, U.S.A. Their church is called the Church of Jesus Christ of Latter-Day Saints, with the belief of a restored church after the breakdown of traditional Christian churches. There is a strong emphasis on family and traditional social values.
- *Paganism:* Based upon a reverence of nature and established throughout the world with a belief in the organic and spiritual nature of the world.
- *Shintoism:* Referred to as a cultural collection of practices in Japan, where people are called to devotion to invisible spiritual entities called "*kami.*" These kami are benevolent spirits that care about human beings and will bring health, success, and good luck as long as humans treat them well. While a Japanese practice, the name Shinto means "Way of the Spirits" and is made up of the characters for "Shen" (divine being) and "Dao" (Way).
- *Sikhism:* Begun in the Punjab district of India and Pakistan by a guru, Nanak, it stresses one's internal religious state along with the importance of doing good rather than merely following rituals. Key components are equality, peace, honesty, and generosity.

- *Zoroastrianism:* An ancient dualistic religion that originated in Iran 3,500 years ago, founded by the prophet Zoroaster, and focused on the cosmic opposing forces within the universe and the moral opposing forces within the mind.

While this brief discussion cannot do any of these religions and belief systems justice, it is nevertheless important to include them in order to review and think about the many differences and similarities. When we broaden our perspective on ideas that are unfamiliar to us, we develop a foundation for personal reflection and then competence building when we meet people with these world views. Hopefully this information will prompt you toward further exploration. Now that we have talked about world view, let us move to the next topic of this chapter, perception.

Perception and Culture

The Science of Perception

Put simply, perception is the neural process involving how our brains select, evaluate, and organize stimuli, thus enabling us to experience the world around us. This can include evaluating things, objects, symbols, people, incidents, beliefs, etc., according to our sensory receptors (sight, sound, smell, touch, taste). We receive stimuli that immediately get stored in our brain, which is one huge data bank of everything we have ever experienced. We filter these stimuli in order to interpret the incoming sensations and use that information to categorize it. We do this without even realizing it—perception is about categorization (Boundless, 2015).

Culture's Influence on Perception

Psychologists also tell us that culture influences our perception. From an article in *Psychological Science,* we can draw specific insight into a study on Western and Eastern perceptions. Here is what the University of Chicago researchers found.

While the ability to appreciate another person's perspective has been proven to be universal according to studies on children, some societies encourage the development of this skill more than others. The reason: people have fundamental differences regarding their perceptions. People from Western cultures focus on finding individual solutions to problems, whereas people from Eastern cultures will use a more collective approach by gaining perspective of the problem. For example, in Japanese society, children are encouraged to learn about "*wa*" which is social harmony, and are taught about the importance of working together in groups in order to maintain this harmony (Griffin & Pustay, 2012). In collectivist cultures, people are more interdependent and define their self-concept through relationships and social obligations. In contrast, members of individual cultures tend to define self-concept through their achievements and independence. Scientists tested their hypothesis that interdependence would make people focus on others rather than the self (Nauert, 2015).

To do this, Mandarin-speaking Chinese and English-speaking North Americans were placed in their language groups and had to work together to move objects on a type of chess board. One person was given the role of director, who would tell the employee where to move the objects. The director's view was partially blocked, whereas the employee had full view. The Chinese subjects focused on what the director was able to see, whereas the North American subjects would pause and try to figure out which object the director could or could not see before moving the correct object. The findings: 65 percent of the North Americans did not consider the boss's perspective at least once during this experiment (e.g., by not asking the boss which object he or she meant).

> Taking into account the other person's perspective was more work for the Americans, who spent on average about twice as much time completing the moves than did the Chinese. Even more startling for the researchers was the frequency with which many of the Americans ignored the fact that the director could not see all the objects.
>
> (Nauert, 2015)

The conclusion—the Chinese interdependence had a strong cultural effect on the pairs trying to work together to move the objects on a board.

Games of Perception

We have all played the game where there are two images and we are asked to choose which we see first—such as the black and white image that could be either two people looking at each other or some type of vase (see Figure 6.3). This goes back to the Gestalt theory of the figure and ground. We all come at such an exercise from a different perspective.

Figure 6.3 Perceptions. (Is it a vase or two people?)

(*Source*: Albert Kok; see https://upload.wikimedia.org/wikipedia/commons/b/be/Gestalt1.png.)

Here is another example, this time one which involves food as the object of our perception. Previously we used a definition of culture by interculturalist Marshall Singer, who identified all people as being "culturally unique." We also used his compelling example about chocolate cake and candy bars. In another vivid explanation, Singer talks about a social experiment he tried during a party. Here is how he told the story (Box 6.4).

Box 6.4 Perceptions and Food by Marshall Singer

My first conscious awareness of the importance of perceptions to human behavior began with an incident when I was still a graduate student. At that time esoteric foods like chocolate-covered ants, fried grasshoppers, smoked rattlesnake meat, and sweet-and-sour mouse tails, were the culinary fad.

Upon moving into a new apartment, I received a housewarming gift from a friend—a whole carton of these canned delicacies. Having at that time rather prosaic food habits, I did not proceed to consume the entire carton.

Indeed, it sat untouched for the better part of a year while I alternately toyed with the idea of trying one of those less-than-tempting "goodies" myself or throwing the entire carton in the garbage (*my* perception of these treats).

One evening while putting out a whole array of cheese and other edibles in preparation for a party, it occurred to me that my opportunity had arrived. Without saying anything to anyone about what I planned, I opened a can of fried caterpillars into a little white dish and set them out on the table along with the other foods. Then I waited to see what would happen.

Halfway through the evening one of the unsuspecting young ladies I had invited to the party came up to me and said, "Marshall, those fried shrimp you put out were delicious." "Fried shrimp?" I asked as innocently as I could. "I didn't serve any fried shrimp." "Yes you did," she insisted. "They were in a little white plate on the table. In fact, they were so good I ate most of them myself." "Oh," I said, pausing for maximum effect, "those weren't friend, shrimp, there were fried caterpillars."

Virtually the moment I said that, the smile disappeared from her face, her complexion turned markedly green, and she proceeded to become terribly sick all over my living room floor. I realized immediately—as I was cleaning up the floor—that what I had done was a terrible trick to play on anyone, and I have never done it again.

But as I reflected on that incident, it amazed me that a food that could have been thought to be so delicious one moment—when it was *perceived* to be fried shrimp—could be so repugnant the next, when it was *perceived* to be something else. Suppose they really had been fried shrimp, and I had merely been joking?

Source: Singer, 1987, pp. 8–9

Food and Perception

Let us continue with food examples. There are some cultures where cheese is important and others that are not. In the United States we eat a lot of cheese—to some palates it is delicious—whether it is a French brie, a Wisconsin cheddar, or a Greek feta; however, in other parts of the world it is considered extremely distasteful. Just as we might be repelled at the thought of eating a skewer of beetles at a Beijing street market (see Figure 6.4), the man who sold it to me would probably wonder *why* anyone would *ever* eat fries, with meat chili and shredded cheese—ugh! Most Asian cultures do not eat much dairy—so taste buds are not accustomed to certain flavors and the effects that food can have on us. Tastes change (e.g., Coca Cola introducing milk products—yogurt drinks—which recently became popular in China—go figure).

It is all about perception and one's experience with norms—those accepted and expected ways of behaving and thinking. If perception is the process that we use to select, evaluate, and organize information, then our perceptions of reality can be more important than reality itself (fried shrimp example).

Without even realizing it, we can cognitively disagree or emotionally feel uncomfortable with something that violates our cultural norms. We all believe that our values are the best—if we did not we would hold other values! Marshall Singer says, "Because no two groups value exactly the same things or rank their values with the same intensity, it is inevitable that there will be basic value conflict between individuals from different groups" (Singer, 1987, p. 3). As leaders how can we communicate successfully? By finding some way to reach an accommodation between those conflicting values. This is why it is critical to understand that everyone has a world view—the starting place of how they, well, view the world! And, when we understand that everyone has a neural response to experiencing something different—the process of perception—we

Figure 6.4 Bugs, Beijing, China

(*Source*: Author.)

> ### Box 6.5 Making Assumptions by Nancy Adler
>
> Interpretation occurs when an individual assigns meaning to observations and their relationships; it is the process of making sense out of perceptions. Interpretation organizes our experience to guide our behavior. Based on our experience, we make assumptions about what we perceive so we will not have to rediscover meanings each time we encounter similar situations.
>
> We make assumptions, for example, about how doors work, based on our experience of entering and leaving rooms; thus, we do not have to relearn how to open a door each time we encounter a new door.
>
> Similarly, when we smell smoke, we generally assume it is the result of a fire. We do not have to stop and wonder if the smoke indicates a fire or a flood. Consistent patterns of interpretation help us to act appropriately and quickly within our day-to-day world.
>
> Because we are constantly bombarded with more stimuli than we can absorb and more perceptions than we can keep distinct or interpret, we only perceive those images that may be meaningful to us. We group perceived images into familiar categories that help us to simplify our environment, become the basis for our interpretations, and allow us to function in an otherwise overly complex world.
>
> Source: Adler, 2008, p. 75

can then tackle the inevitable challenge of stereotyping. This is what we will discuss in the next section (Box 6.5).

Stereotypes and Mental Representations

Definition of Stereotype

The idea of mental representations comes from the field of psychology. We create mental categories, called cognitive maps, which help us categorize what is unfamiliar or complex. As part of the process we compare what is known against what is not in order to categorize and make sense of the intake of information.

Actually, the concept of a stereotype comes from the historical development in printing where little metal pieces called "type" are set together in a frame or mold and, once ink is applied, the type is reproduced identically in another frame. The definition has come to mean a fixed or rigid perception of something that does not vary—it is "set in type" or, as another idiomatic phrase says, "set in stone." It is limited because it is firmly set into that frame in order to be printed exactly as the little metal pieces (the text and punctuation) are laid out.

Stereotypes become dangerous when we determine that *all* people are "this or that" and we become rigid and inflexible with our views. If we meet one person, or have one experience, or if we read about something, rather than think that *everyone* is like that, it would be wise to be open to other possibilities.

Prototypes

We do the same with our mental representations (also called schema) to create categories when we experience something new, unfamiliar, or complex. Without even knowing it, we unconsciously begin to categorize the input data in order to make sense out of it. For example, if you know nothing about the market for fuel cells, for example, but suddenly have an urgent need to know, you begin by organizing the topic into categories: types, their market shares, commercial users (by size, by type), retail market segment prices, parts and equipment suppliers, and so forth. Cognitive psychologists tell us that this same categorizing occurs when you encounter a new culture. If we could not make generalizations and put similar items into categories, we could not make sense of any unfamiliar subject. In the field of intercultural communication, we are encouraged to create prototypes, models that are not rigid. Prototypes are mental representations based on general characteristics that are not fixed and rigid but rather are open to new definitions.

Stereotypes and Generalizations

But, you may argue, is not this entire book about stereotypes? After all, you keep saying, people from culture "x" tend to believe this; people from culture "y" generally do that. You're making one generalization after another. This is an excellent point, so let us make the distinction. A stereotype is a belief about a person or group that puts everyone into a category. When you make a stereotype you tend to reject contradictory information by using selective perception and refusing to change your attitude. However, a generalization is an idea that has a *general* rather than *specific* application that is a hypothesis to be tested and observed. You analyze the data and constantly test your ideas by being open, curious, and willing to learn. A generalization is not set in type as with the old block letters of a 19th-century printing press—rather, you build a prototype—a model that can be molded, designed, or fashioned based upon your experience (Figure 6.5).

Stereotypes about groups of people can be positive, negative, or neutral. For example, a friend invites you to his wedding in Glasgow, Scotland. He wears a kilt. You might have a positive or neutral opinion about kilts if you are an observer; however, if you are asked to participate and have to wear one but are uncomfortable with it, you might classify Scottish people as being odd to allow men to wear a skirt.

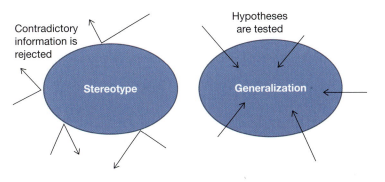

Figure 6.5 Differences Between Stereotypes and Generalizations

(*Source*: Adapted from Cultural Orientations Model, TMC, 1987.)

What about the image of a blonde woman with blue eyes? This could be a positive experience if you think such women are beautiful. However, if you are a blonde-haired, blue-eyed woman and have been stereotyped as a "bimbo" (unintelligent and superficial) then this would be negative.

Watch the clip of the barn-raising from the popular 1980s movie *Witness*. What are the stereotypes that you can identify? Are they positive, negative, or neutral? Why would they be considered stereotypes? Framed differently, how could they become generalizations? Remember, stereotypes are rigid and we apply them to all people regardless. Generalizations are hypotheses to be tested (Box 6.6).

So What Do We Do with Stereotypes?

If we work on being mindful in developing our cultural competence, we become aware of our thoughts and attitudes regarding unfamiliar situations. If we can reassess our reactions to differences and think more openly, we can build a model—like a prototype—in order to test our hypotheses. For example, "I've heard that all Amish people have conservative values and shun the ways of the modern world. I've also read that men are in charge and women submissive—it appeared this way in the movie where the men had the manly jobs of building the barn and the women cooked and served cool drinks. I sure wouldn't want to live in that community." Now this might appear to be a negative statement—but if you examine it closely it is merely stating that this person would not care for that lifestyle, which is perfectly valid. However, if a judgment is passed on all Amish people, "What backward people they are—they don't even know how to live," that is a stereotype. However, we could make a generalization—"I've had this experience concerning 'x.' Hmmm … I'll tuck this away in my thoughts and see what happens next time." Remember, we all make mental

---

Box 6.6 Stereotypes

Why do we find these amusing? Because there is a kernel of truth in each of them.

Heaven

> The cooks are French.
> The mechanics are German.
> The lovers are Italian.
> The police are British.
> And it is all organized by the Swiss.

Hell

> The cooks are British.
> The mechanics are French.
> The lovers are Swiss.
> The police are German.
> And it is all organized by the Italians.

Source: Smith, Jack, 1987

Box 6.7 Generalizations

A generalization is an idea that has a general—not specific application.

When applying to people, countries, or situations, it serves as a hypothesis to be tested and observed.

You analyze the data and constantly test your ideas. You are open, curious, and willing to learn.

---

representations as we try to categorize new experiences. It is natural. The objective is to be open (Box 6.7).

Sophisticated Stereotypes

While we are on the topic of stereotypes and generalizations, it is important to talk about some of the negative implications for sorting out our understanding of culture via the "dimension models" (e.g., Hofstede's and Trompenaars'). It has been argued that the use of cultural dimensions express differences as an "either-or" situation, which is quite extreme. Observations are made by etic (outsider) values as a way to help us make distinctions (in an either-or fashion).

And, cultural dimensions as basic building blocks to cultural understanding have historically come from a Western perspective due to U.S. American influence in the social sciences.

Categorizing entire cultures like this can lead to sophisticated stereotyping—sophisticated stereotyping is basically the classification of *all* people as one entity. We know that there are definite central tendencies for how people behave and act in any culture; however, we also know that people are individuals with many different experiences and world views. Therefore, exceptions and qualifications (both cultural and individual) are necessary since people, life events, and how we communicate across cultures are so complex (Box 6.8).

For example, a sophisticated stereotype might be when we want to find out more about our Indian colleague and seek out Hofstede's dimensions. In reviewing Hofstede's site, we learn that Indian people tend to have high power distance, strong masculinity, and medium individualism. If we think that all people from India are like this, we are stereotyping. But if we use these cultural dimensions *as a guide*, understanding that cultural paradoxes abound and people are individuals, we create a prototype—a model to be tested—rather than a stereotype—an idea that is fixed (Box 6.9).

In working with a group of executives who were establishing a business relation with a Brazilian company in the forestry industry, we initially discussed some of the work preferences of people—in general—from Brazil. From national surveys, in general, time management is quite fluid,

---

Box 6.8 Question for Discussion

How is using a sophisticated stereotype like Hofstede's description of a country's culture any better than the negative stereotypes we often hear about other cultures? Are stereotypes ever helpful?

Box 6.9

Stereotypes, like other forms of categories, can be helpful or harmful depending on how we use them. A more preferred term is "generalizations" because effective generalizing allows people to understand and act appropriately in new situations. But, because stereotypes reflect reality, subconsciously held stereotypes are difficult to modify or discard even after we acquire real information about a person or a group of people. If a subconscious stereotype inaccurately evaluates a person or situation, we are likely to maintain an inappropriate, ineffective, and frequently harmful guide to reality.

Source: Osland & Bird, 2000

more flexible, and a negotiable resource. However, this group considered themselves as typical of the national standard for the United States—they viewed timelines and schedules as critical to meeting production deadlines. Time is to be controlled and managed. In this view, when setbacks occur, it is essential to stick to the schedule, which guides the next course of action. Brazilian attitude toward time—in general—would let the situations and events guide the outcome, being more relaxed in their response to your upcoming project.

Upon checking in with this group a month later, they told me that, while they expected their Brazilian partners would be more "Brazilian" regarding some of the national cultural dimensions we had discussed, that team defied all of the typical attributes of what is deemed Brazilian culture. If anything, the Brazilians were more aggressive than the U.S. Americans! We constantly have to address cultural paradoxes by understanding that our understanding is incomplete. Whether we are business leaders trying to figure out a meeting schedule, what food to serve, or on a deeper level to understand an important world view that a counterpart embraces, we use our perceptions to make quick assumptions about situations so that we can form a hypothesis—to make sense of it—knowing that we are not always right. At any given time we probably do not have all of the information to understand clearly from the other person's perspective (Box 6.10).

Box 6.10 Learning from Mistakes

I had worked at the University in Hong Kong for nearly two years and I just had not learned my lesson. We were a team of about 12 faculty, with about 4 of us who were Westerners (U.S. American, Australian, and Canadian). The very long faculty meetings on Friday afternoons after lunch were agonizing to say the least and it was hard for me to stay alert—ok, actually awake—at times. The meetings were traditionally Chinese—we basically gathered to listen to the director talk about his plans for the program and be reminded of our duties. From time to time my colleagues would ask me, since I was the "direct American," to speak on their behalf about specific concerns within our department. I would listen to their requests and weigh them against one important factor—that when I brought up the issue during the meeting they back me up and provide their opinions. This never happened! After about the third time, I realized that I was only putting myself in a bad position by expressing displeasure—on the part of others—that came off as my own.

It would be easy create a stereotype of my colleagues and to assume the worst—that my colleagues had set me up or possibly even were deceptive by assuring me that they would back me up if I represented their views in an explicit manner to the boss. But that isn't the case—it is likely that my colleagues needed to express that there was discontent—but to do so *explicitly* themselves was not acceptable. Using an intermediary—me—was necessary to get the message across. Since meetings were primarily for the boss to talk and us to listen, there was no need to provide explanations. Merely having an outsider mention that there were unresolved issues was enough to get the message across to the boss.

Universalism and Particularism

Definitions

There are two concepts that relate to world view, *universalism* and *particularism*, which means one either follows the letter of the law or one bends the law. These terms were made famous by Fons Trompenaars, an organizational behavior expert with a Ph.D. from Wharton, a highly respected cross–cultural management consultant, and author of the popular book *Riding the waves of culture: Understanding cultural diversity in business*. He would describe particularism and universalism through this story:

> You are in a car with a friend who is driving. Your friend hits a pedestrian who was walking on the street. You know that your friend was going 50 mph/80 kph in a place where the official speed limit was 30 mph/48 kph. There were no other witnesses, just you. Your friend's lawyer says that if you testify that your friend was only going 30 mph/48 kph that [*sic*] you will save your friend from serious consequences. What right does your friend have to expect that you protect him? (a) My friend has every right to expect me to testify that he was only going 30 mph/48 kph. (b) My friend has some right to expect me to testify that he was only going 30 mph/48 kph. (c) My friend has no right to expect me to testify that he was only going 30 mph/48 kph.
>
> (Trompenaars & Hampden-Turner, 1997, pp. 15–16)

This is a dilemma—do you stay loyal to the universals of not lying under oath, or are you loyal to the particulars of your friend? Dilemmas force us to embrace seemingly contradictory values while aiming for long-term goals. Trompenaars says:

> Once you become aware of cultural differences, you see that everything is one big dilemma. Some companies, especially in the U.S., have solved this by ignoring the differences, calling it "globalization" and running lots of workshops to teach the others how to think. We find that backfires in the long run.
>
> (Kleiner, 2001)

Table 6.2 Characteristics of Universalism and Particularism

Universalism		Particularism	
Characteristics	Strategies	Characteristics	Strategies
Rules or laws that can be applied to everyone.	Explain that you are using an objective process to others.	Emphasis is placed on friendships. Friends will look at the situation to determine what is right or ethically acceptable.	Take time to build relationships, slowly and over time.
Agreements and contracts are used as the basis for doing business.	Provide clear instructions regarding your expectations of all involved.	Deals are made based upon friendships; agreements are changeable.	Be flexible with instructions and be prepared to make compromises.
Rules are used to determine what is right; contracts should not be altered.	Be consistent by keeping promises and giving people adequate time in their decision–making.	Different people hold different views about reality.	Respect the needs of others based upon your growing relationship and knowledge gained.

(*Source*: Adapted from Trompenaars & Hampden-Turner, 1997, pp. 48–9.)

In universalistic cultures, people place a strong value on laws, rules, and obligations and put rules before friendships. On the flip side, in particularistic cultures people put the relationship before the rules, believing that each circumstance and relationship determines how one should behave. For example, in universalistic cultures (such as Anglo and Germanic cultures) it would be necessary to write up a formal contract that spells out every single detail, sign it, and have it vetted by attorneys before closing a deal. If one of the parties breaks one of the clauses in the contract, they could be sued. However, in particularistic cultures (such as Latin and Arab cultures), legal contracts are not as important as the trusting relationship that has been carefully developed over time. A person's word is more important than a signed paper and a hoard of lawyers. Does this mean that particularistic cultures never use contracts? Of course not. Contracts are important; however, the personal relationships that have been developed over time provide a sense of security and a bond when entering into business dealings (Table 6.2).

Example

It is not only regarding legal affairs that universalism and particularism apply. For example, in Chinese culture, there is a strong emphasis of in-groups and out-groups, and whether universal or particular behavior applies. In Chinese tradition, you are obligated only to your in-groups which require strong loyalty yet provide the benefits of a thick web of commitment from members of that intimate group—this comes from Confucian values regarding the filial piety expected of children to parents; employee to boss; citizen to emperor. I remember, back in the fall of 2011, I was accompanying my MBA students on an immersion course in Shanghai and read one morning in the *Shanghai Daily* about a little two-year-old girl, Yue Yue, from Foshan in the southern Guangdong Province, who was hit twice by two different trucks and left on the street until someone intervened. There was public outrage at the lack of Good Samaritan practices and the call for people to be more universal in their approach to helping others. However, a prevailing world view demonstrates that it is customary not to get involved in matters that are beyond one's tight-knit group, which helps to avoid unnecessary trouble (*zuo shi bei e*). As callous as this seems, such a world view influences people to focus on in-group members, which can result in disengagement from other out-groups (Yan, 2009).

This last example can cause shock and a reaction to the heartlessness of the situation. But as we have discussed in this chapter, people approach life from a variety of world views and if we can understand the underlying belief system—whether we agree with it or not—we can begin to develop competence when dealing with challenging issues. We can also keep ourselves in check so that we do not wind up negatively stereotyping an entire group of people based on one practice, or belief, or instance.

Summary

In this chapter we have talked about the fact that everyone has a world view or the vantage point where a person stands to survey their world. As we try to make sense of the world, each of us uses the process of perception to make sense of the external stimuli coming at all five senses. We take in these stimuli, process them, and create mental representations, or schema, in order to make sense of it all. From there we can choose to be flexible by building prototypes, those flexible, organic models that help us understand, or stereotypes, those rigid, static labels that hurt. It is an established sociological need to make understood unfamiliar people, places, things, and situations in order to make sense, so we rely on generalizations. We compare what we know with what we do not know. Such generalizations are all right as long as we view them as hypotheses to be tested rather than rigid judgments that define all people. We have seen how culture influences the way people view the world. As business professionals we need to remember that tacit world views can be invisible forces that impact our lives, professions, and the people with whom we interact.

Answers from Beginning of Chapter

World Religion Symbols

Row 1: Christian Cross; Jewish Star of David, Hindu Aumkar
Row 2: Islamic Star and Crescent; Buddhist Wheel of Dharma; Shinto Torii
Row 3: Sikh Khanda; Bahá'í Star; Jain Ahimsa Symbol.

References

Adler, N. J. (2008). *International dimensions of organizational behavior.* Mason, OH: Thomson Learning.

Bankston III, C. L. (n.d.). Hmong Americans. Retrieved from www.everyculture.com/multi/Ha-La/Hmong-Americans.html (accessed August 4, 2016).

BBC. (n.d.a). Religions: Hinduism. Retrieved from www.bbc.co.uk/religion/religions/hinduism/ (accessed August 3, 2016).

BBC. (n.d.b). Religions. Retrieved from www.bbc.co.uk/religion/religions/ (accessed August 3, 2016).

BBC. (2009a). The basics of Christian beliefs. Retrieved from www.bbc.co.uk/religion/religions/christianity/beliefs/basics_1.shtml (accessed August 3, 2016).

BBC. (2009b). Islam at a glance. Retrieved from www.bbc.co.uk/religion/religions/islam/ataglance/glance.shtml (accessed August 3, 2016).

Boundless. (2015). Introducing the perception process. Boundless Psychology. Retrieved from www.boundless.com/psychology/textbooks/boundless-psychology-textbook/sensation-and-perception-5/introduction-to-perception-39/introducing-the-perception-process-167-12702/ (accessed August 3, 2016).

Brahma Kumaris: World Spiritual Organization. (n.d.). What is Karma? Retrieved from www.brahmakumaris.org/us/whatwedo/courses/fcirym/topics.htm/karma.htm (accessed August 3, 2016).

Dicks, I. D. (2012). *An African worldview: The Muslim Amacinga Yawo of Southern Malaŵi* (p. 22). Zomba, Malawi: Kachere Series.

EuroMedical Link. (n.d.). How culture influences health beliefs. Retrieved from www.euromedinfo.eu/how-culture-influences-health-beliefs.html/ (accessed August 3, 2016).

Fox, M. (2012, September 14). Lia Lee dies: Life went on around her, redefining care. *The New York Times.* Retrieved from www.nytimes.com/2012/09/15/us/life-went-on-around-her-redefining-care-by-bridging-a-divide.html?_r=0 (accessed August 3, 2016).

Gallagher, T. J. (2000). Building institutional capacity to address cultural differences. In R. T. Carter (Ed.), *Addressing cultural issues in organizations: Beyond the corporate context* (pp. 229–40). Thousand Oaks, CA: SAGE.

Gallagher, T. (2001, July). Understanding other cultures: The value orientations method. Paper presented at the Association of Leadership Educators Conference, Minneapolis, MN. Retrieved from www.leadershipeducators.org/Resources/Documents/Conferences/Minneapolis/Gallagher.pdf (accessed August 3, 2016).

Griffin, R. W., & Pustay, M. W. (2012). *International business.* Englewood Cliffs, NJ: Prentice-Hall.

Hills, M. D. (2002). Kluckhohn and Strodtbeck's values orientation theory. *Online Readings in Psychology and Culture, 4*(4), 2–14. Retrieved from http://dx.doi.org/10.9707/2307-0919.1040 (accessed August 3, 2016).

Hofstede, G. (2001). *Culture's consequences: Comparing values, behavior, institutions and organizations across nations.* Thousand Oaks, CA: SAGE.

Jury, L. (1997, June 24). Nike to trash trainers that offended Islam. *Independent.* Retrieved from www.independent.co.uk/news/nike-to-trash-trainers-that-offended-islam-1257776.html (accessed August 3, 2016).

Kleiner, A. (2001). The dilemma doctors. Strategy+Business, 23. Retrieved from www.strategy-business.com/ARTICLE/17251?GKO=444C1 (accessed August 3, 2016).

Kluckhohn, F. R., & Strodtbeck, F. L. (1961). *Variations in value orientations.* Evanston, IL: Row, Peterson.

Kok, Albert. (n.d.). Retrieved from https://upload.wikimedia.org/wikipedia/commons/b/be/Gestalt1.PNG (accessed August 3, 2016).

Nauert, R. (2015). Culture influences perception. Psych Central. Retrieved from http://psychcentral.com/news/2007/07/13/culture-influences-perception/1011.html (accessed August 3, 2016).

New World Encyclopedia. (2014). Henotheism. Retrieved from www.newworldencyclopedia.org/entry/Henotheism (accessed August 3, 2016).

Osland, J. S., & Bird, A. (2000). Beyond sophisticated stereotyping: Cultural sense-making in context. *The Academy of Management Executive, 14*(1), 65–77.

Patheos Religion Library (n.d.). Judaism. Retrieved from www.patheos.com/Library/Judaism (accessed August 2, 2016).

Pew Research Center. (2012, December 18). The global religious landscape. Retrieved from www.pewforum.org/2012/12/18/global-religious-landscape-exec/?utm_content=bufferf682f&utm_source=buffer&utm_medium=twitter&utm_campaign=Buffer (accessed August 3, 2016).

Robinson, B. A. (2009). Buddhism's core beliefs. Retrieved from www.religioustolerance.org/buddhism1.htm (accessed August 2, 2016).

Rokeach, M. (1979). *Understanding human values: Individual and societal.* New York, NY: The Free Press.

Schwartz, S. H. (1992). Universals in the content and structure of values: Theoretical advances and empirical tests in 20 cultures. In M. P. Zanna (Ed.), *Advances in Experimental Social Psychology* (Vol. 25, pp. 1–65). San Diego, CA: Academic Press.

Singer, M. (1987). *Intercultural communication: A perceptual approach.* Englewood Cliffs, NJ: Prentice-Hall.

Smith, J. (1987). Nationality stereotypes deceptive. *The Vindicator.* Retrieved from http://news.google.com/newspapers?id=4pBcAAAAIBAJ&sjid=clYNAAAAI-BAJ&pg=3397,3896549&dq=heaven+chefs-are-french+german+hell&hl=en (accessed August 3, 2016).

Ting-Toomey, S. (1999). *Communicating across cultures.* New York, NY: Guilford Press.

TMC. (1987, February 27). Cultural orientations approach. Retrieved from www.culturalorientations.com/Our-Approach/Six-Levels-of-Culture/55/Smith, J. (accessed August 3, 2016).

Trompenaars, F., & Hampden-Turner, C. (1997). *Riding the waves of culture: Understanding diversity in global business* (2nd edn.). New York, NY: McGraw-Hill.

WorldviewU. (n.d.). Judaism. Retrieved from www.worldviewu.org/judaism/ (accessed August 3, 2016).

Yan, Y. (2009). The good Samaritan's new trouble: A study of the changing moral landscape in contemporary China. *Social Anthropology, 17*(1), 9–24.

Case 6

Nike, Inc.

Air Bakin' Blunder and the Council on American–Islamic Relations[1]

Abstract

In 1997, Nike released a new line of athletic shoes sporting a logo that upset the Muslim community because its design closely resembled the Arabic word for God. This case examines cultural gaps between the world's leader of athletic footwear, and an organization that represents the third-largest faith in the United States. What should Nike have done prior to the release, and what can it do to repair the damage?

Introduction

In June, 1997, Roy Agostino, the spokesperson for Nike, Inc., sat in his Beaverton, Oregon office preparing himself for a difficult press conference that would be held that afternoon. Earlier in the year, the sports footwear and apparel company had released a line of Nike Air athletic shoes with four separate patterns: Air Bakin', Air BBQ, Air Grill, and Air Melt (*The New York Times*, 1997). The entire line of shoes was adorned with a logo that angered the Muslim community because it too closely resembled the Arabic word for God. (See Appendix 1.)

This perception was troubling to Agostino. He knew Nike had intended the logo to resemble flames, hence the association to the names of the shoe line: BBQ, Grill, etc. Additionally, months before the shoe line even went into production, Nike noticed that there might be a small resemblance to the word "Allah," and to mitigate the risk of offense, the company designed a new logo that separated the "A" and the "ir" in the word "Air" (*The Washington Post*, 1997). Agostino grumbled to himself, thinking of how ineffective and inadequate this change had been.

In addition to how he was feeling at the time, Agostino recognized that Nike, Inc. was not a newcomer to controversy and marketing blunders. In 1995, Nike was reprimanded for a billboard placed near the University of Southern California campus depicting a basketball player with the headline, "They called him Allah." (Associated Press, 1997a). This was also offensive to the Muslim community. In response to complaints from the Council on

American–Islamic Relations (CAIR), Nike removed the billboard (Associated Press, 1997b).

Now, only two years later, Nike once again found itself involved in a conflict with CAIR. Frustrated, Agostino realized that a quick and decisive response was of the utmost importance for continued positive relations with the American–Islamic community.

Nike, Inc.—Company Information

Nike, Inc. (Nike) was incorporated in 1968 by Bill Bowerman and Phil Knight. It took Nike 12 years to grow from a start-up athletic footwear company to a listed public company. Thanks to a series of negotiations, innovative products, and excellent marketing campaigns, Nike has now grown to become the world leader of athletic footwear and apparel (United States Securities and Exchange Commission, n.d.a, p. 24).

Nike entered into international markets about ten years after its founding. In fiscal year 1997, the company's non-U.S. sales accounted for 38 percent of its total revenues, compared with 36 percent in fiscal 1996 and 37 percent in fiscal 1995. As of May 31, 1997, Nike had sales distributors, licensees, subsidiaries, and branch offices in about 110 countries in the world. It had 31,000 retail accounts outside the United States.

In the United States, Nike had 19,700 retail accounts (including department stores, footwear stores, sporting goods stores, skating, tennis, and golf shops, and others) along with 26 distribution centers in 1997.

Since 1990, Nike's total sales figures have continued to grow, resulting in a compound annual growth rate of 22 percent. The company's revenue reached $9.19 billion, and its net income reached $796 million in fiscal year 1997. At the time, both numbers were the highest in the company's history (United States Securities and Exchange Commission, n.d.b, p. 21).

In fiscal year 2003, Nike's non-U.S. sales exceeded its U.S. sales for the first time (United States Securities and Exchange Commission, n.d.b). In 2014, its non-U.S. sales accounted for 54 percent of the company's total revenues. Nike's products include eight categories: running, basketball, football (soccer), men's training, women's training, action sports, sportswear, and golf. Its sales network has expanded to almost all countries worldwide. There are now 322 independent retail stores in the United States and 536 retail stores outside of the United States.

Nike's total sales have continued to grow since 2009, resulting in a compound annual growth rate of 11 percent. In 2014, the company's revenue reached $27.8 billion, and its net income reached $2.7 billion, both numbers being the highest in the company's history (United States Securities and Exchange Commission, n.d.c).

Nike is in a highly competitive industry. Its target consumers are people who participate in various sports and fitness activities. These consumers like fashionable athletic styles and change their tastes frequently. Nike has to stay current with new trends and designs and, therefore, develop new products on a timely schedule. Meanwhile, Nike has many competitors in the industry, including Adidas and Reebok. Fortunately, Nike has earned a good reputation for both quality and design. As an industry leader, it is critical that Nike maintain this reputation and brand image (United States Securities and Exchange Commission, n.d.a).

Islam—A Brief Overview

Islam is one of three "Abrahamic" religions, along with Judaism and Christianity, which trace their roots to the agreement God made with Abraham in the Hebrew Bible. Islam is a monotheistic religion that originated in the Middle East and includes a core tenet belief that Muhammad was the last messenger of God. It is now the second-largest religion globally after Christianity, with over 1 billion followers, and it continues to grow rapidly (Religion Facts, n.d.).

Muslims believe the Qur'an is a sacred text because it is the verbatim word of Allah (God). They believe it was revealed to the prophet Muhammad in the 7th century and passed on to the world along with the Hadith (the prophet's teachings and practices) to guide all followers. In Arabic, the definition of the word Islam is "submission." Hence, Muslims believe that the sole purpose of their existence on earth is to submit to and worship Allah now, in anticipation of paradise in the afterlife. They believe that Islam is a complete and untainted religion, and that its teachings and laws can be applied universally.

The faith is based on the Five Pillars of Islam: Testimony (Shahada), Prayer (Salat), Alms-Giving (Zakat), Fasting (Sawm), and Pilgrimage (Hajj), which function as obligatory acts of worship for all believers. Muslims relate nearly every aspect of life to religion and thus first seek the guidance of the Qur'an for all worldly affairs. If the Qur'an's interpretations are unclear, then they seek guidance from the Hadith. Through both, they derive "Sharia Law" and believe that the answers they find are inclusive and can be extended through the ages.

Furthermore, as dictated by the Five Pillars, after declaring their faith, Muslims must pray five times a day facing the prophet Muhammad's burial site (Ka'ba) in Mecca. They are encouraged to do this in their main house of worship, which is known as a mosque, because this strengthens community bonds. The main day of worship is Friday, when all businesses must close for noon prayer and believers gather for a weekly sermon given by an Imam.

Muslims must also fast from dusk to dawn every day for the entire month of Ramadan. Ramadan is the ninth month of the Hijri Calendar, a lunar calendar used by Muslims, which represents the emigration (the Hejira) of the prophet Muhammad from Mecca to Medina and marks the beginning of Islam. (Dates vary in the Gregorian, or Western, calendar. For example, it starts on June 18 in 2015, on June 7 in 2016 and on May 27 in 2017.)

Moreover, Muslims must make a pilgrimage to Mecca once in their lifetime and give alms to the poor yearly.

Islam has many commonalities with Judaism and Christianity; however, there are some notable differences. Muslims believe in the virgin birth of Jesus and consider him a prophet of God whose message has been corrupted with the passage of time. They believe that Jesus did not die, but rather ascended into heaven following his crucifixion. They do not believe in the resurrection of Jesus, but do believe in his second coming.

Muslim Americans

Muslim Americans are considered a minority in the United States, projected to make up just over 1 percent of the population by 2020 (Appendix 2) (Pew Research Center, 2011); however, they represent the third-largest faith in the United States, following Christianity and Judaism. Muslim Americans come from a myriad of backgrounds and cultures.

A study conducted by Gallup Polls in 2008, titled *Muslim American: A National Portrait*, states that Muslim Americans are the most racially diverse religious group in the United States, predominantly composed of African–Americans, who account for 35 percent of the total Muslim population (for a more comprehensive breakdown, see Appendix 3) (Gallup, n.d.). The roots of this dominance can be attributed to the age of slavery in Colonial and post-Colonial America as the slave trade inadvertently sent many Muslims from Africa to the Western frontier. This was followed by an influx of Muslim immigrants into America during the post-Civil War era, initially into blue-collar jobs in New York City and then eventually further west.

Over the past century, some of the most notable migration occurred during the Cold War era as the United States attempted to strengthen its position against the Soviet Union. Although the terror attacks on September 11th caused a slowdown in migration to the United States from the Muslim world, the more recent "Arab Spring" and associated political turmoil is causing many to seek refuge in the West again.

United States and American–Islamic Community

Conflicting Viewpoints

Considering the fundamental nature of the Islamic faith, the Muslim American culture may differ significantly with that of the general population. These distinctions are most apparent when studying how religion relates to aspects of life, such as family, community, gender equality, and political views. It is also worth noting that many aspects of Muslim culture stem from Islam being an inclusive religion.

Muslims are for the most part collectivist in nature. As mentioned before, Muslims incorporate religion into every aspect of their daily lives and are required to pray five times a day. This requires a certain amount of discipline and dedication. This contrasts with the prevailing norm in the United States, where some aspects of worship, such as prayer and confession, may be seen as more of a personal endeavor, separated from most daily affairs.

Muslims pray on rugs and they place great emphasis on cleanliness in the place of worship. It is considered disrespectful to step on prayer mats without clean feet. It is also common for Muslims to extend this tradition into their homes by removing all footwear at the front door before entering.

With this is mind, culturally speaking, Muslims believe that displaying the soles of the feet to others is a sign of disrespect. They teach their offspring not to sit with one leg crossed over the other (thus exposing the bottom of one foot) in social gatherings.

These beliefs about the feet became very public to the Western world in 2008 when a Muslim man threw a shoe at former President George W. Bush while he was giving a speech in Iraq. Throwing a shoe at someone was considered a great insult in the Islamic world. Dr. Faegheh Shirazi, a professor of Middle Eastern studies at the University of Texas, gives an interesting explanation as to why the act of throwing a shoe is negatively perceived through different cultural lenses:

> Perhaps it has to do with the hierarchy of the body position, that is, the relationship between the head and the feet, the head being at the top and not touching the ground and the dirt ... the head carries a more prestigious status in comparison to the feet, which in older times mostly remained bare.

> (Duke, 2013)

Additionally, Muslims, like believers in Judaism, are forbidden to eat pork. This is derived from the Qur'an and is attributed to the filthy nature of the animal itself. Adversely, Muslims eat "halal" meat, which is meat that is slaughtered in an Islamic way, and blessed with the name of Allah. Alcohol consumption is also forbidden.

Muslim Americans view family as the center point of society and community (although, less popular today, their men are encouraged to marry as many as four wives if possible). Men also may aim to have many children and to start building a family from a young age. This stems from the prophet's era when Islam was expanding through wars, and many wives and children of slain fighters were left without someone to provide for them. As it turns out, these traditions and laws have extended into recent times and are in high contrast with the norm of monogamy in the Western world.

Another commonly publicized cultural clash involves Muslim women wearing the burka. The West was built on the notion of freedom, and the concept of the burka is difficult for many Westerners to understand. For Muslim women, modest clothing is the norm, and wearing a hijab or full burka is a mark of devotion and commitment to the faith. In some countries, such as

Saudi Arabia, wearing the hijab is obligatory, while in the United States it is a personal choice. There have been ongoing clashes and misunderstandings surrounding the burka, to the extent that some countries, such as France, have banned it.

Negotiations Between Nike and CAIR

The controversial line of Nike Air athletic shoes went on sale in the United States in March, 1997. Before any of the shoes had moved into retail stores, a shipment was sent to a Muslim distributor, who noticed the ill-fated design. The distributor notified Nike that the logo may be controversial. Nike claimed their original intent was that the word "Air" be written in flames in the logo and there had been no intended malice. Heeding the warning, Nike decided to alter the design to appease the Muslim community and attempted to resolve the situation before it escalated.

Despite Nike's attempt to mitigate the risk, the design was still seen as too closely resembling the Arabic word "Allah." Unfortunately, Nike clearly did not alter the design enough to sufficiently differentiate it from the Arabic reference. As a result, CAIR started receiving complaints from Muslim communities soon after the Nike Air shoe lines were moved into retail stores (Harrington, 1997). As an important representative of the Muslim community, CAIR had a responsibility to address Nike's cultural insensitivity. And, according to CAIR spokesman Ibrahim Hooper, the council responded to the complaints by asking their members "to act in a peaceful way by sending Nike letters, faxes, e-mail and telephone calls" (Harrington, 1997). The spokesman continued on to say that, "a boycott on Nike would have been the next step. But quite frankly, we would never have liked to do that unless there was no other choice" (Harrington, 1997).

So at this point, members of the American-Islamic community proceeded to send correspondence to Nike, expressing their outrage over the use of the word "Allah" on a shoe. First, the word "Allah" is not allowed to be used on a product, and using it on a shoe is a further offense because the foot is seen as unclean (Morrison, 2012). Furthermore, the community was angered because Muslims do not eat pork, and one of the shoes referenced pork (bacon) with the name "Air Bakin'" and its play on words.

Nike responded to the initial complaints and community outrage with a statement from Nike spokeswoman Vizhier Corpuz. In the statement, she claimed that the company had no intention of offending anyone with the shoes and she expressed contrition that the shoes ended up in retail stores. Furthermore, Nike reiterated that they had actually changed the design so "Air" would not be mistaken for any other word (Associated Press, 1997a).

Nike also went a step further by recalling 38,000 pairs of the shoes and diverting a similar number away from "Saudi Arabia, Kuwait, Malaysia, Indonesia and Turkey to 'less-sensitive' markets" (Harrington, 1997). At this point, Agostino believed Nike had done their due diligence and made the appropriate accommodations to renew goodwill between themselves and the Muslim community.

However, CAIR retaliated against Nike's responses to the issue by claiming that the shoes in question had still been seen at stores throughout the United States, and pressed Nike to initiate an investigation. The CAIR executive director accused Nike of having "people at the company who [wanted] to insult Muslims" (Abu-Nasr, 1997). The council was further incensed because Nike had given no assurances that the incident would not happen again. With this latest wave of negotiations, Agostino realized that Nike must go back to the drawing board and come up with a more effective response to CAIR.

The Decision

As Agostino sat in his office making last-minute press release preparations, he thought about the various distinct solutions that Nike management had formulated and that he could announce. Nike had come up with several good ideas for making additional reparations, but Agostino and the company had not yet decided on a decisive approach to mend relations. Among the possible solutions, recalling all the Nike Air shoe lines was a sure win with CAIR, but also the most risky for the company. This solution would hopefully mend fences between Nike and the Muslim community; however, it offered negative financial implications for the company.

The cost of recalling shoes would definitely not sit well with key decision-makers at the company or most stockholders. Instead, Nike just promised to stop producing and distributing the line, leaving thousands of pairs in circulation.

Another possible approach was a public acceptance of guilt—a genuine apology and an offer to donate funds toward the betterment of the affected Muslim community as a show of good faith for the future. "Image is everything in this industry," Agostino thought to himself. If Nike's image is tarnished by this conflict, then it will set a dangerous precedent for the future of the company. Instead, Nike and its stakeholders wanted to set a positive example in the industry, and let consumers know that valid complaints are taken seriously. This press release was critical, and making the right decision for the company had long-lasting implications. Agostino left his office with a feeling of indecision and hoped that he would be making the right choice.

Questions

As Agostino prepared his press release and reviewed all the points he wanted to make, he carefully considered questions similar to the following:

1   What types of communication norms do Americans have? What communication norms do Muslims have? Compare and contrast.
2   How does the concept of due diligence play a role in this case?
3   Why did the Muslim community take offense to the name "Air Bakin'?"

4   Why did CAIR take offense to the shoe, in general?
5   How could Hofstede's Cultural Dimensions model help explain why Nike's Air Bakins were perceived negatively by the Muslim community?
6   Which cultural gaps did the Nike executives experience before rolling out the Air Bakin' shoes?
7   What do you think Nike, Inc., will do to ensure that a similar issue will not occur again in the future? Be specific and give a timeline to implementation for each of your suggestions.
8   What impact, if any, do you think this experience had on Nike, as a company, to individual Nike employees, to Nike's customer base?

Appendix 1

See the following URL for pictures of Nike Air and Arabic "Allah" similarities: http://sneakernews.com/2012/09/28/classics-revisited-nike-air-bakin-1997/.

Appendix 2

See the following URL for information on the estimated Muslim population: www.pewresearch.org/fact-tank/2013/06/07/worlds-muslim-population-more-widespread-than-you-might-think/.

Appendix 3

See the following URL for information on religious breakdown in the United States: www.themosqueinmorgantown.com/pdfs/GallupAmericanMuslim-Report.pdf.

Note

1 Authors: Amin., N., Song, M. Sekardi, K., and Tuleja, E. (Ed.).

References

Abu-Nasr, Donna. (1997, April 24). Nike, Inc. will recall shoes carrying a logo that offends Muslims. Retrieved from www.apnewsarchive.com/1997/WASHINGTON-AP-Nike-Inc-will-recall-shoes-carrying-a/id-0b2daa54895540e366c70e5e6dccdf50 (accessed August 1, 2016).

Associated Press. (1997a, April 10). Nike draws Muslim fire for flamelike shoe logo. Retrieved from www.deseretnews.com/article/554089/Nike-draws-Muslim-fire-for-flamelike-shoe-logo.html?pg=all (accessed August 1, 2016).

Associated Press. (1997b, June 25). Nike, Muslim group reach accord on logo. *Bangor Daily News*. Retrieved from http://news.google.com/newspapers?nid=2457&dat=19970625&id=6v9aAAAAIBAJ&sjid=CU4NAAAAIBAJ&pg=3147,2928141 (accessed October 6, 2014).

Duke, Alan. (2013, February 7). Why shoe throwing is "incredibly offensive." Retrieved from www.cnn.com/2013/02/06/world/meast/shoe-throwing-significance/ (accessed October 7, 2104).

Gallup. (n.d.). *Muslim Americans: A national portrait.* Gallup and The Muslim West Facts Project. Retrieved from www.themosqueinmorgantown.com/pdfs/GallupAmeri-canMuslimReport.pdf (accessed October 7, 2014).

Harrington, J. (1997, June 25). Nike recalls disputed logo: Company apologizes to offended. *The Cincinnati Enquirer.* Retrieved from www.enquirer.com/editions/1997/06/25/bus_nike.html (accessed August 1, 2016).

Morrison, Terry. (2012, October 5). Bad brands and translation blunders. *Business Traveler.* Retrieved from www.businesstravelerusa.com/world-wise/bad-brands-and-translation-blunders (accessed October 5, 2014).

Pew Research Center. (2011, January). The future of the global Muslim population. Retrieved from www.pewforum.org/ (accessed October 7, 2014).

Religion Facts. (n.d.). Retrieved from www.religionfacts.com/islam/ (accessed October 7, 2014).

The New York Times. (1997, April 10). Muslims seek Nike's apology. Retrieved from www.nytimes.com/1997/04/10/sports/muslims-seek-nike-s-apology.html (accessed October 6, 2014).

The Washington Post. (1997, April 10). Apparel. As cited by High Beam Research. Retrieved from www.highbeam.com/doc/1P2-718489.html (accessed October 5, 2014).

United States Securities and Exchange Commission. (n.d.a). Nike's 1997 Form 10-K. Retrieved from www.sec.gov/ (accessed October 6, 2014).

United States Securities and Exchange Commission. (n.d.b). Nike's 2003 form 10-K. Retrieved from www.zonebourse.com/NIKE-INC-13739/pdf/72535/Nike%20Inc_SEC-Filing-10K.pdf (accessed August 1, 2016).

United States Securities and Exchange Commission. (n.d.c). Nike's 2014 form 10-K. Retrieved from www.sec.gov/Archives/edgar/data/320187/000032018714000097/nke-5312014x10k.htm (accessed August 1, 2016).

7 Culture, Cognition, and Reasoning

The capacity to diffuse knowledge is particularly critical within the international context, where firms face a wide range of challenges including culture and political risk.

(Kamoche & Harvey, 2006)

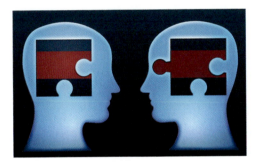

Figure 7.1 Two Heads With Puzzle Piece
(*Source*: Fotolia 63586490, © carlosgardel.)

Chapter Overview

The key questions covered in Chapter 7 will focus on: What have recent neuroscience findings told us about the connection of culture and cognition? Why might people from different cultures approach reasoning in different ways? What are some of the cultural patterns for communicating? How might language play a role in what and how we communicate? (Figure 7.1).

Learning Objective

This chapter looks at non-Western views of intercultural communication by providing culture-specific examples to illuminate human cognition across cultures and why this matters in business. Richard Nisbett's classic study on differences between Eastern and Western thought, as well as some other communication patterns from Kenya and India, demonstrates that the global leader does well to understand why thought, reasoning, and language are key to doing business.

Key Takeaways

— Historical and societal impact on humans results in different methods of reasoning.
— A culture's language influences what, how, and why things are communicated.

Leadership Applications

— Global leaders will deal with difference more effectively if they can identify differences in how colleagues, employees, and business partners think, reason, and rationalize.

Introduction

Neuroscience and Culture

The field of neuroscience is opening up new explanations of the connections between the biological brain and human behavior. Psychologists have long believed that the development of the structure and function of the human brain is shaped by one's environment, and that the environment is naturally shaped by culture. There is now a specific field in the area of cultural neuroscience that studies the interchange between neural and cultural forces which promote human cognition, perception, and behavior (Ambady, 2011). The question is, how does culture, which includes behaviors, communication, and rules, shape the minds (and brains) of people, as well as how is culture shaped by the mind? And, is there a specific part of the brain where such cultural differences are located? Neuroscientists have found that social factors such as group norms and expectations impact the brain regarding the reptilian complex, which is the most basic part of the brain for all breathing creatures. The limbic system, which is related to emotional and social behaviors as well as the neocortex, which is related to language and cognition, are impacted also. As leaders it is critical to understand how people think, so in this chapter we will focus on the connection of cognition (reasoning/ thought) and language.

Because humans are a social species, we have the need to create and maintain groups in order to survive. Think about how our families, communities, associations, and organizations impact our lives through the order and stability that they create. What neuroscientists are telling us is that such sociocultural structures have a major impact on our brains and bodies "through a continuous interplay of neural, neuroendocrine, metabolic and immune factors" (Putz et al., 2014, p. 23). As such, the field of intercultural communication continues to grow in credibility as social and biological scientists give credence to the biological and social factors that influence how we think, communicate, and interact with each other. This is important to the entire discussion woven throughout this book: it is not enough to perform the functional aspects of "doing business" across borders or at home within a diverse organization; rather, it is the hard work of developing both one's EQ and CQ that will help us achieve success in our interactions with others who are different than us.

Beyond neuroscience, some excellent work in the development of scientifically valid and reliable online cross-cultural assessment tools has provided worthy research into how we function as humans regarding culture and communication. The Cultural Orientations Approach (COA), developed by TMC in the 1980s, focuses on three dimensions of culture—interaction style, thinking style, and sense of self. In the latest book about the COA approach, *Maximizing business results with the strategic performance framework,* Putz et al. (2014) explains this interesting connection between neuroscience and culture (Box 7.1).

Cognition

Our thinking style—or cognition—relates to how we reason and perceive. It is the way we process information, react to it, and create our own meaning from that information. Reasoning means that we draw inferences or

---

Box 7.1

Social neuroscience, a relatively new science with an integrative perspective of the social and the biological, has generated innovative insights and applications that change the very nature of established knowledge on the notions of culture, adaptation, globalization, and leadership.

Source: Putz et al., 2014

conclusions and is the process of thinking about something in a logical way in order to form a conclusion. Perceiving is the ability to understand something and is the way we think about something. According to the COA (Schmitz, 2012), there are two forms of reasoning (deductive and inductive) and two forms of perceiving (systemic and linear). Being able to spot a colleague's cognitive style can help you shift your frame of reference for how you might approach them. Have you ever walked away from a meeting utterly frustrated because the point you were trying to get across made sense to you but not to others? Or have you wondered why a colleague was so disorganized in laying out his points? It probably was because each of you had a different way of looking at the problem based upon your cognitive preferences.

Deductive and Inductive Reasoning

In deductive thinking a person instinctively looks for theories and general concepts—to this person it is more important to analyze theories before getting into the details of the data. Think of Einstein and his high-level theory of relativity. A deductive thinker would analyze the overarching theory instead of the details associated with it. In his or her mind it is impossible to even consider the minutia related to the theory because it is the theory that holds the power of meaning in and of itself. For example, a deductive approach would focus on the theory behind $E = mc^2$ and the correlation of energy to matter, and its general concepts of relative space, relative time, matter and energy, and quantum physics. Einstein himself said, "I want to know God's thoughts; the rest are details." (Engel, n.d.) This is what makes sense for the deductive thinker (Prinz, 2016) (Box 7.2).

In inductive thinking a person is more attuned with specific examples and prefers to analyze the details in the data before moving on to the general concepts. An inductive thinker would want to create a mind map of this theory to

---

Box 7.2

Within Western analytic philosophy, culture has not been a major topic of discussion. It sometimes appears as a topic in the philosophy of social science, and in continental philosophy there is a long tradition of "Philosophical Anthropology," which deals with culture to some degree. Within the core areas of analytic philosophy, culture has most frequently appeared in discussions of moral relativism, radical translation, and discussions of perceptual plasticity, though little effort has been made to seriously investigate the impact of culture on these domains. Cognitive science has also neglected culture, but in recent years that has started to change. There has been a sizable intensification of efforts to empirically test the impact of culture on mental processes.

map out its specifics because, without understanding the details, the inductive thinker could not see the logic in the abstractness. That is, you move from the specific to the general. For example, perhaps understanding that "mass and energy are different manifestations of the same thing," or that "space and time are part of one continuum," or that "relativity explains where gravity comes from" will help the inductive thinker grasp the theory of relativity (Tate, 2015).

At work, inductive thinking would mean that you are interested in the specific situations and details surrounding a problem, issue, or event. You are pragmatic and want to interpret the data or information involved with that problem, issue, or event. The inductive thinker is all about the details and to a deductive thinker would be perceived as possibly rushing ahead—or metaphorically putting the cart before the horse (Table 7.1).

At work this would mean that you move from the general to the specific understanding of a situation. For example, when listening to a presentation, you would focus on the quality of the arguments and its credibility because the speaker uses a strong conceptual foundation. If that conceptual foundation is not developed, you would become impatient. Or, after the presentation you would want to examine the conceptual frameworks and key principles by analyzing them. Only then would you want to apply them to individual situations. The deductive thinker is all about the conceptualization of a project or idea rather than its application to particular situations. To the inductive thinker, you would appear to be "lost in the clouds" rather than being "down to earth" and therefore could appear to be unrealistic because of a perceived lack of attention to detail or the current problem. To use another metaphor, you would be "two ships passing each other in the dark"—not on the same wavelength (Box 7.3).

Systemic and Linear Perceiving

The two forms of perceiving are systemic and linear. If reasoning is the process of thinking about something in order to form a conclusion, perceiving is the way you think about something—how you are able to grasp its essence.

Table 7.1 Cultural Orientations Approach—Deductive/Inductive

Deductive thinker	Inductive thinker
Focus on the soundness of theories	Focus immediately on the details of the situation
Think abstractly in order to grasp the situation, problem, or issue	Seek specific example in order to grasp the situation, problem, or issue
First address theories, concepts, and models before getting to specifics	Seek to apply and implement without first understanding underlying concepts
Become impatient with stories or anecdotes that involve examples	Become frustrated if you can't use stories and anecdotes to make specific points

(*Source*: Adapted from Schmitz, 2006, p. 9.)

Box 7.3

In the early 1900s an Indian Chief named Black Elk visited New York City and saw electric lights for the first time and said that the white man had captured the power of the Thunder Beings.

He was describing electricity and, from his point of view, his description was entirely accurate based on his knowledge and frame of reference. We now use terms like "The Big Bang" and "Black Holes" to create a mental picture of something that is beyond our ability to understand from our present frame of reference.

Source: Neihardt, 2008

Systemic thinking is the proclivity to see the big picture and, as a result, structure one's thoughts and solutions based upon that broad view of a problem or situation along with its interconnected parts. In the workplace you would tend to take a "big picture" view of a problem, focusing on the relationships of its various concepts or components. For example, in a presentation you would persuade people by demonstrating the impact on related parts.

Linear thinking looks at the individual components of a problem or situation, structuring one's thoughts and solutions, possibly using a cause and effect structure. A linear-thinking colleague giving the same presentation as a systemic thinker might persuade through laying out the arguments in a linear fashion and then showing the logical simplicity of the argument (fact by fact) rather than showing its interrelated complexity. Both would perceive the other as not getting to the point (Table 7.2).

A Case of Linear Versus Systemic Thinking

The House of Barbie: if you build it, people will come. This is what Mattel thought in 2009 when they built a six-story shop in a prime Shanghai location

Table 7.2 Cultural Orientations Approach– Systemic/Linear

Systemic thinker	Linear thinker
Communicate your point using complexity that demonstrates the interrelatedness of situations, issues, and problems	Communicate sequentially and focus on each issue one by one
Look at the big picture versus the minute details	Examine discrete components and details
Focus on the theoretical outcomes	Focus on cause–effect outcomes

(*Source*: Adapted from Schmitz, 2006, p. 9.)

to sell all-things-Barbie. This novelty store was much more than a toy store because it included a spa, hair and nail salon, a bar, and a restaurant. They even created a new character named Ling. Mattel's reasoning was that, of course, mothers would want to bring their daughters to shop and enjoy a girls' day out. However, only two years later, Mattel was forced to close the store after losing $30 million! What went wrong? One fact that Mattel executives knew was that brands are incredibly important to the rising Chinese middle class (Chadha & Husband, 2006); therefore, this should have been a novel treat for those who had money burning in their pockets.

It was a matter of perspective and Mattel executives did not exercise right thinking. They were too focused on the particular details of all that would go into the many facets of this megastore rather than focus on the big picture—how the Barbie-doll brand might appeal to Chinese women. Mattel misread their market by making an egregious error of dumping too much all at once on a picky consumer—there were the Barbie dolls as well as the themed items, such as clothing, beauty treatment, and other goods. However, the Barbie brand was inconsequential to the female purchasing power. Had Mattel taken a broader view of the market to assess potential conditions they probably would have seen that this idea was doomed for failure. Instead, they forged ahead assuming that what had worked well in one market would work well in another market.

In just a moment we will begin to look at some of the cultural factors that influence our thinking processes. But first, here is a brief summary of some principles of human cognition. I am sure that at some time you have sat in a meeting and wondered why your counterparts just do not "get it." While it all seems perfectly clear and reasonable to you, you wonder why the others are missing your point. Or, you might worry that you lack the mental acuity to get *their* point, all the while wondering why their ideas are so hard to comprehend. It can be quite a relief to realize that each of you is coming at the problem, issue, or situation from a different cognitive vantage point. Knowing these differences in how humans reason helps us move away from simply meaning well to having an action plan for specific situations that inevitably will come up in the workplace. Someone who sees the theory and concepts behind an idea or a plan will reason much differently than one who latches onto the examples and details that come out of the theory. Neither is right or wrong; one way is not better than the other—they are simply different. Current research into neuroscience is helping us to understand how the processes of our brains affect communication, emotions, and social interactions.

Now we will turn our attention to some specific examples of culture's influence on thought processes, reasoning, and language. As we have discussed in previous chapters, all world views are ethnocentric, which means we are socially primed to view events from our in-group perspective; hence we believe (innately) that our ways are the best ways. Since most of the research on intercultural issues over the past several decades has been grounded in a Western or Eurocentric approach, we must step back—figuratively—and try to see things from the perspective of "other." Yoshitaka Miike, professor at the University of Hawaii Hilo, believes that much of our current intercultural dialog is problematic because the Anglo-European perspective has dominated the scene—all other behavior is compared with a Eurocentric view. In this chapter we will take an Asiacentric perspective on how people think and solve problems (Asante et al., 2013).

Historical and Philosophical Backgrounds of the East and West

True or false? There are cognitive differences between Westerners and East Asians. Social psychologist Richard Nisbett set out to find the answer to this question through an interesting experiment he did with hundreds of college students across five countries: Canada, the United States, Japan, China, and South Korea (Nisbett, 2003). It is important to note here that, while each culture is different (e.g., Anglo-European or Asian) they still share common cultural backgrounds—Canada and the United States being similar to each other, and Japan, China, and South Korea being similar to each other. Nisbett separated students into two groups: East and West, and showed them an underwater scene of fish swimming in an aquarium. The results were statistically significant—the Asian students focused on the environment in which the fish swam, along with the plants, rocks, and other marine objects that grounded the scene; however, the Canadian and U.S. students focused on the actual fish, such as counting the number of large fish and small fish in the tank. This is called "field dependence," a term originally coined by 19th-century psychologist Herman Witkin (Vaught, 1972), and indicates that a person's perception of an object will be influenced by the environment in which it rests. Witkin's famous test relied on the rod and frame, and depending on how they were positioned a person would see them differently (Figure 7.2).

Another study, at MIT, examined how Westerners and Easterners made quick perceptual judgments using the same rod experiment but with a

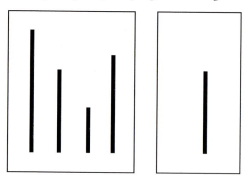

Figure 7.2 Witkin's Rod and Frame Test

(*Source*: Balcetis & Lassiter, 2010, p. 62.)

more technological basis by using a magnetic resonance imaging scanner. Their findings: we all have the same "machinery" (our brains) for cognitive tasks, but our brains are trained in different ways based upon our culture. One of the scientists remarked, "It's fascinating that the way in which the brain responds to these simple drawings reflects, in a predictable way, how the individual thinks about independent or interdependent social relationships." (Nauert, 2015).

In Nisbett's experiment with the fish, he found that Asians, generally, tend to focus on the environment (the "field"), the background variables, and perceive an event more holistically. A field-dependent strategy for learning or problem solving would include sensitivity to other members of the group and their needs for inclusion in the decision-making process. Westerners, generally, look more at the objects individually, isolating details (of the field) and determining what was happening through a cause-and-effect process. A field-independent strategy for learning or problem solving would not pay attention to feelings and opinions but rather focus on the logic of the decision-making process. To this end, Nisbett determined that how people think about and perceive the world was influenced by their social structures, philosophies, and even educational systems as initially formed in ancient Greece and China (Nisbett, 2003).

In another study, people from two groups (Western and Eastern) were shown pictures of a chicken, grass, and a cow. They were instructed to group them—the Western subjects put the chicken and the cow together (they are both animals) and most Eastern subjects put the cow with the grass (the cow eats the grass); hence the majority of Western people focused on the taxonomy of animals and the Eastern people focused on the relationship of the animal to what it eats. Psychologists call this, in the first instance, abstract analytic pairings and, in the second, relational/holistic pairings (a thinking style that embraces contradiction) (Nisbett, 2003).

This research dealing with social development came six years after bio-geographer Jared Diamond published his Pulitzer Prize-winning book *Guns, Germs, and Steel*, which looked at how geography and other environmental phenomena affected certain societies (Diamond, 1999). Diamond argued that the reason why some civilizations grew, prospered, and spread was all due to two things: geography and the great forces of developing civilizations such as agriculture, animal domestication, and immunity to disease. Just as Diamond demonstrated with geography and environment, Nisbett focused on philo-sophical and ecological developments of humans (that is, the study of the relationship between living things with their setting). He proposes that differences in human reasoning are based upon the intellectual history of the ancient Greeks (Plato and Socrates) and the ancient Chinese (Confucius and Lao Tzu). Besides experiments with university students around the world, he drew on historical and philosophical data, as well as the Eastern and Western literature on the nature of thought. As a result, his findings underscored the intersection of social practices with cognitive processes.

For example, there are differences in how mothers interact with their children simply by the language that they use—research has shown that Japanese mothers choose relational words, such as, "I give you the car; now you give it to me. Thank you." U.S. American mothers use object words, such as, "Here is the car; it has nice wheels." It has been said that "[r]elationships become fundamental in Asian thinking and influence a great deal of the way their world is created, where European/Americans tend to be prepared for a world of objects" (Vercoe, 2006, p. 284).

Eastern Orientation

A major influence on Chinese personal agency is harmony—throughout Chinese history, a Chinese person was first and foremost a member of several collectives (family, clan, village). Consequently, individuals did not claim unique and independent identities apart from their family—even within the family, all individuals blended into the main group and found their identity within that group. And while harmony within one's social environment was essential, so was harmony with the natural environment (Figure 7.3).

As was demonstrated in the fish tank experiment mentioned above, the majority of East Asians explained observations in relation to the field (surroundings) of objects—everything in the scene was interrelated. This is exemplary of the general social practice of engaging the social environment as a collective whole versus an individualistic part. Therefore, in any given culture, certain cognitive styles and behaviors are rewarded and reinforced, and others are discouraged, considered as less suitable (Samovar & Porter, 1994). A prime example is the nature of rice farming. Families bonded into clans, which made up the villages, and each community needed to cooperate

Figure 7.3 Longji Rice Terraces, Guangxi Province, China

(*Source*: Fotolia 58592736, © konstantant.)

in order to irrigate the paddies. For example, if you lived down the mountain and did not get along with your neighbor uphill, you might not have a crop to harvest, which meant your family would go hungry. This is still a critical aspect of society today. In fact, you can read about a fascinating research study highlighted in the prestigious *Science* journal by a cultural psychologist on the differences between rice and wheat farming in China. The adage, "Know where your water comes from," makes sense in this context (Talhelm et al., 2014) (Box 7.4).

As harmony within the community is important, as an extension, so is harmony at work. In terms of the Eastern orientation (the collective coming together of people to interact and live harmoniously), we can look at an example of collectivism within in the Japanese. In Japanese, the phrase, "*Deru kui wa utareru*" (出る杭は打たれる) means "The stake that sticks up is pounded down." This implies that one must fit in with the social environment. Japanese people have the group-oriented concept of *wa*, which means social harmony. From an early age, schoolchildren are taught the importance of working on group tasks in order to maintain social harmony. You will find this carried over into adulthood within the business world, with compensation policies rewarding group versus individual performance as well as loyalty to the company (Griffin & Pustay, 2003).

A collective—group—perspective is held by the majority of people in Asian cultures in terms of society, language, and belief systems. This collective focus means that on a job, if you are working with a team and one person of the team gets praised for getting the job done (say the leader or perceived leader of the group) then that person would be embarrassed and possibly lose face because it was the entire group that succeeded, not just

---

Box 7.4

Westerners are seen as prizing individualism, while Asians tend to be creatures who lean on their communities.

If you are looking for an answer as to why, there is the "rice theory." Psychologists say the divide may come down to which crops are historically farmed in different regions.

Researchers have found that people from rice-growing southern China are more interdependent and holistic thinkers, while those from the wheat-growing north are more independent and analytical.

The researchers call it "rice theory," and they believe the psychological differences of southern and northern Chinese stem from their ancestors' subsistence techniques—rice farming needs cooperation and planning; wheat farming requires less cooperation between neighbours.

Source: Meng, 2014

one. Those of us who have an individualist perspective might think that we are helping to promote our colleague by giving praise, whereas we are doing the opposite (Box 7.5).

Harmony with the environment is important as well. The ancient Chinese practice of *feng shui* (literally meaning wind and water) uses the arrangement of furniture or the positioning of buildings to create a positive flow of energy, *chi*. The placement of objects (whether buildings, furniture, decorations, etc.) demonstrates harmony and unity within the "field." All of these entities are interdependent with each other and must preserve the yin and yang—or natural balance. For example, in 1990 when the Bank of China's new building opened, there was harsh criticism about the sharp angles and design of famous architect I. M. Pei's design. It resembles a knife that is cutting other people's business and the building cast "razor sharp" shadows on other buildings, thus "cutting" their business prospects (*New York Times*, 2008). Feng shui is an important practice in Asian culture. Some companies even set aside a portion of the annual budget for feng shui consultant fees (Truong, 2010).

A story was told about an expatriate lawyer who moved to the Shanghai headquarters. She knew a little about Chinese culture and art and purchased a costly painting of the traditional koi fish and hung it near the door so that people walking in would implicitly acknowledge her as a successful attorney— koi represent good luck and wealth. Her clients would be impressed with her knowledge.

However the attorney was puzzled at how uncomfortable her clients appeared and she shrugged it off to being a foreigner. She began to receive pressure from her partners about losing potential business and someone suggested she hire a feng shui master. Luckily, the feng shui master figured out the problem immediately and it had to do with the placement of the painting. While the attorney thought it a good idea to hang the painting at the entrance to her office, it had the opposite effect. The head of the fish faced the door, which meant that luck or prosperity would flow away from the client and escape out the door. A quick and easy fix placed the painting over the attorney's desk. Her luck and success followed (Adler, 2008, p. 27).

Box 7.5

Nisbett said, "East Asian thought tends to be more holistic. Holistic approaches attend to the entire field, and make relatively little use of categories and formal logic. They also emphasize change, and they recognize contradiction and the need for multiple perspectives, searching for the 'middle way' between opposing propositions."

Source: Nisbett, 2003, p. 45

What is your reaction to this story? Does it go against logic? Does it flow with logic? Western and Eastern perceptions clearly differ and it is a matter of perspective. In Eastern cultures people have a need to be in harmony with nature, otherwise life is disrupted, which means prosperity, health, and luck will escape; in Western cultures such matters are not important because it is the individual who controls their own destiny. From the client perspective, the expatriate had failed to achieve the necessary harmony that would bring good luck to themselves and their clients.

This is a vivid example of the main emphasis of this book—knowing *why* something is important to someone from a different world view is even more important than knowing *what* is important. If this attorney internalizes the cultural and social norms behind what was happening, she could then benefit from a deeper appreciation of her clients' perspective, thus being able to communicate and interact more appropriately (Adler & Gundersen, 2008).

Eastern Orientation in Religion and Philosophy

The Eastern orientation toward life blends Confucianism, Daoism, and Buddhism, all of which focus on harmony with people and nature (Box 7.6).

Confucius (552 to 479 BCE) lived during the Early Autumn Era, which was a tumultuous time; hence Confucius wanted to help restore societal order and harmony. His teachings created a system of social and political ethics meant to guide people about how to behave properly in everyday life—it is about practical morality and self-control. Confucian philosophy valued hierarchy, group orientation, and tradition. He taught that it was important to hold to filial piety, kinship, and loyalty as an indication of the important obligations within hierarchical relationships: emperor to subject; husband to wife; parent to child; older sibling to younger sibling; older friend to younger friend. Everyone was expected to know their place, and respect those who were older and had a higher rank—to this day, reverence toward elders and respect for hierarchy are distinguishing values of Chinese society. The main principle is "*ren*" (仁), which translates into "benevolence." Another important principle in Confucian teachings is "*li*" (礼), which one demonstrates through the practice of demonstrating good character. Also important are "*zhōng*" (忠), which is loyalty, "*shù*" (恕), reciprocity, and

---

Box 7.6

A young person's duty is to behave well to one's parents at home and to one's elders abroad, to be cautious in giving promises and punctual in keeping them, to overflow in love to all, and to cultivate the friendship of the good.

(Analects 1:6, Confucius)

"*xiào*" (孝), filial piety, which means taking care of family. All together, these noble aspects add up to virtue (Riegel, 2013).

Daoism is a philosophical system that focuses on becoming one with the environment. It is considered a religion and is attributed to Lao-zi, a Chinese philosopher and poet around 570 BCE, who is purported to have written the philosophical teachings of the Dao De Jing. Daoism is about balance—there must be spiritual harmony within an individual and also between that individual and nature. In all things there are two sides (yin and yang), such as in good and bad. One would not know what good was unless there was bad—reconciling both helps one blend together to create harmony and peace. The Dao literally means, "the way" or "the path" and is a force. It considers compassion, moderation, and humility to be of supreme importance. It is said that Daoism is a nice complement to Confucian filial piety (one's social obligation to family—respect, obedience, and care) and society (Religious-Tolerance.org, n.d.b.) (Figure 7.4).

Buddhism is a major religion, practiced in India, Cambodia, Taiwan, South Korea, Sri Lanka, Myanmar, Vietnam, Thailand, Japan, and China. It is a way of finding peace within oneself through meditation and following a spiritual path to enlightenment. Born a royal prince in 624 BCE, Siddhartha shunned the worldly excess of royalty, becoming a recluse at 29 years of age, and followed a spiritual path to enlightenment, becoming Buddha, a Sanskrit word meaning "awakened one." Reaching enlightenment means that you have overcome the cycle of birth and death, being now liberated from pain and suffering. Buddhism teaches that we need to overcome our negative states of mind, which cause suffering, in favor of positive states of mind, which bring happiness (ReligiousTolerance.org, n.d.a.).

In summarizing the three major belief systems—Confucianism, Daoism, and Buddhism, Confucianism is an ethical and philosophical system that guides people toward harmonious living, while Buddhism is considered a religion. Buddha was a great teacher who demonstrated four noble truths related to human suffering and the eightfold path to Nirvana, needed to achieve enlightenment. Daoism stresses the relationship of humans with nature. These three belief systems are complementary to each other and were instrumental in shaping the world view of people from Eastern orientations as described by Nisbett.

Figure 7.4 Yin and Yang

> Learning *about* cultures is one thing. Learning *from* cultures is another. We can be very arrogant and ethnocentric, but we can still learn about other cultures. Learning *from* cultures, on the other hand, requires us to be humble and modest in order to understand and appreciate other cultures. The former approach is an attempt to describe, interpret, and evaluate a different culture through the world view that is *not* derived from the culture.
>
> (Miike, 2009, p. 67)

As previously mentioned, Yoshitaka Miike, professor at the University of Hawaii Hilo, writes about the Asiacentric world view and its implications for communication. He believes that we can learn from others because of their different traditions, beliefs, and modes of communication. They are "alternative visions" of reality and can be opportunities for learning and growth rather than forces for separation and misunderstanding.

Miike uses the Confucian notion of harmony without uniformity—that humans can attain "the balanced integration of different elements" (Miike, 2009, p. 66). Moving away from a Eurocentric view of the world with core values that include rationality, individual agency, and linear logic, the Asia-centric view focuses on intuitive, holistic, and circular logic. Miike examines five unique propositions regarding an Asiacentric world view in order to contrast with the Eurocentric world view, to understand different perspectives for perceiving, reasoning, and communication. These include circularity, harmony, other-directedness, reciprocity, and relationality. There is an acceptance of contradictory beliefs, or what is called dialectal thinking. Issues are never see as an "either/or" problem; rather, as a challenge to be understood from both sides. The important point here is that neither the Asiacentric or Eurocentric (Western) viewpoints are better than the other—they are simply different and are grounded upon millennia of social development and change (Table 7.3).

An Asiacentric form of communication is iterative, focusing on the interaction of ideas and their complementing nature, while an Anglo-European form of communication emphasizes opposites, or polarity of ideas, such as "either/or," "right or wrong," "good or bad," "correct or incorrect" (Leiberman, 1994). For example, from a Western perspective, the process of negotiation is about winning—and is also linear—you have an objective and know what you want to get; you then set the plan with an agenda that should be followed; then you try to change anything that might get in the way of the plan. A negotiator focuses on the task and not necessarily on the relationship, which can be seen as an either/or focus. From a Japanese perspective it is about control or harmony. This would be known as *erabi*, which means that you can manipulate and control your environment. Said another way, one has personal agency of the ability to

Table 7.3 Asiacentric Communication

Propositions: Asia-centric view of communication: a process in which . . .		Propositions: Eurocentric view of communication: a process in which . . .
1. We are interdependent and interrelated with humanity and the universe.	It is the universe that connects everyone with everything across space and time. The focus must be on interdependence rather than independence.	1. Western thinking proposes self-expression, independence, and individuality.
2. Our goal is to diminish self and rid our focus on egocentrism.	To coexist with others, we need to release our innate tendency for self-centeredness—we do this through self-discipline.	2. Western thinking proposes that communication is a process that we use to prove ourselves in order to enhance our self-esteem.
3. We connect to others who suffer.	The Chinese term "*rénqíng*"—means "whole heartedness." In Japan, there is a concept of "*ninjo*" and in Korea, "*cheong*." It is essential to notice the suffering of others as well as share in their joy (to employ emotion and not just rational thought).	3. Western thinking proposes that communication be focused on rational and logical thought rather than emotions.
4. We realize that what we get we must also give back.	Since our existence depends on all beings—we must show gratitude and respect not only for fellow humans, but for the physical and spiritual environment (ancestral spirits) because of our mutual obligation.	4. Western thinking proposes that communication is used as a means to give or get information where the responsibility is on the self and not on the mutual obligation (at future dates) to others.
5. We consider our moral obligation within society and the universe.	This is an ethical appeal for our sense of duty to cooperate and demonstrate moral integrity—we must be outward versus inward focused through whole-hearted concern (*rénqíng*) for all.	5. Western thinking proposes that we speak for the sake of self-interest (e.g., "debating in the public square," as Aristotle stated).

Note: Discussion: Compare/contrast these five Asiacentric propositions to the Eurocentric/Western viewpoint of communication. How might the Asiacentric and Eurocentric propositions complement each other? What application would they have for you in the workplace?

(*Source*: Adapted from Miike, 2009, pp. 40–5.)

initiate, execute, and control what is needed in order to reach one's goals. The opposite would be *awase*, which looks to fit into the environment.

Negotiations are set up to be long term and ongoing, and never an either/or situation (Yamada, 1997).

Western Orientation

According to Nisbett's research, during the development of Western philosophy (think Socrates, Plato, and Aristotle) the formation of agency was based on the individual versus the group. Greek personal agency was based upon individuality—unique individuals with distinct attributes and goals. Personal agency gave someone a sense that they were in control of their own lives and free to act as they please. Therefore, personal fulfillment and satisfaction to a person in ancient Greek times meant that he was able to pursue his goals without any interference from others (Nisbett, 2003). And often these goals included pursuing knowledge of the world. Greeks used their curiosity about the world by categorizing objects and then crafted rules for a specific and systematic explanation of those objects they were intent on categorizing. Anything could be explained through inquiry and then categorization of underlying principles. For example, the ancient Greeks are known for advancements in physics, astronomy, and formal logic to name a few.

Western Orientation in Philosophy

Debate was a big deal to the ancient Greeks and we owe it to three famous Greek philosophers—Socrates, Plato, and Aristotle. Socrates of Athens is known for his famous saying, "The unexamined life is not worth living." As an intellectual he liked to ask probing and incisive questions as he debated with people in the public square (for which he was eventually forced to drink hemlock, a form of execution of the day). His method is known as the Socratic Method, which is a dialog between teacher and student whereby a series of questions forces students to question their assumptions in order to eliminate contradictions. We also call this "playing devil's advocate" (Ambury, n.d.).

A student of Socrates, Plato (aka Aristocles) was known for his verbal wrestling. Speaking of verbal wrestling, his friends gave him the "nick name" Plato, which in Greek (Πλατων, or *Platon)* meant "broad shouldered" (Behind the Name, n.d.). Plato was sharp (as well as handsome) and wrote his famous thesis, *The Republic,* which described the ideal society as adhering to justice. In *The Republic,* Plato seeks to answer the question, "What *is* justice?"

After Plato came Aristotle (Plato's best student—did you know that Aristotle was the tutor of Alexander the Great?) who believed that happiness was life's goal and is called the father of Western philosophy, having founded logical theory—according to Aristotle it was the highest human endeavor to be able to reason logically. Logic contained proofs (we will discuss this shortly) and persuasion was critical to advancing the logic of an argument. In fact, we

> **Box 7.7**
>
> The word "ethnocentric," which we have been discussing throughout this book, was coined by the Greeks. Ethnocentrism is a belief about one's superiority to that of another. They believed their ways were the best. Of course all people in cultures around the world believe that they are the best—the center of the universe. In fact, the character for China, (*zhong guo*) literally means "middle kingdom." The ancient Chinese—and, perhaps it can be argued, the current Chinese government—still consider China to be at the center of the world.

owe the three elements of persuasion; *ethos*, *logos*, and *pathos* to Aristotle. Debate was important to the Greeks—it is said that this sense of agency "fueled debate" in the public square. People were relatively free to challenge someone in a higher position through the rhetorical strategy of laying out an argument and then proving one was right. Nisbett (2003) explains that being adept with mind and tongue during a debate was just as important as being deft with handling a sword in battle (Box 7.7).

Public debate emphasized argumentation where people would present ideas and opinions and then justify them through a series of proofs—supplying evidence for one's opinions. Western rhetoric is deductive—going from general to specific. There is an overview—or road map—of what will be discussed; then a discussion of related literature and theories; a hypothesis to be proved; analysis of both sides of the argument, with a refutation waiting to sway one toward the hypothesis; and a conclusion that refers back to the original purpose. This direct approach is called deductive reasoning.

Western Orientation in Communication

Deductive reasoning begins with a statement that applies to all members of a group or class and concludes with the notion that "what applies to all must apply to one." It is a form of reasoning that moves from the general to the particular. The principal mechanism for deductive argument is the *syllogism*. A syllogism is basically a series of statements or premises that lead to a valid conclusion:

Major Premise: All men are mortal.
Minor Premise: Socrates is a man.
Conclusion: Socrates is mortal.

What is true of all in the category must certainly be true of individuals within the category. To refute a categorical syllogism, you would either have to prove that not all men are mortal or that Socrates is not a man. The ancient Greeks

> **Box 7.8**
>
> *"ethno"* = race, people, cultural group
>   *"semantic"* = relates to meaning in language

were interested in formulating conclusions and building their knowledge based upon empirical evidence and linear thinking (Box 7.8):

> The Greek language itself encouraged a focus on attributes and on turning attributes into abstractions . . . every adjective can be granted noun status by adding the English equivalent of "ness" as a suffix: "white" becomes "whiteness"; "kind" becomes "kindness." A routine habit of Greek philosophers was to analyze the attributes of an object—person, place, thing or animal—and categorize the object on the basis of its abstracted attributes. They would then attempt to understand the object's nature, and the cause of its actions, on the basis of rules governing the categories. So the attributes of a comet would be noted and the object would then be categorized at various levels of abstraction—*this* comet, *a* comet, a heavenly body, a moving object. Rules at various levels of abstraction would be generated as hypotheses and the behavior of the comet explained in terms of rules that seemed to work at a given level abstraction.
>
> (Nisbett, 2003, p. 9)

Western orientation generally allows for analysis, categorization, and rule development in order to predict something's outcome. Eastern orientation focuses on the dialectic—or the seamless interaction of things. We can even see this in how an influencer analyzes their audience. Aristotle claimed that there were three injunctions for all speaking events: Audience, Purpose, and Occasion. If you knew your audience and could tell them what your purpose was, which was crafted to fit the occasion, then convincing others of your point would follow. This is a Western frame for persuasion, and analyzing an audience within this cultural frame would be important. For example, one study dealing with caffeine consumption showed that European Americans were more likely to be convinced with a cause/effect structure by showing that caffeine was unhealthy and their health would be affected by overconsumption. From an Eastern framework, Asian Americans, however, were more likely to be convinced when shown that their health depended on relational obligations such as the social consequences of becoming a burden. What is interesting is that they would be a burden because they couldn't fill their role as caregiver (Uskul & Oyserman, 2010). Or what about a Western problem-solving approach that is rule-based where one could find titles in every book store on *Three Steps to Lowering Your Taxes*, or *How to Be Healthy By Eating Healthy* (Table 7.4).

Table 7.4 Western and Eastern Persuasion Styles

Greek persuasion	Asian persuasion
+ *Ethos, logos, pathos*	+ Dialogic
+ Formal logic	+ Interdependent (Collective logic)
+ Syllogistic reasoning	+ Harmony (Yin/Yang depicting balance)
+ Cause and effect	+ View on a seamless continuum
+ Break down into discrete components	

World View Revisited as Cognitive Themes

As we have discussed examples of varying world views in the previous chapter, we have talked a lot about culture's norms, behaviors, and values. A given culture's attitudes and values can be demonstrated by how they categorize what is important to them as well. So here is something interesting that can help us understand cognition and reasoning vis-à-vis attitudes expressed by categorizing certain things considered important. What do cows, women, and girls have in common? Depending on your world view, they could have a lot in common or nothing at all!

The Ethno-Semantic Test

Take a look at these words and think about categories. How would *you* group them together?

rock–angel–woman–lion–trees–sand–man–cow–God/god–bush–fish–girl

Once you have grouped them, come up with a category description for each group—for example "animals" or "make-believe" things. This was an actual study performed by a cultural anthropologist, Paul Hiebert (2008), who asked people from different cultures to categorize words and then to explain why they grouped the words the way they did. He wanted to find out how people organized words into a larger system of thought—that is, how might one's cultural perspective (world view) affect how items were categorized? This is called an ethno-semantic test, which seeks to understand the meaning behind the language that people use. Such a study can help us understand the meaning associated with words, how people group and categorize them (domains), and then how these categories relate—so that we might understand the underlying world view of a group of people.

Table 7.5 is an example of the categorization of words from a people group—the Masai—from Kenya. Here is how people in that culture grouped the words and their explanations for them (Table 7.5).

To a young man in the Masai tribe in Kenya, the first column would represent rulers. The second column relates to marriage traditions. When an eligible bachelor wants to marry, he must give the parents cows as a gift for the

Table 7.5 Masai World View in Kenya: Word Domains

Rulers	Marriage traditions	Unknown until taken	Lethal forces
Man	Woman	Rock	God/god
Lion	Girl	Sand	Angel
Whale	Cow	Tree	Demon
		Bush	Ancestor
		Fish	Virus
		Deer	

Note: The words in any given language will reflect the things that are important to its people.

bride. In Masai culture, cows are valued highly because of their milk and because they represent life, therefore this is the most valuable gift he can give in exchange for the gift of a bride. Young men will work long and hard to be able to afford such a prestigious gift—the actual number of cows he is able to give the future father-in-law represents his value as a suitor and his ability to take care of his future bride. If the young man gives too many, the father-in-law will give any extras to his extended family in the following order—his brothers, sons, and then others—a nice form of collectivism. By giving and receiving these practical and precious expressions of life, it creates a social obligation that seals the deal between the families as well as demonstrates a measure of the young man's ability to care for his new wife and future family. The third column represents things that do not belong to anyone until someone takes them (catching a bird or a fish; picking fruit from a tree). The fourth column items are grouped together because they are powerful forces that can kill humans.

If we contrast the Masai groupings to Indian Hindus, the groupings would be different. Hindus arrange words along a hierarchy of life—their belief being that "all of life is one" (Hiebert, 2008). These words, representative of animate and inanimate objects, are considered units of life, and only fragments of present life. Some of these fragments have more purity than others, therefore ranking higher on the scale (gods, angles, and demons rank the highest; followed by other beings, such as humans) all of which have their rankings in castes (categorized into priests, warriors, merchants, workers, and untouchables); and finally the other beings—animals, plants, and rocks have "less" life. All of these "units" are recycled through the belief of continuous rebirth:

God → Angel → Demon → Man → Woman → Girl → Cow → Lion →
Deer → Fish → Tree → Bush → Rock → Sand

The Ethno-Semantic Test shows that the words in any given language reflect the kinds of things its speakers deal with in their lives. Now look at how *your* groupings compared to those of this young man in Kenya. *How* were they different—or similar? What surprised you? What conclusions might you draw from this?

Now you might be asking—What does the anthropology of language have to do with me being a business person who has to figure out how to best manage my virtual team across three different countries, five time zones, and as many languages?!

Everything!

It is a perfect example of what Chip and Dan Heath talk about in their book *Made to stick: Why some ideas survive and others die* (Heath & Heath, 2007). It is a vivid illustration to help you remember that we all frame things differently because of our culture and our language and our world view—woman + girl + cow—who would have thought?! As we have established from the start, we need to move to the backstage view of culture and get an insider's view so that we can explore the "why" and not just the "what." So many of the current books about global management give the reader the essentials of *what* to do because you are a busy business leader; however, this book provides the *why* of what you do—we are building knowledge with the intent that such vivid examples will stick as you practice mindful reflection on what you do in your intercultural encounters.

So, the next time you are tempted to think that the way someone thinks is strange or the way they say something is not exactly the way you would say it in your language, remember that a person's language and culture and world view are intertwined. It will help you frame things differently and pause before you react so that you create a positive script versus one that is negative.

And, you may be wondering why this example on world view of the Masai belongs in a chapter on cognition and reasoning. The point I am trying to make is that culture encapsulates so many things—the lines blur and overlap—culture is complicated and this is why, if we are going to become culturally competent, we need to work on developing knowledge and practicing mindfulness in our culture learning. In summarizing this example, see what Hiebert says about world view and its connection to cognitive themes:

> Worldviews have a cognitive dimension. This dimension includes the deep assumptions about the nature of reality shared by the members of a group. It includes the mental categories and logic people use for thinking and the cognitive themes and counter themes that underlie the culture, It provides a culture with the fundamental mental structures people use to define and explain reality. For example, Christians speak of God, angels, and demons, sin, and salvation. By the latter they mean eternal life with God in heaven. Hindus speak of devas (gods), rakshasas (demons), karma (the cosmic law of good and evil that punishes and rewards gods, humans, and animals and determines their future lives), samsara (the cycle of rebirths), and moksha (salvation). By the latter they mean deliverance from endless life and merger back into the cosmic whole. The Tiv of Nigeria speak of God, ancestors, spirits (good and bad), and life force. They attribute many diseases to witches. Without shared beliefs, communication and community life are impossible.
>
> (Hiebert, 2008, p. 50)

Examples of Cognition and Reasoning Across Cultures

An Indian Perspective

Remember the example of how to interpret if an Indian colleague is agreeing or disagreeing with you? Steve Mazak, one of the founding partners of *Accelerance*, a software development and outsourcing company, provides a perfect example of why global leaders and managers need to understand cultural differences in reasoning and communicating. The key is in listening for how Indian counterparts avoid saying "no" and to try and interpret the subtext of the meaning (Mezak, 2012).

Let us look at some of the underlying reasons for why people might communicate like this. Knowing that you must understand what you could face when interacting with an Indian counterpart, you would do some research to learn about *why* people from this culture might refrain from giving a definitive "no." You would learn that India is a high-context culture that places emphasis on the context surrounding what is conveyed via verbal communication, but especially through nonverbal communication. Additionally, you would learn that all communication is shaped by the nature of personal relationships, and communication patterns will follow a hierarchical order where one's status is important. Why? India is a traditional culture with around 5,000 years of history. Therefore what happened in the past affects what happens in the present because of the respect afforded by such an impressive ancient past.

Ideologic Communication

You would also learn two other important factors regarding India and communication patterns: ideologism versus pragmatism and abstractive versus associative (Kumar & Sethi, 2009). An ideological communicator would assume that everyone has the same point of view, whereas the pragmatic communicator's reason for communicating is to achieve a particular goal. The ideological viewpoint stems from the long history where people have had to fit into the collective whole in order to be accepted by society, although with modernization this is changing. So asking an Indian counterpart if the project will be finished by Thursday is a pragmatic communication strategy—you are seeking a particular goal and you may not get the answer you want (Table 7.6).

Associative Communication

An associative communicator sees a person as a whole—both as a person and a professional—these two aspects go hand in hand. This means that your colleague is not just someone who works with you to achieve your organizational goals, but a person who has feelings that can be hurt, so you need to be sensitive to that person; hence, saving face, avoiding open disagreement, and considering the status of all involved. An abstractive communicator sees a

Table 7.6 Ideologic and Associative Communication

Ideologic Communication

Ideologism – share a vision	**Pragmatism** – achieve a goal
• Communication takes into consideration the group	• Communication's purpose is to consider the task

Associative Communication

Associative – the whole person	**Abstractive** – separate persons
• Cannot separate the person from the profession	• Separates the person from the profession

person in two ways—first, the professional who has to get the work done, and second, as a person. If the professional doesn't do the job right, then that person should be told about the mistake, so there is no separation of people from the problem, as we have learned from Fisher and Ury's famous work *Getting to Yes* (Fisher & Ury, 1991). If you are an abstractive communicator then you will need to be aware of how you delegate tasks and then give feedback to them, as your associative counterparts will be functioning on their norms and not necessarily yours. If you do not distinguish the *who* from the *what*, you might offend.

Better awareness leads to better handling of emotions and, when we can handle our emotions, we can have more realistic expectations of others. Makes sense, right? Then why is it so difficult to accomplish? When you realize that an employee cannot say no because of an ingrained (and tacit) norm, then you can plan for it. Rather than be upset or annoyed, you know that it is part of their style. Through experimentation—I like to call it "cultural improv"—you could avoid questions such as, "You'll get it to me by Friday, right?" and more appropriately frame the question, "Can you tell me where we are in the process at this moment?" Then patiently allow for some elaborateness expressed in several different ways. Large cultural gaps increase our assumptions that people should receive, process, and respond in a similar fashion to us. Awareness, understanding, and skill building helps us to look inward, check our responses, and prevents us from developing an attitude toward others who think and reason differently.

Summary

Why is this chapter's discussion on cognition, reasoning, and language pertinent to today's global leader? These colorful examples will help you remember the next time you want to "write someone off" as not being competent because they do not communicate on your terms.

This chapter has demonstrated that culture and cognition are interconnected, influencing problem-solving approaches and patterns of thought.

As lessons from the field of neuroscience indicate, people from different cultures approach reasoning and perceiving differently. Some are more direct, others indirect; some are more deductive, others inductive; and some are more systemic, others linear. Such patterns of thinking and problem solving vary with individuals, situations, and contexts; these general patterns, however, are linked to cultural conditioning. It is useful to understand that culture can influence logic and reasoning, which, in turn, can affect individual thought and behavior. This awareness may offer some insight into the puzzling circumstances that can arise unexpectedly in the workplace and that may seem inexplicable.

However, just because a co-worker comes from France (identified by a more circuitous approach to problem solving), does not mean that he or she will always be thinking in what appears to be a tangential manner, nor will all Asian speakers be circular in their thought patterns.

References

Adler, N. (2008). *International dimensions of organizational behavior* (5th edn.). Mason, OH: Thomson Higher Education.

Adler, N. J. & Gundersen, A. (2008). *International dimensions of organizational behavior* (5th edn.). Mason, OH: Thomson Learning.

Ambady, N. (2011). The mind in the world: Culture and the brain. *Association for Psychological Science Observer, 24*(5). Retrieved from www.psychologicalscience.org/index.php/publications/observer/2011/may-june-11/the-mind-in-the-world-culture-and-the-brain.html (accessed August 6, 2016).

Ambury, J. M. (n.d.). Socrates. Internet encyclopedia of philosophy. Retrieved from www.iep.utm.edu/socrates/ (accessed August 6, 2016).

Asante, M. K., Miike, Y., & Yin, J. (2013). *The global intercultural communication reader.* New York, NY: Routledge.

Balcetis, E., & Lassiter, G. D. (Eds.). (2010). *Social psychology of visual perception.* East Sussex, UK: Psychology Press.

Behind the Name. (n.d.). Plato. Retrieved from www.behindthename.com/name/plato (accessed August 1, 2016).

Chadha, R. & Husband, P. (2006). *The cult of the luxury brand: Inside Asia's love affair with luxury.* London: Nicholas Brealey International.

Diamond, J. (1999). *Guns, germs, and steel: The fates of human societies.* New York, NY: W. W. Norton & Company.

Engel, J. (n.d.). What did Einstein mean by his famous quote "I want to know God's thoughts, the rest are details?" Retrieved from www.quora.com/What-did-Einstein-mean-by-his-famous-quote-I-want-to-know-Gods-thoughts-the-rest-are-details (accessed August 1, 2016).

Fisher, R., & Ury, W. L. (1991). *Getting to yes: Negotiating agreement without giving in.* New York, NY: Penguin Books.

Griffin, R. W., & Pustay, M. W. (2003). *International business: Managerial perspective: Forecast 2003* (3rd edn.). Upper Saddle River, NJ: Prentice Hall International.

Heath, C., & Heath, D. (2007). *Made to stick: Why some ideas survive and others die.* New York, NY: Random House.

Hiebert, P. G. (2008). *Transforming worldviews: An anthropological understanding of how people change*. Grand Rapids, MI: Baker Academic.

Kamoche, K., & Harvey, M. (2006). Knowledge diffusion in the African context: An institutional theory perspective. *Thunderbird International Business Review*, 48(2), 157–181.

Kumar, R., & Sethi, A. K. (2009). Communicating with Indians. In Samovar, L. A., Porter, R. E., & McDaniel, E. R., (Eds.), *Intercultural communication: A reader* (12th edn., pp. 155–61). Belmont, CA: Wadsworth.

Leiberman, D. (1994). Ethnocognitivism, problem solving, and hemisphericity. In Samovar, L. A., & Porter, R. E. (Eds.), *Intercultural communication: A reader* (p. 179). Belmont, CA: Wadsworth.

Meng, A. (2014, May 10). Why China's wheat-growing north produces individualists and its rice-growing south is clannish. *South China Morning Post*. Retrieved from www.scmp.com/news/china/article/1508726/why-chinas-wheat-growing-north-produces-individualists-and-its-rice (accessed August 6, 2016).

Mezak, S. (2012, April 11). The 7 ways an Indian programmer says "no." *Accelerance*. Retrieved from www.accelerance.com/blog/the-7-ways-an-indian-programmer-says-no (accessed August 6, 2016).

Miike, Y. (2009). Harmony without uniformity: An Asiacentric worldview and its communicative implications. In Samovar, L. A., & Porter, R. E. (Eds.), *Intercultural communication: A reader* (12th edn., p. 37). Belmont, CA: Wadsworth.

Nauert, R. (2015). Culture affects the way we use our brain. *Psych Central*. Retrieved from http://psychcentral.com/news/2008/01/11/culture-affects-the-way-we-use-our-brain/1773.html (accessed August 6, 2016).

Neihardt, J. G. (2008). *Black Elk Speaks: Being the life story of a holy man of the Oglala Sioux*. Albany, NY: SUNY Press.

New York Times. (2008). Feng shui at work. *New York Times* Travel. Retrieved from www.nytimes.com/fodors/top/features/travel/destinations/asia/china/hongkong/fdrs_feat_74_10.html?n=Top%2FFeatures%2FTravel%2FDestinations%2FAsia%2FChina%2FHong+Kong (accessed August 1, 2016).

Nisbett, R. (2003). *The geography of thought: How Asians and Westerners think differently . . . and why*. New York, NY: The Free Press.

Prinz, Jesse. (2016). Culture and cognitive science. *The Stanford Encyclopedia of Philosophy*. Retrieved from http://plato.stanford.edu/cgi-bin/encyclopedia/archinfo.cgi?entry=culture-cogsci (accessed August 6, 2016).

Putz, L. E., Schmitz, J., & Walch, K. (2014). *Maximizing business results with the strategic performance framework: The cultural orientations guide*. Saline, MI: McNaughton & Gunn.

ReligiousTolerance.org. (n.d.a.). Buddhism. Retrieved from www.religioustolerance.org/buddhism7 (accessed August 1, 2016).

ReligiousTolerance.org. (n.d.b.). Taoism (aka Daoism). Retrieved from www.religioustolerance.org/taoism2 (accessed August 1, 2016).

Riegel, J. (2013). *Stanford Encyclopedia of Philosophy*. Retrieved from http://plato.stanford.edu/entries/confucius/ (accessed August 1, 2016).

Samovar, L. A., & Porter, R. E. (1994). *Intercultural communication: A reader*. Belmont, CA: Wadsworth.

Schmitz, J. (2006). *Cultural orientations guide: The roadmap to cultural competence* (5th edn.). Princeton, NJ: Princeton Training Press.

Schmitz, J. (2012). Understanding the cultural orientations approach: An overview of the development and updates to the COA. TMC. Retrieved from www.culturalorientations.com/SiteData/docs/ArticleUnd/616d3a22b5d5d472/Article%20-%

20Understanding%20the%20Cultural%20Orientations%20Approach.12.06.2012.pdf (accessed August 6, 2016).

Talhelm, T., Zhang, X., Oishi, S., Shimin, C., Duan, D., Lan, X., & Kitayama, S. (2014). Large-scale psychological differences within China explained by rice versus wheat agriculture. *Science, 344*(6184), 603–8.

Tate, Karl. (2015, March 5). Einstein's theory of relativity explained (infographic). Retrieved from www.space.com/28738-einstein-theory-of-relativity-explained-infgraphic.html (accessed August 6, 2016).

Truong, A. (2010, December 14). Corporate feng shui: The good and the bad. *The Wall Street Journal.* Retrieved from http://blogs.wsj.com/hong-kong/2010/12/14/corporate-feng-shui-the-good-and-bad/ (accessed August 6, 2016).

Uskul, A. K., & Oyserman, D. (2010). When message-frame fits salient cultural frame, messages feel more persuasive. *Psychology and Health, 25*(3), 321–37.

Vaught, G. M. (1972). The rod-and-frame test in perception. *Journal of Modern Optics, 19*(5), 389–90.

Vercoe, T. (2006). Taking advantage of cognitive difference of Asians and Westerners in the teaching of English. *The Asian EFL Journal Quarterly, 8*(3), 283–93.

Yamada, H. (1997). *Different games, different rules: Why Americans and Japanese misunderstand each other.* Oxford: Oxford University Press.

Case 7

Groupon

Advertising at Super Bowl XLV[1]

Abstract

A Super Bowl commercial advertising Groupon, in February of 2011, was not only a big flop, it was blatantly offensive to Tibetans and those who sympathize with the country's fight for independence from China. This case study helps students identify what went wrong in this intercultural mishap, and why. How can Groupon, the highly successful leader in consumer group purchasing, recover and move on? What can other companies with their own subculture of quirkiness and fun learn from Groupon's mistakes?

Introduction

It was the evening of Saturday, February 6, 2011, and Aaron Cooper had just settled into his recliner at his home in Chicago. He flipped on his television set to FOX just as the pre-game content was beginning—it was the start of Super Bowl XLV, the eagerly anticipated matchup between the Green Bay Packers and the Pittsburgh Steelers. He took a sip of his beer, ate a few chips, and let himself relax for what felt like the first time in months.

Aaron Cooper joined Groupon in June 2010 as the Vice-President of Consumer Marketing (Naymz, n.d.). Prior to Groupon, Aaron worked for both optionsXpress and Orbit Worldwide, but nothing could have prepared him for the high-profile task on which he was about to embark. He had just been notified that Groupon planned to purchase airtime during the Super Bowl for a three-part advertisement, an investment of well over $10 million dollars. The pressure was mounting and Aaron knew that the success or failure of the campaign was his responsibility.

Over the course of the next few months, Aaron worked very closely with Crispin Porter + Bogusky (CP+B), the advertising agency, and Christopher Guest, the director of the commercials (Patel, 2011a). It was finally time for the general public to see the results of their efforts. The football game had just gone to a commercial break when Timothy Hutton appeared on the screen.

The commercial began by talking about the plight of the Tibetan people and how their culture is at risk, raising concern for a serious social issue. It then switched to a lighthearted tone, with Hutton saying, "they still whip up an amazing fish curry" (Sportsmetro, 2011). The commercial concluded by showcasing how Groupon could provide discounts at many of people's favorite restaurants by leveraging the power of group purchasing. Aaron breathed a sigh of relief. The commercial could not have been more of a success. First of all, it poked humor at Groupon in a lighthearted fashion, which should raise awareness for the company. Even more importantly, the commercial contained an altruistic component: any users that visited Groupon's website were given the opportunity to donate—which Groupon would match—to the following three charities: Tibet Fund, Rainforest Action Network (RAN), and Greenpeace (Farnham, 2011).

Walking into work on Monday morning, Aaron was looking forward to hearing the positive reaction from his co-workers and seeing the metrics skyrocket for charitable donations and the number of Groupon users. However, as he walked through the work area to his office, his co-workers seemed to have a muted reaction. He had just reached his desk and pulled out the metrics when the CEO, Andrew Mason, walked into the room. He had a rather stern look on his face as he said: "We've got a problem. . . ."

The Rise of Groupon's Business Model

Andrew Mason, the current CEO, founded Groupon in November 2008 in Chicago, IL (Groupon, n.d.). The company grew out of Mason's earlier start-up venture "ThePoint.com" that allowed individuals to contribute to a campaign or initiative by making pledges that would only be honored if a tipping point in total contributions was reached. Groupon works on a similar principle, allowing partner companies to offer "Group Coupons" through the Groupon website. The coupons, or "Groupons," are discount deals only valid if a certain number of people sign up.

Upon sign up, subscribers' credit card accounts are stored and automatically charged once the tipping point for a deal is reached. The proceeds are then split between Groupon and the merchant (generally on a 50/50 basis) (Investor, 2011). Typically, only one deal is offered daily for each city in which Groupon operates. In return for partnering with Groupon to offer the discount, merchants are guaranteed a minimum volume of sales, as well as publicity on Groupon's website and access to their subscriber base. Partnering merchants come from a wide variety of industries; products as diverse as yoga classes and automobile purchases have been advertised through Groupon (Chicago Automobile Trade Association, 2011).

Competitive Landscape

Online group discounts are a phenomenon that has become increasingly popular from 2008 to 2011, with Groupon emerging as the market leader. Its closest competitor in this sphere is LivingSocial, which offers a similar service but provides a more favorable split of the proceeds for merchants (Patel, 2011b). In addition to LivingSocial, several smaller and locally based services make up the bulk of the competition in the market. Both Groupon and LivingSocial have grown by making a number of acquisitions of smaller competitors during 2011 (Stein, 2012).

The popularity of social networking sites and smartphone applications has been a major driver behind the success of group discounts by allowing for convenient consumer-to-consumer marketing. The demographics of these group discount services reveal that their customers are primarily young women who are well connected on social media and likely to share deals over their social network, ensuring a promotion's success (Schonfeld, 2011). The threat of social networking websites like Facebook and Google starting their own group-discount services remains a serious concern for companies like Groupon.

Recent History

Since its inception, Groupon has rapidly expanded and diversified its customer and geographic demographic. As of December 2010, it had more than 44 million subscribers in 39 countries, generating revenues in excess of $312 million (36 percent of which was generated overseas) (United States Securities and Exchange Commission, n.d.). Revenues were expected to increase significantly in 2011 as Groupon established itself in new markets, particularly in high-growth regions. As of February 2011, Groupon was gearing up to start operations in China in collaboration with a local partner. It was expected to face fierce competition from local firms, with an estimated number of 4,000 local group-buying companies in the Chinese marketplace (Kan, 2011).

Groupon's growth has also necessitated an increase in total staff, growing to over 4,000 employees in over 560 cities, compared with 120 employees in 30 cities in 2010. Large marketing, acquisition, and expansion costs ate into Groupon's revenues in 2010, leaving it with a net loss of $413 million. Some analysts have also raised concerns about the sustainability of its business model, noting that it takes a substantial portion of revenue away from merchants. Despite concerns over its financial performance and the soundness of its business model, Groupon's executive team remains optimistic about the future, reportedly turning down a $6 billion acquisition offer from Google in December 2010. As a result, speculation has been mounting that the company is preparing to launch an Initial Public Offering.

Corporate Culture

Groupon's unique corporate culture has attracted interest from several news and media outlets. Though most online businesses are expected to have their share of quirks, Groupon is notable for retaining the "typical start-up culture" even after its rise to international prominence (Carlson, 2011). Activities such as faux-holidays, employee pranks, or table tennis matches before corporate meetings have been encouraged within the company (Groupon, n.d.).

Much of the culture at Groupon comes from its young staff (average age of 25) and its enigmatic CEO. Andrew Mason (b. 1980) has tried to develop a creative environment by encouraging an audacious sense of humor in the workplace (Bury et al., 2010). He has led the way by personally introducing several unconventional practices and has been described as "eccentric, an inspiring genius, quirky, smart, driven—but with a very weird sense of humor" (Briggs, 2010).

Despite their irreverent culture, several observers also note that Groupon employees want to contribute to society through their efforts. Groupon itself had grown out of a philanthropic venture, and that sense of altruism has survived. A *Wall Street Journal* article describes the corporate culture as follows:

> Irreverence is core to the culture—their offices had a monkey dressed in a Santa suit and a male actor strutting through the office in a tutu for a week—totally mute. There is no dress code or vacation policy. Because "surprise" is also core to the business—a surprise deal of the day—this desire to surprise is core to how people do their work. . . . Mason realizes that a company's purpose may not initially feel altruistic, but companies in business to make money are really equally in business to make a contribution that does good for others.
>
> (Weiss, 2012)

Super Bowl Commercial

The Super Bowl Game might be the single most highlighted sports event in the United States. It is the annual championship game of the National Football League (NFL), and pits the winner of the American Football Conference (AFC) against the winner of the National Football Conference (NFC). In 2011, the Super Bowl matchup was between the Pittsburgh Steelers and the Green Bay Packers, and it attracted more than 111 million viewers on the FOX network (Sweney, 2011).

Given the importance of the game, the commercials during the Super Bowl for any given company are instrumental to their marketing and advertising strategies. Research showed that companies airing three or more TV commercials during the Super Bowl broadcasts experience a permanent 0.45 percent abnormal increase in stock price (Fehle et al., 2005). For that reason, the price of Super Bowl advertising has been increasing dramatically (Smith, 2012). In 1995, the cost of a 30-second commercial reached $1 million for the first time. In 2011, the price was about $3 million. The trend seems to continue (see Appendix 1).

Aaron expected that their $3 million new commercial would pay dividends by generating buzz and driving more customers to the Groupon website.

Culture Backgrounds and Potential Conflicts

Tibet Culture

Eating Habits and Burial Ceremonies

A traditional Tibetan's food includes baked items made from barley flour, yak meat, mutton, and pork. Consumed dairy products include butter, milk, and cheese (Richardson, 2012). Most Tibetans, especially those from East Tibet, do not consume birds or fish. This taboo is closely related to the beliefs of traditional Tibetan Buddhism that worships water and sky as sacred vehicles where supernatural beings reside. All animals related to the water and the sky are considered to have supernatural powers and thus are taboo items to consume.

Two traditional Tibetan burial ceremonies are a sky burial and a water burial. In both cases, people believe humans are created by nature and should return to nature after life ends. In a typical sky burial, the dead body is blessed in a death rite and processed so that it is easily consumed by vultures. The body is then placed in an open space, usually on the top of a hill, awaiting the arrival of the birds.

The water burial is very similar, where the body, after being wrapped, is released into a river. Since the fish in the water typically eat the corpse, they are believed to possess the dead's spirit.

To an outsider, sky and water burial ceremonies might seem barbaric, but they reflect Tibetans' awe of nature and belief in life cycles.

Sensitive Relationships Between Tibet and Beijing

After the 1912 Xin Hai Revolution[2] and before the Chinese central government took over, Tibet was a politically independent region, ruled by the Dalai Lama, the leader of Tibetan Buddhism, the dominant religion in the area.[3] Then, after the Chinese Communist Party (People's Republic of China) took control of China in 1949, Beijing claimed sovereignty over Tibet and tension immediately arose between the theocratic government of Tibet and the central government of China. In 1951, the 14th Dalai Lama sent a delegation to Beijing, where representatives of the two parties signed the "Seventeen-point Agreement." The Agreement gave the Dalai Lama the right to maintain his throne as well as his power but also allowed Beijing to settle troops in Tibet and to establish a local communist government under complete autonomy. However, the Dalai Lama claimed that his delegation signed the Agreement under coercion and that the Agreement worked against the best interests of Tibetans (Powers, 2004).

These tensions between the governments continued to develop. In March of 1959, large crowds of pro-Tibet activists surrounded the Potala Palace to protect the Dalai Lama from being escorted into the hands of the pro-Beijing autonomous government. The unrest caused by those supporters was challenged by the Chinese Army and the Dalai Lama fled to India where he obtained political asylum from the Indian Government. In 1960, a government-in-exile for Tibet was established in Dharamsala, India (Jackson, 2009). Beijing denounced the legality of the exiled government and, to this day, accuses the Dalai Lama of deliberately leading secession activities against China's territorial integrity (Armstrong, 2013).

The recognition of the Dalai Lama by the Western world, however, directly triggered the uneasiness of the Chinese government. In response, Beijing launched a series of nationwide campaigns to defy his reputation, depicting him as a dissident who engaged in activities that jeopardize China's political stability. The tension between the Tibetan locals and the Chinese government exists as of today. The dispute is still a controversial issue within China and among many other countries with whom China has foreign relations (Stokes, 2010).

Beijing's Stronghold on Tibetan Territories and People's Minds

Within China, the government censors all Tibet-related information from either international or domestic sources; only pro-Beijing sources are redirected to the public. As a result of this mass media, most citizens in China view the Dalai Lama and Tibetan activists as negative figures and consider all acts and propaganda by them anti-sovereignty and anti-revolution.

There has been evidence to indicate that many Chinese nationals, under the influence of the communist government and isolated from outside news sources, would easily cultivate strong sentiments of nationalism against activities that support democracy and freedom for Tibet. For example, in April 2008, a Duke University student who was also a Chinese national, received hate mail after expressing empathy for Tibetan independence.

During a pro-Tibet vigil held on campus, Grace Wang, then a freshman, wrote "Free Tibet" on a student's back to reflect her understanding of Tibetan's outcry for democracy. Not expecting she would choose the other side, some Chinese students argued with Ms. Wang angrily. Her action spurred a huge wave of extreme criticisms from Chinese citizens who regarded her as a traitor. Some of the criticisms contained obscenity and even life threats toward Ms. Wang and her parents, who still lived in China. "If you return to China, your dead corpse will be chopped into 10,000 pieces," one person wrote in an e-mail message to Ms. Wang. "Call the human flesh search engines!" another threatened, using an Internet phrase that implies physical, as opposed to virtual, action (Dewan, 2008).

Making Matters Worse

As a response to initial criticism, Groupon disclosed that it would offer to match donations to the three non-government organizations, including the Tibet Fund, up to $100,000 each on their official blog (Andrew, 2011). The Tibet Fund, established by "a small group of U.S. citizens and Tibetan immigrants living in the United States" (The Tibet Fund, n.d.) set as its mission preservation of the distinct "cultural and national identity of the Tibetan people" (The Tibet Fund, n.d.).

Many audiences would feel uncomfortable with the flippancy of the commercial, even without considering any underlying symbolism of fish in Tibetan culture. As one commentator pointed out, it seemed that "these people are losing their culture, but we can get a great deal on their food!" (Andrew, 2011).

But Groupon made matters worse by contriving an entree that generally does not exist in the region—and which would be against the Tibetans' religious beliefs. "An amazing fish curry" was portrayed as something they could "whip up" quickly, as well as eat. The damage to credibility was therefore passed on to the Tibet Fund, beyond Groupon's control.

Internet Contagion

When Groupon's commercial first aired during the Super Bowl in February of 2011, it was viewed by an estimated audience of 111 million individuals (Media and Entertainment, 2011). However, this was by no means the extent of the audience. It was posted to YouTube in a matter of minutes and available for individuals in countries around the world to view.

Within the United States, 85 percent of all adults use the Internet in some capacity (PewInternet, n.d.). Many, especially the younger generation, are involved on social network services such as Twitter and Facebook that keep people digitally connected across time and place. Brand Bowl 2011, a website that tracked tweets related to various corporations during the Super Bowl, identified nearly 18,000 tweets regarding Groupon's advertisements. These tweets, which were overwhelmingly negative in nature (75 percent), quickly tarnished Groupon's brand image and linked people to YouTube so that others could view the controversial commercial.

This negative feedback was not limited to the United States, a country that is quite isolated from the conflict in Tibet. The China Internet Network Information Center (CNNIC, 2012) estimates that over 513 million Chinese use the Internet. And while popular websites such as YouTube, Twitter, and Facebook are censored in China, many alternatives exist (Hutong School, n.d.). As in the United States, Groupon's commercial was quickly posted to Youku (YouTube equivalent) and the word was being spread via Weibo (Twitter equivalent) and RenRen (Facebook equivalent) within minutes.

Groupon and other companies in similar situations have no control once these marketing and outreach strategies are out of their hands. Globalization and the exponential increased use of technology are bringing the consumer to the forefront of information transmission and dissemination.

Conclusion

Outside the window, the snow storm was growing but Aaron was still sweating. The 30-second commercial, led by his most reliable team, created by a first-class agency, and filmed with a renowned director, was designed to be one of the key drivers for revenue growth in this fiscal year.

"Andrew, something went wrong," Aaron paused for a second, "but I think we can make it right."

Discussion Questions

1   Given general knowledge about the cultural orientation of people of American, Indian, and Chinese descent, how do you think Groupon's commercial was received?
2   What are the different ways of thinking and perceiving of the various nation groups involved?
3   What are the historical, philosophical, and political backgrounds of each group that influenced and shaped the way they approach life?
4   Compare and contrast the subgroup culture (Groupon) with the culture in the United States. Do you believe these differences would have been further amplified as they tried to expand to foreign markets (e.g., China)?
5   To what degree did the ethnocentrism of Groupon's leadership team contribute to this mishap?
6   How should Groupon address the critics of this commercial?

Appendix 1

Super Bowl 30-Second Advertisement Cost

See the following URL for an article and graphic on the cost of Super Bowl ads from 1967 to 2012: www.businessinsider.com/chart-the-incredible-inflation-of-super-bowl-ad-prices-since-67-2012-1.

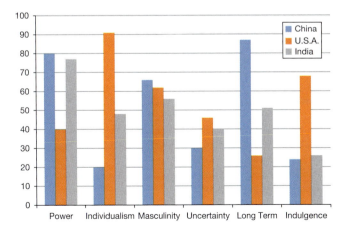

Figure 7C.1 Hofstede's Comparison of China, India, and the United States

(*Source*: https://geert-hofstede.com/china.html.)

Notes

1 Authors: Chen, B., Jiang, S., Koehler, M., Zafar, A., and Tuleja, E. (Ed.).
2 Xin Hai Revolution ended thousands of years of feudalism in China and was an inflection point of Chinese modern history.
3 Dalai Lama is the title for the superior leader of Tibetan Buddhism and practically ruled Tibet prior to Beijing.

References

Andrew. (2011, February 6). GrouponBlog. Groupon Super Bowl ads. Retrieved from https://blog.groupon.com/cities/groupon-super-bowl-ads/ (accessed August 28, 2012).

Armstrong, Paul. (2013, July 10). Fight against Dalai Lama will continue, top Chinese official says. *CNN World*. Retrieved from www.cnn.com/2013/07/10/world/asia/china-tibet-dalai-lama/ (accessed August 8, 2016).

Briggs, Bill. (2010, December 10). U.S. business on NBCNews.Com. Quirky CEO "genius" behind Groupon's success. Retrieved from www.msnbc.msn.com/id/40494597/ns/business-us_business/ (accessed August 28, 2012).

Bury, Chris, Kimberly Kaplan, & Eric Johnson. (2010, September 20). Groupon.com: Internet fairy tale or the next fabulous flameout? *ABCNews*. Retrieved from http://abcnews.go.com/Business/groupon-grows-leaps-bounds/story?id=11681785 (accessed August 28, 2012).

Carlson, Nicholas. (2011, October 31). Inside Groupon: The truth about the world's most controversial company. *Business Insider*. Retrieved from www.businessinsider.com/inside-groupon-the-truth-about-the-worlds-most-controversial-company-2011-10 (accessed August 28, 2012).

Chicago Automobile Trade Association. (2011, August 19). Dealer's use of Groupon offers for vehicle sales a no-no: BBB. Retrieved from www.cata.info/dealers_use_of_groupon_offers_for_vehicle_sales_a_no-no_bbb/ (accessed August 28, 2012).

CNNIC. (2012). [In Chinese]. Retrieved from www.cnnic.net.cn/hlwfzyj/hlwxzbg/201201/P020120709345264469680.pdf (accessed August 28, 2012).

Dewan, Shaila. (2008, April 17). Chinese student in U.S. is caught in confrontation. *The New York Times*. Retrieved from www.nytimes.com/2008/04/17/us/17student.html?_r=2&oref=slogin& (accessed August 28, 2012).

Farnham, Alan. (2011, February 7). Groupon's controversial TV commercial. *ABCNews*. Retrieved from http://abcnews.go.com/Business/groupon-super-bowl-commercial-ignites-controversy/story?id=12856998#.UGL57Pk-v5h (accessed August 28, 2012).

Fehle, F., Tsyplakov, S., & Zdorovtsov, V. (2005, November). Super Bowl commercials and stock returns. Can companies influence investor behaviour through advertising? *European Financial Management*, *11*(5), 625–47.

Groupon. (n.d.). The world of Groupon. Retrieved from www.groupon.com/pages/world-of-groupon (accessed August 28, 2012).

Hutong School. (n.d.). Social networking sites in China. Retrieved from www.hutong-school.com/social-networking-sites-china (accessed August 28, 2012).

Investor. (2011, November 29). Briefing. Ahead of the curve archive: How Groupon works. Retrieved from www.briefing.com/investor/our-view/ahead-of-the-curve/how-groupon-works.htm (accessed August 28, 2012).

Jackson, Peter. (2009, February 27). Witness: Reporting on the Dalai Lama's escape to India. *Reuters*. Retrieved from www.reuters.com/article/2009/02/27/us-witness-jackson-dalailama-idUSTRE51Q4OB20090227 (accessed August 28, 2012).

Kan, Michael. (2011, August 25), Groupon's struggle in China no surprise, say analysts. IDG News Service as cited in *PC World*. Retrieved from www.pcworld.com/article/238774/groupons_struggle_in_china_no_surprise_say_analysts.html (accessed August 28, 2012).

Media and Entertainment. (2011, December 21). Nielsen's tops of 2011 television. *Nielsen*. Retrieved from http://blog.nielsen.com/nielsenwire/media_entertainment/nielsens-tops-of-2011-television/ (accessed August 28, 2012).

Naymz. (n.d.). Aaron Cooper profile. Retrieved from www.naymz.com/aaroncooper 1161324 (accessed August 28, 2012).

Patel, Kunur. (2011a, February 21). Can consumers forgive Groupon's ad gaffe? *Crain's Chicago Business*. Retrieved from www.chicagobusiness.com/article/20110219/IS-SUE01/302199994/can-consumers-forgive-groupons-ad-gaffe (accessed August 28, 2012).

Patel, Romil. (2011b, April 21). Why Groupon sucks for merchants and LivingSocial doesn't. *Venture level: Text*. Retrieved from http://venturelevel.com/post/479828 5366/why-groupon-sucks-for-merchants-and-livingsocial (accessed August 28, 2012).

PewInternet: Pew Internet and American Life Project. (n.d.). Internet adoption, 1995–2012. Retrieved from http://pewinternet.com/Trend-Data-(Adults)/Internet-Adoption.aspx (accessed August 28, 2012).

Powers, John. (2004). *History as propaganda: Tibetan exiles versus the People's Republic of China*. Oxford: Oxford University Press.

Richardson, H. E. (2012). Tibet. In *Encyclopædia Britannica*. Retrieved from www.britannica.com/EBchecked/topic/594898/Tibet (accessed August 7, 2016).

Schonfeld, Eric. (2011, March 22). Groupon buying industry in U.S. estimated to grow 138 percent to $2.7 billion this year. *TechCrunch*. Retrieved from http://techcrunch.com/2011/03/22/group-buying-138-percent-2-7-billion/ (accessed August 28, 2012).

Smith, Chris. (2012, February 1). Super Bowl ad rates can double within ten years. *Forbes*. Retrieved from www.forbes.com/sites/chrissmith/2012/02/01/super-bowl-ad-rates-can-double-within-ten-years/ (accessed August 28, 2012).

Sportsmetro. (2011, February 6). Groupon Super Bowl ad: Save money—Tibet. *YouTube*. Retrieved from www.youtube.com/watch?v=vVkFT2yjk0A (accessed August 28, 2012).

Stein, Jake. (2012, June 1). Groupon vs. LivingSocial customer acquisition debate. *The eTail blog*. Retrieved from www.theetailblog.com/featured/groupon-vs-livingsocial-customer-acquisition-debate/ (accessed August 28, 2012).

Stokes, Dustin. (2010, March 10) Conflict over Tibet: Core causes and possible solutions. The Beyond Intractability Project, The Conflict Information Consortium, University of Colorado, Boulder. Retrieved from www.beyondintractability.org/casestudy/stokes-tibet (accessed August 28, 2012).

Sweney, Mark. (2011, February 8). Super Bowl 2011 draws highest ever audience for US TV show. *Guardian*. Retrieved from www.guardian.co.uk/media/2011/feb/08/super-bowl-highest-ever-audience (accessed August 28, 2012).

The Tibet Fund. (n.d.). Retrieved from www.tibetfund.org/aboutus.html (accessed August 28, 2012).

United States Securities and Exchange Commission (n.d.). Groupon financial filing 10-k for the fiscal year ended December 31, 2011. Retrieved from http://investor.

groupon.com/secfiling.cfm?filingid=1445305-12-922&cik=#GROUPON10-K_
HTM_S023DAAE6D5FBE58386D660B662D68EBA (accessed August 7, 2016).

Weiss, Bari. (2012, December 20). Groupon's $6 billion gambler. *The Wall Street
Journal*. Retrieved from http://online.wsj.com/article/SB10001424052748704828
104576021481410635432.html (accessed August 28, 2012).

8   Culture and Leadership

Being global is not just about where you do business.
(Robert House, The Wharton School, Principle Investigator of
the GLOBE Study)

Figure 8.1 Handshake
(*Source*: Fotolia 39364115, © FotolEdhar.)

Chapter Overview

Chapter 8, Culture and Leadership, examines the questions based upon the work of the last 15 years regarding the GLOBE Study and defines global leadership based upon new findings in cultural dimensions, leadership scales, and organization of cultures according to society clusters. Are there global norms for leadership? How does leadership differ from one cultural group to another? Are there best practices for certain leadership attributes? These are the key questions we will address in Chapter 8 (Figure 8.1).

Learning Objective

Chapter 8: Culture and Leadership ties everything in the book together by discussing four myths to being a culturally competent leader and then refuting them by examining the latest research on global leadership. A cross-cultural team of social scientists from around the world studied leadership attributes and reinforced that leader effectiveness is contextual. They determined a leader's efficacy is drawn from the norms of a society, its organizations, as well as the values and beliefs of its people. We discuss the definition of leadership that comes from the attributes researched: a leader is "exceptionally skilled at motivating, influencing, or enabling you, others, or groups to contribute to the success of the organization or task."

Key Takeaways

— There are certain universal global leadership norms; however, *how* these norms are carried out depends on the context and situation across cultures. People in different societies have different criteria when assessing leadership success.
— Strong scientific research conducted over a decade across many cultures has created the most comprehensive analysis of global research to date.

Leadership Applications

— Managers and leaders need to compare their own cultures with those of others in order to understand what is different *and* what is similar. This can lead to more successful interactions.
— It is not enough to be aware, open-minded, and respectful of the management practices of other cultures. The successful global leader understands both culture-general and culture-specific norms and is able to use this knowledge to effectively navigate what they do not know.

Introduction

Why in a book called *Intercultural Communication for Global Business* is leadership addressed in the last chapter? Well, every chapter *is* about leadership, because communication is the key to leadership. We cannot be leaders if we cannot communicate. We *can* be culturally competent leaders when we understand the interconnection between culture and communication. This is what we have been discussing throughout the previous chapters. Communication is grounded in cultural and social norms, beliefs, values, attitudes, and behaviors.

In the following scenario, think about what you would do as a global leader if faced with the challenge of managing a global team for a major international product launch. What might be some of the logistical, business, and relational needs for communicating with a wide range of constituents both internally and externally? What would you do? After a discussion on the latest research in global leadership, we will revisit this scenario and walk through how a culturally competent global leader would handle this challenge.

Case: What Would You Do?

You have been assigned to lead a virtual team to launch a new product line overseas. Your product has a cutting-edge manufacturing process and technological design elements that will overtake your competitors in leaps and bounds. Naturally, your company leaders are pushing to move the project forward and meet tight deadlines.

On your team are regional sales and marketing managers in the United Kingdom, Chile, and South Korea. You also have two new channel sales partners in Dubai and Australia. Other team members will include a customer service manager in India, an IT director in Taiwan, and a managing director of manufacturing in China who also oversees Hong Kong.

You are proud of being selected for this challenge—certainly one that could prove to be a career builder. So you begin to list all of the key considerations that it will take in order to establish a cohesive and committed team that will work together to produce a successful launch of the product. There are three considerations that you would need to immediately focus on: logistic, business, and relationship. The wise leader would realize that all of these considerations overlap and could possibly differ for each of the nine cultures (mentioned above) with which you will work.[1]

If you have ever been in a situation similar to this, you know that it is a challenge to work with a cross-functional team, but a cross-cultural team comprising people from different cultures can be the ultimate challenge. Why? Because cultural differences play a significant role in how we think, act, and communicate. If you are going to be successful working with people on a global level, there are four culture myths that you need to debunk.

There are four myths to being a global leader. This discussion will be an effective way to wrap up the book while at the same time introducing some important research and concepts regarding leadership across cultures.

Culture Myth #1

Customs May Differ, But We Are All Basically the Same Deep Down Inside

It is human nature to think that all people are just like us. We'd rather assume that we are more similar than different—after all, we are all human—right? When we believe in this myth, we expect that others will think the same way, perceive the same way, and behave the same way we do. While the motivating goal probably is to be accepting of all people, in actuality by reducing everyone to "the same," we are trying to maintain stability in our own lives. So we try to figure out others based upon who we are. This takes on an ethnocentric perspective where we evaluate other people and their cultures based on our particular cultural standards.

In order to interact successfully with people who hold different world views and different perceptions as to what is legitimate (e.g., what is right or wrong in one's eyes) we need to unblock this tendency to ignore difference. Only then can we begin the process of understanding intercultural differences.

Culture influences the norms of every group. These norms, or unstated rules, are the accepted and expected ways of behaving and interacting with other people. Culture is something that we learn early on as we are conditioned to act, react, and learn about how people in our world do things from watching them, conversing with them, and interacting with them. Culture includes a group's communication patterns; how a group solves problems; and how a group perceives and passes on its shared values, beliefs, attitudes, and behaviors, including its perception of self, group, environment, authority, and power. All of us learn different ways of "being" from our cultural group and that influences how we interact with others, so we *have* to become comfortable with difference so that we can learn to interact more successfully with others.

For example, in the United States, we generally tend to be direct with our communication—being direct is a manner of saying what you see and what you mean, directly, without disguising the message. When handling conflict there is a preference for explicit communication where you are straightforward in identifying the problem, diagnosing and then managing it. Part of this can be a personality trait, but part of it can also be a cultural preference. If your colleague is from Japan, their manner of dealing with conflict might be entirely different—perhaps they will use indirect communication that is more implicit in order to mitigate the negative impact of being so straightforward. A common strategy for handling conflict would be avoidance, which is grounded by deeply held historical and societal dynamics. To expect that your colleagues would handle conflict in the same way that you do would be counterproductive—and ethnocentric. We need to remember that customs differ and so do people.

Culture Myth #2

My Technical Expertise Will Help Me Succeed—After All, That Is Why They Have Selected Me

At first glance, the notion of a global leader is someone who has the knowledge to comprehend the many details of international accounting and financial practices; to have the skills to deal with the multifaceted operations of global supply-chain management; or to be able to handle the complex process of a merger and acquisition. While it is critical to possess the functional business skills necessary to do business in the global business environment, functional skills are not enough.

A global leader today must be able to readily adapt to change in an ambiguous environment and deal with the complexity that comes with interpersonal relationships. Global leadership means that a person possesses intercultural competence, that we have defined as CQ. CQ is the ability to recognize and understand the beliefs, values, attitudes, and behaviors of others while simultaneously adapting your behavior according to that knowledge.

Another common misconception is that successful leadership skills practiced in one's own culture are naturally transferable when applied in another cultural setting. We learn of many cross-border deals and negotiations that fall flat simply because not enough due diligence has been performed or key players are unable to adapt readily to the challenges found in cross-cultural relations—even though such high performers may have done well with their previous assignment. Current management research has shown that there are many differences involved in the transfer of such leadership capabilities because what may be meaningful and appropriate in one context could be insulting and improper in another based upon the cultural norms for living.

Let us say you are experienced working in Brazil and you are comfortable with the expressiveness of the Brazilian culture regarding personal space and physical touch, understanding that the *abrazo*, or embrace upon greeting someone, is important in developing personal trust. You now have the opportunity to do business in Dubai and you are aware that—between men— there is also some form of physical interaction when greeting. It is not enough to transfer the meaning of what happens in one culture directly to another. While this is a rather simplistic, low-risk example, the point is rather profound. Simply being aware of the importance of physical space and touch in the process of developing relationships is not enough. One must do their due diligence to understand the reasons for why the norms of a culture are what they are. It is important to have confidence in one's functional expertise but to also possess both the awareness and the knowledge of what is needed to succeed in different cultural situations.

Culture Myth #3

I Lived Abroad for a Semester in College, It Will Be Easy To Adapt

While having prior experience living, working, or even traveling abroad can open our eyes to the many differences of people and their ways of living, it is not enough to think that one experience—or even a series of experiences— is a predictor of future success. There are just too many variables concerning situation and context. Intercultural problems arise from differences in behavior, thinking, assumptions, and values between people with whom they associate. These cultural differences often produce misunderstandings and lead to ineffectiveness in face-to-face communication. A deeper understanding of the nature of cultural differences would increase the effectiveness of anybody in intercultural situations.

For example, let us say you are an accountant and have risen through the ranks within your organization. Because of your expertise, you are selected to go to Chile to work on a partnership with another company. You figured that you would easily adjust to Chilean culture because you enjoy the Latin culture overall—you had studied Spanish in high school, spent a semester in Seville, Spain, during college, and now enjoy vacationing in Mexico with your family. However, once you get to Chile, have to set up your household, get your family settled, and have to learn to adapt *daily* to another way of thinking and behaving as you manage a team of junior accountants, you realize that what you signed up for was not what you expected. Your expectations for efficiency, consistency, and accuracy are not the same as your employees or colleagues. It becomes harder and harder to accomplish the goals of the joint venture because of the day-to-day struggles to communicate and fit in with your counterparts.

In order to reach our goal of understanding others, we must first become more conscious and knowledgeable about how our *own* culture has conditioned our ways of thinking and planted within us the values and assumptions that govern behavior. Becoming a cultural detective by taking time to reflect on what are your own personal values, beliefs, and attitudes and where/from whom you developed these, will help you to understand your own behaviors and reactions to certain events and situations. Values are the things that are important to you and are reflected in how you live your life; a belief is something that you consider to be right or wrong; and an attitude is a state of mind—what you think about something. When you reflect on these core aspects of who you are and try to connect with why you do things the way you do, you begin to see identifiable patterns which you can then compare with those of others. Consider the following questions:

- What are my core values, beliefs, and attitudes? How are these reflected in my behavior?
- How has my culture (family or nation) influenced who I am?
- How do these values, beliefs, and attitudes affect the way I interact with people? The way I do business?
- What assumptions do I make about others on a daily basis? What drives these assumptions?
- How flexible and adaptive am I in ambiguous situations?

Why is this important? Constant reflection on your thoughts, beliefs, values, and even feelings as you act and interact in unfamiliar environments will help to move you toward greater intercultural competence.

Culture Myth #4

I Am the Boss, So Others Will Have To Adapt To Me

Did you know that the phrase "When in Rome, do as the Romans do" comes from a dialog between St. Ambrose of Milan and his follower St. Augustine back in 387 CE? St. Augustine had a question about differing liturgical practices in Rome and Italy. The Church in Rome fasted on Saturdays but the Church in Milan did not. Ambrose gave his advice to Augustine to follow the customs of the Church wherever he went. Thus, "When you are in Rome ... " (Martin, n.d.). Today's world has become complex and this age-old adage has been challenged: Whose Rome is it anyway? If we are the one leading the project, do we expect that everyone will comply with our standards? If the shoe is on the other foot, does that mean that we have to conform 100 percent with our counterpart's ways? The bottom line, when a guest, it is both polite and to your advantage to follow your host's customs (Box 8.1).

Martin J. Gannon, popular author and interculturalist, has said, "these days, a non-Roman in Rome meets non-Romans as well as Romans and encounters Romans outside of Rome" (2001, p. 157). He is basically saying that the world and its people are so complex that we have to be ready for culturally responsive strategies. We cannot simply define a country as "one size fits all." When we talk about cultures, we often think in terms of a national culture—e.g., "the Italians do this" and "the British do that." As we try to make sense out of the differences between these national cultures, we are often drawn to generalizations in order to categorize unfamiliar information. We have talked about how cognitive psychologists tell us that this is a way of making mental maps. Using generalizations can be a good way for global managers to make sense of the complexities of confusing cultural practices, but they must be informed generalizations that are based upon combining cultural knowledge with openness to individual differences.

Box 8.1 When in Rome ...

Cum Romanum venio, ieiuno Sabbato; cum hic sum, non ieiuno: sic etiam tu, ad quam forte ecclesiam veneris, eius morem serva, si cuiquam non vis esse scandalum nec quemquam tibi.

When I go to Rome, I fast on Saturday, but here [Milan] I do not. Do you also follow the custom of whatever church you attend, if you do not want to give or receive scandal?

Letter 54 to Januarius

Source: Martin, n.d.

Here is why: In every culture there are dominant cultural patterns that can generally describe the standard values, practices, and behaviors of any given group of people; but there are also many sub- and co-cultures within that dominant culture. These could be ethnic, religious, political, economic, and social class influences, among others. It is hard to know all of the many differences in people and their groups, so generalizations can be used as a hypothesis to be tested and observed. That way, we will not expect all Romans to be the same. We neither want to fully adapt to our preconceived idea of who the other person is within our assumptions about the culture, nor do we want to expect that, since we are the boss, others will fall at our feet and do everything the way we want them to—in today's global marketplace we need to adapt and work together.

We have been addressing these four myths throughout this book as we seek to understand the underlying values, beliefs, attitudes, and behaviors of people who are different than we are. We will come back to these four myths at the end of the chapter but, for now, let us focus on important research findings about leadership attributes across cultures. This chapter is a culmination of all that has been discussed so far but helps us to hone in on the *specific* aspects of how people from different societies around the world view leadership.

The GLOBE Study of 62 Societies

This final chapter focuses on another important database of significant findings in the GLOBE Study of 62 Societies. GLOBE stands for "global leadership organizational behavior effectiveness" and a cross-cultural team of social scientists from around the world collaborated to study leadership attributes. Though this study found definite leadership patterns across cultures, the main finding was that leader effectiveness is contextual, that is, a leader's efficacy is drawn from the norms of a society and its organizations, as well as the values and beliefs of its people.

While this basic finding might seem unremarkable—that leadership is contingent upon situational contexts which are embedded in any given culture—it is actually quite remarkable in that it extended the original work of Kluckhohn, Hofstede, Schwartz, and others (House et al., 2004), and once again came up with a massive amount of quantitative data that they analyzed using the highest standards of statistical analysis. The leader of the study, the late Robert House, professor of management at the Wharton School, mobilized 170 social scientists from 62 countries around the world to survey thousands of middle managers about leadership attributes. He described the definition of a leader as: "exceptionally skilled at motivating, influencing, or enabling you, others, or groups to contribute to the success of the organization or task" (House et al., 2004, p. 15). There were three distinct classifications that emerged from both the quantitative and qualitative methods: (a) distinct leadership scales; (b) distinct cultural dimensions; and (c) distinct groupings of the societies being studied.

GLOBE Study Leadership Styles

The research team analyzed the responses of 17,300 employees from 951 organizations to determine the characteristics of a global leader. From this data they came up with 112 leader characteristics and, with further analysis, generated 21 leadership scales by taking the mean of the societies and recording the "most/least desirable" attributes, such as integrity, autonomy, or humaneness. Through statistical and conceptual analysis they further refined these scales in order to reach a manageable six universal leader styles (see Table 8.1). This study follows the theory of Implicit Leadership, which says that "individuals hold a set of beliefs about the kinds of attributes, personality characteristics, skills, and behaviors that contribute to or impede outstanding leadership" (Javidan et al., 2006, p. 72). In other words, how does someone accept and respond to their leader?

The GLOBE Study measured cultural practices and values regarding leadership attributes—with cultural practices being the way things are and values as the way people would like things to be. This makes it possible to capture the similarities and differences in the norms, values, beliefs, and practices among societies (House et al., 2004).

This is helpful to understand that leadership attributes are desirable in some cultures and not in others—therefore they are contingent upon the cultural and social norms of a group of people. Knowing the general tendencies when doing

Table 8.1 Six Leadership Styles: GLOBE Study Findings

Charismatic/ Valued-based	Stresses high standards, decisiveness, and innovation; seeks to inspire and motivate people around a vision; creates a passion for performance centered on core values.
Team-oriented style	Instills pride, loyalty, and collaboration among organizational members; and highly values team cohesiveness and a common purpose or goals. Leader is administratively competent in order to motivate and garner trust.
Participative style	Encourages input from others in decision-making and implementation; and emphasizes delegation and equality; is opposite of being autocratic.
Humane style	Stresses compassion and generosity; it is patient, supportive, and concerned with the well-being of others. The nature of communication aims to avoid conflict; the process of communication focuses on supporting others and therefore maintaining cohesion.
Autonomous style	Is characterized by an independent, individualistic, and self-centric approach to leadership (reported as a hindrance to outstanding leadership and only mildly helpful in others).
Self-protective style	Focuses on the safety and security of the leader as well as the group; self-centered and face-saving in its approach (reported as a hindrance to outstanding leadership).

(*Source*: Adapted from GLOBE Study, House et al., 2004, p. 14.)

business will help you predict and react appropriately for the behavior that you might encounter. For example, the attribute of being ambitious was highly rated by some cultures (6.73 out of 7) and poorly rated by others (2.85 out of 7). Not only did the study collect thousands of surveys, but the international team of researchers throughout the 62 countries held focus groups (House et al., 2004). For example, in the Netherlands and Switzerland the notion of being a leader was negative, because societal norms indicate that people are suspicious and fearful of people in authority since they are expected to abuse their power. Therefore, those who rise to a leadership position face all sorts of restrictions to limit what they can and cannot do. Accordingly leaders are not supposed to expect or be given special treatment or privileges.

The GLOBE Study found that certain leadership traits such as being trustworthy, fair, honest, decisive, and compassionate, are global; however, *how* these traits are conveyed can differ based upon cultural norms. For example, in Anglo cultures, such as the United States, a leader is decisive if they can make a quick decision. Being quick is more important than being 100 percent accurate as long as you take action. Leaders from Germany or France probably will take a different approach since the tendency is to be deliberate and precise when making decisions.

GLOBE Study Cultural Dimensions

Additionally, the GLOBE Study found nine cultural dimensions that were consistent across cultures, many of them similar to Hofstede's original research (see Table 8.2). The important thing to remember is that this is the most comprehensive, large-scale *leadership* study of its kind that was performed by an international team that sought out—as its main construct (concept to be studied)—the study of leadership styles across cultures. Take a few moments to study Table 8.2 and see what feels typical to your attitudes and assumptions about the way things *should* be and perhaps actually *are* from your society's perspective in the workplace. What have you experienced? Have you ever thought about this before? At the end of the chapter you will be asked to reflect on how you might deal with global counterparts who have been conditioned to accept different assumptions and perspectives, which will make this study come into sharper focus.

GLOBE Study Society Clusters

The study was able to use the data of 61 of 62 countries (due to pervasive response bias from the Czech Republic) (Jesuino, 2002) and created "society clusters." This means that societies with the most similarities "clustered" together. The farther apart the societies were, the more differences they possessed (House et al., 2004) (see Table 8.3). Within each of these paired clusters, the desired behaviors are listed in the relative importance as reported by these societies. For example, in Eastern European countries, the leaders are

Table 8.2 Nine Cultural Dimensions: GLOBE Study Findings

Power distance	*The degree to which members of a collective expect power to be distributed equally. Therefore, societies tend to ...*

Higher
— *Many social classes with certain differences*
— *Power provides social order and role stability*
— *Upward social mobility is limited*
— *Information is controlled*
— *Civil liberties are weak*
— *Democracy doesn't mean equal opportunity*

Lower
— *Large middle class*
— *Power represents corruption and coercion*
— *Upward social mobility is high*
— *Information is shared*
— *Civil liberties are strong*
— *Democracy promotes opportunities for all*

Uncertainty avoidance	*The extent to which a society, organization, or group relies on social norms, rules, and procedures to alleviate unpredictability of future events. Therefore, these societies tend to ...*

Higher
— *Rely on formalized policies/procedures*
— *Rely on legal contracts and agreements*
— *Keep precise records*
— *Take moderate calculated risks*
— *Tight control when developing new idea*
— *Resistant to change*
— *Need to establish rules to predict*

Lower
— *Rely on informal interactions vs. procedures*
— *Rely on the word of our trusted colleague*
— *Less concern keeping precise records*
— *Take risks with less calculating*
— *Lighten up on the controls to push through*
— *Less resistance to change*
— *Fewer rules to dictate every behavior*

Humane orientation	*The degree to which a collective encourages and rewards individuals for being fair, altruistic, generous, caring, and kind to others. Therefore, these societies tend to ...*

Higher
— *Other-interest is critical (family, friends, community, work, even strangers)*
— *Benevolence, kindness, and generosity are valued*
— *People are motivated by need for belonging and affiliation*
— *Family and personal relationships provide protection for the individual*
— *Paternalistic norms are expected (e.g., the boss as a benefactor who expects loyalty)*

Lower
— *Self-interest comes before others*
— *Pleasure, comfort, self-enjoyment are valued*
— *Material possessions and power motivate people*
— *The State provides social and economic support*
— *Welfare institutions replace paternalism*

(Continued)

Table 8.2 (continued)

Collectivism I: *institutional*	*The degree to which organizational and societal institutional practices encourage and reward collective distribution of resources and collective action. Therefore, these societies tend to …*

Higher

— *Members know they are interdependent on their organization and must make personal sacrifices to meet obligations of the group*

— *Employees develop long-term relationships because of obligation to the organization*

— *Organizations are responsible for employee welfare (and by extension, their families)*

— *Decisions are made by group consensus*

— *Compensation and promotion come from what is good for the group and based on seniority*

— *Motivation is socially influenced and employees must fulfill obligations to the group*

— *Employees are accountable for the success or failure within their groups*

— *Dealing with conflict requires avoiding, compromising, and accommodating tactics*

Lower

— *Members know that they are independent of the organization and are expected to bring their unique skills and abilities to the organization*

— *Employees develop short-term relationships and are not obligated to the organization*

— *Organizations are interested in the work that employees perform (not their personal or family welfare)*

— *Decisions are made by individuals in power*

— *Compensation and promotion are achieved based on equity that rewards the work of an individual regardless of rank*

— *Motivation is intrinsically based to serve one's interests and needs*

— *Accountability for success or failure of an organization is within the individual*

— *Dealing with conflict requires direct and solution-based tactics*

Collectivism II: *in-group*	*The degree to which individuals express pride, loyalty, and cohesiveness in their organizations or families. Therefore, these societies tend to …*

Higher

— *Individuals are first and foremost part of a cohesive group*

— *Individuals make clear distinctions between in-groups and out-groups*

— *One's self is dependent on the group*

— *Group goals trump individual goals*

— *Duties and obligations to the group are of utmost importance*

— *Societies often have a slower pace of life*

— *People emphasize oneness and relationships*

— *Extended family structures are vital to life*

— *Love has less emphasis in marriage*

Lower

— *Individuals look out for themselves and immediate families*

— *Individuals don't think much about in-groups and out-groups*

— *One's self is autonomous*

— *Individual goals trump group goals*

— *Personal needs take precedent over group*

— *Societies are often more fast paced*

— *People emphasize rational and objective thought*

— *Nuclear family structures are important*

— *Love has more emphasis in marriage*

(Continued)

Table 8.2 (continued)

Assertiveness	*The degree to which individuals are assertive, confrontational, and aggressive in their relationships with others. Therefore, these societies tend to ...*

Higher
— *Assertiveness, domination, and tough behavior are expected*
— *Values competition—praises the strong*
— *Success is progress*
— *Reveals thoughts and is expressive with emotions*
— *Control one's environment*
— *Communicates directly and explicitly*
— *Pay for performance motivates*
— *Results are more important than relationships*

Lower
— *Assertiveness, domination, and tough behavior are socially unacceptable—favors modesty and tenderness*
— *Values cooperation—cares for the weak*
— *Relationship building with people is progress*
— *Is cautious and reserved with personal emotions and thoughts*
— *Live in harmony with one's environment*
— *Communicates indirectly, appreciates subtlety, and concerned with saving face*
— *Pay for performance hinders harmony*
— *Relationships are more important than results because of loyalty, integrity, and cooperation*

Gender egalitarianism	*The degree to which a collective minimizes gender inequality. Therefore, these societies tend to ...*

Higher
— *Women are in positions of authority and power*
— *Women have higher status in society*
— *Women have role in community decision-making*
— *Women participate in labor force*
— *Have less occupational gender segregation*
— *Have similar educational opportunities for women/literacy rates higher*

Lower
— *Few women are in positions of authority and power*
— *Women have lower status in society*
— *Women have little or no role in community decision-making*
— *Fewer women participate in labor force*
— *Have more occupational gender segregation*
— *Have fewer educational opportunities for women/literacy rates lower*

Future orientation	*The extent to which individuals engage in future-oriented behaviors such as delaying gratification, planning, and investing in the future. Therefore, these societies tend to ...*

Higher
— *Economic success can be achieved*
— *Save for the future*
— *People are more intrinsically motivated*

Lower
— *Lower levels of economic success are achieved*
— *Spend now rather than save for the future*

(Continued)

Table 8.2 (continued)

— Organizations have strong strategic focus	— People are less intrinsically motivated
— Organizations and leaders are more flexible and adaptive	— Organizations have shorter strategic focus
— Combine both material success and spiritual fulfillment	— Organizations and leaders are less flexible and adaptive
— Leadership is visionary (sees stability in the midst of chaos)	— Material success and spiritual fulfillment are dualities and result in trade-offs
	— Leadership is repetitive (follows routines in order to maintain stability)

Performance orientation	The degree to which a collective encourages and rewards group members for performance improvement and excellence. Therefore, these societies tend to …

Higher	Lower
— Values training, development	— Values family relationships and societal connections
— Emphasizes results versus the person	— Emphasizes loyalty and belongingness more than results
— Rewards performance	— Quality of life is more important than performance
— Values assertiveness, competitiveness	— Values seniority and experience
— Expects work completed on time	— Respects harmony with environment
— The best employee is one who has a "can-do" attitude and is in control	— The best employee works for the good of the group
— Expects, values, and rewards individual achievement	— Expects, values, and rewards group effort with assertiveness being socially unacceptable
— Performance appraisals are used to achieve results	— Performance appraisals should emphasize one's integrity, loyalty and cooperation—feedback is seen as judgmental
— Taking initiative shows "drive"	— Taking initiative is risky and self-promoting
— Values directness, clarity, and sense of urgency	— Values indirectness, subtlety in communication, and takes time to get things done

(*Source*: Adapted from GLOBE Study, House, et al., 2004, pp. 30, 302, 359, 405, 454, 459, 462, 536, 570, 618.)

autonomous by making decisions unilaterally, somewhat inspiring and somewhat team oriented. The opposite would be a Nordic leader, who would be charismatic by demonstrating vision and participation but is not expected to take a personal interest in employees. A Confucian Asian leader would practice self-protective leadership that focuses on saving face yet at the same time being the benevolent caretaker of their employees. Its opposite would be a Germanic European style of leadership that would focus on autonomous leadership that is independent and individualistic.

Table 8.3 Leadership Attributes: GLOBE Study with Ten Country/Society Clusters

Eastern Europe	Middle East	Confucian Asia	Southern Asia	Latin America
Albania, Georgia, Greece, Hungary, Kazakhstan Poland, Slovenia, Russia	*Egypt, Kuwait, Morocco, Qatar, Turkey*	*China, Hong Kong, Japan, Singapore, South Korea, Taiwan*	*India, Indonesia, Iran, Philippines, Thailand*	*Argentina, Bolivia, Brazil, Columbia, Costa Rica, Ecuador, El Salvador, Guatemala, Mexico, Venezuela*
Leaders should be independent and protect their position. Desired behaviors: <ul><li>Autonomous leadership</li><li>Self-protective leadership</li><li>Charismatic/value-based leadership</li><li>Team-oriented leadership</li><li>Humane-oriented leadership</li><li>Participative leadership</li></ul>	Leaders should demonstrate status and saving face. Negative attributes include being charismatic, value-based, or group oriented. Desired behaviors: <ul><li>Self-protective leadership</li><li>Humane-oriented leadership</li><li>Autonomous leadership</li><li>Charismatic/value-based leadership</li><li>Team-oriented leadership</li><li>Participative leadership</li></ul>	Leaders should care about others, yet can use status to make unilateral decisions. Desired behaviors: <ul><li>Self-protective leadership</li><li>Team-oriented leadership</li><li>Humane-oriented leadership</li><li>Charismatic/value-based leadership</li><li>Autonomous leadership Participative leadership</li></ul>	Leaders should be collaborative and sensitive to others. Saving face and respecting status are important. So is being inspirational. Desired behaviors: <ul><li>Self-protective leadership</li><li>Charismatic/value-based leadership</li><li>Humane-oriented leadership</li><li>Team-oriented leadership</li><li>Autonomous leadership</li><li>Participative leadership</li></ul>	Leaders should be charismatic. While they should be value-based they also can be self-serving. They should also inspire and collaborate. Desired behaviors: <ul><li>Charismatic/value-based leadership</li><li>Team-oriented leadership</li><li>Self-protective leadership</li><li>Participative leadership</li><li>Humane-oriented leadership</li><li>Autonomous leadership</li></ul>

(Continued)

Table 8.3 (continued)

Nordic Europe	Anglo	Germanic Europe	Latin Europe	Sub-Saharan Africa
Denmark, Finland, Sweden	*Australia, Canada, Ireland, New Zealand, South Africa (White sample), U.K., U.S.A.*	*Austria, Germany-East, Germany-West, Netherlands, Switzerland (German)*	*France, Israel, Italy, Portugal, Spain, Switzerland (French)*	*Namibia, Nigeria, Zambia, Zimbabwe, South Africa (Black sample)*
Leaders should be inspired, yet involve people in decision-making. Negative attributes include saving face and focusing on others. Desired behaviors: • Charismatic/value-based leadership • Participative leadership • Team-oriented leadership • Autonomous leadership • Humane-oriented leadership • Self-protective leadership	Leaders should motivate and provide a clear and confident vision. Desired behaviors: • Charismatic/value-based leadership • Participative leadership • Humane-oriented leadership • Team-oriented leadership • Autonomous leadership • Self-protective leadership	Leaders should be charismatic, display autonomy, and expect participation. Negative attributes include saving face and focusing on others. Desired behaviors: • Autonomous leadership • Charismatic/value-based leadership • Participative leadership • Humane-oriented leadership • Team-oriented leadership • Self-protective leadership	Leaders should inspire through self-confidence, collaboration, and participation. Desired behaviors: • Charismatic/value-based leadership • Team-oriented leadership • Participative leadership • Self-protective leadership • Humane-oriented leadership • Autonomous leadership	Leaders should be caring and collaborative; inspirational without being self-centered. Desired behaviors: • Humane-oriented leadership • Charismatic/value-based leadership • Team-oriented leadership • Participative leadership • Self-protective leadership • Autonomous leadership

Note: Countries opposite each other (top and bottom on each page) differ the most from each other.

(*Source:* Adapted from House et al., 2004, pp. 178–203.)

It is useful to note that the GLOBE Study uses the term "society," instead of "country" or "nation," because the data showed that there are many cultural groups within a given nation state. For example, the study distinguished between Western and Eastern Germany due to the political and historical events after World War II where Germany was split into four sections, with Eastern Germany being controlled by the then Soviet Union. Regarding language differences, Switzerland was divided into German- and French-speaking groups; racial differences in Africa were distinguished by the Black sample and the White sample; and religious differences by Israel's inclusion in Latin Europe (this relates to the social and business ties that the Jewish community maintained in Spain before migrating to Eastern European countries) (House et al., 2004).

Clustering societies is an important way of distinguishing groups from each other. Societal clusters are therefore described as "unifying themes linking societal cultures together within distinct regions of the world" (House et al., 2004, p. 178) that help summarize both similarities and differences of such groups. The three effects that will influence any given society are physical geography, migration, and religious/linguistic practices, yet geography has had the biggest influence on how we determine a society (a nation, a country). For example, Africa is made up of many countries and even if you looked at a particular country such as Nigeria or Uganda you will find many different views on cultural identity via language, ethnicity, religion, region, etc. It is the same for Europe, for Asia, for everywhere. We can say that certain countries, regions, or societies have more in common than others. For example, northern Africa—made up of Islamic countries—have more in common with each other than sub-Saharan cultures. It is similar to the analogy of the chocolate candy bar and the chocolate cake—both have chocolate in them (similarities) but both are completely different kinds of confections (differences) (Box 8.2).

The reasons behind the research are important for business leaders since we need to know that what we are learning about cultural competence has a strong history of sound theoretical development. Otherwise, why should people listen to us?

> There has been almost a half century of effort to identify clusters of societies using the analysis of international-level data. Clusters provide important information regarding societal variation and are a useful way to summarize intercultural similarities as well as intercultural differences. Cluster-based information can assist in theory development. Judicious sampling within and across societal clusters can test potential boundary conditions for management theories and interventions. Clusters may also be used to guide the sampling strategy for cross-cultural research to ensure that an adequate sampling of cultural variability is included in the samples. Researchers can also test the generalizability of empirical findings obtained in one culture to other cultures.
>
> (Gupta et al., 2002, p. 11)

Box 8.2 How Many Countries Are in the World?

How do we define what a country or a nation is?
  According to Political Geography Now (2016), there are six definitions:

195 Sovereign states (UN)
201 States with partial recognition
204-207 De facto sovereign states
206 Olympic nations
209 FIFA countries eligible for World Cup*
249 Country codes in the ISO standard list**

The most common definition of country or nation is a sovereign state which is an area that has an independent government and borders. These are the countries that belong to the United Nations and it is said that membership in the UN means that such countries "mostly accept each other as sovereign states."

One can debate about what constitutes a "state with partial recognition," such as in the case of Taiwan, or as a "UN observer state," such as in the case of Palestine. There are definite tensions regarding groups of people within certain borders that have an independent government.

The world is constantly changing.

Notes: *FIFA stands for Fédération Internationale de Football Association; **International Standard for Country Codes www.iso.org/iso/country_codes

Source: Political Geography Now, 2016

In a nutshell, the societal clusters could be broadly described as in Table 8.4.

In sum, through the data collected from the surveys, researchers were able to develop an in-depth sketch (818 pages) of an exceptional leader, who has integrity, charisma, values, and good communication skills. An ineffective leader is someone who is withdrawn, mean, and self-important. In a subsequent publication a decade later, *Strategic leadership across cultures: GLOBE study of CEO leadership behavior and effectiveness in 24 countries,* the researchers once again drew on surveys and statistical data to illuminate, in a 464-page sequel, what leaders actually do (House et al., 2013).

Overcoming the Four Cultural Myths as a Global Leader

So how do we create success with our cross-functional and intercultural team? The answer is to develop our CQ. We must be forewarned, though,

Table 8.4 GLOBE Study Societal Clusters

Anglo societies are generally competitive and results oriented; less attached to families and in-groups compared to other societies (high performance orientation; low in-group collectivism).

Confucian Asia societies have a tendency to be high performers, expecting impeccable performance; they focus on the good of the group rather than the individual, and are highly devoted to their families (high performance orientation, institutional, and in-group collectivism).

Eastern Europe societies strongly support colleagues and promote gender equality; they are less achievement oriented than other societies, yet rely on rules and laws to keep order (high-assertiveness, in-group collectivism and gender egalitarianism; low performance orientation, future orientation, and uncertainty avoidance).

Germanic Europe societies adhere to schedules, plan for the future, and prefer rules and laws in order to control their social environment; they are not as group focused but more individual oriented. Leaders are participative but can also be independent and inspirational (high performance orientation, assertiveness, future orientation, and uncertainty avoidance; low humane orientation, institutional, and in-group collectivism).

Latin America societies are extremely loyal to their families and in-groups, yet less so with institutional and societal groups. Leaders are charismatic/value-based, team-oriented, and self-protective. They are moderate in terms of their employees' participation and decision-making (high in-group collectivism; low performance orientation, institutional collectivism, and uncertainty avoidance).

Latin Europe societies value individuality in order to watch out for themselves and family rather than promote the goals of their society. Leaders are charismatic/value-based, team-oriented, and participative. While leaders can be inspiring, collaborative, and self-oriented, they are not necessarily compassionate (moderate on most scales and have low humane orientation and institutional collectivism).

Middle East societies are deeply devoted to their families and in-groups, yet women do not have the same status as men. Orderliness and policies are relaxed in order to enjoy the moment. While collective societies, the approach to leadership holds self-attributes such as status and saving face, and does not respect charismatic/value-based or group-oriented leadership (high in-group collectivism; low gender egalitarianism, future orientation, and uncertainty avoidance).

Nordic Europe societies place priority on social preservation with less emphasis on family groups; they concentrate on long-term success with everyone sharing equally in power—cooperation is critical. Women share equal status to men and it is more important to be caring than competitive. Leadership is participative but doesn't overdo it with too much compassion—they balance it (high gender egalitarianism and institutional collectivism; low in-group collectivism, power distance, and assertiveness).

Southern Asia societies differ from the charismatic Confucian Asia countries and believe that effective leadership is more autocratic rather than participative (look out for the welfare of the group and demonstrate strong loyalty to their families and in-groups (high humane orientation and in-group collectivism)).

Sub-Saharan Africa societies (Black sample) demonstrate sensitivity toward others and strong humaneness deriving from the practice of Ubuntu (I am because of who you are). This relates to caring for others more than caring for self (high humane orientation).

(*Source*: Adapted from Northouse's interpretation of the GLOBE Study, Northouse, 2015, pp. 309–13.)

that developing CQ is a challenge because most of us group people who live and work with others like themselves. However, becoming an interculturally competent leader *is* possible as we learn more about the world. But how can we do this with our busy schedules? It is not possible to know every custom or every fact and figure about a particular culture, but you *can* develop a global mindset. Having a global mindset is an ongoing process of self-learning.

If you have been assigned to lead that cross-functional intercultural team, hopefully you can now challenge your assumptions so that you do not fall prey to cultural myths. We become interculturally competent when we increase awareness of who we are while developing knowledge about the practices and behaviors of others. This way we can identify differences and become comfortable with them. Also, if we are open to learning new things, we can acknowledge that we do not know everything and become inquisitive about others and the world around us. Then, we can become adaptive as we collaborate with others to achieve successful intercultural interactions.

Using the GLOBE Study

Knowing what you now know about the nature of global leadership styles, cultural dimensions, and societal norms, you could begin to analyze your situation.

The following discussion is based upon a society—a group of people—that over time has developed the assumptions and practices that are accepted, expected, and rewarded by their society. If we view situations from our own lens, results could be disastrous, so seeing the other side is critical. But that does not necessarily mean we have to change who we are completely—we need to be adaptive. This is called culturally endorsed implicit leadership theory (House et al., 2002, p. 8), which calls for contingency and flexibility. Everyone has assumptions, stereotypes, and mental frameworks that influence how we view someone's leadership or management abilities. Since people across different cultures have different expectations about what makes a good leader, knowing what you know now will help you bridge your style with the expected styles. I agree with Professor Javidan of the Thunderbird School of Global Business and his colleagues from the GLOBE Study in that intercultural communication is a two-way street. It is not about immediately changing the way you do things. It is about reflecting deeply on how you do things based upon your cultural conditioning and then reflecting on the extra layer of complexity regarding how your counterparts will do things and expect to do things based upon their cultural conditioning. The culturally competent leader will figure out how to balance this human challenge of being a competent communicator.

For example, if you know you have certain leadership attributes that do not match the style of your counterparts within their society, it would be wise to have an open and specific conversation about your expectations. This can be a valuable learning experience for all. Using all of the information provided by the GLOBE Study, you could figure out how to balance what you will say, how you will say it, and how you will respond to your counterparts' reactions. You will constantly stay on top of the subtle nuances of what happens when people with different expectations interact (Javidan et al., 2006). It would also be wise to begin establishing trusted relationships (this takes time) so that you have confidants who can give advice and guide you along the way.

The following is what I would do in terms of beginning my research for dealing with our hypothetical global team.[2]

Step One Analysis

The societies with which I'm working include: the United States, the United Kingdom, Australia, Dubai, South Korea, China, Hong Kong, Taiwan, India, and Chile. This will be a challenge because of the many different societal clusters with which I will be dealing. Since I am in the Anglo society cluster, I would examine the leadership attributes of my own cluster first. If I go through Tables 8.1, 8.2, 8.3, and 8.4 presented in this chapter and think about my "gut" reaction to how I would handle a situation when interacting with people from those areas, I will notice a few things. Anglo societal clusters tend to have a charismatic/value-based leadership style that promotes high standards, decisiveness, and innovation; seeks to inspire people around a vision; and creates a passion for performance centered on core values. It is also participative, encouraging input from others in decision-making and implementation; and emphasizes delegation and equality.

Through careful reflection, I would then consider if these were my primary leadership styles as well. Maybe yes, and maybe no. Comparing the leadership styles in Table 8.1 to the cultural dimensions in Table 8.2 can be enlightening as I think through whether my culture has influenced my own personal leadership style. I could make a list of how these styles play out in my workplace interactions; my personal life; and my overall societal environment. Plotting out these leadership styles and cultural dimensions is a strong first step to reflecting on how I interact with and manage people (Table 8.5).

Step Two Analysis

Now I would look at Table 8.3 in terms of the society clusters that are directly opposite of mine—this would be Middle East. When dealing with my counterparts in Dubai, as a woman I would have to be cognizant of the differences in gender equality. While Dubai is not as conservative as Saudi Arabia, it still is a society that favors male leadership over female, so I might have to work with a male colleague as a potential intermediary. I would need to be aware of strong in-group collectivism, and the pride and security that this brings to the group. I would build my legitimacy by working with my male

Table 8.5 Determining My Own Leadership Styles Across Cultures

Leadership	Societal value	Workplace value	Self-value
Six leadership styles:			
+ *Charismatic/Value-based*			
+ *Team-oriented style*			
+ *Participative style*			
+ *Humane style*			
+ *Autonomous style*			
+ *Self-protective style*			
Nine cultural dimensions:			
+ *Power distance*			
+ *Uncertainty avoidance*			
+ *Humane orientation*			
+ *Collectivism I: Institutional*			
+ *Collectivism II: In-group*			
+ *Assertiveness*			
+ *Gender egalitarianism*			
+ *Future orientation*			
+ *Performance orientation*			

colleague while also developing relationships within the tight-knit group before making any decisions. According to the GLOBE Study, Middle East society clusters tend to be self-protective, humane oriented, and autonomous in their leadership practices. This means that generally my counterparts might focus on the safety and security of the leader as well as the group; are autonomous and will do what is good for their group; and are humane oriented—toward their group.

Step Three Analysis

Then I would group the other societies with their GLOBE Study clusters—Confucian Asia consists of China, Hong Kong, Taiwan, and South Korea; South East Asia consists of India; Latin America consists of Chile.

Confucian Asia counterparts would probably be protective of their group, yet use a team-oriented and humane approach. The boss is seen as the benevolent protector and, while they would use a team-oriented approach, this means that there would be strong collaboration among team members for the good of the group, not necessarily for decision-making. The benevolent boss would make the decisions and expect loyalty from team members.

Latin America-style leadership would be charismatic/value-based, team oriented, and self-protective. Although stressing high standards while inspiring and motivating, the leader would, like Confucian Asia leaders, focus on the team cohesiveness and protect their interests.

Southern Asia—my counterparts from India would be more like my Chilean colleagues, being self-protective, charismatic, and humane in their leadership approaches. Probably the biggest challenge would be that Anglo leadership attributes focus on the participative leadership style, expecting employees to join in with the decision-making and innovation. I would need to pay attention to the delicate balance of protecting the group from potential harm (being benevolent) yet still exerting guidance that leads the group (making the decision).

As with all cultures, we need to understand the general characteristics of a society—based upon the research—and be ready for the paradoxes that certainly will abound. I was recently coaching a group of executives preparing for a business venture in Argentina. We talked about the need to prepare for the possible impact of time when expecting their colleagues to return e-mails and other forms of communication. They reported back that their Argentine counterparts were more on time and accurate with communiques than they were. Another group working with a nonprofit organization in Chile had the opposite experience and was frustrated at how long procedures took. Be prepared yet be ready for surprises. Culture and its effect on leadership cannot be put into a prescriptive recipe.

Step Four Analysis

Now I would need to do a little research and find out about the historical, political, social, and cultural backgrounds of these societies. Because cultural competence is more than merely a list of do's and don'ts, it would be wise to understand a little about the background of each society's world view and history. Such knowledge provides context, a backdrop of sorts, for helping us make sense of why people might have certain leadership practices.

U.K. and Australia

If I were coming from an Anglo perspective (United States), I would need to realize that, while I might share more commonalities with my British and Australian counterparts, there still would be differences. I would need to research the specifics of these societies in order not to assume that my counterparts would react the same as I would. Anglo societies tend to be more individualistic and competitive in decision-making and assigning tasks while at the same time trying to narrow the gap with informality.

However, certain differences exist if I were to be interacting with counterparts from the United Kingdom and Australia. A common language does not mean you'll have a common culture. While we can chuckle about the differences between chips and crisps or trunks and boots, going deeper means we need to analyze values—those things that are important to us and guide our daily living. For example, in the United States, when you go to a job interview or network at a social event, you are expected to be self-promoting. Whether you are comfortable with selling yourself or not, it is expected and endorsed in order to get ahead. However, if you are working with British counterparts you would need to "dial back" a bit as people from the United Kingdom disdain self-promotion, or even being praised by someone else in public. It simply is not a value that is practiced. The same with expression, as Brits are more reserved and instrumental versus publicly enthusiastic than their U.S. counterparts. It would also be important to understand how Australia was first colonized by the Dutch and then the British, and the significant political and social issues surrounding the Aboriginal people of Australia (Australian Government, n.d.).

Chile

Chile's history is fascinating and quite diverse. The main inhabitants were the Mapuche, a pre-Columbian people with records as early as 600–500 BCE who may have been related to Polynesia cultures from the western Pacific (Storey et al., 2007). The Incas extended their empire from Peru toward the Mapuche area in the late 1400s and then less than a hundred years later the Spanish explorer Pedro de Valdivia arrived. Chile gained its independence from Spain in 1817 after years of war. In the early 1900s, Chile, like Argentina, saw migration of immigrants from Europe (Spain, Italy, Germany), but not on the same scale as was experienced in Argentina and Uruguay (Hutchinson et al., 2013). The government was basically stable until the 1970s, with the entrance of Salvador Allende and his Marxist government, which was taken over in a coup by the right-wing government of General Pinochet in 1973 (with help from the U.S. CIA), who ruled until 1990, when the country was able to have its own independent elections (Geographia, n.d.). Those years under Pinochet were filled with terror and fear, when thousands of people, "*desaparecidos*" or "disappeared ones," were systematically rounded up as political parties holding views contrary to Pinochet. They were suppressed and dissidents were persecuted. Since the 1990s Chilean politics has remained stable but there still exists tension between the military and the government because of the extreme human rights violations of Pinochet. And, Chile has made great strides in mitigating poverty, which is much lower than other South American countries; however, an aging demographic creates constant challenges. Other social problems include classism, which is more of an issue than race, since much of the country is "*mestizo*," a "mixture" of people due to the long history of colonization and immigration (Central Intelligence Agency, 2016a).

China, Taiwan, Hong Kong, and South Korea

Regarding Confucian Asia, it would be important to understand that *Confucian Asia* and *Southeast Asia* have different world views. South Korea, China, and Taiwan have been influenced by both Confucian philosophy and Buddhism. Confucius focused on practical conduct and self-control, which created a system of social and political ethics meant to guide people toward proper behavior in everyday life (6th–5th CE). Confucian philosophy valued hierarchy, group orientation, and tradition, and emphasized that it was important to hold to filial piety, kinship, and loyalty as an indication of the important obligations within the established order of relationships. About the same time, Buddhism originated in India and eventually found its way to other parts of Asia, such as South Korea, China, Nepal, and Japan. Buddhism seeks to purify one's soul from the suffering in the world and tries to transcend the yearnings of the material world (About Buddhism, n.d.).

In addition to knowing about the philosophical underpinnings of Confucian Asia, it would also be necessary to note some of the history and sociopolitical conflicts between the societies. For example, China claims Taiwan as part of its own; however, Taiwan views itself as its own country—this dates back to the clash between Mao Zedong, founder and chairman of the Chinese Communist Party, and nationalist Kuomintang leader, Chiang Kai-shek, who fled in 1949 to Taiwan. It would also be critical to understand Hong Kong's relationship to the United Kingdom regarding the two Opium Wars of the mid-1800s, the unequal Treaty of Nanjing, and its return to China in 1997 (Pletcher, 2015).

Not only this, but what might I need to know about South Korea and its different history from China? Just because it is in the Confucian Asian cluster does not mean that South Korean and Chinese societies are the same! And what about its communication patterns that might differ from China? While South Korea follows the same filial piety and harmonious relationships as China, the society as a whole uses a very different and complex form of addressing people, called "honorifics." This concept carries the connotative meaning for the level of respect that must be used when addressing or referring to a person with higher status. In South Korean speech practice, there are also grammatical "speech levels" used to reflect the formality or informality of the situation. Koreans use titles in place of personal names and avoid certain pronouns because of the intimacy they carry. For example, the second-person pronoun "you" and the third-person pronoun "he" or "she" are often not used. Most often, if you do not know someone's name, you use a title based upon their appearance, or how you "size them up." For example, "*ajumma*" refers to a married, middle-aged woman; "*samonim*" refers to a teacher's wife. Professional women may not appreciate either term because they imply dependence on the man. The word for grandmother, "*halmeoni*," can be used for a woman who is a professional, well-educated, and who might appear to be 65 or older. A more neutral term would be "*seonsaengnim*" or teacher (Jin-sung, 2007). Honorifics is not only an important phenomenon in South Korea, it is also a method to differentiate between genders, with paternalism projected onto women (Javidan & House, 2001).

India

Additionally, what is India's history? What is India's relationship with the United Kingdom and its colonization in 1858, the formation of modern India and Muslim Pakistan in 1947, and the India–Pakistan War of 1965? What are

Brahmanism and Hinduism, and how have these philosophies informed the world view of such a vast society? India has always had a complex religious and philosophical history because of the many world views held by its people. It is important to note that, as a society, India has been tolerant of many religions in order to create harmony with each other. Brahmanism predates Hinduism, and comes from the Brahman class of priests, which is the highest class in Indian society. They migrated from the areas of the Black and Caspian Seas and were known as the Indo-Europeans (also called Aryans, which means noble). Brahmans believe in the rebirth of the soul, as do Hindus. There is a belief that both people and gods are mutually obligated to each other, with people sacrificing and gods responding by fulfilling earthly needs; when this happens there is equilibrium in the universe. This has a tremendous impact on India's humane-oriented leadership style; however, the paradox of strict caste systems also exists (James, 2007).

United Arab Emirates

The United Arab Emirates (U.A.E.) is made up of seven "emirates," or a federation of seven states (Abu Dhabi, Ajman, Dubai, Fujairah, Sharjah, Umm al Quwain, and Ras al-Khaimah), which came together in 1971–2 after gaining independence from the United Kingdom. Once a quiet land mass on the eastern part of the Arabian Peninsula (about the size of the state of Maine in the United States), it is now one of the most important economic centers and bustling areas in the Middle East. The population is over 8 million people, whose major language is Arabic and religion, Islam. Sheikh Khalifa bin Zayed is President of the U.A.E. Federal Council and established Zayed University in several locations including Dubai and Abu Dhabi. These universities provide education for women because of bin Zayed's reputation as a pro-Western modernizer (*BBC News*, 2015). The U.A.E. is an international community— only 19 percent of its people are Native Emirati, with 23 percent being other Arabs and Iranians, 50 percent South Asian, and 8 percent other expatriates such as Westerners and East Asians. While this makes for an international mix of leadership styles, and while the U.A.E. is known for its liberalization in comparison to other Arab societies, it is nevertheless grounded in the Middle East society cluster (Central Intelligence Agency, 2016b).

There is definitely so much to learn—but these historical and world view points are critical to understanding the reasoning behind the many lists produced in this chapter. And, when you think about it—these are only brief synopses of historical, societal, and religious events. This is why becoming a CQ leader is a challenge!

Step Five Analysis

Finally, I would employ one of the many useful cross-cultural assessment tools that are available in order to look at my individual tendencies toward hidden bias, ability to deal with uncertainty and complexity, as well as how my particular communication preferences would affect my interactions with the people on my teams. At the end of this chapter, Table 8.6 lists the various cross-cultural assessment tools that can be used in developing CQ capabilities.

And of course, one could use all of the information garnered by the research in this book, to explore the cultural makeup of various societies through Hofstede's website, the GLOBE Study, practicing the Cultural Sense-Making Model, thinking through paradoxes, and so on. Once the research is done, it will be up to the savvy global leader to be flexible in realizing that, while it is good to do one's homework, the people and situations encountered will probably not play out like a script—therefore "cultural improv" will be necessary.[3]

Conclusion

Global leadership is a tall order. This chapter's discussion on current research into global leadership attributes and societal clusters demonstrates how complicated human communication is. However, it *is* possible to become a CQ leader.

Jack Welch, CEO of General Electric, once said:

> The Jack Welch of the future cannot be me. I spent my entire career in the United States. The next head of General Electric will be somebody who spent time in Bombay, in Hong Kong, in Buenos Aires. We have to send our best and brightest overseas and make sure that they have the training that will allow them to be the global leaders who will make GE flourish in the future.
>
> (Javidan & House, 2001, p. 289)

The two key investigators in the GLOBE Study responded to Mr. Welch's comment quite aptly:

> To be successful in dealing with people from other cultures, managers need knowledge about cultural differences and similarities among countries. They also need to understand the implications of the differences and the skills required to act and decide appropriately and in a culturally sensitive way.
>
> (Javidan & House, 2001, p. 293)

Today's leader needs to meet the increasing demands of dealing with cross-cultural differences. It is not enough to live in Austria, speak four languages, and interact across borders every day.

Model of Cultural Competence Revisited

What makes the CQ leader is the three-step iterative process discussed at the beginning of this book (see Chapter 2) (Thomas & Inkson, 2009) (Figure 8.2).

Figure 8.2 Model of IC Competence

(*Source*: Thomas & Inkson, 2009.)

Knowledge is what the culturally intelligent person needs to learn. This includes being aware of the fundamental principles of intercultural inter-actions: knowing what culture is, how cultures vary, and how culture affects behaviors. The premise is that: basic knowledge is *not* enough—there are many subtleties with cultural differences and the global leader must go beyond learning of facts. This leads us to the next phase.

Reflection is what the culturally intelligent person needs to consider: this means paying attention in a mindful way to the cues in intercultural situations and also observing one's own reactions and emotions. This moves us from abstract to concrete experience when we encounter an interaction that is ambiguous. The premise is that: because the essence of culture is subtle and based upon context and situations, cultural behaviors are expressed in com-bination with the unique personalities of the individual at a particular moment within a particular context.

Competence is what the culturally intelligent person needs to practice: this means improvising and revising thoughts, reactions, and behaviors in order to become competent—skillful—across a wide range of situations. A person chooses the appropriate behaviors from a well-developed repertoire of both knowledge and behaviors that are appropriate for different intercultural situations. The premise is that: when one goes beyond learning facts to reflecting deeply to experiencing interactions with people who are different, one can develop skills, and eventually, competence.

In a nutshell, this three-step process is what this book is all about: know-ledge, mindfulness, and skills. While such a notion of a three-step process is certainly a Western construct for creating a framework for understanding, it can also be an Eastern framework if we make it iterative, and hopefully dia-logic, as well. One thing is for sure, understanding culture's consequences is

Table 8.6 Intercultural Assessment Tools

Cultural Orientations Inventory (COI)
www.culturalorientations.com

The Cultural Orientations Indicator is a web-based, self-reporting tool designed to foster self-awareness and other-awareness so users can effectively communicate and collaborate in a global team environment. It is part of the cross-cultural platform, the Cultural Navigator, which hosts a variety of web-based learning tools. The assessment illuminates an individual's particular communication preferences through a non-evaluative report that provides recommendations and suggests relevant resources for building effective skills and cultural aptitude. This tool is non-evaluative and helps to identify a person's work-style communication preferences that can impact communication on a multicultural and global level.

The COI was developed over 30 years ago and undergoes constant revalidation by Training Management Corporation (TMC) and is designed to measure difference in cultural values, beliefs, and attitudes. This assessment tool has been developed by experts in the behavioral science field and demonstrates high validity and reliability, and has been translated into 13 languages.

The COI's three dimensions provide a way in which users can understand and discuss with their colleagues how they prefer to interact, process information, and view themselves in their work environment.

- *Interaction Style*: Orientations that impact how you communicate and engage with others in work situations.
- *Thinking Style*: Orientations that impact how you conceptualize and process information in work situations.
- *Sense of Self*: Orientations that define how you view yourself and are motivated in the workplace.

Because the COI tool provides an assessment of individual *preferences* (likings, affinities, biases) it helps people understand as they explore culture based differences in themselves and others. The goal is to help participants develop cultural competence, which is the *ability to reduce the risks and maximize the opportunities inherent in cultural differences and similarities*. High levels of cultural competence allow individuals and organizations to understand, manage, and leverage culture at work. These capabilities enable responsiveness and adaptability, which are critical in today's dynamic global marketplace.

Intercultural Development Inventory (IDI)
http://idiinventory.com/products/the-intercultural-development-inventory-idi/

The Intercultural Development Inventory (IDI) is a cross-culturally valid and reliable assessment that assesses intercultural competence by showing one's own orientations toward cultural difference and commonality (how you make sense of and respond to similarities and differences). The instrument is easy to complete and it can generate an in-depth graphic profile of an individual's or groups' predominant level of intercultural competence along with a detailed textual interpretation of that level of intercultural development and associated transitional issues. It is built upon the theory of the Developmental Model of Intercultural Sensitivity DMIS (see below).

The Intercultural Development Inventory (IDI) is a cross-culturally valid and reliable assessment tool that assesses intercultural competence by showing one's own orientations toward cultural difference and commonality (how one makes sense of and respond to similarities and differences). The instrument generates an in-depth graphic profile of both an individual's or group's predominant level of intercultural competence.

(Continued)

Table 8.6 (continued)

Intercultural competence is *the capability to accurately understand and adapt behavior to cultural difference and commonality.* Intercultural competence reflects the degree to which cultural differences and commonalities—in values, expectations, beliefs, and practices—are effectively bridged from a mutual adaptation perspective as people work together to achieve inclusiveness based upon mutual respect and understanding.

People are different in their ability to recognize and respond effectively to cultural differences and commonalities. The intercultural development continuum adapted from the Developmental Model of Intercultural Sensitivity originally proposed by intercultural theorist, Milton Bennett, identifies specific orientations that range from more mono-cultural to more intercultural or global mindsets.

This continuum indicates that individuals who have a more intercultural mindset have a greater capability for responding effectively to cultural differences, recognizing and building upon real commonalities. That is, your success in achieving workplace goals is better served when you are able to more deeply understand culturally learned differences, recognize commonalities between yourself and others, and act on this increased insight in culturally appropriate ways that facilitate performance, learning and personal growth among diverse groups.

Each participant receives an Individual Report that highlights their individual phase on this developmental model along with in-depth discussion of relevant issues for consideration. In addition, each participant receives a Development Plan that provides five steps for improving intercultural competence. It is available in 17 languages and has the highest level of cross-cultural reliability and validity as tested through rigorous psychometric analysis.

The Global Competencies Inventory (GCI)

www.kozaigroup.com/global-competencies-inventory-gci/

The Global Competencies Inventory (GCI) is designed to assess your personal qualities associated with effectiveness in environments where there are cultural norms and behaviors different from your own. The information contained in this feedback report can provide a basis for understanding both your current competencies as well as point to opportunities for future development and growth.

This scientifically validated and reliable report focuses on three main factors and sixteen dimensions of intercultural adaptability:

Perception Management: How an individual mentally approaches cultural differences:
- Non-judgmentalness
- Inquisitiveness
- Tolerance of ambiguity
- Cosmopolitanism
- Interest flexibility

Relationship Management: An individual's orientation toward developing and maintaining relationships with, and awareness of, culturally different others:
- Relationship interest
- Interpersonal engagement
- Emotional awareness
- Self-awareness
- Social flexibility

(*Continued*)

Table 8.6 (continued)

Self-Management: The strength and clarity of an individual's sense of self-identity and ability to effectively manage thoughts, emotions, and responses to stressful situations:
- Optimism
- Self-confidence
- Self-identity
- Emotional resilience
- Non-stress tendency
- Stress management

This tool can be used for:
- Executive coaching for personal and professional development
- Selection and promotion criteria for different levels of management
- Pre- and post- measurements for changes in intercultural competencies
- Cross-cultural and diversity courses to increase awareness and self-analysis for improvement

Seven different languages are reflected in the GCI: Arabic, Mandarin, English, French, German, Japanese, Spanish.

The Global Mindset Inventory (GMI)
http://globalmindset.thunderbird.edu/home/global-mindset-inventory/three-capitals

The Global Mindset Inventory (GMI) is an assessment tool that measures a person's ability to better influence individuals, groups and organizations who have different values, beliefs, behaviors, and norms for living.

Intellectual Capital: One's capacity to understand how one's business works on a global level with three key attributes:
- Global business savvy: a strong grasp of how the industry operates worldwide, how global customers behave, how your competitors target their needs and habits, and how strategic risk varies by geography.
- Cognitive complexity: the ability to piece together multiple scenarios with many moving parts, without becoming paralyzed by the number of options.
- Cosmopolitan outlook: an active interest in the culture, history, geography, and political and economic systems of different parts of the world.

Psychological Capital: One's receptiveness to new ideas and experiences. There are with 3 key attributes:
- Passion for diversity: a penchant for exploring other parts of the world, experiencing other cultures, and trying new ways of doing things.
- Thirst for adventure: an appreciation for the ability to thrive in unpredictable and complex environments.
- Self-assurance: self-confidence, a sense of humor, a willingness to take risks in new contexts, and high levels of energy; the ability to be energized, rather than drained, by a foreign context.

Social Capital: Helps build trusting relationships with people who are different from you. The 3 most important attributes are:
- Intercultural empathy: the ability to engage and connect emotionally with people from other parts of the world.
- Interpersonal impact: the ability to bring together divergent views, develop consensus, and maintain credibility; and skill at building networks – not just with peers and seniors but with other, less obvious potential contacts.
- Diplomacy: listening to what is said and what is not said, eases in conversations with people who are different from you, and a greater inclination to ask than to answer.

(Continued)

Table 8.6 (continued)

Intercultural Effectiveness Scale (IES)
http://kozaigroup.com/inventories/the-intercultural-effectiveness-scale/

The Intercultural Effectiveness Scale (IES) was developed specifically to evaluate the competencies critical to interacting effectively with people who are from cultures other than our own. This instrument is used primarily by non-profit organizations, including government agencies and educational institutions. The competencies assessed by the IES are equally applicable to evaluating how well people work effectively with people who are different from them (gender, generation, ethnic group, religious affiliation, etc.)

Continuous Learning. This dimension assesses our interest in learning and general curiosity as well as our interest in better understanding ourselves. To appreciate and understand those who are different from us, we need to be willing and motivated to learn about them and their culture. In addition, to set a good foundation for interacting effectively with them, we also need to understand ourselves well, including our values, beliefs and behavioral tendencies.

Interpersonal Engagement. It evaluates our interest in understanding various peoples and places in the world and developing actual relationships with people who are different from us. Developing positive relationships with people who are not like us depends in large part on our interest in learning about and from them. The more we learn about the world around us, the various peoples, their backgrounds, the issues they face, and so forth, the more we are able to interact with people who are different from us.

Hardiness. Interacting with people who differ from us culturally, generationally, religiously and so forth entails psychological effort. This effort in turn always produces varying levels of stress, uncertainty, anxiety, and sometimes fears. To interact effectively with those who are different from us requires an ability to cope with these psychological and emotional stresses. Coping can be accomplished by having a natural resilience to stress and also by better understanding the nature of the differences. Understanding differences increases our confidence, enables us to find more common ground, and decreases the psychological effort involved when interacting with people who differ from us.

Note: For more information visit the specific websites or check them out on my website: http://globalbizleader.com

complex, uncertain, and ambiguous. But we *can* crack the cultural codes by following this process of gaining knowledge, practicing mindfulness, and developing our skills through trial and error—think of it as cultural improv—you are constantly creating and recreating learning opportunities for developing your global leadership. May we all aim to be CQ leaders.

Notes

1 Adapted from Jason Moehring, International HR/OD Leader and Education Specialist, Chiang Mai, Thailand, and used with permission.
2 In writing this final chapter on research and global leadership attributes, I planned for the following: start off with a real-world scenario via a discussion of the myths about global leadership, present the research findings, and end with my solution for how I would manage a global team based upon the GLOBE leadership attributes. To my

delight, as I wrapped up my research, I came across an excellent article by my much-respected colleague, Professor Mansour Javidan, who took a similar approach. I have therefore incorporated some of their information as well(Javidan et al., 2006).

3 In my teaching and consulting I use a variety of scientifically validated and reliable cross-cultural assessment tools that are a powerful way to learn about communication preferences and competencies.

References

About Buddhism. (n.d.). What is Buddhism? Retrieved from www.aboutbuddhism. org/what-is-buddhism.htm/ (accessed on August 2, 2016).

Australian Government. (n.d.). European discovery and colonization of Australia. Retrieved from www.australia.gov.au/about-australia/australian-story/european-discovery-and-colonisation (accessed on August 2, 2016).

BBC News. (2015, November 18). United Arab Emirates country profile. Retrieved from www.bbc.com/news/world-middle-east-14703998 (accessed on August 3, 2016).

Central Intelligence Agency. (2016a, February 25). The world factbook—Chile. Retrieved from www.cia.gov/library/publications/the-world-factbook/geos/ci.html (accessed February 25, 2016).

Central Intelligence Agency. (2016b). The world factbook—Middle East United Arab Emirates. Retrieved from www.cia.gov/library/publications/the-world-factbook/geos/ae.html (accessed February 25, 2016).

Gannon, M. J. (2001). *Cultural metaphors: Readings, research translations, and commentary*. Thousand Oaks, CA: SAGE.

Geographia. (n.d.). Chile—history. Retrieved from www.geographia.com/chile/chilehistory.htm (accessed October 21, 2016).

Gupta, V., Hanges, P. J., & Dorfman, P. (2002). Cultural clusters: Methodology and findings. *Journal of World Business*, *37*(1), 11–15.

House, R., Javidan, M., Hanges, P., & Dorfman, P. (2002). Understanding cultures and implicit leadership theories across the globe: An introduction to project GLOBE. *Journal of World Business*, *37*(1), 3–10.

House, R. J., Hanges, P. J., Javidan, M., Dorfman, P. W., & Gupta, V. (Eds.). (2004). *Culture, leadership, and organizations: The GLOBE study of 62 societies* (3rd edn.) (Chapters 13–19). Thousand Oaks, CA: SAGE.

House, R. B., Dorfman, P. W., Javidan, M., Hanges, P. J., & de Luque, M. S. (2013). *Strategic leadership across cultures: GLOBE study of CEO leadership behavior and effectiveness in 24 countries*. Thousand Oaks, CA: SAGE.

Hutchinson, E. Q., Klubock, T. M., Milanich, N. B., & Winn, P. (Eds.). (2013). *The Chile reader: History, culture, politics (the Latin America readers)*. Durham, NC: Duke University Press.

James, M. S. (2007). Asia/philosophy 105. Retrieved from www.gossamerstrands.com/Asia105/lecture1.htm (accessed February 25, 2016).

Javidan, M., & House, R. J. (2001). Cultural acumen for the global manager: Lessons from project GLOBE. *Organizational Dynamics*, *29*(4), 289–305.

Javidan, M., Dorfman, P. W., de Luque, M. S., & House, R. J. (2006). In the eye of the beholder: Cross cultural lessons in leadership from project GLOBE. *The Academy of Management Perspectives*, *20*(1), 67–90.

Jesuino, J. C. (2002). Latin Europe cluster: From south to north. *Journal of World Business*, *37*(1), 81–89.

Jin-sung, Yang. (2007, October 2). Korean way of addressing people. *The Korea Times: Opinion*. Retrieved from www.koreatimes.co.kr/www/news/opinon/2008/04/162_11170.html (accessed on August 2, 2016).

Martin, G. (n.d.). The meaning and origin of the expression: When in Rome, do as the Romans do. Retrieved from www.phrases.org.uk/meanings/when-in-rome-do-as-the-romans-do.html (accessed on August 2, 2016).

Northouse, P. G. (2015). *Leadership: Theory and practice* (7th edn.). Los Angeles, CA: SAGE.

Pletcher, K. (2015, April 17). Opium wars. *Encyclopaedia Britannica*. Retrieved from www.britannica.com/topic/Opium-Wars (accessed February 25, 2016).

Political Geography Now. (2016, January 10). How many countries are there in the world in 2016? Retrieved from www.polgeonow.com/2011/04/how-many-countries-are-there-in-world.html (accessed February 25, 2016).

Storey, A. A., Ramírez, J. M., Quiroz, D., Burley, D. V., Addison, D. J., Walter, R., Anderson, A. J., Hunt, T. L., Athens, J. S., Huynen, L., & Matisoo-Smith, E. A. (2007). Radiocarbon and DNA evidence for a pre-Columbian introduction of Polynesian chickens to Chile. *Proceedings of the National Academy of Sciences*, *104* (25), 10335–9.

Thomas, D. C., & Inkson, K. (2009). *Cultural intelligence: Living and working globally* (2nd edn.). San Francisco, CA: Barrett-Koehler.

Case 8

Brew Time

Starbucks in the Indian Market[1]

Abstract

In January of 2012, Starbucks was preparing for a full-scale entry into the Indian market. The head of Starbucks Coffee Asia Pacific division, however, realizes that India—given its history—may be more like the U.K. than its neighboring China. This case study summarizes changes in Indian government, business, and culture, and will help students examine global leadership and management from a unique cultural perspective.

Introduction

On January 18, 2012, John Culver was late to work due to an unusual winter ice-storm in Seattle, Washington. The President of Starbucks Coffee China and Asia Pacific got out of his car and reached for his blackberry.

The first e-mail caught his attention. The message—from Howard Schultz, the chairman, President, and CEO of Starbucks Corporation—was perfectly clear, yet complex: "John, we're going ahead with the Tata partnership. We're announcing it a week from Monday in Mumbai. Get a flight booked. India's your baby. If you've got any remaining concerns, come and see me ASAP."

Culver had steadily risen through the ranks at Starbucks from his initial employment in 2002 until his appointment as head of Starbucks Coffee International in December 2009. Having joined the food service group in 2002, he did not have an extensive background in international markets. Yet by 2007, management had been impressed with his work ethic and leadership ability and promoted him to lead Starbucks Coffee Asia Pacific, where he learned a good deal about East Asia. Starbucks had already scrapped a prior effort by Martin Coles to expand into India in 2007, the man Culver would succeed in 2009 as head of Starbucks Coffee International (Starbucks Corporation, 2011a).

On July 11, 2011, following an internal review, Starbucks announced a new organizational and leadership structure. As of October 2011, Starbucks

Coffee International and Starbucks U.S., the previous distinction, were combined and then divided into three new segments:

1   Starbucks Coffee Americas and U.S. (led by former head of Starbucks U.S., Cliff Burrows), focusing on markets within North and South America;
2   Starbucks Coffee EMEA (headed by Michelle Gass), focusing on markets within Europe, the United Kingdom, the Middle East, Russia, and Africa; and
3   Starbucks Coffee China and Asia Pacific (headed by Culver), focusing on all Asia Pacific markets, including China (Starbucks Investor Relations, 2011).

In a conference call to investors on July 28, 2011, Schultz explained the rationale for the restructuring:

> In moving to a new 3-region global structure, we are matching our best talents to our biggest opportunities around the world. In this new structure, one president will oversee all operations within each of the 3 distinct regions with responsibility for the performance of company-operated stores as well as working with license and JV partners in each market with their respective region.
>
> (Seeking Alpha, 2011a)

At the time of the division, Culver knew that the expansion of Starbucks into India would be under the purview of Starbucks Coffee China and Asia Pacific. In early 2011, Starbucks established a strategic partnership with India-based Tata Coffee Limited, a subsidiary of the Tata Group (Seeking Alpha, 2011b).

Now, after much thought and planning, Starbucks was going to launch a full-scale entrance into the market through a joint venture with Tata Coffee Limited. Inasmuch as India is geographically closer to China than Europe, the rationale to include the Indian venture under Starbucks Coffee China and Asia Pacific made sense.

However, Culver remained unconvinced that India's culture was more like China's culture than it was like Europe's culture. After all, India had been a part of the British Empire until 1947 and remained a constituent state of the British Commonwealth.

Perhaps the synergies would be better if the expansion were organized under Starbucks Coffee EMEA instead of Starbucks China and Asia Pacific. Perhaps an expansion model predicated on a European prototype would be more ideal. Perhaps Indians had more similar tastes and views with Europe than with East Asia. Perhaps success in India depended on the division under which the operation was organized.

Culver had expressed some concerns to Schultz and had independently looked at the issue in some detail in his exceedingly rare downtime, but he had yet to come to a firm conclusion about where the Indian expansion should be located and what unique aspects of India might impact Starbucks' success. Now with the looming announcement, he knew he had one last chance to assure himself and the company that the current structure and plan were both sound and correct.

As Culver walked into the lobby of Starbucks' headquarters, he knew he had no time left to vacillate between the different options. He had to come to a firm decision and let Schultz know whether he had any remaining concerns about how Starbucks could be successful in India. He boarded the elevator and pressed the button for Schultz's floor, deep in thought about his research and the impending impact his choice would have on the Indian coffee retail market and the nation's coffee culture.

Starbucks from Seattle to India

Starting Out

In 1971, Jerry Baldwin, Gordon Bowker, and Zev Siegel opened a store devoted to coffee connoisseurs like themselves. Pike's Place, a neighborhood within Seattle, Washington, was the original home of Starbucks Coffee, Tea, and Spice Company which sold dark roast beans (Schultz & Yang, 1997). A decade later, Howard Schultz entered the picture. After one cup of Sumatra, he was interested and joined Starbucks in 1982 (Schultz & Yang, 1997).

However, the Starbucks as it is known today really began in 1987. It took several years to get to this point. Schultz visited Italy in 1983 and was enthralled by the coffee culture and knowledgeable baristas. He decided to try to bring this model back to the United States and ventured into this area solo before acquiring Starbucks in 1987 (Schultz & Yang, 1997).

His vision was a "third place" between work and home where people could gather (Starbucks Corporation, n.d.). Despite his passion, success at Starbucks was slow as coffee was seen by many investors as just a commodity (Starbucks Corporation, n.d.).

With 165 stores in four states, Starbucks went public in 1992 (Lexisnexis. com, 2003). Since perceptions about coffee had not changed, numerous skeptics claimed that a "$3 coffee [w]as a West Coast yuppie fad" (Lexisnexis. com, 2003). Local diners were still leading the coffee market but that would change with the growth of Starbucks. Since the initial public offering, Starbucks became aware of the need to grow in order to keep ahead of the competition and satisfy Wall Street (Starbucks Corporation, n.d.).

Formula for Growth

Starbucks paid close attention to quality, community, and real estate in its quest to grow and truly become the "third place." As the third place, "[w]e changed the way people live their lives, what they do when they get up in the morning, how they reward themselves and where they meet," said Starbucks veteran Orin Smith (Lexisnexis.com, 2003).

After entering a new market, the retail stores would act as the billboards for the brand. Clusters of Starbucks locations would open to ensure efficiency and convenience (Starbucks Corporation, n.d.). Starbucks encouraged stores to be close together: even on opposite street corners, "[a] new store will often capture about 30 percent of the sales of a nearby Starbucks but the company considers that a good thing" (Lexisnexis.com, 2003).

What other companies would see as cannibalization, Starbucks saw as an advantage in delivery and management costs, as well as a way to manage waiting times and increase customer satisfaction. To understand the deeper significance of this, consider how this strategy has become their signature. This is now associated with the Starbucks business model in many other parts of the world as well (Lexisnexis.com, 2003).

Despite increasing the size of the coffee market, by 2003 Starbucks had "captured just 7 percent of the coffee-drinking market in the U.S. and less than 1 percent abroad" (Lexisnexis.com, 2003). By 2005, Schultz charged Starbucks with the goal of operating over 10,000 locations worldwide (Lexisnexis.com, 2003). In order to achieve this number, opening successful international locations was imperative.

International Expansion

Starbucks' first venture abroad was in 1995 when it partnered with Sazaby Inc. to open stores in Japan (Mathee, 1995). Japan was slated as the first international location since it represented the "third-largest coffee-consuming country in the world" (Mathee, 1995). To break into the international markets, Schultz recognized the importance of partnerships with national companies. To him, national companies brought immense value in terms of language, culture, and real estate knowledge (Mathee, 1995).

When Starbucks opened its first café in Japan, it also had its eye on China. In 1999, Starbucks first entered China after four years of careful strategizing. Since China is primarily a tea culture, placing great emphasis on the tea ceremony, Starbucks originally partnered, in 1995, with Beijing Meida Coffee Co., to sell roasted beans to major hotels.

Tea consumption far outpaces coffee consumption in China, but that fact did not deter Starbucks, because even a small percentage of the populace amounts to a large customer base in such a populated country. Starbucks would not target older generations, especially given the stigma associated with coffee. In this era, only the wealthy would indulge in espresso.

While the coffee culture spread as income levels rose, it was the upper class that still dominated consumption of this beverage (Cunningham, 2010). When Starbucks opened its first store, it offered coffees at a lower price point, only to be matched by the local competitors (Cunningham, 2010). All of these efforts entailed significant investment into understanding the Chinese market for Starbucks. Cultural competence and an informed strategy were imperative to capitalize on the unique aspects of the people and their immediate customer base.

Understanding foreign cultures led Starbucks to impressive growth in the 2000s. In 2003 the company operated 6,000 stores in 30 countries, growing at a pace of three stores a day (Lexisnexis.com, 2003). At this time Starbucks had "1,460 stores outside the U.S., scattered around Europe, the Pacific Rim, the Middle East and Mexico" (Lexisnexis.com, 2003). By 2008, Starbucks was present in 43 foreign countries, which represented 4,500 of their stores (Adamy, 2008). As of 2011, the total number of Starbucks locations has risen even more, totaling 10,787 in the United States and 6,216 abroad (Starbucks Corporation, 2011b). Yet there is room for even more growth. To continue their expansion, Starbucks planned to open 50 new stores in India in 2012.

The Retail Coffee Industry in India

Key Concerns with Developing India's Tastes

Starbucks' current initiative was certainly not its first attempt to access the growing Indian market. In 2007, Starbucks halted its venture with its Indonesian franchise partner and Kishore Biyani of the Future Group (Kumar & Bailey, 2012). A second public failure would not be ideal for Starbucks' reputation, so Culver was aware that Starbucks needed to carefully review the legal, societal, and business frameworks of India to succeed.

Indian Legal Considerations

WORKING WITHIN THE INDIAN GOVERNMENT SYSTEM

India is a country with a long, disparate history interrupted in modern years by a period of British colonialism, evidenced first by the East India Company's gain of power in approximately 1820 until control switched to the full British Crown in the late 1850s (Prakash, 1999). In 1947, India achieved independence from British rule and set course to be the largest constitutional republic in the world.

Since its independence, India has experienced government and political stability. There has been little political turmoil, which has helped the business environment. India's government has protected its local industries by limiting Foreign Direct Investment ("FDI") in India (Prakash, 1999).

The current government has been more accommodating toward the business environment and foreign investors in particular. As of 2011, the government was seeking ways to increase the permitted level of FDI for retail operations (Agarwal & Bahree, 2011). In addition, liberalized rules relating to FDI in real estate started to occur in 2001 (Tyagi & Kapur, 2008). Despite the potential for a unilateral approach into India, Starbucks continued to go forward with its joint venture partnership with Tata Coffee Limited.

Other governmental concerns impact Starbucks: for instance, India's enforcement of copyright and trademark laws has been questionable. It is relatively easy to skirt trademark policies, and intellectual property rights are not strictly enforced. For example, Starbucks has entered into litigation with a company using the name "Starstruck" (Parikh, 2009).

India remains on the Office of the United States Trade Representative's priority list, which identifies countries that have trade barriers relating to intellectual property rights (Kirk, 2012). Also, India has yet to approve the United Nations-backed World Intellectual Property Organization Copyright treaty (Business Software Alliance, 2012).

Despite all of this, what maintains the country's viability is India's adoption of the Geneva Convention, which requires it to enforce international legal proceedings (Geneva Academy of International Humanitarian Law and Human Rights, n.d.). Moreover, India formed the International Centre for Alternative Dispute Resolution to help better resolve disputes (Shah & Singh, 2011). It is clearly making strides in its litigation processes and system to foster fruitful relationships with multinational corporations like Starbucks.

Indian Societal Considerations

A TEA-DRINKING NATION?

Beyond the governmental considerations, Starbucks must also deal with India's societal norms. With a population of approximately 1.2 billion people as of 2011, India approaches China's population of 1.3 billion (Government of India, 2011). The population has grown approximately 1.7 percent per year over the past decade, which explains its youthful median age of approximately 25 years (compared to the United States' median age of approximately 37 years and China's median age of approximately 36 years) (Central Intelligence Agency, n.d.).

India's population, while still primarily rural, has become more urban in the recent past: 30 percent of the population—roughly 360 million people—now lives in an urban setting which Starbucks can seek to target (NationMaster.com, n.d.).

India has been a predominantly tea-drinking nation (Jain, 2012; Ani, 2012). However, according to a recent report in the *Indian Express*, Indians' consumption of coffee is increasing like never before in the country; this is due to various reasons including an increased presence of Western media, as well as a shift toward more imports and higher standards of living (Bailay & Das, 2012).

Especially keen on the coffee shop experience are the young: "For this segment, particularly those with steady, disposable incomes, coffee shops serve as a social hub." (K@W, 2011). Indians do not greatly respect the social use of alcohol so the coffee shops have provided a great location for people to meet up for a drink.

> It has also helped facilitate the country's growing dating culture—having a girlfriend or boyfriend at a young age is frowned upon by many, so secret trysts at a coffee shop have become the norm for many young Indians, and serve as a suitable rendezvous away from the prying eyes of parents.
>
> (Vaidyanathan, 2012)

With half of India's population under the age of 25, coffee shops have a large populace to target.

The International Coffee Organization has acknowledged the trend of increased favorability for coffee stores. In 2010, the level of coffee consumption in India was approximately 1.71 million 60-kg bags. In 2011, that figure increased by 3 percent to 1.76 million 60-kg bags (Bailay & Das, 2012). The increase is all the more significant when that data are compared with coffee consumption at the beginning of the millennium. In 2001, Indians only consumed 1.02 million 60-kg bags (Bailay & Das, 2012). One of the most significant rises in consumption occurred in 2010, when the level grew by roughly 6 percent. Industry experts believe there is still plenty of room for more expansion. Significant margins remain in capturing this growth.

The increase in coffee consumption in India has spurred Starbucks' interest in the country. "Coffee has changed from being a traditional beverage, consumed mainly in south India, to a mainstream beverage with a national presence," noted Culver (Panchal, 2012).

Indian Business Considerations

The Current Competitive Landscape

Despite the increase in India's partiality to coffee in the past decade, Starbucks had not yet made gallant strides into the market. Governmental and societal considerations have played a role in that decision, but business factors also impact Starbucks' entry into the Indian market.

Other companies have filled the void left by Starbucks' absence and have set up an existing foothold in India. Starbucks will need to be mindful of the three major competitors that currently exist in India and determine the best way to take the market share from them. (Table 8C.1, in Appendix 1, shows the chief competitors of Starbucks in India and other pertinent information relating to them.)

> *Café Coffee Day:* Café Coffee Day ("CCD") was the pioneer of the Indian retail coffee market, opening its first store in Bangalore in 1996 (Café Coffee Day, n.d.). A subsidiary of India's own Amalgamated Bean Coffee

Trading Company, CCD now operates over 1,200 stores in over 100 cities in India, leading its nearest competitor by 1,000 stores (Choudhury, n.d.). CCD also has a smaller international presence in countries such as Pakistan and Austria (Choudhury, n.d.).

Barista Lavazza: CCD's main current competition is Barista Lavazza, a chain store owned by Italy's largest coffee company, Lavazza (Barista, n.d.). Though only one-fifth the size of CCD, Barista Lavazza has a strong presence in many of the major cities of India. Barista Lavazza aims to "ensure that our espresso bars reflect the warmth and character of traditional Italian coffee houses" (Barista, n.d.).

Costa Coffee: Unlike Barista Lavazza which acts more like an independent sister company to Lavazza, Costa Coffee is a dependent child of its larger United Kingdom-based parent. Costa Coffee entered the Indian market in 2005 and has since opened approximately 90 stores in major cities in India (Costa Coffee, n.d.).

Other competition: The three main retail coffee companies face their own growing competition from the already-present Gloria Jean's of Australia and the Coffee Bean & Tea Leaf from the United States (K@W, 2011). In addition to the announced entrance of Starbucks into the market, rumors exist that several other international companies may soon follow, including the U.S. Dunkin' Donuts, the United Kingdom's Coffee Republic, Australia's Coffee Club, and France's Alto Coffee (K@W, 2011).

Existing and potential competition in India is not the only economic consideration for Starbucks. Starbucks must contend with significant retail real-estate costs in certain urban cities, including Mumbai, India's chief business city, where property prices in recent years have soared (Sharma, 2012). One Indian analyst stated: "The prohibitive costs ... could affect store profitability and make (achieving) break-even more challenging," further noting that entering smaller cities and towns might be even more challenging due to these costs (Bailay & Das, 2012). Further, the increase in coffee bean costs—up 60 percent from 2010 to 2011—may hurt the bottom-line for new entrants (K@W, 2011).

Cultural Dimensions

Since joining the Starbucks international team in 2007, Culver learned many things about global business. One of the key things he quickly discovered was that business knowledge does not necessarily translate into business success when working with people from other cultures. Culture not only includes people's observable behaviors, but also goes much deeper below the surface to include cognitive interpretations and emotions. Each culture is composed of its own values and norms. Understanding these intercultural differences as well as developing the cross-cultural skills and competencies was crucial to Culver's past success. Therefore, he knows that the success of Starbucks in India will depend heavily on the ability to understand the Indian culture and to prepare for potential gaps or tensions caused by cultural differences among India, the United States, and other countries—particularly India's close neighbor China—where Starbucks currently does business. Culver used several tools to help this process, including the cultural dimensions framework outlined by Dutch sociologist Geert Hofstede (see Figure 8C.1, Appendix 2) (Hofstede, n.d.).

The first thing that Culver did when he began his international work was to learn more about himself and the U.S. American culture in which he grew up. Culver is known at Starbucks for his organization and structure. Everyone in the office knows that they are expected to be at meetings on time and that Culver likes to closely follow agendas. Like many U.S. Americans, Culver prefers a controlled environment in which focus is placed on taking initiative to find solutions to problems. Culver also came to understand additional aspects of the U.S. American culture. U.S. Americans tend to prefer low-context and direct communication. They often are also more individualistic, focusing more on personal accomplishment and independence. This is seen in the Hofstede index where the United States has a high score at 91 for individualism.

The United States also has a low Hofstede score of 29 for long-term orientation, reflecting its preference for equality and creativity over traditions (Hofstede, n.d.). In the GLOBE Study (Table 8C.3, Appendix 3), the United States was grouped in the Anglo cluster with Canada, Australia, Ireland, the United Kingdom, South Africa, and New Zealand. "These countries were high in performance orientation and low in in-group collectivism. This means it is a characteristic of these countries to be competitive and results oriented but less attached to their families or similar groups than other countries." (Northouse, 2013, p. 310). These cultural characteristics helped Culver earn success in business in the United States, but proved to be a challenge during his work in Asia.

Through his work in Asia in recent years, Culver learned much about the culture of China, Asia's largest and fastest-growing economy. Unlike the United States that is very individualistic focused, China is much more collectivist focused with a low Hofstede score of 20 for individualism. People in China usually place more importance on relationships. Successful business is a result of patience in taking time for relationship building. China is part of the Confucian Asian cluster in the GLOBE Study. Leaders in China are team oriented yet make decisions based on status and hierarchy (Northouse, 2013). This strong sense of hierarchy within business and society is also reflected in China's Hofstede power distance score of 80.

Traditions are also very important in China. This means the Chinese people are likely to base future decisions on the past and see change as a threat (Northouse, 2013). Clearly, the United States and China differ greatly in several areas of culture.

As Starbucks contemplated entry into the Indian market, Culver recognized that he must also understand the Indian culture. Given that India was once part of the British Empire, he began by looking at British culture with the thought that it may help provide a background for Indian culture. Since the United Kingdom is also part of the Anglo cluster in GLOBE, it is very similar to the United States. As expected, Culver found that the United States and the United Kingdom also have very similar scores on all aspects of the Hofstede dimensions: 40 and 35 on power distance, 91 and 89 on individualism, 62 and 66 on masculinity, 30 and 35 on uncertainty avoidance, and 29 and 25 on long-term orientation respectively (Northouse, 2013).

However, there are some differences between the two countries. For example, the United Kingdom tends to be more harmonious than the United States, has a higher context for communication, and an indirect form of communication. They also tend to be more formal and hierarchical (Northouse, 2013). Culver was uncertain how these British cultural values may have transferred to India.

Differing from the United States, the United Kingdom, and China, India is part of the southern Asia cluster according to GLOBE (Northouse, 2013). Culver found that India shares many cultural characteristics with China, but differs in several key areas as well. On the Hofstede dimension, India has a high power-distance score of 77, indicating its preference for hierarchy and centralization similar to that in China. Its individualism score of 48, however, is between that of the United Kingdom (89) and China (20). Additionally, its long-term orientation score of 61 is also between that of the United Kingdom (25) and China (118).

Culver also noted several areas where India is different from all three countries he already analyzed. For example, India tends to be an expressive culture, meaning people show emotion in the workplace. India also tends to be more cooperative than competitive, and views space in a more public manner:

> Indians tend towards a public orientation when taking into account personal space and are not averse to frequent interruptions during meetings, physical proximity when standing, and touching one another when communicating. They are also not averse to asking personal questions around marriage, salary, etc. in the initial stages of interaction.
>
> (Cultural Navigator, n.d.)

Having reviewed the various aspects of different cultures, Culver knew that the Starbucks team needed the ability to shift when they entered India. India's culture is inextricably tied with various other countries' culture, and this is crucial when assessing the potential dimensions to explore.

He saw several potential areas of cultural conflict for the Starbucks business during its expansion into the Indian market. For example, the joint venture with Tata required the ability to successfully conduct business, build trust and relationships, and manage projects with leadership and top corporate management (Bahree, 2012).

Additionally, each individual Starbucks location would need to be run effectively, with success highly dependent on the manager and the baristas. Starbucks also planned to source everything locally and would be dealing with Indian suppliers and farmers. And, no coffee shop can be successful without customers. Starbucks needed to make sure that it connected to the Indian consumer.

The Decision

Schultz's e-mail had made it clear that Culver would be in charge of the expansion into India unless he said something. Exiting the elevator, Culver made his way to his boss's office, determined to make a decision prior to reaching his boss's door. As Culver turned a corner he nearly ran into Schultz. "Hey, are you coming to see me?" Schultz asked.

Questions

1 What are the cultural differences among the United States, the United Kingdom, China, and India that are relevant to Starbucks' entry into the Indian retail coffee market?
2 What leadership traits and styles would be most effective in India? Does it differ for leaders at the corporate level and the retail level?
3 How would a customer's experience at Starbucks differ in each of the four cultures?
4 What should Culver recommend to Schultz for where the Indian division should be located within Starbucks' organizational structure?

Appendix 1

Retail Coffee in India

Table 8C.1 India's Café Culture

Company	Number of Stores
Café Coffee Day	1,232
Barista Lavazza	184
Costa Coffee	90
Gloria Jean's Coffees	24
The Coffee Bean & Tea Leaf	15

(*Source:* CNBC graph, www.youtube.com/watch?v=SOI-MtWS4Y8.)

Appendix 2

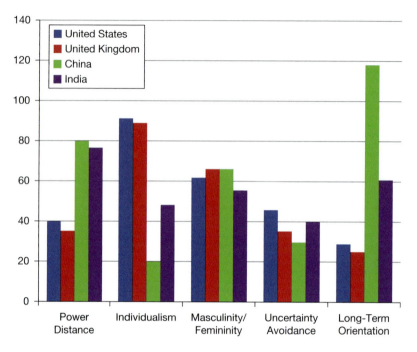

Figure 8C.1 Hofstede's Cultural Dimensions of Countries

(*Source:* Hofstede, n.d.)

Appendix 3

GLOBE Study

Table 8C.3 Leadership Attributes: GLOBE Study with Ten Country (Society) Clusters

Eastern Europe	Middle East	Confucian Asia	Southern Asia	Latin America
Albania, Georgia, Greece, Hungary, Kazakhstan Poland, Slovenia, Russia	Egypt, Kuwait, Morocco, Qatar, Turkey	China, Hong Kong, Japan, Singapore, South Korea, Taiwan	India, Indonesia, Iran, Philippines, Thailand	Argentina, Bolivia, Brazil, Columbia, Costa Rica, Ecuador, El Salvador, Guatemala, Mexico, Venezuela

(*Continued*)

Table 8C.3 (continued)

Nordic Europe	Anglo	Germanic Europe	Latin Europe	Sub-Saharan Africa
Denmark, Finland, Sweden	Australia, Canada, Ireland, New Zealand, South Africa (White sample), U.K., U.S.A.	Austria, Germany–East, Germany–West, Netherlands, Switzerland (German)	France, Israel, Italy, Portugal, Spain, Switzerland (French)	Namibia, Nigeria, Zambia, Zimbabwe, South Africa (Black sample)

Note: Countries opposite each other (top and bottom) differ the most from each other.

(*Source:* Adapted from House et al., 2004, pp. 190–1.)

Note

1 Authors: Anumah, R., Feehan, J., Hoekstra, E., Kalinauskas, K., and Tuleja, E. (Ed.)

References

Adamy, J. (2008, December 6). Starbucks brews growth abroad. *Wall Street Journal.* Retrieved from www.wsj.com/articles/SB10001424052970204740904577192500354456184 (accessed September 20, 2016).

Agarwal, V., & Bahree, M. (2011). India retreats on retail. *Wall Street Journal.* Retrieved from http://online.wsj.com/article/SB10001424052970204903804577083343062468240.html (accessed August 4, 2016).

Ani. (2012). India to declare tea national drink in 2013. *The Times of India.* Retrieved from www.indiatimes.com/national/india-to-declare-tea-national-drink-in-2013_-20921.html (accessed August 4, 2016).

Bahree, Megha. (2012, January 12). Starbucks will open cafes in India. Coffee retailer forms joint venture with Tata Group; pair plans to open 50 stores by year-end. *Wall Street Journal.* Retrieved from www.wsj.com/articles/SB121494400432420449 (accessed September 20, 2016).

Bailay, R., & Das, S. (2012). Coffee chains to pre-empt Starbucks success strategy. *The Indian Express.* Retrieved from www.indianexpress.com/news/coffee-chains-to-preempt-starbucks-success-strategy/957993/ (accessed August 4, 2016).

Barista. (n.d.). *Worldwide.* Retrieved from www.barista.co.in (accessed August 4, 2016).

Business Software Alliance. (2012). Country Report: India. Retrieved from http://portal.bsa.org/cloudscorecard2012/assets/pdfs/country_reports/Country_Report_India.pdf (accessed August 4, 2016).

Café Coffee Day. (n.d.). About Café Coffee Day. Retrieved from www.cafecoffeeday.com/our-business.php?mnid=3&lmids=1 (accessed August 4, 2016).

Central Intelligence Agency. (n.d.). *The world factbook.* Retrieved from www.cia.gov/library/publications/the-world-factbook/fields/2177.html (accessed August 4, 2016).

Choudhury, S. (n.d.). Coffee retail: More than just a sip. Retrieved from www. indiaretailing.com/coffee-retail.asp (accessed August 4, 2016).

Costa Coffee. (n.d.). Retrieved from www.costacoffee.com/ (accessed August 4, 2016).

Cultural Navigator. (n.d.). India Cultural Norms: Public and Private Space. Retrieved from www.culturalnavigator.com/CN7/login.aspx (accessed August 1, 2016).

Cunningham, M. E. (2010). China's Coffee Culture. Retrieved from www.forbes.com/ 2010/04/28/starbucks-china-consumers-markets-economy-coffee.html (accessed September 20, 2016).

Geneva Academy of International Humanitarian Law and Human Rights. (n.d.). India: International treaties adherence. Retrieved from www.geneva-academy.ch/ RULAC/international_treaties.php?id_state=107 (accessed August 4, 2016).

Government of India. (2011). Provisional population total: India: Census 2011. Retrieved from www.censusindia.gov.in/2011-prov-results/indiaatglance.html (accessed August 4, 2016).

Hofstede, G. (n.d.). Retrieved from http://geert-hofstede.com/ (accessed September 23, 2012).

House, R. J., Hanges, P. J., Javidan, M., Dorfman, P. W., & Gupta, V. (Eds.). (2004). *Culture, leadership, and organizations: The GLOBE study of 62 societies* (3rd edn.). Thousand Oaks, CA: SAGE.

Jain, V. (2012). Tea time. Foodservice: India edition. Retrieved from http://tapri.net/ pdf/26_37_Cover20Story.pdf (accessed August 4, 2016).

K@W. (2011). Capturing India's percolating coffee market. Retrieved from http:// knowledge.wharton.upenn.edu/india/article.cfm?articleid=4607 (accessed August 4, 2016).

Kirk, R. (2012). 2012 Special 301 Report. Retrieved from www.ustr.gov/webfm_send/ 2849 (accessed August 4, 2016).

Kumar, A., & Bailey, R. (2012). Starbucks set for festive season flag-off from Mumbai. *Economic Times.* Retrieved from http://articles.economictimes.indiatimes.com/2012-06-26/news/32424796_1_starbucks-flag-festive-season (accessed August 4, 2016).

Lexisnexis.com. (2003). Starbucks: Today Fortune 500, tomorrow the world. *The business.* Retrieved from www.lexisnexis.com.proxy.library.nd.edu/lnacui2api/results/ docview/docview.do?docLinkInd=true&risb=21_T15546348350&format=GNBFI& sort=DATE,A,H&startDocNo=76&resultsUrlKey=29_T15546340944&cisb=22_ T15546349969&treeMax=true&treeWidth=0&csi=222278&docNo=81 (accessed August 4, 2016).

Mathee, I. (1995). Starbucks sees big things brewing from joint venture with Japanese. *The Ottawa Citizen.* Retrieved from www.lexisnexis.com.proxy.library.nd.edu/ lnacui2api/results/docview/docview.do?docLinkInd=true&risb=21_T15562672736 &format=GNBFI&sort=DATE,A,H&startDocNo=1&resultsUrlKey=29_T1556267 2709&cisb=22_T15562672708&treeMax=true&treeWidth=0&csi=397220& docNo=8 (accessed August 4, 2016).

NationMaster.com (n.d.). *People > Percentage living in rural areas.* Retrieved from <www.nationmaster.com/graph/peo_per_liv_in_rur_are-people-percentage-living-rural-areas (accessed August 4, 2016).

Northouse, P. G. (2013). *Leadership: Theory and practice.* Los Angeles, CA: SAGE.

Panchal, S. (2012). Coffee giant Starbucks taps into tea-loving India. *Business Inquirer.* Retrieved from http://business.inquirer.net/79878/coffee-giant-starbucks-taps-into-tea-loving-india (accessed August 4, 2016).

Parikh, B. (2009). Starbucks in India: The time is just right. Retrieved from www. slideshare.net/b_a_d_bad/15173068-internationalbusiness-starbucksinindia (accessed August 4, 2016).

Prakash, G. (1999). *Another reason: Science and the imagination of modern India.* Princeton, NJ: Princeton University Press.

Schultz, H., & Yang, D. J. (1997). *Pour your heart into it: How Starbucks built a company one cup at a time.* New York, NY: Hyperion.

Shah, K., & Singh, A. (2011). Is ADR set to become the preferred method of dispute resolution in India? Practical law. Retrieved from http://arbitration.practicallaw. com/2-504-6921 (accessed August 4, 2016).

Sharma, S. (2012). Soaring rents worry retail chains. *Daily News and Analysis.* Retrieved from www.dnaindia.com/money/report_soaring-rents-worry-retail-chains_1653244 (accessed August 4, 2016).

Seeking Alpha. (2011a). Starbucks' CEO discusses Q3 2011 results—Earnings call transcript. Retrieved from http://seekingalpha.com/article/282938-starbucks-ceo-discusses-q3-2011-results-earnings-call-transcript?page=2 (accessed August 4, 2016).

Seeking Alpha. (2011b). Tata Coffee & Starbucks sign MoU for strategic alliance in India. Retrieved from http://investor.starbucks.com/phoenix.zhtml?c=99518&p= irol-newsArticle&ID=1515804&highlight (accessed August 4, 2016).

Starbucks Corporation. (2011a). John Culver inducted to Florida State University College of Business Hall of Fame. Retrieved from https://news.starbucks.com/ news/john-culver-inducted-to-florida-state-university-hall-of-fame (accessed August 16, 2016).

Starbucks Corporation. (2011b). 10-K. Retrieved from http://investor.starbucks.com/ (accessed August 4, 2016).

Starbucks Corporation. (n.d.). Our heritage. Retrieved from www.starbucks.com/ about-us/our-heritage (accessed August 4, 2016).

Starbucks Investor Relations. (2011). Starbucks announces new leadership structure to accelerate global growth. Retrieved from http://investor.starbucks.com/phoenix. zhtml?c=99518&p=irol-newsArticle&ID=1584009&highlight= (accessed August 4, 2016).

Tyagi, S., & D., Kapur . (2008). FDI in real estate development sector—The hindrance in the blessing. National realty. Retrieved from www.zeus.firm.in/Journals/ FDI20in%20Real%20Estate.pdf (accessed August 4, 2016).

Vaidyanathan, Rajini. (2012). Coffee v Tea: Is India falling for the cappuccino? *BBC News Magazine.* Retrieved from www.bbc.co.uk/news/magazine-16932747 (accessed August 4, 2016).

Index